DEVELOPMENTAL PSYCHOPHYSIOLOGY
OF MENTAL RETARDATION

DEVELOPMENTAL PSYCHOPHYSIOLOGY OF MENTAL RETARDATION

Concepts and Studies

Edited by

RATHE KARRER, Ph.D.

Illinois State Pediatric Institute
Chicago, Illinois

Foreword by

John I. Lacey, Ph.D.

Fels Research Institute
Yellow Springs, Ohio

Introduction by

Donald B. Lindslcy, Ph.D.

University of California
Los Angeles, California

CHARLES C THOMAS · PUBLISHER
Springfield · Illinois · U.S.A.

Published and Distributed Throughout the World by
CHARLES C THOMAS • PUBLISHER
Bannerstone House
301-327 East Lawrence Avenue, Springfield, Illinois, U.S.A.

© 1976, by CHARLES C THOMAS • PUBLISHER
ISBN 0-398-03414-1
Library of Congress Catalog Card Number: 75-2061

*With THOMAS BOOKS careful attention is given to all details of
manufacturing and design. It is the Publisher's desire to present books that are
satisfactory as to their physical qualities and artistic possibilities and
appropriate for their particular use. THOMAS BOOKS will be true to those
laws of quality that assure a good name and good will.*

Printed in the United States of America
C-1

Library of Congress Cataloging in Publication Data

Karrer, Rathe
    Developmental psychophysiology of
mental retardation: concepts and studies

    Includes indexes.
    1. Mental deficiency. 2. Psychology, Physiological.
3. Developmental psychobiology. I. Title.
[DNLM: 1. Mental retardation—Physiopathology. WM300
K18s]
RC570.K35   616.8'588'07   75-2061
ISBN 0-398-03414-1

For

BETTY, TANA, DANA, and PHILLIP

Man being a unit is artifically analyzed, for study's sake, into his three prominent vital expressions, activity, intelligence, and will. We consider the idiot as a man infirm in the expressions of his trinity. . . . Contrarily to the teachings of various mythologies of the brain, and with the disadvantage of working against the prevalent anthropological formula, we were obliged at the same time to use most of its terms; we have developed our child, not like a duality, nor like a trinity, nor like an illimited poly-entity, but as nearly as we could like a unit. It is true that the unity of the physiological training could not be gone through without concessions to the language of the day, nor to necessities of analysis, quite repugnant to the principle; it is true that we have been speaking of muscular, nervous, or sensorial functions, as of things as distinct for us as muscles, nerves, and bones are for the anatomist; but after a long struggle with these difficulties, psychophysiology vindicated its rights against the feebleness of our understanding, and the mincing of our vocabularies.

EDWARD SEGUIN
Idiocy and its treatment by
the physiological method, 1866.

CONTRIBUTORS

Edward C. Beck, Ph.D.
Director, Neuropsychology Research, Veterans Administration Hospital, and Research Professor, University of Utah, Salt Lake City, Utah.

Jytte Busk, Ph.D.
Assistant Research Psychologist, Neuropsychiatric Institute Pacific State Hospital Research Group and University of Southern California School of Medicine, Los Angeles, California.

Johs Clausen, Dr. Philos.
Chief Research Scientist, Department of Psychology, New York State Institute for Basic Research in Mental Retardation, Staten Island, New York.

Jerome Cohen, Ph.D.
Professor, Departments of Psychology, and Neurology, Northwestern University Medical School, Chicago, Illinois.

J. P. Das, Ph.D.
Director, Centre for the Study of Mental Retardation and Professor, Department of Educational Psychology, University of Alberta, Edmonton, Canada.

Robert Dustman, Ph.D.
Associate Director, Neuropsychology Research, Veterans Administration Hospital, and Research Associate Professor, University of Utah, Salt Lake City, Utah.

Fred Fehr, Ph.D.
Associate Professor, Department of Psychology, Arizona State University, Tempe, Arizona.

vii

Gary C. Galbraith, Ph.D.
Associate Research Psychologist, Neuropsychiatric Institute Pacific State Hospital Research Group, Los Angeles, California.

Jack Gliddon, Ph.D.
Assistant Research Psychologist, Neuropsychiatric Institute Pacific State Hospital Research Group, Los Angeles, California.

Judy Ivins, M.A.
Psychologist, Illinois State Pediatric Institute, Chicago, Illinois.

John Johnson, Ph.D.
Psychologist, Greenville-Green County School System, Greenville, Tennessee.

Rathe Karrer, Ph.D.
Administrative Research Scientist, Illinois State Pediatric Institute, Chicago, Illinois.

Antoinette Krupski, Ph.D.
Assistant Professor, Graduate School of Education, University of California, Los Angeles, California.

Arnold Lidsky, Ph.D.
Associate Research Scientist, Department of Psychology, New York State Institute for Basic Research in Mental Retardation, Staten Island, New York.

Donald B. Lindsley, Ph.D.
Professor, Departments of Psychology, Physiology, and Psychiatry, and Member, Brain Research Institute, University of California, Los Angeles, California.

John Locke, Ph.D.
Research Associate Professor, Children's Research Center, Associate Professor, Department of Speech and Hearing Science; Department of Psychology, University of Illinois, Champaign, Illinois.

Russell Lockhart, Ph.D.

Director, Psychophysiology Research Laboratory, Camarillo-Neuropsychiatric Institute Research Program, and Associate Research Psychologist, Department of Psychiatry, University of California, Los Angeles, California.

Thomas Schenkenberg, Ph.D.

Clinical Psychologist, Veterans Administration Hospital, and Research Assistant Professor, University of Utah, Salt Lake City, Utah.

Eugene Sersen, Ph.D.

Associate Research Scientist, Department of Psychology, New York State Institute for Basic Research in Mental Retardation, Staten Island, New York.

FOREWORD

ALTHOUGH AN OVERALL SYNTHESIS which successfully leads to an understanding of mental deficiency is not yet attainable, this book is a valuable attempt at a more fundamental synthesis, namely the integration of behavioral and physiological descriptions and interpretations. I was both reassured and stimulated to find again—but this time within the confines of a detailed consideration of a major kind of behavioral disorder characterized by attentional and cognitive deficits—that behavioral and electrophysiological investigations can be complementary and mutually supportive methods for understanding the human organism, its development, deviations, and malfunctions.

The nervous system of the mentally retarded person must possess some unique features. Can the psychophysiologist and neuropsychologist measure, assay, describe and interpret specifically relevant features of neural functioning? In so doing, can he satisfy both the scientific aim of understanding the neural substrate of behavior and the therapeutic aim of providing soundly based suggestions for intervention and amelioration? Positive answers are not inevitable because we are limited in our ability to evaluate and understand the intimate and important details of neural processes, and because, for technical and ethical reasons, we are limited to peripheral, external measurements. Scalp recordings of the electroencephalogram and of evoked potentials may or may not tap relevant processes; electrodermal and cardiovascular aberrations may or may not be specific or interpretable. I expect the reader to find, as I did, continued support and encouragement for the belief that such peripheral measurements indeed can be revealing and useful; but also expect the reader to find, as I did, that much remains to be done.

The studies and information in this book surely will challenge the reader to exercise his own powers of synthesis, for they are largely descriptive and analytical, and the hypotheses under test are diverse. This is inevitable in our current state of knowledge about mental retardation itself, and about the specificity and interpretability of peripheral measures of physiological activity. Contradictory facts abound; the fundamental genesis of electroencephalographic activity is not entirely understood; the significance of autonomic activity is hotly debated; and available models and miniature theories seem more valuable as heuristic guides than as explanations of a satisfyingly wide range of empirical observations.

The individual chapters in the book were written by active and highly competent investigators, who utilize the most modern technologies, and who base their investigations upon a modern and sophisticated understanding of the interplay between behavioral and electrophysiological observations. There is hardly an issue or technique in current psychophysiology that is not touched upon in this book, often in illuminating and insightful ways. Hemispheric asymmetries, the significance of EEG coherence measures for cognitive functioning, the variable spatial and temporal aspects of evoked potentials, biofeedback, electromyography, the differential significance of skin resistance and heart rate, the orienting reflex, the contingent negative variation, attention, speed of response, the effects of stimulus parameters, nosological uncertainties—each of the topics, and others, is considered in greater or lesser detail. Behavioral observations suggest searches for new psychophysiological facts; psychophysiological observations suggest searchers for new behavioral facts. In more than one instance, reassuring—albeit imperfect—parallelisms are found.

The book leaves little doubt in my mind that psychophysiological investigations can and will lead to improvements in diagnosis, intervention, and evaluation of therapeutic procedures, as well as to increases in basic understanding. Much remains to be done, however. And this book, with its reviews and overviews, its detailed presentation of specific investigations and its sophisticated suggestions for future research, serves as an important statement of where we are now, and of where we can and should go to fulfill the aims both of science and therapy.

JOHN I. LACEY

PREFACE

A QUICK PERUSAL through the mental retardation (MR) literature is enough to demonstrate that a psychophysiological
approach to understanding mental retardation is rare. A similar
scan of the neuroscience literature reveals little consideration of
MR as relevant to understanding brain-behavior relations. Nor
is there a wide appreciation of the role of macro-physiological
events to behavior. These three implicit orientations impede
basic work on developmental brain-behavior relations relevant
to understanding developmental defects like MR.

The neglect of psychophysiological relations grows out of at
least two conceptions. First, there is disenchantment with macro-
physiological activity as capable of rendering any but the most
superficial analysis of behavior-physiology relations. On the contrary, macro-physiological activity is inherently and meaningfully bound into the ongoing behavior chain. It constitutes an
interface between micro-physiological mechanisms and the organism's psychological processes.

Second is the assumption that cognitive function, or intelligence (usually an IQ derived from a diverse battery of subtests)
and/or social factors are the *sine qua non* of MR. This conceptualization often results in treating intelligence and cognition as if they are epiphenomena unrelated to physiology and
brain function affected by various developmental factors. It also
tends to ignore the motor and sensory involvement often present
in MR as well as the affective nature of experience and action.
This has biased research efforts for decades. The recent emphasis
on adaptive behavior is a somewhat balancing trend to this assumption.

The purpose of this book, then, is to present a cross-section of
representative work and concepts and to stimulate further work
in the developmental psychophysiological analysis of MR. It
should also demonstrate to psychophysiologists that MR research

xiii

can give rise to fruitful questions and answers to behavior-physiology relations.

To accomplish these aims current work from the main lines of psychophysiological analysis of MR has been selected. This work falls primarily into two categories: studies of autonomic activity, or of electrocortical activity. Studies utilizing animal models and studies primarily of pharmacological nature have not been included even though both approaches may contribute to the psychophysiological analysis of MR. It was felt that these approaches are more prevalent and currently accepted.

The book grew out of conversations with most of the present authors. They were very helpful during an ambivalent period back in 1971 when the decision to organize this book was germinating. Drs. Herbert M. Kohn, Johs Clausen, and Gershon Berkson gave freely of their time to read and reread various chapters and gave useful suggestions during the conceptualization and editing. My wife, Betty, provided moderation, encouragement, and many suggestions during the whole trying period of editing and organizing the diverse approaches.

In the last analysis it is up to the reader to decide if the ideas, concepts and methods to be found herein are heuristic and viable. If the book acquaints others (especially graduate students) with an approach of which they had little awareness and stimulates a few to question and follow up some of the ideas it will have been a success.

RATHE KARRER

CONTENTS

DEVELOPMENTAL PSYCHOPHYSIOLOGY
OF MENTAL RETARDATION

CHAPTER 1

MENTAL RETARDATION: HISTORICAL AND PSYCHO-PHYSIOLOGICAL PERSPECTIVE

DONALD B. LINDSLEY

INTRODUCTION

THIS BOOK IS UNIQUE in that it brings to bear upon the problem of mental retardation new concepts of brain organization and behavior, of orienting, conditioning and learning, and new and modern technologies for exploring the psychophysiology of brain function during information processing. It looks for differences in the relation of psychophysiological process and behavioral performance between intellectually normal and retarded persons with respect to information processing capacities. On the behavioral side, it examines orienting, attention, perception, conditioning, learning and motor performance. It seeks ways to differentiate the functioning of the autonomic nervous system in normal and mentally retarded individuals during these behaviors. Finally, and importantly, it describes various methods of employing modern computer technology to study the electroencephalogram (EEG) and its most recent derivatives, average evoked potentials (AEPs) and steady (DC) potentials (e.g. the

3

contingent negative variation, CNV). These latter derivatives provide potentially powerful means of tuning in on brain activity during information processing ranging from simple perceptual to higher cognitive functions. They afford a means of assessing specific sensory input and also the arousal, activating and integrating aspects of nonspecific sensory mechanisms, which underlie the attentive, associative and temporal sequencing or multiplexing functions so important to information processing.

This introduction will attempt to broaden the perspective of information processing so far as our understanding of the complexities of the brain and other parts of the nervous system are concerned. In doing this, it will concentrate, by way of example, primarily upon the visual system and its mechanisms and how these relate to other regulating mechanisms of the nervous system such as those concerned with orienting, arousal, alerting, and attention which are now believed to play critical roles in the processing of information. As yet, these mechanisms are poorly understood, but the concepts emerging from their study at various levels of phylogenetic and ontogenetic development are challenging. Hopefully, they will lead to new and better understanding of normal, as well as retarded, development and function. The various chapters of this book indicate the extent to which some of these new methods and concepts are being employed in an effort to find a basis of understanding of mental retardation.

Obviously, mental retardation is a complex and multifaceted problem. How do we define it? How do we assess it? How do we categorize it? In kind or degree? What are its causes? Are they primarily genetic in origin, or environmental? If genetic, what form does the genetic factor take? Are there genes for intelligence, per se, and if so, what precisely is meant by intelligence? Do genes determine the number of brain cells, the number and extent of their ramifying dendrites, or the number of spines which will sprout on the apical dendrites of pyramidal cells? What about the neurochemistry such as the enzymes and the monamines? Or the ultrastructure, such as the locus and stores of neuro-transmitter substances? If causative factors are environmental and deprivational, how do these operate to depress information processing? There is gradually accumulating evidence that the stimulation of an enriched environment seems to be capable of modifying the structural and physical characteristics of the brain as well as its neurochemistry. There is evidence that brain trauma, before, during or after birth can affect intellectual and behavioral performance. Likewise, infectious processes, certain inborn errors of metabolism and iso-immunization processes, to mention only a few, seem able to affect intellectual and behavioral performance. Imbalances in the functioning of the autonomic system, the endocrine systems, the acid-base regulating systems, and others can have a devastating effect upon the central nervous system and presumably upon the performance of the brain, whether in intellectual or other adaptational functions. Finally, it should be mentioned that psychological factors related to experience, training and the environment can be influential in retarding or accelerating the development of processes upon which intellectual performance depends, such as perception, learning, memory storage and retrieval. There seems to be such a thing as learning to learn, learning to attend, or learning to be motivated when reinforcement is appropriate.

Thus, there are potentially a multiplicity of causative factors. While more and more of these factors are being identified as responsible for, or contributory to, what we call mental retardation, the vast number of cases are still unexplained. This is in part due to the fact that we do not know exactly how to define this broad and complex problem. Definitions are often concerned with the disposition of a case, rather than with its cause, prevention or treatment.

Some have sought to classify the mentally retarded in socio-economic and personal self-sufficiency terms so as to separate the most deeply or severely affected and to provide for their care and protection in institutions. Some efforts have been directed toward separating those who cannot profit from any formal education experience in the schools from those who might go the equivalent of a few grades in school with the aid of special tutoring or special classes. These social, cultural and educational problems which were originally looked upon as criteria for diagnosis, classification, segregation and treatment, have in recent years taken on a "new look" as potential causes of mental retardation through deprivation in subcultural environments (see Sarason, 1963; Sarason and Gladwin, 1958).

How do you prevent something when you don't know its causes, or when you don't even know the nature of the thing which you want to prevent? If the nature and mechanisms of intelligence, ability to learn, or ability to process and use information were known, and could be divided and subdivided to bring them into manageable dimensions for research study, perhaps further progress could be made in understanding and doing something about mental retardation. However, there have been persistent problems in attempting to define intelligence, to measure it, to estimate its heritability and to determine its dependence upon the social, cultural and educational environment.

Before elaborating upon a psychophysiological perspective of information processing in normal and mentally retarded persons, it seems desirable to present a brief historical purview of the concept of mental retardation.

HISTORICAL PURVIEW

Historically, a variety of terms have been applied to the conditions under which vast numbers of people suffer some degree of cognitive inability to adjust to the basic and common requirements of life's exigencies, including personal, social and economic welfare. These conditions may be due to *endogenous* (hereditary) or *exogenous* (environmental, deprivational, traumatic, or disease) factors, or a combination of the two and their interactions. The cognitive inabilities may vary qualitatively and quantitatively. They may vary in the extent of their pervasiveness, as well as in their susceptibility to modification under certain environmental circumstances and interventions.

For over three-quarters of a century there has been much concern in England with predominantly legal and social definitions of *mental deficiency* or *mental defectiveness*. In 1899 the Elementary Education Act first legally defined the concept of "mentally defective children." The Mental Deficiency Act of 1913 provided definitions for three grades of mental defectiveness: *idiots, imbeciles,* and the *feebleminded.* The emphasis in these definitions was primarily upon social and occupational adequacy.

In about the same timeframe at the beginning of the century, an educational, rather than a social-occupational problem motivated action which was to become of considerable importance for the concept of mental retardation. French authorities commissioned a psychologist, Alfred Binet, and a psychiatrist, Théophile Simon, to develop a measuring device for separating those children in the overcrowded schools who could profit from further schooling from those who could not. The result was an individual, age-scale, intelligence test which appeared in 1905, with revisions in 1908 and 1911 (Binet and Simon, 1914, 1916). Goddard (1914) was quick to see the advantage of such an instrument for quantifying intellectual capacity and classifying retarded trainees, but it was Terman, with Merrill, who did a major job of providing an American standardization. The 1916 Stanford-Binet Intelligence Test (Terman, 1916) and its subsequent revision and extension (Terman and Merrill, 1937) employed statistical concepts in an effort to develop a reliable and valid instrument for measuring "intelligence." Terman is mainly responsible for the adoption and popularization of the IQ concept, first introduced by William Stern (1914). The Stanford-Binet test became the workhorse of the school and the clinic, whenever an individual assessment of intelligence was needed, and when its dependence upon verbal and language abilities was not inappropriate. In 1939, it was supplemented and complemented by the Wechsler-Bellevue Adult Intelligence Scale (Wechsler, 1939), which afforded both a verbal and nonverbal assessment, and subsequently by a children's version, the Wechsler Intelligence Scale for Children (WISC).

The quantitative, psychometric approach in the measurement of intelligence and the development of the concept of the IQ was primarily an American contribution. It held great appeal because the IQ provided a basis of classification of the mentally retarded and led to the establishment of ranges of IQ values which delineated roughly the previously established socio-legal categories of mental deficiency defined by the British commissions and carried on upward to the other half of the intellectual distribution curve. IQ classifications were approximately as follows: Idiot 0-25; Imbecile 25-50; Moron or Feebleminded 50-70; Borderline 70-80; Dull normal 80-90; Normal 90-110; Superior 110-120; Very Superior 120-140; Genius 140 and upward.

A further development of the psychometric movement was the introduction of group tests. The army Alpha and Beta, for example, were constructed to meet the need during World War I for screening recruits. Subsequently, group tests for children were developed. Such intelligence tests were supplemented with achievement tests for which an educational quotient (EQ) and an achievement quotient (AQ) could be calculated. Thus, the penchant to quantify and classify in terms of a single number, no matter how varied the *content* of the intelligence or achievement tests, or under what conditions they might have been taken, typifies the extent to which a concept of intelligence as a discrete and exact quantum was held. There was, of course, some merit in such evaluations, both in terms of the ease and administrative utility of the measurement and the fact that such evaluations were generally more objective than any others that could be made.

Despite their great usefulness in winnowing retarded, borderline, and dull normal children from the group who could make normal progress in school, standardized intelligence tests, especially verbal ones, penalized children and adults from low socioeconomic levels, different cultural environments or language groups, as well as those with minimal school experience. To remedy these difficulties attempts to develop culture-free tests were launched, e.g. the Cattell Culture-Free Tests, and the Raven Matrices Tests.

The concurrent and gradual development of psychometric methods for more objectively classifying children and adults with respect to intelligence in terms of mental age and IQ opened up questions which seemed to supercede those of mental retardation per se, namely, what is intelligence and how should it be measured. In general, the psychometric view seemed to be predicated mainly on the belief that intelligence, at least as measured by tests, is normally distributed in the population and that the mentally retarded represent one end of the continuum. Others have questioned this and felt that the performances of many mentally retarded reflected not just differences in degree, but differences in kind. This latter view is complicated by the fact that many of the more severely retarded manifest brain damage or malfunction of unknown relation to their intellectual deficits.

During the era of extensive measurement and investigation of intelligence, several prominent theories were developed which emphasized general and/or specific factors. Spearman (1927) emphasized a general or G-factor in intelligence and several specific factors. It was felt that the G-factor was largely an hereditary contribution, and that specific factors, though having hereditary components, were subject to considerable environmental and training influence. Examples might be special aptitudes and skills in music, art, mathematics and so forth. Accordingly, he recommended that general intelligence tests attempt to evaluate the G-factor, and many who developed omnibus-type intelligence tests felt that the diversity and all-inclusiveness of their tests was an indication that they were assessing the G-factor. With respect to definitions of intelligence, there were many. In essence they generally reduced to a simple statement that intelligence is the mental ability to solve problems and to adjust or adapt to the many situations found in one's daily living and working environment.

In an effort to determine just what it is that intelligence tests measure, and, if possible, to determine what kinds of specific abilities exist so that better tests of such specific factors could be designed, L. L. Thurstone and J. P. Guilford utilized factor analytic techniques. These techniques were applied to the performances on all kinds of test items found in standard intelligence tests as well as upon specially constructed items. Thurstone (1935, 1938, 1944) came to the conclusion that there were eight or ten factors. Among these were such factors as verbal comprehension, word fluency, numerical ability, spatial ability, reasoning ability, and memory.

Guilford's (1956, 1967a, b) extensive and valuable work with factor analysis has led him to a rather complex model of the structure-of-intellect. He recognized that empirical work along multiple factor analytic lines had turned up a rather large number of supposedly unique intellectual abilities, and that some of them followed rather parallel courses. In order to cope with these varied abilities in some systematic and logical way he developed the structure-of-intellect model, the most recent version of which I have seen comprised a cube containing 120 cells. This model represents intellect as being composed of four types of informational content (figural, symbolic, semantic and behavioral), five types of operations which may be performed with respect to the informational content (cognition, memory, divergent production, convergent production, and evaluation), and six formal types of informational products (units, classes, relations, systems, transformations and implications). Thus, according to Guilford, information processing ability (intellect or intelligence) can be analyzed and classified according to *content* or type of information processed, the *operations* by means of which it is processed, and the *products* or end results of information processing. In the light of the empirical evidence from multiple factor-analytic studies of intelligence tests and his theoretical model of the structure-of-intellect, Guilford proposed that "intelligence is a systematic collection of abilities or functions for processing information according to logical principles."

Guilford acknowledges that his model does not take into account motivational and emotional factors. No doubt he also would admit that it does not attempt to appraise level of arousal or activation, or the role of attention and expectancy in the processing of information. It is precisely such factors which psychophysiological approaches, such as are dealt with in this book, attempt to measure and evaluate. It is well known that some of these factors, especially arousal and activation, and perhaps also emotion and motivation, are dependent upon the reticular formation of the lower brainstem. There is a distinct possibility that this important structure, at the crossroads of input to, and output from, the brain, which regulates sleep and wakefulness and, indeed, our consciousness and awareness of the world about us, may be in some manner impaired or deficient in some forms of mental retardation.

Thus far this sketchy historical review of mental retardation and the concept of intelligence and its measurement has been confined to the twentieth century. Early medical and neurological views of the nineteenth century recognized the problem diagnostically and even advocated rehabilitative training in selected cases. Let us now have a brief review of the problem from the neurological viewpoint.

History records that Itard, a French physician successfully employing "sense training" with the deaf, became interested in a boy who had existed in isolation more or less as an animal in the wild. This boy, about whom Itard (1932) wrote the book, *The Wild Boy of Aveyron,* was discovered in 1799 and was diagnosed by the psychiatrist, Pinel, as an incurable idiot. Itard thought otherwise, and while he did not succeed in restoring the boy to normality, his success in generating more adequate sensory functions and some intellectual understanding, along with social adaptation, was sufficiently promising to challenge others to look for ways of training and rehabilitating those with severe intellectual defects rather than writing them off as hopeless and without any potential for improvement.

Seguin, a French neurologist, was one of those inspired by Itard's concepts and early efforts. Seguin lived during a period of considerable excitement and ferment about the new knowledge of the brain and nervous system that was developing in the nineteenth century. It is, perhaps, not surprising that in the midst of the new and stimulating ideas about the nervous system that Seguin (1907) should have developed what might be called an early neurophysiologic viewpoint of the feebleminded. He described two types of idiocy; superficial, and profound. Superficial idiocy meant that one or more motor or sensory avenues manifested impairment but that central brain structures were

believed to be intact. Profound idiocy, on the other hand, involved damage or impairment to the brain itself. In both instances, Seguin felt that sensory stimulation and motor activity
would help to open up input and output channels, that nerve
pathways and brain cells would develop under the influence of
sensory stimulation, a view widely held today. In any case, the
notion of Seguin was that the deaf or otherwise sensory defective, the retarded and the normal all required sensory stimulation to attain the broadest fulfillment of potential development.

Parenthetically, Sechenov, the father of Russian physiology,
in his book, *Reflexes of the Brain*, published in 1863, advocated
the necessity of extensive and varied sensory stimulation for the
normal development of the infant and child. Sechenov (1935)
saw in infancy an instinctive *striving* for sensory stimulation
which broadened the entire base of peripheral reflexes. As the
cerebral cortex developed, these reflexes came under inhibitory
control, but they also continued to elaborate by irradiation into
associated behavioral reflexes and eventually into voluntary manifestations of control. These latter manifestations he referred
to as "psychical reflexes," which in order to develop required
continued external stimulation and response and advanced
through concrete to more abstract expressions. Pavlov (1927) described these more advanced expressions of speech and thought
as belonging to the "second signal system" in contrast to the ex-
ternally controlled conditioned reflexes of the "first signal system." Anokhin (1966) further elaborated some of these conceptions in terms of modern neurophysiology to include return-
afferentation from conditioned reflex excitation. He emphasized
the necessity of the return-afferentation reflecting the precision
and adequacy of the response and fitting, in effect, a template of
what he called the "acceptor of action," residing in the highest
neural centers. Possibly a comparable notion of the internal
neural organization with respect to percepts, learning and
thought, was the so-called schema or schemata of Sokolov (1958,
1966).

Sechenov's ideas, as well as those of his and Pavlov's follow-
ers, have certainly been put into effect in modern-day schools

(nurseries, kindergartens, etc.) for children of workers raised outside the home in the USSR. Within the U.S. there is also widespread use of sensory stimulation in programs designed to facilitate infant development and divert developmental disabilities. The question is, when is it most effective? Early in infancy, or throughout early childhood, and even later? Is it the sensory stimulation and its motor consequences per se, or is it instead a device for learning to attend and develop flexibility in the use of alerting and attentional mechanisms? Psychophysiological investigations in conjunction with such programs could help to answer some of these questions. An important attempt at this kind of research is included in this book (Chap. 7).

As early as 1860, Guggenbuehl, a Swiss physician who founded a school for cretins, found that one of the main difficulties in their management and learning was their inability to attend to instructions or instructional material. To remedy this situation he would suddenly sound a gong, or in a dimly lit room write on a blackboard with a phosphorus pencil creating a brilliant line, hoping to momentarily capture the attention of his charges. Years later, Robert Malmo (1942), while repeating experiments of Carlyle Jacobsen of the early 1930's on the ability of frontal lobectomized monkeys to perform in a delayed response discrimination test, found that monkeys could perform these tests if the performance box was darkened so that there were no distractions. In contrast to Jacobsen's interpretations that such frontal animals manifest impaired memory, Malmo concluded that they have instead impaired ability to attend in the presence of competing sensory distractions. The same result was later confirmed by others, and is a generalization often made about brain-injured humans, namely, that attention tends to be impaired and that distractions interfere with perceptual and learning performances. If attention is an important component in learning to perceive, learning to learn, or learning to think, and even learning to be motivated in any of these tasks, one may well ask whether the mentally retarded and others with specific or general learning difficulties are impaired in their ability to learn to attend. If so, this may be worth investigating developmentally from basic orienting reflexes to general and selective attention, keeping in mind that the reticular formation plays a prominent role in such activities. Five chapters in this book deal with these questions by investigating orienting responses or attention processes (Chaps. 3, 4, 5, 8, 11) while other chapters contribute pertinent results (Chaps. 6, 7, 9, 13).

PSYCHOPHYSIOLOGICAL PERSPECTIVE

In the preceding historical review, despite its cursory nature, we have seen that the concepts of mental deficiency, mental retardation, or mental subnormality have never been very clearly or adequately defined. This has led to much confusion in thinking about the problem, indeed, even in determining what the problem is and what is to be done about it. Naturally, this has led to much diffusion of effort over the years.

It seems important to be able to establish that certain forms of mental retardation are secondary to other more discrete and objective biomedical factors and sometimes of a hereditary or constitutional nature. These factors include diseases of pregnant mother or child, inborn errors related to physiology, endocrinology, immunology, etc. and prenatal, perinatal or postnatal traumas. It is in connection with these factors that gains have been made in prevention (e.g. PKU, Rubella, Down's Syndrome, etc.).

The fact remains, however, that a relatively small percentage of the total population of mentally retarded can be accounted for in these terms. In contrast, some 75 percent are of the "familial retarded" type of unknown etiology, and assumed to be hereditarily and/or culturally determined. Some have argued that an appreciable number of this group might be accounted for in terms of "minimal brain damage," i.e. below the threshold of detection by ordinary neurological examination methods, but with some pathological or physiopathological aberrancy possibly detectable by careful and special EEG study. However, the detection of some "minimal" pathology may add no information as to etiology of the pathology.

"Minimal brain damage," is a deceptive concept. If it cannot be detected by standard neurological examination how is it detected? There may be several minimal or questionable neurological signs, such as slightly depressed or exaggerated reflexes. General or specific motor behavior may be characterized by clumsiness or awkwardness. Speech may not be entirely fluent. Verbal communication may be slow, hesitant, or characterized by lapses. Reading and writing fluency may be below normal. Learning, problem solving and thinking may be slow. But now we are back essentially to a definition of intelligence, namely, inadequate learning ability or information processing. We infer by this that "something" is wrong with brain function, and that "something" is probably "brain damage" or "minimal brain damage." It is easy to see how this logic develops by an analogy from impaired motor behavior.

In cerebral palsy, whether due to prenatal or postnatal trauma, disease or other factors, there is weakness or palsy in one or more limbs, depending upon the extent of brain damage over the relevant portion of the motor cortex on the side contralateral to the weakness. But, suppose that the same process had affected not the motor area of the cortex, but a comparable area of the cortex of the posterior parietal lobe on the right side. There would in all likelihood be no motor paralysis and perhaps no readily observable deficit. The neurologist generally has no specific items in his standard examination to reveal this as he does the cerebral palsy due to a motor area lesion, even when the palsy or weakness is not widespread or marked. In both cases intelligence tests might have been within normal limits. If he had some reason to expect pathology in this or other regions he might call for a pneumoencephalogram or an arteriogram, or some other modern brain scan procedure, but such expensive and sometimes risky procedures would not be used as a standard routine. He might opt for a standard EEG examination, which might or might not reveal a source of abnormality. However, specialized use of the EEG and its derivatives, the average evoked response (AER) or the contingent negative variation (CNV), and specialized psychophysiological or psychoneurological tests might reveal disturbances localized to this area. The differential effects in the EEG from bilaterally homologous areas are sometimes a sign of disturbance in a particular area, and methods are being worked out to make such bilateral comparisons by computer methodology.

Some years ago, Lindsley and Cutts (1940), and others more recently, reported that 70 to 80 percent of behavior disordered children have certain degrees of abnormality in their EEG's, but none of these children were mentally retarded. Furthermore, although in a follow-up study of some of the same children (Lindsley, unpublished data) four to six years later most showed the same types of EEG disturbances, it has never been unequivocally demonstrated that such disturbances persist into adulthood, and if so, that behavior pathology is an inevitable consequence. In another study (Lindsley and Cutts, 1941), EEG's were reported for a child who was followed for nearly two years after an acute attack of equine encephalitis. For several months following the onset of the attack there were periodic convulsions. The behavior, the EEG, and total protein in the spinal fluid were markedly abnormal, but eventually all of these abnormal signs cleared up, and the IQ was at its pre-attack level of about 150. Since it seems likely that some parts of the brain suffered organic pathology (perhaps diffusely) during the course of this illness because of the generalized EEG abnormality and the persistently high total protein values, it is notable that the intellectual level did not suffer impairment following the illness. Therefore, it is likely that mental retardation, or even impairment in a high IQ level, is not an inevitable consequence of events presumed to result in brain damage; even those events equal to or greater than those usually described in "minimal brain damage." It is well known, of course, that the EEG is sensitive to brain damage in the acute phases, but once brain tissue has been destroyed, unless there are complicating irritations, pressures etc., the abnormality in the EEG may disappear and no longer reflect local disturbances. The same may be true following some brain hemorrhages or minor "strokes" when behavior and EEG may both return to normal.

Berger (1932), the first to study the human EEG in 1929, reported that the EEGs of feebleminded persons resemble those of normal subjects, except for some reduction in amplitude and frequency of the alpha rhythm in the lowest grades. Later (1938), he reported that the EEG of adult feebleminded subjects manifested a more regular and rhythmic alpha pattern than normal adults due, he believed, to their generally passive mental characteristics. Kreezer (1936, 1937, 1939) studied various groups of mentally retarded persons and found that the alpha rhythm increased in frequency, amplitude and amount with mental age in mongolian and hereditary types of mental deficiency. The correlations were generally low, but significant statistically. The increases he found were most prominent in the mental age range from six to eight years. There were marked individual differences within a given mental age level.

Lindsley (1938), in eighty-eight normal children of ten to fourteen years of age, found no significant correlations between intelligence as measured on Stanford-Binet and Otis tests and alpha frequency, amplitude or percent time. Knott, et al. (1942) found a .50 correlation between alpha frequency and intelligence (Stanford-Binet Revision) for a group of forty-eight eight-year-olds. No significant correlation was found for a group of forty-two twelve-year-olds. Overall there appears to have been very little consistent relationship of significance between intelligence and various traditional characteristics of the resting alpha rhythm. It is possible that with modern techniques of frequency analysis and power density spectra that some relations of significance will be noted.

Four chapters in this book report on modern computer analysis of the EEG, average evoked potentials and steady potentials in mentally retarded persons (Chaps. 8, 9, 10, 11). Since these studies review recent literature in each area, no further review will be provided here. These chapters and others employing different psychophysiological techniques or concepts will provide some challenging new thoughts and data on the problem of mental retardation.

In any of the areas where brain-behavior functions are impaired, either by organic pathology or the many possible functional (e.g. physiological, biochemical, psychological) deviancies, it is desirable to have a battery of tests or procedures of objective nature with which to assess and evaluate the systems which are disturbed. One could start with a psychological or neurological model of information processing and plan a series of tests for each sensory input channel, using the experimental literature as a guide to the most important questions to be asked and the most appropriate current methods to be employed. This could take one into the perceptual and cognitive realms and the integrative processes which limit or expand the interactions between modalities. There is more than ample informational content and methodology in the experimental literature from which to make choices of functions to be measured. The problem is to pick and choose the right measures both from the point of view of what one wishes to study and what one can appropriately adapt for use with human subjects whose limitations may impose constraints not encountered in working with normal adults in an experimental setting. Another element of choice is that the measure should be of some reasonably clearly defined basic function or set of parameters which are part of a logically and systematically conceived framework. Once such a battery or set of measures has been implemented and tested for reliability and validity with respect to each individual component, a plan for the accumulation of relevant data should be conceived. My own predilection would be to use this objective set of measures as a basis for classifying patients and normals into subgroups, i.e. those that perform alike on certain measures would be grouped together for further analysis and study.

For example, in a psychiatric population experimenters often select by clinical diagnosis a particular type of schizophrenic to be compared in terms of one or two measures with another type of schizophrenic; or a group of manic depressives to be compared with a group of schizophrenics. If, as often happens, the particular measures do not reliably differentiate between the groups, the measures are abandoned as inadequate. On the other hand, if the measures had been applied across an entire group of the patient population, as well as normals, there might well have been a number of individuals from diverse clinical categories who showed the same basic reactions on these measures. This would mean that they have something in common and if the background of the measure was sufficiently well understood it could lead to the formulation of further hypotheses as to why they were alike in this respect.

There are many factors to be considered in any attempt at subgrouping, including choice of subjects to be studied and choice of tests to be employed. For example, in considering cross sections of a population of mentally retarded to be studied there is the factor of whether physiological maturation should be evaluated and considered as well as chronological age. In the choice of measures to be employed, sensory, perceptual, cognitive, motor, psychoneurological and psychophysiological or electrophysiological, it is desirable to consider carefully what is appropriate for different stages of development. In selecting perceptual and conceptual tests one might wish to consider what has been learned and proposed in this regard with respect to the stages of development in children by Inhelder and Piaget (1958). Or similarly, in the use of the EEG as a physiological measure one should not ignore the changes in the state of development of the alpha rhythm as a function of age from say one to ten years (Lindsley, 1939). In almost every category of measurement some judgment such as this will have to be made before a measure is adopted and included in a battery of tests.

I believe this method of approach would be worth trying with mentally retarded individuals in an effort to find a better method of classifying them for further study. So far only one major attempt has been made to differentiate subgroups of retardates. Clausen (1966) attempted to differentiate functional subgroups with a selective battery of thirty-five sensory, perceptual, motor, and cognitive measures. However, no clear subgroups emerged, and Clausen interpreted his findings in terms of impaired arousal processes (and presumably reticular formation functions) in the retardate. Chapter 2 represents an expansion into a psychophysiological analysis of Clausen's attempt to differentiate subgroups. The results again contribute to a concept of arousal malfunction. This is an important concept that will be returned to later.

One of the ways in which people can get ideas about what is appropriate to measure or to what specific questions one should be seeking an answer, comes from careful observation of individuals. I would like to briefly report one personal example of this which comes to mind in connection with the study of the mentally retarded. It goes back a long way in my experience, but I think it illustrates first how one's curiosity is aroused about a problem, and also how a number of years may go by before you learn enough or get some insight as to what that problem might require in the way of a solution.

About thirty-five years ago, I was teaching a course on psychological methods and measurement at Brown University, when I became aware of a film which left a lasting impression on me. It illustrated performance testing in mentally retarded and normal persons by contrasting the performance of about a twenty-year-old male with a mental age of five with that of a little girl of five years of age with a mental age of five. The test was a Seguin Form Board with ten wooden blocks which fitted into recesses in the board. No language or verbal ability was required. The examiner took one of the blocks and demonstrated how it would fit into a recess in the board of corresponding shape. Then the examiner placed the blocks on the far side of the board but within reach of the subject and indicated by pantomine that the subject was to place the blocks in the board. The little girl very speedily and unerringly placed all ten blocks. The twenty-year-old was shown performing next. He sat looking at the examiner with a friendly but silly grin on his face. After the brief demonstration he slowly reached for a block, let us say an oval-shaped one, and tried to put it in a diamond-shaped recess. He continued to persist in this effort without apparently deriving any feedback information that the block and the recess did not match.

This performance aroused my curiosity and caused me to wonder just what aspects of the information processing system were defective or functioning improperly. From the demonstration he apparently got the idea he was to put the blocks in the recesses. His vision and eye-hand coordination seemed to be adequate for he picked up the block and put in over the recess, but alas, the wrong one. He repeatedly tried to force the oval block into the diamond recess. He seemed to be motivated for the task since he reached for the block and attempted to place it. Attention seemed to be focussed on the task for the block was held over the diamond recess. Was it that attention was too broadly focussed upon the block as a whole, or too sharply focussed upon one given point, so that the discrepancy in the two forms, the recess and the block, could not be detected by scanning or shifting the gaze around the edges? Or was it that an incorrect judgment to act, once initiated, could not be interrupted; the pattern of response was set and perseveration of response was the result? There was no effort to scan the board for a recess more likely to fit the block, and no attempt was made to place the block over another recess in the board. Was it possible that discrepant or nonmatching edges were observed, but the information not stored, even temporarily, until further scanning results could be correlated with the preceding observations so as to be collated and lead to a judgment "wrong." Was there no interplay of excitation and inhibition so that eye fixations and saccadic eye movements would alternate until all edges had been observed or scanned; or so that attention and observation could rapidly shift from one point to another on the block or recess? Was there no flexibility to make trial and error responses and judgments, other than the same essentially stereotyped movement? Was it possible that there was little more information processing than feature detection in its simplest form at the primary visual cortex, or even only at subcortical levels? As I recall there was a lapse in the stereotyped activity long enough for the subject to look up at the examiner with the same silly grin as at the start, as if to say, how do you do this? The examiner than guided his hand and the block to the correct recess. Another block was taken and the same type of error made. Eventually, I believe, a success or two came quite by chance, but there was no continuing series of successes.

The little girl, on the other hand, seemed not to hesitate at all with each serial placement and there was no evidence of deliberate scanning of the entire board in search of an appropriate recess for each block in turn. It was as if she could take it all in at a glance, with a span of apprehension covering most of the board.

It seems to me that the cause was not peripheral or retinal and probably had to be a central process of some kind, possibly attentional in nature. At that time I was aware of the fact that the oscillations of the alpha rhythm of the EEG at about 10 per second might function like a neuronic shutter mechanism or a chopper circuit, and provide a waxing and waning excitability cycle each tenth of a second, so that attentional or scanning shifts might be made at any inexcitable moment. I was not yet aware of the arousal and alerting functions of the reticular formation, and the fact that such activation mechanisms, operating via midline thalamic nuclei and the orbitofrontal cortex, may generally or differentially regulate the state of the cortex (Skinner and Lindsley, 1973, 1967; Lindsley, 1970, 1960) and possibly relate to vigilance or attention and selective attention (Skinner and Lindsley, 1971; Haider, Spong and Lindsley, 1964; Spong, Haider and Lindsley, 1965). After I did become aware of the influence of the reticular formation upon the electrical activity of the cortex and its arousal, alerting, and attentional correlates, I began to think that retardates might have a less than optimally functioning reticular formation (Lindsley, 1957). This could be due to a hereditary or constitutional defect, or because of prenatal or postnatal trauma or disease. It even seemed possible that in prenatal life as the anlage of the reticular formation was being formed, or in early postnatal life, deprivation of stimulation could have partially arrested the development of this structure or altered its functions. A few years later, about 1957, Gershon Berkson and I contrived a project where alpha blockade in the EEG was to be studied in a group of mentally retarded patients. While the project was never completed, Berkson took it up again during a post-doctoral year at the Maudsley Hospital in London (Berkson, Hermelin and O'Connor, 1961).

They found that the length of persistence of the alpha block-ade to sensory stimulation was shorter in mentally defectives than in normal subjects, a result which might be consistent with a defective or undeveloped reticular activating system, and pos-sibly with inability to maintain attentiveness long enough to process information into memory. This, of course, is hypotheti-cal and speculative but it provides food for thought about the mechanisms which underlie information processing.

In keeping with the concept that the role and function of the reticular formation in mentally defective individuals may be de-ficient is a study by Hernandez-Peon and Aguilar-Figueroa (1964) in which they found the average evoked potentials to tactile stimuli repeated at the rate of 1 per second did not mani-fest the characteristic normal pattern of habituation. Further-more, when attention was directed away from the stimuli under conditions of distraction, the evoked responses showed an op-posite effect from that of normals. Instead of the amplitude being reduced when distraction was introduced, as in normals, it was initially enhanced in the retarded subject and required nearly forty seconds to become comparably reduced to the level of the response in normals. These aberrant reactions in mentally retarded subjects suggest deficiencies in reticular-cortical-reticu-lar systems of regulation. In the discussion of a paper by O'Con-nor (1967), Hernandez-Peon further presented and illustrated these results. O'Connor's concepts are especially interesting from the viewpoint of a psychoneurological and psychophysiological approach to mental retardation. He reports on the results of various studies of perception, learning, memory, transfer of training, coding into language and attention. O'Connor conclud-ed that defective children are not handicapped in memory to the extent that others suggest, but probably are in attention func-tions and in the coding of the perceptual world into speech. This latter result corresponds to the difficulty level which In-helder and Piaget (1958) say exists even for normal children as they reintegrate their relatively simple and concrete concepts of the world into the more abstract symbols of language and speech. This may have some relationship to the shift from abstract to concrete cognitive functions emphasized by Goldstein (1939, 1942) which occurs in normal adults under the influence of brain injury.

O'Connor's (1967) emphasis of difficulties with input functions and coding in the retarded, suggests that attentive and integrative mechanisms so essential to intellectual functions are faulty. The question is are they faulty because of faulty arousal, orienting and alerting mechanisms anchored in the reticular formation, or because of malfunctions of associated differential attention mechanisms further integrated via nonspecific thalamic nuclei and orbitofrontal cortex? Or, are they faulty because of a rather different mechanism anchored in the posterolateral thalamus in polysensory nuclei, such as the pulvinar, which are sometimes described as associational nuclei? The function of the pulvinar, which, proportionally, becomes very large in monkey and man, especially, is undoubtedly involved in a part of the information processing function, very possibly with that difficult step mentioned above when perception and cognition progress from the relatively simple, concrete level to the symbolic, semantic, abstract formulation level of speech and thought. These hierarchies of cognitive information processing often involve multi-modal sensory input, the transfer of information from one mode to another, integration and orientation in time and space, and special coding and decoding features, as well as a labile and flexible memory storage system.

Unfortunately, these and other steps in the information processing hierarchy cannot be specified as yet in much detail in neurophysiological and psychophysiological terms. However, some progress has been made, and in what follows there will be an attempt to characterize for one sense mode, vision, some of the elementary information processing features, with special emphasis upon the elaboration of visual input systems via a series of delay paths. More has been worked out along these lines for vision than for the other sensory channels, and no doubt it is the most complex because of its prime importance for information processing.

It is usually considered that the brain, and especially the

cerebral cortex, mediates the processing of information necessary to intellectual development. But is it only the cerebral cortex with which we are concerned? Obviously not. The autonomic nervous system also plays a role in information processing via the OR, specific cardiac processes (Lacey and Lacey, 1971), emotional state and even pupillary responses. Miller (1973) has eloquently described instrumental learning involving the ANS. Much information processing takes place elsewhere in the nervous system and even in specialized receptor mechanisms, the retina and the cochlea, as well as in other less highly specialized and concentrated receptors of other sense modalities. Each sense mode funnels its information to the brain and to its supposedly highest representation, the cerebral cortex, by unique coded messages containing selected and segregated bits of information representing the external world and the body itself. Much of this information does not reach the cerebral cortex directly, and perhaps not even indirectly, for it serves its purposes of reflex integration at spinal, brainstem or diencephalic levels. Even considerable sensory input which does reach the cortex during the waking states does not reach the level of consciousness. In some instances we could be aware of it, but we are not, due to inattentiveness, distraction, etc. Also, during sleep much sensory input reaches the cortex but we are not aware of it and do not react to it.

Not all of the energy changes in the external world around us are sensed, mirrored and stored in our brain, for our cutaneous receptors are not sensitive to all contacts, pressures and vibratory frequencies imposed upon the skin. The dynamic range of the ear of man is very limited with respect to the frequency of the rarefactions and condensations of the atmosphere existing at the tympanic membrane; even much less than for the dog which senses much higher frequencies. The receptors of the eye are sensitive to only an exceedingly narrow bandwidth of the total electromagnetic spectrum. Yet, each of these peripheral sensory mechanisms is capable of some degree of information processing, i.e. the segregation of certain selected properties of the external environment, both qualitative and quantitative.

In the case of the eye, each of the myriad receptors has a certain threshold of excitability. Some fire to the "on," some to the "off" and some to the "on" and "off" of light. There are two synaptic levels in the retina, one, at the junction of receptors and bipolar cells and one between bipolar cells and ganglion cells whose axons comprise the optic nerve. Few or many receptor influences may converge upon bipolar cells, providing focal or areal representation. Just as the brain has "interneurons," the retina has intervening connector cells, the horizontal cells and amacrine cells. There may be temporal and spatial summation at retinal synapses as elsewhere in the nervous system. Each neural channel has an excitatory or inhibitory receptive field which may be large or small and an inhibitory or excitatory surrounding field.

A consequence of all of this intricate mechanism, not unlike that of the cerebral cortex, is that a certain degree of information processing is going on in the retina. Microelectrode recordings from one of the 500,000 optic nerve fibers in the monkey reveals, as it has in the cat and rabbit, and undoubtedly would also in man, that each single unit or optic nerve fiber conveys a certain type of information. It may respond to only one, or it may respond to more than one, feature of the visual environment exposed to the eye—its wavelength, its spatial locus or orientation, its contrasting borders, its spatial frequency, and so on. While a single optic nerve fiber may convey one or more kinds of information, collectively, several, or many more such fibers may add other sensory characteristics, both of qualitative and quantitative nature. Thus information processing, including separation and segregation of units of information, both of kind and quantity, may go on at the retinal level. In general, the projection of these fibers upon the lateral geniculate body and primary visual cortex maintains a topographical organization consistent with its spatial origin on the retina.

Where these optic nerve fibers synapse upon other nerve cells in the lateral geniculate body, the relay nucleus of the thalamus for vision, there is additional selective feature detection and information processing. As in the retina, there are interacting and integrating interneurons; there are also intrusions from other brain centers, including the reticular formation which may enhance or inhibit responsiveness. Thus, there is further information processing at this level of the visual system. The axons of these lateral geniculate cells comprise the optic radiations, a broad but thin band of fibers, looping along the inner boundaries of the temporal lobe to the primary visual cortex, a receiving area known as the striate cortex, or in Brodmann's architectonic terminology as area 17 of the visual cortex.

It is here in area 17 of the visual cortex in cat and monkey that Hubel and Wiesel (1962, 1965, 1968) have demonstrated that single visual cortical cells respond electrically in a selective and differentiated manner to specific characteristics of the visual environment. These feature-detecting cells, by their highly selective response, manage to abstract certain properties of the stimulus, such as line length, orientation and movement. But the process of "abstraction" does not end here in area 17 with the so-called "simple" cells. Hubel and Wiesel have also recorded from what they call "complex" and "hypercomplex" cells of areas 18 and 19 of the visual cortex of monkeys, a narrow circumstriate belt surrounding the spatially extensive area 17 or striate cortex in the monkey. Here they find single cells which respond to more refined features of the visual stimulus such as angles, curvature and other components which go to make up a pattern. But despite these fascinating discoveries of progressively more elaborate feature-detecting properties which differentiate stimuli impinging upon the retina as lines of different orientation, direction of movment, or angles and combinations thereof, which seem to be building blocks for pattern perception, Hubel and Wiesel (1965) are forced to conclude, in discussing the relevance of it for perception, that it goes "only a short way toward accounting for the perception of shapes encountered in everyday life." They are not able to tell us where and how form and pattern perception takes place in the brain, and how the differentiated forms take on meaning: that this form is a sphere or ball, and this one a cube or pyramid. Even for the simple feeding dish from which a cat or dog is fed daily, and which they soon come to discriminate from other nonfeeding dishes and respond to enthusiastically when presented, there is little evidence as to where and how recognition of the dish is stored.

There is, however, some evidence in the monkey which suggests that memory for visual form or pattern may be critically dependent upon a small region on the lateral and inferior surface of the temporal lobe. Farther back along the temporal lobe in a region approaching the circumstriate belt of the anterior visual cortex and the posterior parietal cortex, there are small areas of the inferotemporal cortex which are believed to be important in the discrimination of visual patterns, and, possibly even more important, critical for visual attention (Mishkin, 1972).

These presumably auditory discrimination and association areas of the temporal lobe which serve visual functions are regions to which the pulvinar nucleus of the thalamus is known to distribute some of its projections, as it does also to other association zones of the parietal and occipital cortex. The junctional regions of the occipital, parietal and temporal lobes are believed to be important integrating centers and the pulvinar and other posterolateral association nuclei of the thalamus appear to have two-way connections with them. The pulvinar nucleus of the thalamus is a polysensory convergence center for visual, auditory and somatosensory input and has been shown to respond electrically to stimuli of any of these modalities (Huang and Lindsley, 1973).

The pulvinar is known to receive input from the superior colliculus and pretectal region of the midbrain. These regions of the midbrain receive visual input from fibers of the optic nerve and tract. While most of the optic nerve and optic tract fibers go directly to the lateral geniculate nucleus and are relayed to the primary receiving area of the visual cortex, some of the optic tract fibers pass by way of the brachium of the superior colliculus to the superior colliculus and the adjacent pretectal region. The former route, known as the geniculo-striate pathway, is the direct or specific visual sensory projection pathway; the latter via the superior colliculus will contribute to two important time-delay pathways which affect the processing of information in the cortex. One of these delay paths goes from the superior colliculus to the pulvinar (and nucleus lateralis posterior), and from the pulvinar to the inferotemporal cortex and to the circumstriate belt of the visual and parietal cortex in the monkey. The other delay pathway for visual input is believed to be via the superior colliculus or pretectal region of the midbrain to the midbrain reticular formation which lies just below this region.

The reticular formation is also a polysensory center, receiving input from all sense modalities, and, as shown by Moruzzi and Magoun (1949) has among other things, an ascending activating function. That is, stimulation of the reticular formation by natural sensory input from any of these modalities, or by direct electrical stimulation, causes the synchronized electrical activity of the cerebral cortex to become desynchronized or activated. Behaviorally, such stimulation of the reticular formation arouses the sleeping animal and alerts a drowsy one. Thus, sensory input via the reticular formation has an activating influence upon the cerebral cortex generally and through it an arousal effect upon behavior. A unique or novel stimulus, which is unexpected, usually causes an orienting response, that is, the animal orients its body, head and receptors optimally to receive and appraise the source and nature of the unexpected stimulation. The ascending reticular activating system, operating through the midline thalamic nuclei (so-called nonspecific nuclei because of their generally diffuse influences upon the entire cortical mantle), the inferior thalamic peduncle and the orbitofrontal cortex, appears to control and regulate the excitatory and inhibitory level of various cortical regions and therefore apparently the receptivity of these regions to incoming messages over sensory specific pathways such as the geniculo-striate system for vision (Skinner and Lindsley, 1973).

The midline thalamic nuclei probably serve as pacemakers for cerebral rhythms, such as the familiar alpha rhythm of the electroencephalogram of man. As the alpha rhythm slows a person becomes drowsy and with still further slowing of the synchronized waves he may attain a stage of deep sleep and be relatively immune to the influences of sensory stimulation around him unless it becomes intense. In such a stage he is not able to process sensory information and derive meaning from it. Only in a unique state of paradoxical or REM (rapid eye movement) sleep, when the EEG pattern reverts to one resembling a waking state is there an awareness and temporary memory for the dream. During such a state an animal or human appears to be in one of his deepest stages of sleep, but the EEG pattern is very different from that of ordinary slow wave deep sleep, hence its paradoxical character.

These relatively brief periods of paradoxical or REM sleep occur usually several times during the course of a night's sleep and may last several minutes or longer. In a state of deep slow wave sleep, or under the influence of an anesthetic, the excitability of the reticular formation appears to be depressed, for its response to sensory stimulation is markedly diminished. Its ascending influences upon the nonspecific midline thalamic nuclei are diminished and therefore do not desynchronize their rhythmic activities. Without the influence of reticular activation the midline pacemaker nuclei, tonically driven from visceral or other sources but at a relatively low level, tend to pace or regulate cortical rhythms at a relatively low rate, more so than when high frequency, irregular, activating discharges from the reticular formation impinge upon them. The result is relaxation, inattention, drowsiness and sleep. During wakefulness it appears that there can be some differential and localized effects of nonspecific input upon the various regions of the cerebral cortex. Such effects, especially those of a brief and phasic character, may be responsible for the ability to shift attention from one sensory mode to another, or even within a given sense mode.

It is important to note that when the reticular activating system is depressed in sleep or under an anesthetic and the cerebral cortex manifests large amplitude slow waves characteristic of sleep or of the anesthetic state, there can be no processing of sensory information. The impulses or messages get through via the specific sensory systems to the cerebral cortex, for their effects can be registered as evoked potentials. However, they are not perceived or remembered and conditioning or learning of specific responses to them cannot take place.

Information processing (perception, learning, memory, concept formation, problem solving and thinking) can best take place when the brain and its cerebral cortex are in states which correspond with behavioral wakefulness, alertness and attentiveness. One might also add that in order to be attentive and perceptive it is generally conceded that there must also be some pervasive motivating influence, i.e. some task or reason to process the information with the expectation that there will be some kind of reward for doing so, either escape from pain, discomfort, or, some satisfaction, pleasure or reduction of need or drive state.

This brief, and incomplete, description of one of the sense modes, vision, has been presented as an example of how complex the receptive and neural mechanisms are that transform events in the physical world and the organism's relation to them into experience, or stored information. Such information, or intelligence, has a dynamic quality because it is constantly being utilized in the processing of new information and revising or adding to the previous store of information. In this sense intelligence is not merely a static "something" a given or endowed structural "something," say 10 billion brain cells in a black box, organized in some immutable pattern with billions upon billions of inter-connections or synapses. Within the organism (in contrast to a cell culture) brain cells could not survive without all of the other organs and organ systems of the body as a whole upon which the brain is dependent for its nourishment and viability. But the supporting and housekeeping functions which surround the brain are not enough. Sensory receptors, their neural pathways to the brain, and the terminal synapses on dendritic spines of cortical brain cells would not develop or retain their structure and functional capacities in the complete absence of stimulation.

Riesen (1970) has discussed the detrimental effects of light and pattern deprivation upon the ganglion cells of the retina, on the electroretinogram and upon behavioral performances in visual tasks. These results indicate that damage to the peripheral mechanism of the eye through lack of stimulation can affect its role in information processing at that level. In addition Valverde and Ruis-Marcos (1970) have shown that central neuronal structure in the visual cortex of mice can be adversely affected by rearing the mice in the dark. Dendritic spines of apical dendrites in the striate cortex either do not develop or deteriorate as a function of the lack of visual experience. O'Connor (1968) has discussed the effects of restricted environments on the social and intellectual behavior of developing children, and Casler (1968) has argued that institutional environments have a similar adverse effect because of perceptual deprivation. Mason (1970) has presented a biological perspective on the effects of experiential deprivation in relation to information processing. In general, most deprivational situations of long duration are detrimental to the development and efficiency of information processing systems. However, much shorter periods of selective treatment may be effective either positively or negatively if occurring during so-called critical periods (Scott, 1962) for the development of social behavior and learning.

In contrast to deprivation and restriction of environment, Rosenzweig, Krech, Bennett and Diamond (1968) have described for the rat the effects of an enriched environment upon brain chemistry and anatomy, showing that brain weight and cortical thickness increase, acetylcholinesterase activity is enhanced and problem-solving ability is improved. Thus we see that both the structure and function of neural information processing systems can probably be altered significantly by decreasing or increasing the amount of environmental stimulation.

In relation to information processing and learning ability as indicators of intelligence, Fantz (1970) indicates that visual exploration and information processing begin at birth or shortly thereafter. The opportunity for experiential effects is present long before the human infant is in a position to learn much from his environment by manual and locomotor activities, or verbal communication. He points out something I think may be very important. Whereas an infant may be able to detect and discriminate visual forms and patterns at a simple level, a more important aspect may be the development of a process of selective attention. Since selectivity is very much a part of information processing at all subsequent levels of development this may be a crucial place in which to attempt to exercise it and encourage it. Not only would this be an important step in learning to attend but would go hand in hand with learning to learn. Fortunately, there has been a recrudescence of interest and effort in early experience and development on the part of experimental child psychologists, pediatric neurologists, physiological and comparative psychologists and neurobiologists (see books by Newton and Levine, 1968; Young and Lindsley, 1970). There is greater investigation of psychophysiological measures such as the EEG, evoked potentials, as well as sucking and heart rate components of orienting. The consequence will be an expansion of our knowledge and predictive power of early cognitive development.

As will be observed in various chapters of this book modern instrumentation and technology, far in advance of the 1930's, 1940's and 1950's may now be brought to bear on mental retardation and information processing concepts of intelligence. Mental retardation is, as we have seen, a complex problem with multiple causes. This is probably true of any psychological and behavioral impairment. Even if they have common underlying systems, these must interact with other systems to produce the great variety of syndromes and symptoms which characterize the many different disorders. The goal would be to attempt to functionally isolate systems or subsystems by selective stimulus and behavioral control. There are many ways of accomplishing this and sufficient progress has been made along many experimental lines to make this seem feasible. Some of the studies described in this book are representative of initial steps in this direction, combining psychological and psychophysiological methods.

Despite all of the technological advantages of the modern era, the problems and unanswered questions remain pretty much the same as in days of yore. There is still no substitute for a keen mind in the head of the investigator to formulate the questions to be answered by our advancing technology and to have the wit to know when he has obtained an answer. The subsequent chapters are cogent presentations with this purpose.

REFERENCES

Anokhin, P. K.: Special features of the afferent apparatus of the conditioned reflex and their importance to psychology. In: A. Leontiev, A. Luria, and A. Smirnov (Eds.): *Psychological Research in the U.S.S.R.* Moscow, Progress Publishers, 1966.

Berger, H.: Ueber das Elektrekephalogramm des Menschen. I. *Arch Psychiat Nervenkr, 87:*527-570, 1929.

———: Ueber das Elektrekephalogramm des Menschen. V. *Arch Psychiat Nervenkr, 101:*452-469, 1932.

———: Ueber das Elektrekephalogramm des Menschen. XIV. *Arch Psychiat Nervenkr, 108:*407-431, 1938.

Berkson, G.; Hermelin, B., and O'Connor, N.: Physiological responses of normals and institutionalized mental defectives to repeated stimuli. *J Ment Def Res, 5:*30-39, 1961.

Binet, A., and Simon, Th.: *Mentally Defective Children.* (Translated by W. B. Drummond). London, Edward Arnold, 1914.

———: *The Development of Intelligence in Children.* Baltimore, Williams and Wilkins, 1916.

Casler, L.: Perceptual deprivation in institutional settings. In: G. Newton and S. Levine (Eds.): *Early Experience and Behavior: The Psychobiology of Development.* Springfield, Thomas, 1968.

Clausen, J.: Ability structure and subgroups in mental retardation. Baltimore, Spartan, 1966.

Fantz, R. L.: Visual perception and experience in infancy: Issues and approaches. In: F. A. Young and D. B. Lindsley (Eds.): *Early Experience and Visual Information Processing in Perceptual and Reading Disorders.* Washington, D.C., National Academy of Sciences, 1970.

Goddard, H. H.: The Binet measuring scale of intelligence, what is it and how is it used. *Training School Bulletin,* 86-91, 1914.

Goldstein, K.: *The Organism: A Holistic Approach to Biology Derived from Pathological Data in Man.* New York, American Book Co., 1939.

———: *After-Effects of Brain Injuries in War; Their Evaluation and Treatment.* New York, Grune and Stratton, 1942.

Guggenbuehl, H.: The cretins of Abendberg. *Amer J Insanity, 17:*335, 1860.

Guilford, J. P.: The structure of intellect. *Psychol Bull, 53:*267-293, 1956.

———: *The Nature of Human Intelligence.* New York, McGraw-Hill, 1967a.

———: Creativity and learning. In: D. B. Lindsley and A. A. Lumsdaine (Eds.): *Brain Function and Learning. Brain Function,* Vol. IV. Los Angeles, Univ. of California Press, 1967b.

Haider, M.; Spong, P., and Lindsley, D. B.: Attention, vigilance and cortical potentials in humans. *Science, 145:*180-182, 1964.

Hernandez-Peon R., and Aguilar-Figueroa, E.: Electrophysiologic recordings in mentally retarded subjects. (Incorporated in an article by Hernandez-Peon, R.: Attention, sleep, motivation and behavior.) In: R. G. Heath (Ed.): *The Role of Pleasure in Behavior.* New York, Hoeber, 1964.

Huang, C., and Lindsley, D. B.: Polysensory responses and sensory interaction in pulvinar and related posterolateral nuclei in cat. *Electroenceph Clin Neurophysiol, 34:*449-462, 1973.

Hubel, D. H., and Wiesel, T. N.: Receptive fields, binocular interaction and functional architecture in the cat's visual cortex. *J Physiol (Lond), 160:* 106-154, 1962.

————: Receptive fields and functional architecture in two nonstriate visual areas (18 and 19) of the cat. *J Neurophysiol, 28:*229-289, 1965.

————: Receptive fields and functional architecture of monkey striate cortex. *J Physiol (Lond), 195:*215-243, 1968.

Inhelder, B., and Piaget, J.: *The Growth of Logical Thinking from Childhood to Adolescence.* London, Routledge and Kegan Paul, 1958.

Itard, J. M. G.: *The Wild Boy of Aveyron.* (Translated by G. and M. Humphrey), New York, Appleton-Century, 1932.

Knott, J. R.; Friedman, H., and Bardsley, R.: Some electroencephalographic correlates of intelligence in eight-year- and twelve-year-old children. *J Exp Psychol, 30:*380-391, 1942.

Kreezer, G.: Electric potentials of the brain in certain types of mental deficiency. *Arch Neurol Psychiat, Chicago, 36:*1206-1213, 1936.

————: Electrical phenomena of the brain among the feeble-minded. *Proc Amer Assn Men Def, 42:*130-141, 1937.

————: Intelligence level and occipital alpha rhythm in the Mongolian type of mental deficiency. *Amer J Psychol, 52:*503-532, 1939.

Lacey, J. I., and Lacey, B. C.: Some autonomic-central nervous system interrelationships. In: P. Black (Ed.): *Physiological Correlates of Emotion.* N.Y., Academic, 1971.

Lindsley, D. B.: Electrical potentials of the brain in children and adults. *J Gen Psychol, 19:*285-306, 1938.

————: A longitudinal study of the occipital alpha rhythm in normal children: frequency and amplitude standards. *J Genet Psychol, 55:*197-213, 1939.

————: Psychophysiology and Motivation. In: M. R. Jones (Ed.). *Nebraska Symposium on Motivation.* Lincoln, Univ. Nebr., 1957.

————: Attention, consciousness, sleep and wakefulness. In: J. Field, H. W. Magoun, V. E. Hall (Eds.): *Handbook of Physiology-Neurophysiology,* Sect. 1, Vol. III, Washington, D.C., Amer. Physiological Society, 1960.

————: The role of nonspecific reticulo-thalamo-cortical systems in emotion. In: P. Black (Ed.): *Physiological Correlates of Emotion*. New York, Academic, 1970.

Lindsley, D. B., and Cutts, K. K.: The electroencephalograms of "constitutionally inferior" and behavior problem children: Comparison with normal children and adults. *Arch Neurol Psychiat, Chicago, 44*:1199-1212, 1940.

Lindsley, D. B., and Cutts, K. K.: Clinical and electroencephalographic changes in a child during recovery from encephalitis. *Arch Neurol Psychiat, Chicago, 45*:156-161, 1941.

Malmo, R. B.: Interference factors in delayed response in monkeys after removal of frontal lobes. *J Neurophysiol, 5*:295-308, 1942.

Mason, W. A.: Information processing and experiential deprivation: A biologic perspective. In: F. A. Young and D. B. Lindsley (Eds.): *Early Experience and Visual Information Processing in Perceptual and Reading Disorders*. Washington, D.C., National Academy of Sciences, 1970.

Miller, N. E.: Autonomic learning: clinical and physiological implications. In: M. Hammer, K. Salzinger, S. Sutton (Eds.): *Psychopathology*. New York, Wiley, 1973.

Mishkin, M.: Cortical visual areas and their interactions. In: A. G. Karczmar and J. C. Eccles (Eds.): *Brain and Human Behavior*. New York, Springer-Verlag, 1972.

Moruzzi, G., and Magoun, H. W.: Brain stem reticular formation and activation of the EEG. *Electroenceph Clin Neurophysiol, 1*:455-473, 1949.

Newton, G. and Levine, S. (Eds.): *Early Experience and Behavior: The Psychobiology of Development*. Springfield, Thomas, 1968.

O'Connor, N.: Mental retardation and learning. In: D. B. Lindsley and A. A. Lumsdaine (Eds.): *Brain Function and Learning. Brain Function*, Vol. IV, Los Angeles, Univ. of California Press, 1967.

————: Children in restricted environments. In: G. Newton and S. Levine (Eds.): *Early Experience and Behavior: The Psychobiology of Development*. Springfield, Thomas, 1968.

Pavlov, I. P.: *Conditioned Reflexes*. Oxford, Clarendon Press, 1927.

Riesen, A. H.: Effects of visual environment on the retina. In: F. A. Young and D. B. Lindsley (Eds.): *Early Experience and Visual Information Processing in Perceptual and Reading Disorders*. Washington, National Academy of Sciences, 1970.

Rosenzweig, M. R.; Krech, D.; Bennett, E. L., and Diamond, M. C.: Modifying brain chemistry and anatomy by enrichment or impoverishment of experience. In: G. Newton and S. Levine (Eds.): *Early Experience and Behavior: The Psychobiology of Development*. Springfield, Thomas, 1968.

Sarason, S. B.: *Psychological Problems in Mental Deficiency. 2nd ed.* New York, Harper, 1963.

Sarason, S. B., and Gladwin, T.: Psychological and cultural problems in mental subnormality. Part II, In: R. L. Masland, S. B. Sarason and T. Gladwin, *Mental Subnormality: Biological, Psychological and Cultural Factors.* New York, Basic Books, 1958.

Scott, J. P.: Critical periods in behavioral development. *Science, 138*:949-958, 1962.

Sechenov, I. M.: *Reflexes of the Brain,* 1863. Reprinted in *Sechenov: Selected Works.* (Translated by A. A. Subov) Leningrad, State Publishing House, 1935.

Seguin, E.: *Traitment Morale, Hygiene Et Education Des Idiots.* (2 vols) Paris, 1846.

————: *Idiocy and Its Treatment by the Physiological Method.* (Originally published in 1864.) Reprinted New York, Columbia University, 1907.

Skinner, J. E., and Lindsley, D. B.: Electrophysiological and behavioral effects of blockade of the nonspecific thalamo-cortical system. *Brain Res, 6*:95-118, 1967.

————: Enhancement of visual and auditory evoked potentials during blockage of the nonspecific thalamo-cortical system. *EEG Clin Neurophysiol, 31*:1-6, 1971.

————: The nonspecific mediothalamic-frontocortical system: Its influence on electrocortical activity and behavior. In: K. H. Pribram, and A. R. Luria (Eds.): *Psychophysiology of the Frontal Lobes.* New York, Academic, 1973.

Sokolov, E. N.: *Perception and the Conditioned Reflex.* Moscow, Univ. of Moscow, 1958 (Translated version: Oxford, Pergamon, 1963).

————: Orienting reflex as information regulator. In: A. Leontiev, A. Luria, A. Smirnow (Eds.): *Psychological Research in the U.S.S.R.* Moscow, Progress Publishers, 1966.

Spearman, C.: *The Abilities of Man.* New York, Macmillan, 1927.

Spong, P.; Haider, M., and Lindsley, D. B.: Selective attentiveness and cortical evoked responses to visual and auditory stimuli. *Science, 148*:395-397, 1965.

Stern, W.: *The Psychological Methods of Testing Intelligence.* Baltimore, Warwick and York, 1914.

Terman, L. M.: *The Measurement of Intelligence.* Boston, Houghton-Mifflin, 1916.

Terman, L. M., and Merrill, M. A.: *Measuring Intelligence.* Boston, Houghton-Mifflin, 1937.

Thurstone, L. L.: *The Vectors of Mind.* Chicago, Univ. of Chicago, 1935.

————: *Primary Mental Abilities.* Chicago, Univ. of Chicago, 1938.

————: *A Factorial Study of Perception.* Chicago, Univ. of Chicago, 1944.

Valverde, F., and Ruis-Marcos, A.: The effects of sensory deprivation on dendritic spines in the visual cortex of the mouse: A mathematical model of spine distribution. In: F. A. Young, and D. B. Lindsley (Eds.): *Early Experience and Visual Information Processing in Perceptual and Reading Disorders.* Washington, National Academy of Sciences, 1970.

Wechsler, D.: *The Measurement of Adult Intelligence.* Baltimore, Williams and Wilkins, 1939.

Young, F. A., and Lindsley, D. B. (Eds.): *Early Experience and Visual Information Processing in Perceptual and Reading Disorders.* Washington, National Academy of Sciences, 1970.

CHAPTER **2**

MEASUREMENTS OF AUTONOMIC FUNCTIONS IN MENTAL DEFICIENCY

Johs Clausen; Arnold Lidsky; and Eugene A. Sersen[*]

[*] This project was supported in part by NIH grant 5 R01 HD 02744. The contributions of all who assisted in the study are gratefully acknowledged. Ivar Floistad participated in the early stages of the project. Carol Hulnick Woodruff assisted in collecting and editing the major portion of the data. Deborah Burke, Sally Hyland, and Charles Miezejeski contributed to various aspects of the study, as did Steven Richman and Alan Kluger, who also prepared the illustrations for publication. Diamantis Skinitis was responsible for the computer analysis and assisted with computer programs. Douglas Andersen assisted by maintaining the equipment. Appreciation is also extended to the nursing staff of the Institute. We thank Dr. James Block for critically reading an early version of this manuscript. We are indebted to the late Dr. Jack Hammond, Director of Willowbrook State School, and his staff for their support of the project. Thanks to their complete cooperation, we could efficiently screen, select, and bring to the Institute the majority of the patients included in the study. We also acknowledge the assistance of Dr. George A. Jervis, former Director of the Institute for Research in Mental Retardation, for making available the noninstitutionalized PKU patients. We also acknowledge with gratitude the cooperation of the directors and staffs of the State Schools who made it possible to transfer PKU patients to the Institute: the late Dr. Jacob Schneider of Letchworth Village, Dr. Frank R. Henne of Newark State School, Dr. Charles Greenburg of Rome State School, Dr. Oleh H. Wolansky of Suffolk State School, Dr. George F. Etling of Wassaic State School, Dr. Samuel Feinstein of West Seneca State School and Dr. Emanuel Rechter of Wilton State School.

M ENTAL DEFICIENCY IS a condition which results from a wide variety of causes, with impairment of CNS and disturbance of metabolic processes as prominent features in several diagnostic subgroups. Such physiological or biochemical impairments probably involve autonomic nervous system (ANS) functioning as well. The need to examine ANS functioning in mental deficiency is reinforced by the frequent suggestion that impairment of arousal is a central characteristic of mental deficiency (Berkson, 1961; Baumeister and Ellis, 1963; Baumeister and Kellas, 1968; Clausen, 1966, 1972; Crosby, 1972; Holden, 1965; Horowitz, 1965; Lindsley, 1957; Rosvold, 1967; Samuels, 1959). Autonomic variables were used as indices of arousal in the early animal studies (French, 1960; Hernandez-Peon, 1966; Moruzzi and Magoun, 1949) and have been emphasized in Russian studies of the orienting response (Luria, 1961a, 1961b; Sokolov, 1960). Nevertheless, large scale and systematic studies of the autonomic correlates of mental deficiency have been exceedingly rare.

LABORATORY STUDIES OF AUTONOMIC ACTIVITY

Karrer, in 1966, reviewed the handful of studies conducted up to that time. There seemed to be fairly substantial evidence that mental defectives, with the possible exception of Down's syndrome cases, have lower skin resistance than normals. There was also evidence, mostly from studies of skin resistance, that defectives are less reactive to simple stimuli of weak to moderate intensity. Karrer suggested that the situation may be different for stimuli of strong intensity. Several authors have proposed that latency (Grings, et al., 1962; Kodman, et al., 1959) and recovery time (Berkson, et al., 1961; Vogel, 1961) of autonomic responses may be shorter in defectives. These authors, however, have not related recovery time to response amplitude. The paucity of comparative studies of autonomic function in retardates with different etiologies was also emphasized by Karrer.

Berkson, Hermelin, and O'Connor (1961) compared eighteen adult normal males and three groups of mental defectives with respect to skin resistance and heart rate, under resting conditions, and in response to light flashes. Their Feebleminded and Imbecile groups had significantly lower resistance than the Normals, while Down's cases had slightly higher resting levels. Consistent with the other mentally defective groups, the Down's cases showed significantly less resistance change in response to stimulation. The Down's group also showed elevated heart rate compared to Normals (93 vs. 82 beats per minute), although this difference did not reach significance; the remaining groups were intermediate in heart rate. In a later publication, O'Connor and Hermelin (1963) found lower than normal skin resistance in all defectives, although their Down's cases did not differ significantly from the Normals.

In the laboratories of the Training School at Vineland, Clausen and Karrer conducted two studies which were reported in several publications (Clausen and Karrer, 1968, 1969, 1970; Karrer, 1965; Karrer and Clausen, 1964). In the 1964 publication, comparisons between mentally deficient and normal subjects were made in terms of resting levels of systolic blood pressure, galvanic skin resistance, heart rate, heart rate variability, and changes in blood volume of the finger. Changes in these variables were also recorded in response to auditory stimuli. It was found that, at rest, the mentally deficient subjects had generally lower skin resistance, higher systolic blood pressure, and greater blood volume changes of the finger than the normal subjects, but only the skin resistance difference reached significance. In addition, the autonomic resting level and reactivity measures of the patient group were statistically more concordant than those of the Normals. Compared to the Normals, the defectives were generally less reactive to stimuli, with significant differences in heart rate and heart rate variability.

The 1970 publication added blood volume changes of the head, respiration amplitude, and respiration period to the preceding measures, and Normals, Nonorganic Defectives, and Organic Defectives were compared on two occasions. The data again indicated lower skin resistance and higher blood pressure for the patients. This time, however, the differences in skin resistance were not significant, while the blood pressure difference was significant between Normals and Organics on the first day of recording. The data were also scored for the occurrence of orienting responses—simultaneous vasoconstriction in the periphery (finger) and vasodilation in the head—when a series of sound stimuli was applied (Clausen and Karrer, 1968). Fewer orienting responses were found for the mental defectives, particularly on the first day. Latency, time to maximum response, and recovery time for skin resistance and blood volume changes for the finger and the head, did not vary significantly between the groups (Clausen and Karrer, 1969).

Wallace and Fehr (1970) found no differences in resting skin resistance or heart rate when they compared nine Down's cases and ten Normal Controls (Chap. 7). When subjects responded to a 70 dB buzzer by pressing a key, the Normal group showed a significantly greater resistance decrease and a nonsignificant trend toward greater heart rate response.

Comparing skin resistance responses of 160 mentally retarded with 160 normal adults, Lobb (1970) found the responses of the retardates to be characteristically smaller and less frequent. Contrary to suggestions of Berkson, et al. (1961) and Vogel (1961), Lobb reported no differences between the groups in persistence of the skin response.

With the exception of Down's syndrome, undifferentiated populations of the mental defectives were generally tested in the previous studies. Some of the inconsistencies of the studies reviewed may be attributed to the heterogeneity of the patient groups. It would therefore be desirable to compare various etiological groups for autonomic activity recorded under identical conditions.

SOME RELATED CLINICAL OBSERVATIONS

The mental deficiency literature contains some indirect suggestions regarding autonomic functions in specific etiological categories. With regard to phenylketonuria (PKU), Penrose (1963) observed a tendency to excessive sweating, whereas Menkes (1965) suggested that in many PKU's the skin is rough and dry. Penrose and Menkes agree, however, that PKU's manifest excessive movements, and have accentuated reflexes resulting in brisk responses similar to those observed in hyperthyroidism. These characteristics are relevant for autonomic recordings, as movements are the greatest source of artifacts. Menkes (1965) and Jervis (1963) called attention to the light pigmentation in PKU

—a factor which could result in low baseline values for blood volume measures, when photoelectric transducers are used. While these authors also mentioned relatively high incidence of abnormal EEG patterns in PKU's, Jervis found no distinctive pattern, whereas Menkes reported frequent hypsarrhythmia.

Reports concerning the condition of the skin in Down's cases tend to be contradictory. Brousseau (1928) reviewed early reports, and in an attempt to reconcile the conflicting views, concluded that the skin of the infant Down's cases was lightly colored, soft, delicate, and very smooth to the touch, but as they grew older their skin became dark, dry, and eczematous. In another section of the book, however, the general comment is made that the skin is mottled and clammy. Penrose (1963) and Benda (1969) mentioned dry skin as a characteristic. Øster (1953, p. 23) stated that: "The sweat secretion was reduced in twenty mongols between the ages of 6.1 and 58.1 (years). The parents, no doubt correctly, attributed this to the inactivity of the patients." At another point (p. 43) Øster noted dry skin in 233 (or 44%) of his patients. Benda (1969) suggested that the thick, dry, and rough skin of some Down's syndrome cases is due to thyroid deficiency, and that various degrees of myxedema may be found. If the impressions of dry skin are correct, high skin resistance should be obtained in Down's cases.

Most authors seem to agree that Down's patients are prone to respiratory infection (Benda, 1969; Brousseau, 1928; Kirman, 1965), and have a high incidence of congenital heart defect (Benda, 1969; Breg, 1970; Brousseau, 1928; Kirman, 1965; Øster, 1953). Brousseau recorded respiration and found shallow and exceedingly irregular breathing. Øster found loud and harsh systolic murmur, while Benda reported a high rate of septum defect. Benda also observed that the peripheral vascular system appeared distended and congested, with underdeveloped peripheral capillaries, and thin and narrow vascular branching. Brousseau found the extremities cold and frequently cyanotic.

It remains to be demonstrated whether the proneness to respiratory diseases will be reflected in measurements of respiration rate and amplitude, or whether congenital heart disease will influence heart rate. Benda's observations on the vascular system could lead to an expectation of reduced blood volume changes and increased peripheral blood pressure in Down's syndrome patients.

The great degree of variability in physical and developmental abnormalities among Down's cases has been stressed by many authors (Brousseau, 1928; Lillienfield, 1969; Tredgold, 1914). While the superficial similarity among Down's cases might suggest less inter-individual variability, these observations may imply greater variability in autonomic variables among Down's syndrome cases than among normals.

PURPOSE OF THE PRESENT STUDY

Whereas the literature provides partial answers to the question of autonomic functioning in some categories of mental deficiency, conclusions must be qualified because of inconsistencies in the data, frequently small subject samples, limited diversity of autonomic variables and etiological groups, and absence of test-retest reliability data. The objectives of the present study, therefore, were to

1. Compare autonomic activity in Normals and four groups of mental defectives—Familials, Down's cases, PKU's, and Encephalopathies due to mechanical injury at birth.
2. Determine autonomic activity during rest and in response to stimulation.
3. Determine reliability of autonomic variables by recording over four sessions.
4. Record autonomic activity and reaction time during a vigilance task, in order to compare physiological and behavioral aspects of arousal.

METHOD

Variables and Apparatus

To assess levels of autonomic functions and patterns of activity in mentally deficient subjects, the following variables were recorded: Systolic blood pressure (BP), blood volume changes of the forehead (HV) and finger (FV), skin resistance (SR), heart period (HP), respiration period (RP), and respiration amplitude (RA).

BP was measured from the right hand by means of a Biophysical Electronics Model SM2 Continuous Systolic Monitor. A digital occlusion cuff placed on the proximal phalanx of the middle finger of the right hand was inflated with each pulse beat. The triggering pulse beat was detected by a sensor placed against the distal phalanx of the same finger, until the cuff occluded the artery. A controlled air leak in the system decreased the cuff pressure until the cuff and arterial pressure were equal, thus indicating the systolic BP. The rate of pressure fall determined the sampling frequency, which in the present study was one reading for every two to three pulse beats. The particular advantage of this system is that it allows a frequent sampling cycle and can be used for recording BP responses as well as resting levels. The monitor output was fed into a Grass 7P1A amplifier.

HV and FV were determined from resistance changes in Lafayette E4 Photoelectric transducers measured by the PGR circuit of a Grass 7P1A preamplifier. The transducer bulbs were supplied with 1.4 volts from a regulated DC power source. The head transducer was placed in the middle of the forehead by means of a headband and was covered with a piece of black leather to prevent the room light from interacting with the transducer bulb. FV was recorded from the index finger of the left hand, with a black cloth mitten over the hand to prevent light interference; during the vigilance task the transducer was on the right index finger. While this method does not permit the recording of absolute blood volumes, changes are detectable, i.e. an increase in blood volume results in reduced reflectance and higher photocell resistance.

SR was recorded using the PGR circuit of a 7P1A Grass preamplifier with a current of 50 μA. Two 20 mm diameter zinc electrodes and paste (Yellow Springs Instrument Co.) were applied to the right arm, one to the palm, and the other to the dorsal surface of the wrist. The palm was dryrubbed with a gauze pad, and the wrist was cleaned with acetone and thoroughly rubbed with electrode paste.

HP was determined from intervals between EKG R-waves, recorded from left forearm and right calf (standard lead II position) using Johnson and Johnson Telectrodes and Grass electrode paste. A Grass 7P1A or a 7P3A AC preamplifier was used.

Respiratory movements were recorded with a mercury strain gauge (Parks Electronics Laboratory) placed at the level of the sternum. The signal was fed into a Grass 7P1A preamplifier in the DC 20K mode.

The recordings were made with an 8 channel Grass Polygraph. Paper speed was 2.5 mm/sec or 5 mm/sec, depending upon experimental conditions. One channel recorded slow code from a Systron Donner H1-150 Time Code Generator (TCG). Simultaneously with polygraph recording, the data and fast time code were recorded on a 7 channel Sanborn 3900 tape system.

The subject rested on a bed located in a double walled RF shielded acoustic chamber (8 × 8 feet) which was maintained at 70° F (±1°) and 50 percent (±5%) relative humidity. The chamber was dimly lit, and the subject's movements were directly registered on the polygraph record by a research assistant in the chamber with the subject. The subject could also be observed by the experimenter by means of a closed circuit television system.

A Hewlett Packard sine wave oscillator, a Dynakit amplifier, a Hewlett Packard attenuator, and a Lafayette interval timer were used to produce auditory stimuli through an Acoustic Research AR4 speaker. The speaker was mounted on one wall of

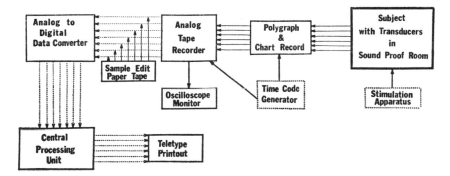

Figure 2-1. Block diagram of apparatus.

the acoustic chamber, two feet above the subject's head. The same equipment, plus a Stoelting 5 channel programmer provided tones with varying interstimulus intervals for a vigilance task. In the latter, the subject responded to the tones by pressing a telegraph key which activated an electronic counter (Hewlett Packard 5223L) connected to a digital recorder (Hewlett Packard 5050A).

A block diagram of recording and processing equipment is shown in Figure 2-1.

Procedure

The subject was instructed to relax and to remain as still as possible, while resting levels of autonomic activity were recorded for fifteen to twenty min. Following the Rest condition, a series of auditory stimuli was presented, after which a mild degree of hyperventilation was attempted. Auditory Stimulation consisted of a series of 3-5 1,000 Hz tones of 1 sec duration, spaced approximately 2 min apart. Intensity was 40 db above established hearing threshold. As much as possible, the tones were presented during artifact-free periods and at the point of maximum exhalation in the respiratory cycle. For Hyperventilation the subject was instructed to blow up a Number 10 balloon, beginning approximately 2 min after presentation of the final auditory stimulus. The degree of hyperventilation, however, could not be fully controlled, since the rate of the balloon inflation varied with the different subjects, and some subjects were incapable of following instructions. Recording continued for about 5 min following hyperventilation. The total duration of the continuous record comprising one session was thirty to forty minutes. Standard recordings were obtained in four sessions, ordinarily one week apart, but in a few cases the interval between sessions was as short as two days.

A fifth session was added for the Vigilance Condition, in which motor reaction time (RT) and autonomic activity were simultaneously recorded. Following Semmel (1965), a total of 18 stimuli were presented in three blocks of six randomly arranged intertrial intervals: 15, 30, 60, 90, 180, and 240 sec. The auditory stimuli were 1,000 Hz tones of 3 sec duration and 10 db above threshold. To determine baseline RT, the same stimulus was presented six times before and six times following the vigilance series, with 15 sec intervals and an oral warning signal 1 to 3 sec prior to stimulation. The subject remained in a supine position during the task, and pressed the key with his left hand. When the subject failed to press the key within 4 sec of stimulus onset, a maximum RT of 4,000 ms was assigned for that trial.

Hearing threshold for a 1,000 Hz tone was established prior to the first recording session, using standard audiometric procedure, and served as a reference for stimulus intensity. For those subjects who could not be tested, particularly some of the PKU's, hearing threshold was grossly estimated. The subjects were also given a practice session with simple auditory reaction time, using the same type of response key as in Vigilance. Those who could not perform in the practice reaction time tests were not given the vigilance task; some, who performed adequately in the reaction time test, however, did not respond during Vigilance.

Sampling of Data

For the resting data, the first 10 sec of every 30 sec period of the record was selected for analysis. In case of movement artifact the sample was advanced or delayed up to 15 sec, but if that did not result in an artifact-free sample, the sample for that 30 sec segment was omitted. The number of samples in a single session ranged from six to thirty-five. For Auditory Stimulation, data for 10 sec just prior to, and up to 10 sec following the stimulus were analyzed. Hyperventilation sampling consisted of a 10 sec period just prior to hyperventilation, and alternate 10 sec periods for 2 min following balloon inflation. For Vigilance, 7 sec samples before and after stimulation were analyzed.

The data were processed using a Hewlett Packard 2115A laboratory computer. During Rest, BP in mm Hg units was determined from approximately four values per sample. HV and FV were determined at the troughs between pulse beats. Blood volume changes were obtained by subtracting mean value of the first sample (baseline) from all subsequent samples. RP was computed as duration (in 1/100 sec units) between corresponding points in a cycle, either at the beginning or peak of inhalation, whichever came first in each sample. Typically, two full cycles were contained in a sample, but deep sighs or respiration pauses could result in incomplete cycles within the time limit and such data were excluded. RA was registered as the voltage difference between extreme points in a respiration cycle. SR in ohms was measured once at the beginning and once at the end of each sample. HP was measured as time (in 1/100 sec units) between successive R-waves throughout the sample. The number of values per sample varied from 10 to 20. For each sample, the program provided mean values for each of the seven variables, which were used in all statistical analyses of the Rest and Hyperventilation conditions.

With respect to Auditory Stimulation, pre- and poststimulus values were compared to obtain measures of response. A good part of the data which were recorded following the presentation of stimuli was lost because it was difficult to prevent many of the mentally deficient subjects from making motor responses to the stimuli. When the assistant who was with the subject in the recording room signalled movements, all variables within that data analysis period were rejected regardless of whether the data channels showed movement artifacts. In addition, the pre- and poststimulus records were carefully examined for indication of movement artifact for each variable separately. A single variable displaying any type of artifact was rejected, while the other variables within the sample were retained. To preserve as much of the data as possible, the 10 sec poststimulation period was maintained for the values with low periodicity, BP, RP, and RA, but reduced to a 5 sec period for the remaining variables. Nevertheless, because of the strict criteria, the data available for analysis were substantially reduced, and it was not always data for the same subjects or stimuli that were included in the analyses of each variable for each session. Unfortunately, responses of largest magnitude tended to be accompanied by movement artifact, requiring rejection of some of the largest patient responses.

For SR response, three additional parameters were considered:

Latency from stimulus onset to detectable resistance decrease; Time to Peak (TTP) from stimulus onset to maximum resistance decrease; and Percent Recovery at the end of a 20 sec post-stimulus period.

Subjects

Four groups of mental defectives, Cultural Familial, Down's Syndrome, Encephalopathy due to mechanical injury at birth, and PKU, as well as a group of Normal controls, participated in the study. The diagnoses of the patients were obtained from their medical records, and were in accordance with the AAMD classification system (Heber, 1961).

Patients who according to their record had spasticity, heart anomalies, hearing impairment, extreme hyperactivity, or recent seizure activity, were excluded from the study. Psychotropic medication was discontinued at least forty-eight hours before testing. Where anticonvulsants, such as phenobarbital, were prescribed their administration was not interrupted.

The study was planned for fifteen subjects of each sex in each group, with an age range from ten to thirty years. The actual number of subjects in each group contributing data to one or more conditions of the study, their mean age, and IQ, are included in Table 2-I. The discrepancies from intended numbers result from rejection of some subjects because of excessive movements during recording, equipment failure, or unavailability of testable male PKU's. The patients used in this study constitute all PKU's from New York State institutions, who met our criteria, were presumably capable of being tested, and for whom parental permission was obtained.

The IQ's were obtained from the patients' records. The range within each group was 33 to 76 for Familials, 15 to 45 for the Down's subjects, 15 to 74 for Encephalopathies, and 13 to 56 for the PKU's. IQ matching for the various patient groups was not achieved since institutionalized PKU's characteristically have low IQ while the Familials are in the upper range of the institutional IQ distribution. The majority of the IQ's were obtained with the WISC or the WAIS. Some of the IQ's may be questioned because of lack of verbal facility on the part of the patient, be-

TABLE 2-I

AGES AND IQ's OF GROUPS

	Normal			Familial			Down's Syndrome			PKU			Encephalopathy		
	M	F	Comb.	M	F	Comb.	M	F	Comb.	M	F	Comb.	M	F	Comb.
N	15	15	30	14	15	29	15	15	30	8	17	25	16	15	31
Age Mean	19.7	18.7	19.2	19.6	19.6	19.6	18.6	18.6	18.6	17.8	21.0	20.0	19.7	20.8	20.2
Age SD	5.1	5.3	5.2	5.1	5.3	5.2	4.7	5.3	5.0	6.0	8.4	7.9	4.4	6.3	5.4
IQ Mean				52.6	50.3	51.4	28.4	29.9	29.1	37.2	30.5	32.6	44.8	33.9	39.5
IQ SD				12.8	9.1	11.1	11.1	6.6	9.1	17.5	14.7	16.0	10.8	16.5	14.9

cause the test was administered as much as six years prior to the study, or because the patient's age and mental status at the time of testing required use of less reliable scales. The Normal subjects were primarily employees of the Institute, or children of employees. While information about IQ was not available, mean IQ was presumed to be at least 100.

The patients, mainly from Willowbrook State School, were brought the short distance to the Institute, usually in pairs, so that they spent a morning or an afternoon at the Institute. One patient remained in a waiting room under supervision of a ward attendant, while the other was tested. In order to control for time of day, two of the subject's weekly sessions were scheduled for the morning, and two for the afternoon. Most patients seemed to enjoy their visits to the laboratories. Fewest problems in recording were encountered with the Down's Syndrome and Familial cases.

Autonomic data from PKU patients were extremely difficult to obtain, both because of the unavailability of such patients and because of their inability to cooperate in the recording situation. Many PKU's were not so diagnosed in the central register of New York, and few in the State Schools were in the ten to thirty-year range. Since Willowbrook could not supply sufficient numbers of PKU's, we screened the PKU populations of other state schools and requested parental permission for temporary transfer of the patients to the Institute. None of the institutionalized patients had been on a dietary regimen. Three private patients, however, had been on a diet with reduced phenylalanine. They still excreted an excess amount of phenylalanine, and were still intellectually subaverage, but in terms of abilities and cooperation they were distinctly superior to most of the institutionalized PKU's.

The difficulties in recording from the institutionalized PKU's resulted from their lack of speech and inability to comprehend the instructions to remain quiet during recording. Some PKU's have a tendency to exhibit stereotyped motor discharges, or movements of a more purposeful nature such as grabbing for the experimenter's hand. When the movements were so extensive as to threaten electrode attachment, attempts were made to restrain the patients. Occasionally this developed into a struggle, and it may be a euphemism to include such recording under the term Rest condition. By careful selection of samples, however, and by comparison of calm and hyperactive PKU's we have attempted to distinguish stable PKU characteristics from movement-induced autonomic activity.

It will be no easy task to improve on the quality or quantity of the PKU data. Since many of these patients are maintained on drug regimens in the institutions, a screening procedure does not always give a correct impression of potential for cooperation. Thus, of the thirty-three PKU's with whom testing was attempted, a maximum of twenty-five provided adequate autonomic data for inclusion in statistical analyses.

RESULTS

Rest Condition

Following the editing procedures described above, 13,799 ten-second data samples were analyzed. The average number of samples per session ranged from 20.4 in PKU's to 28.8 in Normals.

Some statistical analyses required constant sex ratios between groups, and therefore some subjects had to be excluded. In such cases data from subjects who had the fewest samples were dropped.

Analyses of Means

The group means for the seven variables, for each diagnostic group as well as for males and females separately, are entered in Table 2-II. F-ratios from Analysis of Variance of the sample means for each variable, are summarized in Table 2-III.

GROUP DIFFERENCES. Table 2-III shows significant main effects for Group for all variables but the two blood volume measures. Further specifics about the location of the differences are seen in Table 2-IV, which gives the *t*-values for all comparisons (Tukey *a*-procedure, Winer, 1962).

From Tables 2-II and 2-IV it may be seen that Down's and PKU cases have shorter HP than Normals and Familials. Down's

TABLE 2-II

GROUP MEANS FOR REST BY VARIABLE

	N	HP	BP	HV	FV	RP	RA	SR
		.01 sec	*mm/Hg*	*10K ohms*	*10K ohms*	*.01 sec*	*mV*	*K ohms*
Normal								
Males	14	85.7	125	3.49	2.73	374.0	.55	150.6
Females ...	14	75.0	120	3.17	1.74	319.2	.50	166.7
Total	28	80.3	123	3.33	2.23	346.6	.53	158.6
Familial								
Males	14	81.6	122	3.45	2.84	322.7	.35	163.9
Females ...	14	79.8	114	3.45	2.09	300.9	.41	182.1
Total	28	80.7	118	3.45	2.46	311.8	.38	173.0
Down's								
Males	15	73.4	104	6.59	3.23	311.8	.31	119.0
Females ...	15	69.8	114	4.68	1.53	302.9	.26	151.4
Total	30	71.6	109	5.64	2.38	307.3	.29	135.2
PKU								
Males	8	70.5	115	4.43	2.39	306.3	.70	110.2
Females ...	8	71.4	109	1.59	.25	351.4	.44	135.9
Total	16	70.9	112	3.01	1.32	328.8	.57	123.1
Encephal.								
Males	14	75.0	119	4.58	3.30	309.9	.48	120.8
Females ...	14	75.5	114	3.71	2.00	309.5	.31	165.4
Total	28	75.2	117	4.15	2.65	309.7	.40	143.1

cases have significantly lower BP than Normals, Familials, and PKU cases. Normals have higher RA than Down's cases and PKU's have higher RA than Familials, Down's cases, and Encephalopathies. With regard to SR,* the Familials have higher values than Down's and PKU cases. The significant F-ratio for RP was not reflected in the more stringent follow-up t-test involving paired group comparisons.

The four variables which gave significant differences (Table 2-IV), expressed as z-scores relative to the means and standard deviations of the Normal group are illustrated in Figure 2-2. The data are arranged so that positive scores suggest "sympathetic-like" activity, and negative scores suggest "parasympathetic-like"

* Since measurement was in resistance units, and since statistical comparisons of the distribution of resistance and its transformations to conductance and log conductance revealed no consistently greater normality in different groups, resistance has been retained as the unit.

TABLE 2-III

SUMMARY OF ANALYSES OF VARIANCE

(F's for Rest data)

	Group 4/120 df	Sex 1/120 df	Group × Sex 4/120 df	Session 3/360 df	Group × Sess 12/360 df	Sex × Sess 3/360 df	G × Sex × Sess 12/360 df
HP	5.05†	3.31	1.34	8.86†	1.12	1.34	.66
BP	6.99†	1.52	3.20*	1.57	1.23	.50	1.19
HV	2.08	2.51	.54	.91	2.35†	2.09	1.57
FV	1.13	12.75†	.39	2.42	1.13	.26	1.70
RP	2.56*	1.85	2.29	3.66*	1.90	1.18	1.02
RA	7.61†	4.93*	2.06	.42	1.07	.90	2.08*
SR	4.07†	11.17†	.42	8.04†	1.67	2.56	.93

* p < 0.05.
† p < 0.01.

TABLE 2-IV

FOLLOW-UP *t*-TESTS OF GROUP DIFFERENCES FOR REST DATA
(Tukey's *a*-Procedure)

Comparisons	HP	BP	RA	SR
Norm.—Fam.	.19	2.27	3.57	1.52
Norm.—Down's	4.19*	6.50†	5.82†	2.47
Norm.—PKU	4.54*	4.93†	.99	3.76
Norm.—Encephal.	2.46	2.72	3.16	1.64
Fam.—Down's	4.38*	4.23*	2.24	3.99*
Fam.—PKU	4.73†	2.65	4.56*	5.27†
Fam.—Encephal.	2.65	.45	.41	3.16
Down's—PKU	.34	1.57	6.81†	1.28
Down's—Encephal.	1.73	3.78	2.66	.83
PKU—Encephal.	2.08	2.21	4.15*	2.11

* $p < 0.05$.
† $p < 0.01$.

activity. There is little argument that short HP, high BP, and low SR represent the "sympathetic-like" direction. For a high RA, however, there would be argument for a sympathetic as well as a parasympathetic interpretation, depending upon whether amplitude is considered independently or as compensation for a slower RP. In the present situation, it was the energetic breathing of the PKU cases that led us to regard high amplitude as a "sympathetic-like" indicator.

The curves in Figure 2-2 invite several comments. While never differing significantly, the z-scores of the Familials are consistently on the parasympathetic side of the normals. It should also be noted that while BP was below the Normal value for all patient groups (parasympathetic direction), three of the groups (Down's Syndrome, PKU's, and Encephalopathies) had higher than Normal z-scores for HP and SR (sympathetic direction).

Finally, the figure indicates differences in autonomic patterns between the various etiological categories. The PKU group is distinguished by large RA and low SR; the Down's group by low BP and small RA; and the Encephalopathies (with the least distinctive features) by BP and RA values similar to the Familials, and HP and SR above the Familials. To determine the extent to which individual subjects within groups resembled the group

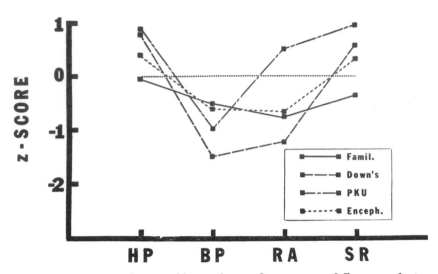

Figure 2-2. z-scores for variables with significant group differences during Rest.

patterns illustrated in the figure, z-scores for each variable, relative to the means and SD's of the Normals, were ranked within an individual, and coefficients of concordance were obtained (Siegel, 1956). A significant degree of concordance was found for every patient group ($p < .01$). Thus, the patterns are not the results of a few extreme scores, but reflect the pattern of the individuals within each group.

Plotting the z-scores for males and females separately gave essentially the same patterns for the two sexes. The main difference was that the males showed greater deviations from their control group than did the females.

Specific questions pertaining to the homogeneity of the PKU group and the role of excessive movements during recordings were examined by subdividing the PKU's into Cooperative (4 males and 4 females) and Uncooperative (4 males and 10 females) groups for each sex, based on degree of movement artifact and experimenter's judgment. A Group by Session analysis of variance gave no significant F's for any variable. Since it is difficult to reach statistical significance with such small numbers of subjects, however, the group means were inspected for trends.

There was little suggestion of consistent differences between the Cooperative and Uncooperative groups. While the Uncooperative males showed lowest SR and BP among the four PKU groups, the Cooperative PKU's had SR's as low as the Down's and Encephalopathy groups. In view of these results, and the significant concordance within the total PKU group, it is unlikely that the resting pattern of PKU's in Figure 2-2 has motor activity as its primary cause.

Session Differences. The main effect of Session (Table 2-III) was significant for HP, RP, and SR. However, *t*-tests of intersession means for all four variables were significant only between session one and sessions two, three, or four. For HP, and SR, this finding was similar for all subgroups, inasmuch as none of the Group × Session interactions (Table 2-III) was significant. This implies that a single session is adequate for group discrimination with respect to HP and SR.

Sex Differences. Tables 2-II and 2-III show significant sex differences for three variables with males showing consistently higher FV changes, lower SR, and higher RA. The general trend toward a sympathetic-like pattern in males relative to females is also evident, although not significant in HV.

Interactions. One significant Group x Sex interaction was obtained, with males in all groups except Down's having higher BP than females. Only HV yielded a significant Group x Session interaction, which is primarily attributable to the fact that the means for session one in Down's cases are considerably lower than their means for the other three sessions. Finally, the significant Group × Sex × Session interaction for RA stems from differences between sessions for the male PKU's only.

Intercorrelations of Autonomic Measures. To determine the relationship between autonomic variables, correlations were obtained for *within* subject as well as *between* subject data. The between subject analysis used the means for each of the variables over the four sessions, for each subject within a diagnostic group. This type of correlation indicates the degree to which subjects within a group tend to be consistent with regard to level of autonomic variables. Of the 105 correlations (21 per group) only seven were significant beyond the .05 level, and these were so scattered that they did not constitute solid trends. Only three pairs of variables were significantly correlated for more than one group: HP-RP in Down's cases ($r = .48$, $p < .01$) and PKU's ($r = .46$, $p < .05$); HV-FV in PKU's ($r = .61$, $p < .01$) and Encephalopathies ($r = .75$, $p < .01$); and FV-SR in Down's cases ($r = .47$, $p < .01$) and Normals ($r = .45$, $p < .05$). All groups showed negative correlations between HV and SR, and FV and RA, and positive correlations between RP and RA, although these were not significant.

The within subject correlations examine relationships between variables within a single individual. High correlations would indicate uniformity of ANS activity. The data consisted of the means of each variable from each of the 10 sec analysis segments for each subject. The correlations were averaged over each session for each group, using an r to z transformation with the Fisher correction for bias (Edwards, 1950). The vast majority of the within correlations were statistically significant, in part because of the extremely large number of degrees of freedom. Most of the significant correlations were small, however, with only ten of the 105 correlations indicating a shared variance between variables of more than 10 percent. The largest and most consistent correlation was that between HV and FV, ranging from .14 in the Down's to .85 in the Encephalopathies. We had noticed, however, that volume readings tended to increase systematically between the beginning and end of a session. This observation was confirmed by correlating the volume measures with sampling time within sessions. Thus there was a possibility that the transducers were subject to a common drift or that the heat from the bulbs produced a gradual vasodilation in the tissue under the transducers. Correlations between the variables were therefore determined with time partialled out. The correlations between volumes were substantially reduced, ranging from a low of .14 in the PKU's to a high of .29 in the Normals. The intercorrelations of the other variables were not appreciably changed by partialling out time. The largest of the remaining unpartialled correlations were those between HP and RA, which ranged from −.20 in the Encephalopathies to −.30 in the Familials. Thus, neither the between nor the within subject correlations are suggestive of a high degree of interrelationship between autonomic variables.

Analysis of SD's

It is conceivable that variability of autonomic functions may differ between normals and patient groups. For some of the patients one might expect higher variability during a recording session due to a greater tendency toward movement, and less stability in attitude and mood. To examine this problem, the standard deviations (SD's) of the subject's sample means within sessions were obtained.

Five of the seven variables showed a significant Group effect in the Analyses of Variance. However, the patient groups were not consistently more variable than the Normals for most measures. Furthermore, no single group was consistently most variable across all measures. It is interesting to note that for RP and SR, for example, the PKU's showed the greatest variability, while for HP and HV they were least variable.

Thus, while several group differences were found, the rank order of the groups with respect to variability differed from measure to measure. The mentally deficient groups, therefore, are not consistently more variable in autonomic functioning at rest than are normals. The lack of consistent variability was also supported by the fact that the great majority of correlations between SD's was not significant.

Intersession Reliability

The correlations between pairs of sessions, for each variable, were obtained for each group separately. The averaged group correlations indicated that all but one of the correlations were significant beyond the .05 level. Magnitude of the correlation coefficients for the different variables appeared to fall into two clusters. RP, HP, and SR showed the largest correlations, generally greater than .65, while the correlations for the remaining variables were below .50.

Within Session Changes

To determine if any group differences existed with respect to trend within a session, an analysis of variance was performed for the differences between the first and last quarter of the samples with Group and Sex as main effects. This was done for each variable and each session separately. Only the first session reflected significant group differences in more than one variable, namely RP ($F = 4.25$, $p < .01$) and SR ($F = 3.30$, $p < .05$). In both cases Normals showed the largest relative reduction from start to end of session in activation level—i.e. reduced respiration rate and increased skin resistance. All groups, however, showed a similar direction of change for SR.

A significant sex difference was found for RP in the first session ($F = 5.53$, $p < .05$) and for FV in the first ($F = 4.93$, $p < .05$) and second ($F = 4.97$, $p < .05$) sessions. Specifically, the males showed greater reduction in respiration rate than the females, and had a greater change in FV.

It may be concluded that, beyond the first session, changes in autonomic activity during a recording session apparently do not differ in patients and normals.

Relationships of Variables to Age and IQ

The correlation coefficients of each autonomic variable with age and IQ were based on all sessions combined. Correlations with age included all subjects in the study, while the correlations with IQ included only patients. Consistent with developmental physiology, age was significantly correlated with HP ($r = .23$, $p < .01$) and BP ($r = .32$, $p < .01$) indicating longer HP and higher BP with increasing age. FV was also found to increase with age ($r = .18$, $p < .05$). It is interesting that subjects ranging in age from ten to thirty do not systematically show an increase in RP with age. Similarly, an increase in SR with age might have been expected; however, the lack of significant correlation is in accord with Ellis and Sloan's (1958) reported correlation of −.07 between conductance and age in 125 mental defectives ranging between eight and fifty-four years. With respect to IQ in the patient population, a significant positive correlation was obtained only for HP ($r = .29$, $p < .01$), indicating lower heart rate in subjects with higher IQ.

In the cases where either age or IQ correlated significantly with an autonomic variable for all subjects combined, the sign of the correlation was consistent when determined for each diagnostic group separately, with the sole exception of the Age-FV relationship in the PKU's, which was negative but not significant.

Stimulus Conditions

Auditory Stimulation

Data from this condition were examined by means of two separate sets of analyses, one for the average of all usable responses to stimuli for each subject in each session, and the other for the first available response sample in each session. The results were not essentially different, and the presentation and discussion have therefore been limited to the former. Because of the number of deleted samples, a sequential analysis of response within a session, as an indication of habituation, was not feasible.

For BP, which was measured every second or third heart beat, and for the slowly recurring respiratory measures, mean levels pre- and poststimulation were analyzed. For the remaining faster changing variables, maximum rather than mean response was selected for analysis. Directionality of response for SR is well established, and consists of a resistance decrease. HP, HV, and FV, however, could go in either direction, i.e. the heart rate might either accelerate or decelerate following stimulation, and blood volume might increase or decrease. To determine the direction of response, therefore, separate analyses of poststimulus levels covaried for prestimulus levels were performed for maximum and minimum values of these three variables. These analyses indicate that for HV the responses clearly consisted of increased blood flow, with no group means indicating a decrease. For HP, the majority of group means also indicated an increase (deceleration) following stimulation. The results were less clear with regard to FV, with an approximately equal number of group means over the four sessions suggesting increase and decrease. Since significant differences for FV appeared only in the analysis of the maximum values, presentation of the HP, HV, and FV results will be restricted to the analyses of the maximum values for all three of these variables.

The poststimulus autonomic measures were analyzed by means of Factorial Analyses of Covariance (Winer, 1962), with pre-stimulus level as the predictor variable, in order to compensate for possible differences in magnitude of response as a function of prestimulus level of the variables. This type of analysis has been shown to be identical to a covariance analysis of the difference between pre- and postlevels (Benjamin, 1967; Block, 1964). The three temporal measures of SR—Latency, Time to Peak, and Percent Recovery 20 sec following stimulation—were analyzed by means of Factorial Analyses of Variance, with Group and Sex as main effects. Each Session was treated separately in all analyses in order to maximize the number of cases.

DIFFERENCES BETWEEN VARIABLES. Only SR yielded significant differences in all four sessions, with F-ratios ranging from 4.39 to 6.86 ($p < .01$ in all cases). The magnitudes of response adjusted for prestimulus levels are shown in Figure 2-3. The Down's cases were significantly less reactive than Normals in all four sessions, and Familials were less reactive than Normals in three sessions. Figure 2-3 indicates a trend toward greater SR reactivity and intersession variability in the PKU group than in the Familials, Down's cases, and Encephalopathies, although the PKU's are generally less reactive than the Normals.

There were no significant group differences for any of the temporal characteristics of the SR response, probably because of the sparsity of the data. Females had significantly longer Latencies than males in the last two sessions and longer TTP in session three. One significant Group × Sex interaction was found for Latency in the fourth session, where Familial females had substantially longer Latencies than Familial males, and males and females of other subgroups.

The SR findings in this condition contrast sharply with those from all other variables, where significant effects were few, occurred in no more than one session, and generally did not exceed the .05 level.

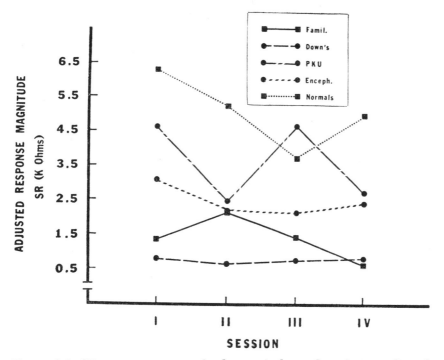

Figure 2-3. SR response magnitude during Auditory Stimulation, adjusted for prestimulus level.

INTERCORRELATIONS. Between subject intercorrelations of autonomic responses to auditory stimulation (pre minus postlevels), averaged over stimuli in all sessions for all groups combined, showed only a single significant coefficient, that between HP and RA ($r = -.21$, $p < .05$). The general conclusion is that there is little relationship between response magnitudes for the different variables.

Hyperventilation

The covariance design for the hyperventilation data was exactly the same as for Auditory Stimulation, with level of the first available post-hyperventilation sample adjusted for level prior to hyperventilation. As before, much of the data had to be excluded because of excessive movement artifact, resulting occasionally in rejection of the first actual posthyperventilation sample. Comparisons of groups for time between end of hyperventilation and first available sample, however, revealed no significant differences.

With regard to autonomic variables, significant differences were obtained in at least two sessions for the main effect of Group for SR, RA, HP, and BP. The two respiratory measures may be regarded as an index of degree of hyperventilation. While no group differences were found for RP, significant RA differences were obtained in three sessions ($F > 3.84$ in all cases, $p < .01$). Both measures tended to increase relative to the pre-hyperventilation sample in all groups, with the exception of RP in the Down's cases. The amplitude change was statistically significant in all four sessions only for the Normals, and was significantly greater than that of most patient groups; it was not, however, consistent with the direction of change expected as a result of hyperventilation. Whether or not hyperventilation was produced, autonomic equilibrium was affected by the procedure.

For SR there was a general significant decrease in all groups except Down's. Group differences were consistent over all four sessions ($F > 6.0$ in all cases, $p < .01$) and follow-up t-tests with a Tukey a-procedure showed that the Normals decreased more than either the Familials, the Down's, or the Encephalopathies. The resistance drop in the PKU's was greater than in any of the other patient groups, attaining significance in comparison with the Down's cases in two sessions, and differing significantly from the Normals in session two.

Significant HP decreases in all four sessions were found for all groups except Normals and Familials. Significant differences between groups for HP were found only for session one ($F = 2.61$, $p < .05$) and session two ($F = 3.59$, $p < .01$). The general trend was for the Down's, PKU, and Encephalopathy groups to show greater decreases than the Normals and Familials in HP.

Although significant group differences for BP occurred in sessions 1 and 3, they stemmed primarily from increases in PKU's greater than those of the other groups. Since the increase was more apparent for males in one of the sessions, and for females in the other, and since PKU means resembled those of the other groups in the remaining two sessions, artificial triggering of the pulse detector by minute finger movements may be responsible for the differences.

Intercorrelations of differences between the pre- and first post-hyperventilation sample for all subjects showed only two correlations significant beyond the .05 level: $r = -.24$ between HV and FV, and $r = -.22$ between BP and RA. Correlations between responses in corresponding variables during the two conditions of Auditory Stimulation and Hyperventilation were significant only for RP at the .05 level ($r = .24$), and SR at the .01 level ($r = .45$).

In summary, only two variables seemed to reflect in a reasonably consistent way the effect of balloon inflation, namely SR and HP. SR, and to a lesser extent HP, indicate different response magnitudes in the Normals and the patient groups even after adjustment for differences in prehyperventilation levels. Surprisingly, the changes were in opposite directions with the Normals having greater SR but lesser HP changes than the patients.

Vigilance Condition

On the basis of Semmel's (1965) findings, the patient groups should show poorer vigilance performance than the Normals, manifested in relatively longer vigilance reaction time. If retardates are more dependent on external stimuli for maintenance of arousal, then greater difference between RT's for long and short interstimulus intervals (ISI) would also be predicted. That is, the patients should be less vigilant than Normals to begin with and, in addition, should be less able to sustain their vigilance during protracted intervals. Furthermore, if arousal is related to autonomic activity, and maintenance of arousal is a prerequisite for vigilance, then there should be a relationship between vigilance and autonomic activity.

Reaction Time

BASELINE RT. The baseline RT's (Pre in Fig. 2-4), which represent the mean of combined pre- and postvigilance trials, reflect a hierarchy of groups. The relative positions are, with a single exception, sustained throughout all ISI's.

F-ratios from Analyses of Variance for the RT data are presented in Table 2-V. For the baseline RT, significant Group and Sex main effects were obtained. Follow-up *t*-tests showed that the Normals and Familials have significantly shorter RT's than either the Down's, PKU, or Encephalopathy groups. The commonly found faster RT for males was also confirmed.

The similarity in rank order of the mean RT's and IQ's of the patient groups raised the possibility that the differences between the groups might be accounted for on the basis of IQ. Since IQ's were not available for Normals, the baseline RT data of the patient groups only were reanalyzed by means of covariance analysis with IQ. Differences between groups in RT were not affected by adjustment for differences in IQ.

INTERVAL. The mean RT's of the five diagnostic groups, as a function of ISI, are presented in Figure 2-4.

Analysis of Variance of the Vigilance RT's also showed significant group differences which, according to follow-up *t*-tests, reflect the faster RT in the Normals as compared to Down's, PKU, and Encephalopathy groups, and the faster RT in the Familials than in the Down's and PKU groups. The significant sex difference found in baseline RT was not maintained during Vigilance, because of a relatively greater increase in male RT.

The main effect of Interval was significant, with *t*-tests show-

TABLE 2-V

F-RATIOS FOR RT DATA

	Baseline Anova	Vigilance Anova	Ancova
Group	14.19†	15.29†	2.40
Sex	4.89*	1.63	2.45
G × S	.99	2.28	2.30
Interval	—	5.43†	5.42†
I × G	—	1.87*	1.86*
I × S	—	.50	.49
I × G × S	—	.73	.73

* $p < 0.05$.
† $p < 0.01$.

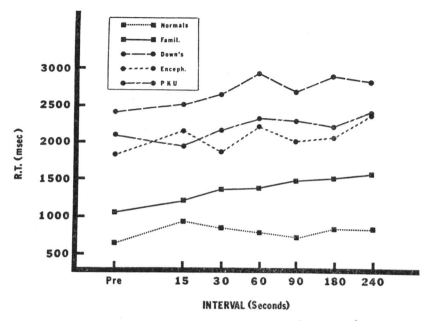

Figure 2-4. RT as a function of interstimulus interval.

ing faster RT's at 15 sec than at 60 and 240 sec, as well as faster RT at 30 than at 240 sec. The significant I × G interaction resulted from significant differences between intervals for Down's, Encephalopathy, and PKU groups, but not for Normals or Familials.

The Covariance Analysis examines the vigilance RT data adjusted for differences in baseline RT's. Table 2-V shows no significant main effects or interaction for Group and Sex. Since the covariance adjustment does not affect the relative difference between intervals, the main effect of Interval remains as in the unadjusted analysis. Follow-up *t*-tests of the I × G interaction again showed that while performance of the Down's, Encephalopathy, and PKU groups declined over intervals, that of the Normal and Familial groups did not.

The adjusted means for each group and interval are presented in Figure 2-5. It may be observed that there is considerable overlap between Normals and patients at the 15 sec ISI, but greatest

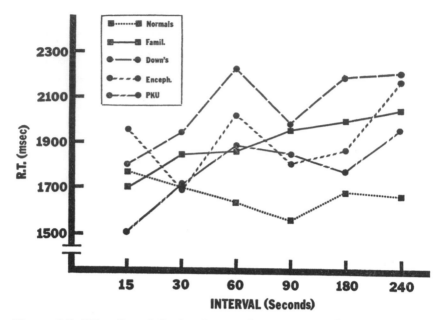

Figure 2.5. RT, adjusted for baseline performance, as a function of inter-stimulus interval.

divergence at the longest ISI. The reduction in group differences as a result of covariance adjustment demonstrates that the general slowness of the patients in a vigilance setting is largely accounted for by their longer baseline RT's. As ISI's increase, however, the patients become relatively more deficient compared to the Normals in adjusted vigilance performance, indicating difficulty in maintaining arousal or attention.

RELATION TO AUTONOMIC VARIABLES. To assess the relationship between RT and autonomic variables, two types of correlational procedures were applied, one based on a comparison of within subject data and the other on a comparison of between subject data. For the latter, product-moment correlations between mean RT for each interval and corresponding mean level of autonomic activity for each variable, pre- as well as poststimulation, were determined for each diagnostic group. The blood volume measures were not considered because of the relative nature of their measurement. Because of the short period of analysis (7 sec), and the requirement that a respiratory cycle begin with the start or peak of inhalation, respiration data were often missing and were therefore excluded in order to maximize the number of available samples for the other variables. While no relationships were consistent over all groups and intervals for the pre- or post-stimulation levels, RT and prestimulation levels yielded significant correlations for two groups at more than three intervals. When significant, the RT-SR correlations for PKU's ranged from −.57 to −.60; for Familials the RT-HP correlations ranged from −.45 to −.50.

Reaction times were correlated with prestimulus and with poststimulus autonomic levels for the eighteen vigilance trials of each individual in the within subject comparisons and averaged for each diagnostic group. For prestimulation data the objective was to determine whether RT could be predicted from the subject's level immediately prior to stimulation. The correlations were uniformly small, despite the fact that for the patient groups a few correlations were significant. The largest correlations, those with BP ($r = -.14$) and with HP ($r = .14$) in Familials, each accounted for less than 3 percent of the variance in RT. Correlations tended to be consistent in sign across groups; however, variation from subject to subject within each group was quite large, e.g. the correlations with HP in individual Familial subjects ranged from −.48 to .72. Similarly for post-stimulation data, few correlations with RT were significant and variability between subjects was considerable. The largest correlations were with HP in the Familial ($r = .17$), Encepalopathy ($r = .17$), and PKU ($r = .16$) groups. While the data suggest a slight tendency for longer HP's to follow longer RT's, the common variance is again less than 3 percent.

Thus, there is only limited evidence for consistent linear relationships between RT and these autonomic variables, whether one considers absolute level across subjects (between subject comparison) or concomitant variation within a subject.

Autonomic Variables

RESPONSE AS A FUNCTION OF INTERVALS. Since an auditory stimulus was used in the present task, Vigilance may be regarded as a variation of the Auditory Stimulation condition. Covariance Analyses of poststimulus autonomic level adjusted for level prior to stimulation were performed.

Group differences were found for BP, RP, and SR at the .01 level (F = 3.84, 3.59, and 6.05 respectively). For BP, the adjusted response magnitude was significantly smaller for the Down's than for the Normal and Familial groups. RP response was least for the PKU group, differing significantly from that of the Down's group.

SR again showed significant group differences, as in previous conditions of the study. The responsiveness of the Normals was significantly greater than that of all groups except the PKU's. A significant Interval effect was also found for SR (F = 3.61, $p < .01$), with the response for the 240 sec interval being larger than for the 15 sec interval, and the response for both the 180 and 240 sec intervals larger than for the 30 sec interval. The average magnitude of responses adjusted for prestimulus level of resistance for each diagnostic group and interval are presented in Figure 2-6.

The occurrence of negative responses is a result of a smaller actual response than would be predicted on the basis of the prestimulus value of the particular group. For all groups, response magnitude increases in a stepwise fashion across the three successive pairs of intervals.

While there were no significant sex differences, significant Group × Sex interactions were obtained for HP (F = 3.87, $p < .01$) and HV (F = 3.35, $p < .05$). The HP interaction resulted from significantly longer HP in the Normal males relative to all patient groups except the Familials, with no group differences among the females. The HV interaction stemmed from differences between Down's and Normal males, and between Down's and PKU females.

A summary of the autonomic data and vigilance RT, in terms

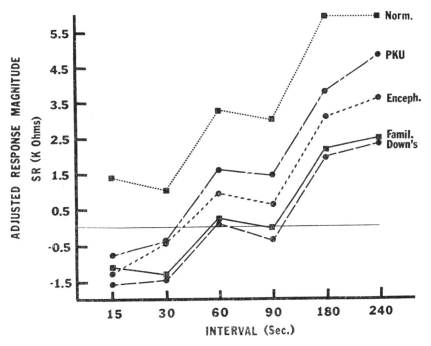

Figure 2-6. SR response magnitude, adjusted for prestimulus level, as a function of interstimulus interval.

of z-scores, is presented in Figure 2-7, which expresses the adjusted group means, averaged over all intervals, relative to the adjusted means and standard deviations of the Normals. Direction of scores is arranged such that poststimulation levels reflecting larger responses are upward, e.g. higher BP and lower SR. It is clear that all patient groups responded less in autonomic variables and yielded longer RT's than did the Normals.

INTERCORRELATIONS. Relationships between levels of autonomic variables were also examined in terms of within and between subject correlations. Between subject correlations were determined for each interval separately, for both pre- and poststimulus levels. The correlations were generally not consistent for intervals or groups.

The average of the within subject correlations for the groups

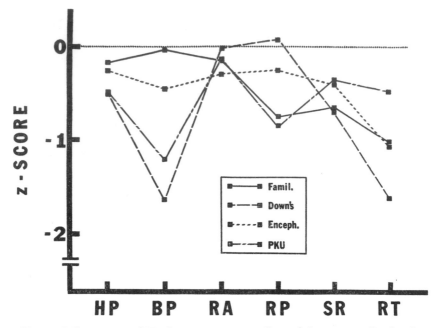

Figure 2-7. *z*-scores of Vigilance responses, adjusted for prestimulus level.

for poststimulation levels of all variables, except respiration, indicated several significant correlations although the magnitudes of the relationships were relatively small. The largest correlations, between HV and FV, were significant for four groups and ranged from .23 to .56. As in the Rest condition, this correlation may have resulted from transducer drift or temperature effects on the blood vessels. Other correlations which were significant and consistent for at least three of the five groups occurred between SR and HP ($r = .18$ to .35), BP and HP ($r = -.17$ to $-.22$), and between HP and FV ($r = .18$ to .24). A relatively larger number of significant correlations in the Normal and Familial groups suggested a somewhat greater uniformity of autonomic responsivity, in contrast to the Down's, Encephalopathy, and PKU groups.

In general, the evidence for association between autonomic variables is somewhat stronger when based on within individual than between individual comparisons. Nevertheless, the shared variance between measures once again appears slight.

Other Relationships

Correlations were also obtained between RT for each interval and IQ and age. Neither age nor IQ correlated significantly with RT at any interval.

In order to determine whether vigilance performance changed over time, Covariance Analyses of the means of the three Blocks, each containing the six intervals, were performed for RT and each autonomic variable. A significant main effect for Blocks occurred only for HP, with all groups showing longer HP's as the experiment progressed. Changes over blocks for the other variables tended to be similar for all groups inasmuch as the Group × Blocks Interactions were generally nonsignificant.

One additional set of analyses sought to determine whether the group differences in RT during vigilance could be accounted for on the basis of prestimulus levels of autonomic activity. Analyses of RT, covaried for prestimulation level of each autonomic variable, however, yielded essentially the same results as were obtained in the unadjusted analysis of RT, confirming the lack of relationship indicated in the other correlational results.

In summary, a number of differences are apparent between Normals and patients in the Vigilance task. The most pronounced finding is the general slowness of the retarded subjects in the baseline reaction time situation. With respect to vigilance performance, the greatest difference between most patient groups and the Normals appears to be a decrease in vigilance on the part of the patients with increasing ISI. The relationships between vigilance performance and level of autonomic functioning were generally slight. In terms of magnitude of autonomic response as a function of vigilance interval, findings were similar to those obtained in the reactivity condition, with Normals manifesting largest responses. Also similar to the reactivity findings was the superiority of the SR measure in terms of group discrimination. Finally, the Vigilance data confirmed the slight degree of relationship among autonomic measures obtained in other segments of the study.

Discriminant Analysis

In order to determine the maximum discriminative potential of the vast quantity of data available from this study, and whether each group could be characterized by a particular pattern of scores, a series of Two-Group Discriminant Analyses was performed, utilizing the Hewlett Packard adaptation of the Goddard Computer Science Institute program GCSL 020. The Discriminant Analysis calculates a single score for each subject from the sum of several weighted measures. The weights are mathematically selected in order to produce a distribution which maximally differentiates between pairs of groups. Fifteen measures were selected to represent all conditions of the study. Emphasis was placed on those which were most reliable, appeared to give greatest group differences, and for which loss of data was minimal. Specifically, measures of HP and SR from all four experimental conditions were chosen, along with the means of RP, RA, and BP from the Rest Condition, and both baseline and longest ISI Vigilance RT's. Resting level scores consisted of means, while Auditory Stimulation and Hyperventilation scores utilized pre-poststimulation differences for HP and SR averaged over all four sessions. The Vigilance HP and SR scores were pre-stimulation levels and pre-post differences from the longest ISI. Groups were compared, two at a time, in all possible combinations, for the fifteen measures.

The distributions of Discriminant scores for all pairs of groups are presented in Figure 2-8. The abscissa expresses the score in standard deviation (SD) units, in order to provide a common scale for all comparisons. It can be seen that the overlap between the Normals and each patient group is relatively small, with the greatest amount between the Normals and the Familials (three and four S's respectively) at the mean (zero SD) of their combined distribution. Comparing the patient groups with each other, the most striking discriminations involve PKU's, who are completely separated from the Familial and

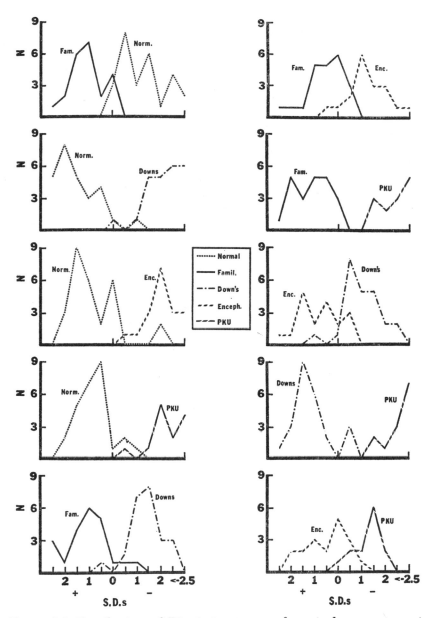

Figure 2-8. Distributions of Discriminant scores for paired group comparisons.

Down's cases. The Encephalopathy group seems most difficult to distinguish from other patient groups.

Examination of weights entering into the Discriminant Analysis suggested different patterns for the various discriminations. Only a few indications of consistency were apparent. RT for the longest vigilance interval, for example, appeared to contribute relatively heavily to the separation of the Normals from the patient groups, while HP during Rest and Vigilance appeared to differentiate the Familials from the other patients. Furthermore, both RA during Rest and SR during Auditory Stimulation appeared to contribute substantially to discrimination of PKU's from the other patient groups. In general, however, there seemed to be no strong evidence for a single pattern which distinguished one group from all the other groups, nor a single measure which weighed heavily in all discriminations. Since the technique tends to capitalize on chance differences, these findings require replication with an independent group of subjects.

DISCUSSION
Empirical Considerations

The present study has demonstrated a number of differences in autonomic functioning between mentally deficient subjects and normal controls. In general, the patient groups, with the exception of the Familials, showed elevated sympathetic scores during rest. The Rest data are consistent with those of previous studies for SR (Karrer, 1966) and heart rate (Karrer and Clausen, 1964; Clausen and Karrer, 1970; Berkson, et al., 1961). Although Karrer and Clausen found higher systolic BP in defectives, all patient groups in the present study manifested lower than normal blood pressure, a discrepancy which may be the result of previously discussed problems of recording. In contrast to the lack of differentiation in RA between Normals and Organic or Nonorganic defectives obtained by Clausen and Karrer (1970), the present study, using more specific diagnostic groups and larger sample sizes, did yield significant differences.

With respect to responsivity our results are also consistent with previous findings of generally reduced SR responses in mental defectives (Karrer, 1966). The lack of significant differences in the temporal aspects of the SR response is in agreement with Clausen and Karrer's (1969) report. Response differences in the other autonomic variables were not as consistent as in SR.

Semmel's (1965) observation of impaired vigilance of the mental defectives at all ISI's was not confirmed in the present study, using adjusted RT's as the measure of vigilance perform-ance. The two studies, however, differed in several respects; the mean IQ of Semmel's subjects was higher, his experimental and analytical procedures differed in that he used a visual stimulus and a detection score, and his subjects responded from a seated position. Perhaps as important as the patient-normal differences in vigilance RT at the longer ISI's, in our study, is the overall sluggishness of the patients manifested even in the baseline performance.

Of the autonomic measures in the various conditions of this and other studies SR and HP appear to be the most productive in discriminating between groups. Both have the merits of high intersession reliability and ease of recording. BP and respiration measures yielded fewer differences and had lower intersession correlations in the present study, but may be useful because of their relationships to HP and SR. Failure of the photoelectric measures of blood volume to discriminate between groups, the relative nature of their measurement and their proneness to artifact, question their usefulness.

In addition to the general differences between defectives and normals, it is clear that defectives differ in autonomic activity as a function of diagnostic classification. The Familials were char-acterized by a low sympathetic-like resting level and small reac-tivity scores, particularly with respect to SR under all conditions, and the respiratory measures in the vigilance condition. Sample variability within sessions tended to be particularly low for RA and SR. The low SR reactivity separated the Familials from the Normals, and their similarity to normal resting level for all variables—most prominent for SR—distinguished them from the other patient groups. With regard to baseline RT, the Fa-milials were again closest to Normals in performance (Fig. 2-4).

Their adjusted RT during vigilance, however, was frequently poorer than that of the other patient groups (Fig. 2-5). As the Familials constitute the most cooperative group of patients, their data are least likely to be influenced by artifact. Familial mental deficiency may be an exception to the general finding summarized by Sternbach in 1966, that parasympathetic dominance has not characterized any psychopathological group. Since sweat glands are exclusively innervated by the sympathetic nervous system, however, it may be that the Familials are characterized instead by inhibition of sympathetic activity; BP and HP responses during vigilance are less consistent with but do not contradict this interpretation.

The Down's cases tended to have extreme values of autonomic functions, but the direction relative to the Normals was not uniform. While there have been no previous reports of significant differences from normals in either SR or heart rate under resting conditions, Berkson, et al. (1961) and Wallace and Fehr (1970, Chap. 7) reported slightly higher SR and faster heart rate, whereas O'Connor and Hermelin (1963) reported lower than normal skin resistance in Down's subjects. The present findings, based on a larger number of subjects, and consistent over four sessions, indicated significantly faster heart rate, and confirmed O'Connor and Hermelin's finding of lower skin resistance. The clinical reports of dry skin in Down's patients which appear contradictory may refer to a scaly condition of the epidermal layers, rather than to a reduction of sweat secretion and autonomic activity. In addition, Down's cases in the present study showed low BP and low RA. These differences in respiration, heart rate, and BP in relation to the higher incidence of respiratory and circulatory diseases in Down's cases remain to be explored. The vascular abnormalities of the Down's patients described by Benda (1969) were not manifested in group differences in the blood volume changes of the present study. On the other hand, initial photocell resistance, which varies with skin thickness and pigmentation, as well as absolute blood volume, indicated least light reflection in the Down's cases.

Compared to the Familials the Down's group displayed significantly faster heart rate, lower BP, and lower SR at rest. Their autonomic pattern, with the exception of SR during vigilance, was in direct contrast to that of the Familials, in that HP and BP were most different from Normals while respiratory measures were most similar. They showed the least response to auditory stimulation and hyperventilation. Their baseline RT, as well as their adjusted RT, were the slowest of all groups. As most of the Down's cases were cooperative in the recording situation, their data can also be regarded as relatively valid.

On the surface, the Down's patients present a mixed picture in terms of sympathetic effects. The short HP and low SR during rest are suggestive of elevated sympathetic activity, while the low BP and low RA suggest higher parasympathetic-like activity. Although parasympathetic dominance would fit the behavioral stereotype of placidity, resting level of SR appears contradictory unless it can be accounted for on the basis of peripheral structural differences, such as higher ion concentration or density of sweat glands. Assuming sympathetic dominance, the low reactivity scores across all variables could be the result of sympathetic activity already at a virtual maximum. The results of Reiss, et al. (1965), showing higher basal metabolic rate in Down's cases compared to Familials, support the interpretation of sympathetic dominance in Down's cases.

The PKU's differed from Normals more in their resting pattern than in responsivity during stimulation and hyperventilation, where they tended to be the most responsive of all patient groups. During vigilance they showed substantial changes in SR with minimal HP and RP responses. Despite the disparity in baseline RT, the adjusted vigilance RT's of the PKU's were closest to those of the Normals. They were more variable than the Normals in BP, FV, RP, and SR, while less variable in HP and HV. The PKU's, like the Down's cases, differed from the Familials by a relatively faster heart rate, lower BP, and lower SR at rest, and minimal reactivity in HP and BP during vigilance. Their SR reactivity under all stimulus conditions was the greatest of all patient groups. Relative to all groups, PKU's showed the largest RA and the least changed RP during vigilance.

The observation of light skin pigmentation in PKU's by Menkes (1965) and Jervis (1963) was examined by comparing groups for initial photocell resistance of the blood volume transducers. The PKU's values were lowest of all groups, indicating greatest light reflection, although the differences were not significant. Penrose's (1963) report of moist skin in the PKU's, rather than Menkes' (1965) contrary observation, is more in accord with our finding of low SR at Rest.

Any conclusion with respect to PKU autonomic activity must be tentative, as this was the group where movement artifact was most evident. Nevertheless, since no significant differences were found between cooperative and noncooperative PKU's, a characterization of the PKU's in terms of sympathetic dominance seems appropriate and is in accord with their motor activity.

The Encephalopathy subjects were the least distinctive of all groups, with intermediate scores in all measures. They present the greatest difficulty of interpretation in terms of autonomic mechanisms. Although the validity of their data exceeds that of PKU's, it is less than that of the Familials and Down's cases. The difficulty in separating them from any other group in the discriminant analysis also suggests that they represent greater heterogeneity of etiology and mechanism.

The differences between groups in the present study appear to apply equally to both sexes in view of the few signficant Group × Sex interactions. The numerous differences between the sexes, however, point to a need for consideration of sex as a factor in future studies, or at least for maintenance of equal sex ratios between groups. Inconsistencies in previous findings may have resulted from neglect of this factor.

A major question regarding the diagnostic categories of mental deficiency concerns the degree to which the obtained differences between groups reflect variations in IQ. Previous reports in the literature have been contradictory with respect to the relationship between IQ and resting levels of SR. Collman (1931) reported a negative correlation in defective and dull children, O'Connor and Venables (1956) found a positive relationship (negative with conductance), whereas Ellis and Sloan (1958) found virtually no relationship. The present findings are consistent with those of Ellis and Sloan, and indicate that the group differences in SR are independent of differences in IQ. Although a significant correlation between IQ and HP was found in the present study, and although the rank order of the patient groups was the same for both variables, it is also unlikely that these group differences were solely a function of IQ, in that the Normals were between the Familials and the other patient groups with respect to HP. Furthermore, the size of the correlation was relatively small. Also similar to the rank ordering of IQ's were the baseline RT's of the groups; covariance analysis with IQ, however, did not result in the elimination of differences between patient groups. In addition, analysis of vigilance RT, adjusted for differences in baseline RT, revealed significant differences between the groups in the slope of RT across intervals. Finally, the degree of differentiation between patient groups obtained in the discriminant analysis, most notably between Down's and PKU's who are most comparable in IQ, suggests that the differences between groups are not merely a function of level of intelligence, degree of understanding, or institutionalization.

Theoretical Implications

Different aspects of the data are compatible with a number of interpretations of patient deficiency. The general tendency to sympathetic-like activity in the patients could, for example, represent either greater fearfulness in the test situation, a delay in biological maturation correlated with mental age, or chronic stress resulting from metabolic, chromosomal, or neural pathology. The data for the Familials, however, would be inconsistent with these hypotheses. Another possibility involves differences in the various organ systems innervated by the ANS. While heart rate, for example, reflects the degree of sympathetic-parasympathetic innervation, it is also a function of differences in heart structure, sensitivity to neurotransmitters, amount of local transmitter substance, and number of effector neurons. The lack of correlation between variables would be consistent with such a hypothesis, and undoubtedly some of the variation in the data is attributable to such sources. Except for Benda's (1965) report of vascular anomalies in the Down's cases, however, we have no evidence of specific abnormalities in the other patient groups which would produce the ordering of groups in terms of auto-nomic variables.

One of the major approaches to the problem of mental defi-ciency has involved the concept of arousal. The traditional view, generally based on response data, suggests that mental deficiency is characterized by a low arousal level (Berkson, 1961; Baumeis-ter and Ellis, 1963; Clausen, 1966; Horowitz, 1965; Lindsley, 1957; Rosvold, 1967). While this notion is consistent with the response data from the present study, it has difficulty accounting for the ordering of patient groups with respect to resting level, and would require the assumption that either resting levels are unrelated to arousal or that the arousal deficiency is manifested in reduced responsiveness to external stimulation only.

An alternative formulation is that mental deficiency involves a departure in either direction from an optimal level of arousal. Characterization of the arousal level of a particular group would require specification of the relationship between arousal and its autonomic and behavioral manifestations. The simplest hypothesis would posit a monotonic relationship between degree of arousal and level of autonomic activity. In terms of the auto-nomic measures in the present study, higher arousal would be manifested by increased sympathetic activity. From this view-point the most adequate measure would be skin resistance, since it reflects only sympathetic activity. The relationship between arousal and the dually innervated functions, such as blood pres-sure and heart rate, would be more complicated since compensa-tory parasympathetic actions might mitigate the sympathetic ef-fects. Regarding the relationship of behavioral measures to arousal, an inverted U-function has been suggested (Hebb, 1955; Malmo, 1959), i.e. improvement in performance up to some op-timal level of arousal, followed by a decline. In terms of reac-tion time, therefore, fastest response should occur at moderate levels of arousal.

The SR data during Rest suggest the following order of the

groups in terms of increasing arousal level: Familials, Normals, Encephalopathies, Down's cases, and PKU's. Except for the Down's group, the order reflects what we would expect from observation and from clinical reports of behavior of these groups. Thus the hyperactive PKU's are at the upper extreme. As previously mentioned the Down's cases present an apparent paradox between the behavioral stereotype and the autonomic levels of HP and SR. From their easygoing and friendly manner, somewhat flabby musculature and relaxed posture, they would appear to have a low sympathetic level. While their HP could be considered a compensation for low BP, SR could not be so readily accounted for. In the absence of a demonstrated peripheral difference to explain the low SR, their resting arousal level must be considered similar to that of the PKU's. More specifically, the Down's cases may represent a combination of heightened sympathetic activity and muscular atonicity.

In contrast to the Rest data, where the means of the patient groups are generally located on either side of those of the Normals, the SR reactivity data during Auditory Stimulation, Hyperventilation, and Vigilance uniformly indicate a smaller change in arousal for all patient groups. In rank order the PKU's are most reactive, followed by the Encephalopathies and Familials, with Down's cases least reactive.

It is possible to integrate the resting level, stimulation, and RT data by postulating an ogival relationship between SR levels and arousal on the one hand, and the U-shaped relationship between RT and arousal on the other. The hypothetical relationships and the relative positions of the different groups are indicated in Figure 2-9. The ogive shows that equal increments of arousal would produce largest changes in SR at moderate SR levels (Normals), and smaller responses toward either extreme (patients). The Familials at the extreme left showed both high resistance at Rest and small response during stimulation, the Normals had moderate resistance and the largest response, and the remaining three groups, to the right of the Normals, showed low resting resistance level and smaller than Normal responses. Because of the extremely small responses of the Down's group and

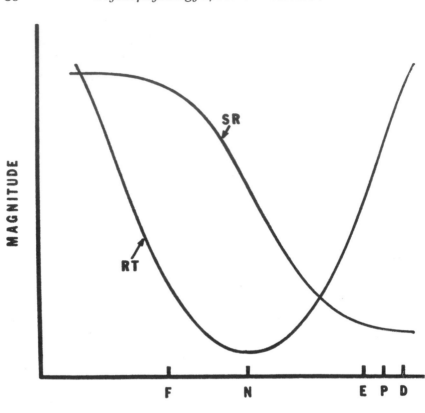

Figure 2-9. Hypothetical relationship of SR and RT to arousal. (F = Famili-al, N = Normal, E = Encephalopathy, P = PKU, and D = Down's Syndrome.)

their low SR at Rest they have been placed at the extreme right of the curve.

The baseline RT data of the groups do follow the order expected from the hypothetical U-shaped curve. The adjusted vigilance RT data, however, indicated a much better performance on the part of the PKU's than the curve suggests. In addition, for the adjusted RT as a function of interval (Fig. 2-5), the PKU's and the Encephalopathies should theoretically have decreased their RT with increasing interval and decreasing arousal, whereas in fact they tended to show an increased RT.

Implications of our version of the hypothesis may be tested by manipulating the arousal level of groups on either side of the normals where changes in arousal should produce opposite effects. Specifically, increases in the arousal level of the Familials and decreases in the Down's, PKU, and Encephalopathy cases should lead to autonomic and behavioral performance levels more closely approximating the normals. Especially desirable would be parametric studies of the effects of different stimulus intensities upon various performance and autonomic variables in groups such as the Familials and Down's. Confirmation of these predictions would have implications for drug treatment and environmental design.

SUMMARY

Autonomic activity including skin resistance (SR), heart period (HP), respiration period (RP), and respiration amplitude (RA), systolic blood pressure (BP), and blood volume changes of the forehead (HV) and finger (FV) were recorded for Normals, Familials, Down's syndrome cases, Encephalopathies, and PKU's. Three experimental conditions, Rest, Auditory Stimulation, and Hyperventilation, were repeated in four sessions, and Vigilance performance was measured in a fifth session.

1. Reliability and stability of autonomic variables were as high in mentally defective subjects as in Normals. In general one recording session produced reliable measures. Of the various measures, the most reliable and productive measures were SR and HP.

2. Intercorrelations of variables both between and within subjects were generally low, contrasting with traditional expectations of unified action of sympathetic activity.

3. Age was positively correlated with both BP and HP during Rest, while IQ was consistently related only to HP. Sex differences were generally similar for all groups and indicated greater sympathetic-like activity in males.

4. Compared to Normals:

a. The Familials were characterized by low sympathetic-like activity in all variables during Rest and reduced reactivity during the other conditions.

b. The Down's group at Rest was generally characterized by extreme autonomic scores with short HP, low BP, and low SR, contrasting with the behavioral stereotype of placidity, along with considerably attenuated responsivity.

c. The PKU's during Rest also manifested a sympathetic pattern and were the most responsive of the patient groups, particularly for SR.

d. The Encephalopathies showed a moderate sympathetic pattern which was less distinctive than that of any other patient group.

5. Vigilance, as measured by speed of response (RT) to irregularly spaced auditory signals, showed a differential effect of interval with all patient groups, except the Familials, declining in performance with longer interstimulus intervals. The pronounced group differences in baseline RT indicated progressively longer RT's for Familials, Encephalopathies, PKU's, and Down's cases.

6. Group differences in SR resting level and reactivity, as well as RT, were related to location of the groups along the hypothetical arousal dimension. Specifically, SR was proposed to have an ogival relationship, and RT a U-shaped relationship to arousal.

REFERENCES

Baumeister, A. A. and Ellis, N. R.: Delayed response performance of retardates. *Am J Ment Defic*, 67:714-722, 1963.

Baumeister, A. A. and Kellas, G.: Reaction time and mental retardation. In N. R. Ellis (Ed.): *International Review of Research in Mental Retardation*. Vol. III, N.Y., Academic, 1968.

Benda, C. E.: *Down's Syndrome*. N.Y., Grune and Stratton, 1969.

Benjamin, L. S.: Facts and artifacts in using analysis of covariance to "undo" the law of initial values. *Psychophysiology* 4:187-202, 1967.

Berkson, G.: Responsiveness of the mentally deficient. *Am J Ment Defic*, 66:277-286, 1961.

Berkson, G.; Hermelin, B., and O'Connor, N.: Physiological responses of normals and institutionalized mental defectives to repeated stimuli. *J Ment Defic Res*, 5:30-39, 1961.

Block, J.: Covariance analysis scale transformation in statistical treatment of nonadditive units. *Percept Mot Skills*, 19:755-761, 1964.

Breg, W. R.: Family counseling in Down's syndrome. In V. Apgar (Ed.):

Down's syndrome (Mongolism). *Ann NY Acad Sci, 171*:645-654, 1970.

Brousseau, K.: *Mongolism.* Baltimore, Williams and Wilkins, 1928.

Clausen, J.: *Ability Structure and Subgroups in Mental Retardation.* Washington, D.C., Spartan Books, 1966.

————: Arousal theory in mental retardation. In M. Hammer, K. Salzinger and S. Sutton (Eds.): *Psychopathology: Contributions from the Biological, Behavioral, and Social Sciences.* N.Y., J. Wiley, 1972.

Clausen, J. and Karrer, R.: Orienting response—frequency of occurrence and relationship to other autonomic variables. *Am J Ment Defic, 73:* 455-464, 1968.

————: Temporal factors in autonomic responses for normal and mentally defective subjects. *Am J Ment Defic, 74*:80-85, 1969.

————: Autonomic activity during rest in normal and mentally defective subjects. *Am J Ment Defic, 75*:361-370, 1970.

Collman, R. D.: The psychogalvanic reactions of exceptional and normal children. *Contr Educ,* No. 469, N.Y., Teachers College, 1931.

Crosby, K. G.: Attention and distractibility in mentally retarded and average children. *Am J Ment Defic, 77*:46-53, 1972.

Edwards, A. L.: *Experimental Design in Psychological Research.* N.Y., Rinehart and Co., 1950.

Ellis, N. R. and Sloan, W.: The relationship between intelligence and skin conductance. *Am J Ment Defic, 63*:304-306, 1958.

French, J. D.: The reticular formation. In J. Field, H. W. Magoun, and V. E. Hall (Eds.): *Handbook of Physiology.* Section 1. *Neurophysiology.* Vol. 2. Washington, D.C., American Physiological Society, 1960.

Grings, W. W.; Lockhart, R. A., and Dameron, L. E.: Conditioning autonomic responses of mentally subnormal individuals. *Psychol Monogr,* 76:39, 1962.

Hebb, D. O.: Drives and the C.N.S. (conceptual nervous system). *Psychol Rev, 62*:243-254, 1955.

Heber, R.: A manual on terminology and classification in mental retardation. *Am J Ment Defic,* Monogr. Suppl., 2nd ed., 1961.

Hernández-Péon, R.: Physiological mechanisms in attention. In R. W. Russell (Ed.): *Frontiers in Physiological Psychology.* N.Y., Academic, 1966.

Holden, E. A.: Reaction time during unimodal and trimodal stimulation in educable retardates. *J Ment Defic Res,* 9:183-190, 1965.

Horowitz, F. D.: Theories of arousal and retardation potential. *Ment Retard,* 3:20-23, 1965.

Jervis, G. A.: The clinical picture. In F. L. Lyman (Ed.). *Phenylketonuria.* Springfield, Thomas, 1963.

Karrer, R.: Comparison of autonomic activity of mental defectives and normals: a sequential analysis of the heart rate response. *J Ment Defic Res,* 9:102-108, 1965.

————: Autonomic nervous system functions and behavior. In N. R. Ellis (Ed.): *International Review of Research in Mental Retardation.* Vol. II, N.Y., Academic, 1966.

Karrer, R. and Clausen, J.: A comparison of mentally deficient and normal individuals upon four dimensions of autonomic activity. *J Ment Defic Res, 8:*149-163, 1964.

Kirman, B. H.: Down's disease (Mongolism). In L. T. Hilliard and B. H. Kirman (Eds.): *Mental Deficiency, 2nd ed.* Boston, Little, Brown and Co., 1965.

Kodman, F.; Fein, A., and Mixon, A.: Psychogalvanic skin response audiometry with severe mentally retarded children. *Am J Ment Defic, 63:* 131-136, 1959.

Lacey, J. I.: The evaluation of autonomic responses. Toward a general solution. *Ann NY Acad Sci, 67:*123-164, 1956.

Lillienfield, A. M.: *Epidemiology of Mongolism.* Baltimore, The Johns Hopkins Press, 1969.

Lindsley, D. B.: Psychophysiology and motivation. In M. R. Jones (Ed.): *Nebraska Symposium on Motivation.* Lincoln, University Nebraska Press, 1957.

Lobb, H.: Frequency vs. magnitude of GSR in comparisons of retarded and non-retarded groups. *Am J Ment Defic, 75:*336-340, 1970.

Luria, A. R.: An objective approach to the study of the abnormal child. *Am J Orthopsychiat, 31:*1-16, 1961(a).

————: *The Role of Speech in the Regulation of Normal and Abnormal Behavior.* J. Tizard (Ed.): N.Y., Liverwright Publishing Co., 1961(b).

Malmo, R. B.: Activation: A neurophysiological dimension. *Psychol Rev, 66:*367-386, 1959.

Menkes, J. H.: Section on abnormalities in protein and amino acid metabolism. In C. H. Carter (Ed.): *Medical Aspects of Mental Retardation.* Springfield, Thomas, 1965.

Moruzzi, G. and Magoun, H. W.: Brain stem reticular formation and activation of the EEG. *EEG Clin Neurophysiol, 1:*455-473, 1949.

O'Connor, N. and Hermelin, B.: *Speech and Thought in Severe Subnormality.* N.Y., Macmillan, 1963.

O'Connor, N. and Venables, P. H.: A note on the basal level of skin conductance and Binet IQ. *Br J Psychol, 42:*148-149, 1956.

Oster, J.: *Mongolism.* Copenhagen, Danish Science Press, 1953.

Penrose, L. S.: *The Biology of Mental Defect, 3rd ed.* N.Y., Grune and Stratton, 1963.

Reiss, M.; Wakoh, T.; Hillman, J.; Pearse, J.; Daley, N., and Reiss, J.: Endocrine investigations into mongolism. *Am J Ment Defic, 70:*204-212, 1965.

Rosvold, H. E.: Some neuropsychological studies relevant to mental retardation. In G. A. Jervis (Ed.): *Mental Retardation: A Symposium.* Springfield, Thomas, 1967.

Samuels, I.: Reticular mechanisms and behavior. *Psychol Bull,* 58:1-25, 1959.

Semmel, M. I.: Arousal theory and vigilance behavior of educable mentally retarded and average children. *Am J Ment Defic,* 70:38-47, 1965.

Siegel, S.: *Nonparametric Statistics.* N.Y., McGraw-Hill, 1956.

Sokolov, E. N.: Neuronal models and the orienting reflex. In M. A. Brazier (Ed.): *The Central Nervous System and Behavior.* N.Y., Josiah Macy, Jr., Foundation, 1960.

Sternbach, R. A.: *Principles of Psychophysiology.* N.Y., Academic, 1966.

Tredgold, A. F.: *Mental Deficiency, 2nd ed.* N.Y., William Wood and Co., 1914.

Vogel, W.: The relationship of age and intelligence to autonomic functioning. *J Comp Physiol Psychol,* 54:133-138, 1961.

Wallace, R. M. and Fehr, F. S.: Heart rate, skin resistance, and reaction time of Mongoloid and normal children under baseline and distraction conditions. *Psychophysiol,* 6:722-731, 1970.

Winer, B. J.: *Statistical Principles in Experimental Design.* N.Y., McGraw-Hill, 1962.

CHAPTER 3

HEART RATE CHANGES DURING REACTION TIME: AN APPROACH FOR UNDERSTANDING DEFICIENT ATTENTION IN RETARDED INDIVIDUALS

ANTOINETTE KRUPSKI[*]

[*] This research was supported by a predoctoral fellowship from the American Association of University Women (1970-1971) and by a NIMH predoctoral traineeship, HD-00158, in mental retardation (1967-1970) both of which were awarded to the author. It was also partially supported by a NIMH Research Grant MH-18655 awarded to Hiram Fitzgerald. Portions of this paper were presented at meetings of the Society for Psychophysiological Research, New Orleans, 1970, the Gatlinburg Conference on Research and Theory in Mental Retardation, 1971, and in a dissertation in partial fulfillment of the requirements for the Ph.D. degree.

The author wishes to express sincere thanks to Fred Beckett of the Okemos, Michigan School System and David Knaggs of the St. Lawrence Community Mental Health Center for their assistance in obtaining subjects and to Gary Connors for his technical assistance.

92

STUDIES OF REACTION TIME (RT) performance in retarded subjects have reliably reported significantly slower RT scores in this group when compared to subjects of normal intelligence (Baumeister and Kellas, 1968). The RT task involves the successive presentation of a warning signal followed by a reaction signal. Typically, the subject is instructed to respond as quickly as possible to the reaction signal. Responses usually involve a button press or similar task. It is generally assumed that if the subject is attending or preparing to respond during the preparatory interval (PI), or a period of time between warning and reaction signals, he will have a fast RT score.

One of the appealing aspects of the basic RT procedure is its flexibility. For example, the duration and/or regularity of the PI can be manipulated. When the duration of the PI is consistent from trial to trial, the procedure is called fixed, or regular RT. When this duration is varied from trial to trial, the procedure is called variable, or irregular RT.

In support of the assumption that the RT task taps some aspect of attention processes, a rather extensive literature has accumulated which demonstrates the sensitivity of response-speed measures in RT tasks to populations that are often clinically defined as having attention problems, such as the mentally retarded. Reports of retardate's performance on RT tasks have been quite consistent: Retardates typically have slower RT scores than normals even on their "best" trials (Baumeister and Kellas, 1968; Berkson, 1960; Czudner and Marshall, 1967; Tizard and Venables, 1956; Wallace and Fehr, 1970). At least one investigator has inferred that such data reflect the retardate's inability to sustain attention during the PI of a trial (Denny, 1964). In addition, retardates typically show greater intra-individual variability on trial-to-trial performance in a number of tasks, including RT (Liebert and Baumeister, 1973). Such inefficiency in retardate performance presumably stems from an inability to sustain attention throughout a task.

Hyperactive children as well as children diagnosed as learning disabled are examples of other clinical populations often identified as exhibiting attention problems. Like retardates, hyperactive children are reported to be slower in RT and more variable in trial-to-trial performance (Cohen and Douglas, 1972).

Sroufe, Sonies, West, and Wright (1973) reported that the mean RT scores of children referred for treatment for learning disability were not significantly different from those of normal control children. However, RT scores of the clinical sample were significantly more variable than were those of control children.

Young, normal children are another group who are thought to be deficient in attention, or at least more distractible than their older counterparts. Consistent with the retardate research, studies of normal children have reported slower RT scores in chronologically younger children when their performance is compared to older children or young adults (Elliott, 1970; Grim, 1967; Sroufe, 1971). In each of these studies, the slower RT performance of younger subjects has been attributed to some deficit in the ability to maintain attention or to maintain an appropriate preparatory set.

In summary, slower and/or more variable RT performance has been reported for subject populations that are often clinically described as having problems in attention, such as mentally retarded, hyperactive, learning disabled, and young, normal children. The most frequent interpretations of these data relate deviant RT performance to an inability to sustain attention, or to maintain an appropriate preparatory set. Taken together, this work appears to be reasonable support for the assumption that RT tasks tap some component of attention processes.

Another dependent measure used to study attention and RT performance is heart rate (HR). The specific nature of this response has been studied most extensively in normal adult male subjects. Essentially, a HR deceleration is reported to occur during the fixed PI which reaches its nadir during the second in which the subject is to respond (Chase, Graham, and Graham, 1968; Coquery and Lacey, 1966; Lacey and Lacey, 1966; Obrist, Webb, and Sutterer, 1969). The degree of this time-locked HR deceleration has been correlated with RT speed such that greater HR decelerations are associated with faster RT speed. Although the functional significance of this HR response is currently being debated (Elliott, 1972; Hahn, 1973), many investigators who have studied this response imply that HR deceleration during RT tasks reflects some component of attention processes (Chase, et al., 1968; Jennings, Averill, Opton, and Lazarus, 1971; Lacey, 1967; Obrist, et al., 1969; Obrist, Webb, Sutterer, and Howard, 1970).

Sroufe (1971) studied HR changes and RT performance in six-, eight-, and ten-year-old children in an attempt to assess changes in these two measures as a function of age. Sroufe reasoned that the HR deceleration response, so reliably observed in adult samples, would provide a useful measure in a developmental assessment of the ability to maintain attention. As predicted, older subjects had faster RT scores than younger subjects in a five-second PI condition. Heart rate decelerations paralleled the RT findings with older children showing more reliable and greater time-locked HR decelerations than did younger children. In general, Sroufe suggests that these data support the notion that time-locked HR deceleration is an index of the ability to maintain attention.

A STUDY OF HEART RATE AND REACTION TIME OF RETARDATES

In view of the reliable relationship between the HR deceleration and RT performance, particularly the developmental trend demonstrated by Sroufe, it appears as though a study of HR changes during RT would also reflect differences between normal and mentally retarded groups. It follows that retarded subjects, who typically respond more slowly in the RT task, might also show attenuated HR decelerations during the reaction signal.

One of the purposes of this study was to examine HR changes during the PI of a RT situation in order to determine where in the PI normal and retarded subjects differ. On the basis of previous work, it was hypothesized that retardates would show less HR deceleration than normal subjects during the second in which the reaction signal occurred. In addition to this response at the reaction signal, a number of studies suggested that retardate's responses to the warning signal would also be of lesser magnitude. After an extensive review of the literature, Karrer (1966) reports that retardates react less than normals to stimuli of moderate or mild intensity, although there is some evidence that they respond equally to intense stimuli. Some authors (Heal and Johnson, 1971) have interpreted such autonomic findings within an orienting response framework where autonomic responses to stimulus onset are interpreted as preparing the organism for optimal reception of stimuli. Using this framework these authors argue that the lower responsivity observed in retardates is related to poorer reception of stimuli and, hence, lower levels of attention to stimulus onset. In the present study a light of moderate intensity was used as the warning stimulus so that lower magnitude HR responses to warning light onset were expected in the retarded group. Such a finding interpreted within the orienting response framework would suggest that retardate's poorer RT performance might be due to impaired reception of stimuli.

In order to observe HR responses to both warning and reaction signals, a minimum PI length of 4 seconds was used in this study. A 4-second PI allows some recovery of HR response to the warning signal so that there is minimal overlap with the heart rate response to the reaction signal. Preparatory intervals of 7 and 13 seconds were also used so as to sample RT and HR changes during conditions which required short, moderate, and sustained levels of attention. These PI lengths were presented in blocks of trials so that all PIs were the same length within trial blocks.

An examination of moderate and sustained levels of attention seemed particularly relevant since young subjects appear to be significantly more impaired in RT performance during fixed PIs that require sustained attention. For example, Sroufe (1971) found no reliable HR decelerations in six-, eight-, or ten-year-old children during a 10-second PI, although many of these same children exhibited reliable HR decelerations during a 5-second PI condition. This finding is like that reported by Elliott (1970) who found that younger subjects in his study performed most poorly in comparison to the older subjects during longer fixed PIs, i.e. 8- and 16-seconds. Elliott has pointed out that the 8- and 16-second PIs can be viewed as being more difficult as the length of these time intervals are harder to judge and because readiness to respond must be maintained for a longer period of time.

Thus, Sroufe and Elliott's work with normal young children suggest that the ability to attend, as measured in fixed RT, is most saliently deficient in sustained PIs of 8 seconds or longer. Sroufe found no reliable HR decelerations during a 10-second fixed PI condition in any of his subject groups, whereas Elliott found slowest RT performance in younger subjects in 8- and 16-second PIs. Similarities between young, normal children and retardates in other characteristics of RT performance imply that retardates might also exhibit greater impairment during PIs of sustained duration. It was hoped that if such differences existed, they would emerge by using PI lengths of short, moderate, and long duration.

One final aspect of the study involved the investigation of individual differences within both retardate and normal groups. Between-subject variance in groups of retardates is typically much greater than that observed for groups of normal subjects in many tasks, including RT (Berkson, 1973; 1966; Denny, 1964; Liebert and Baumeister, 1973). The explanation of these wide individual differences is not clearly demonstrated from etiology or specific neuropathological data. Berkson (1973) has suggested a process oriented approach in order to understand this heterogeneity within retarded groups of subjects. He points out that within-group analyses based on a specific behavior (such as RT) might be useful in providing greater understanding of individual differences. Such an approach was adopted here, so that much of the results section will focus on within-group differences.

In summary, HR changes were examined in groups of normal and retarded subjects during a RT task. The PIs were fixed at either 4, 7, or 13 seconds. Differences between groups found in this study were reported in a previous publication (Krupski, 1975), so that these results will be briefly summarized. Emphasis will be on within-group analyses and the implications resulting from them.

Method

Subjects

Subjects were twelve normal males and twelve noninstitutionalized, retarded males, mean age twenty and twenty-one, respectively. The normal subjects, undergraduate students from Michigan State University, received extra course credit for their participation, while the retarded subjects, from the Lansing, Michigan, metropolitan area, were paid two dollars for their participation. Retarded males had a Wechsler mean IQ of 70 (range 55 to 82). Subjects had no sensorimotor impairments. Neither had they received any drugs or medications for at least two weeks prior to the experiment.

Apparatus

The RT stimulus was a green, 24-volt, DC jewel light located about three feet in front of the subject at eye level. A white light, located two inches below the green light, served as the rest period stimulus and became illuminated only between blocks of trials. The presentation of these stimuli was controlled by two Hunter timers. The response manipulandum was a microswitch placed on the arm of the subject's chair. In this position, the subject's forearm and heel of the preferred hand were supported by the arm of the chair with his index finger extended above the microswitch. Reaction time was measured in milliseconds by a Standard electric clock. Subjects were tested in a sound-attenuated room where the temperature was maintained at approximately 70° F., and the ambient noise level was 51 db (A-scale).

Heart rate (Lead I), RT stimulus signal, and RT responses were continuously recorded on a 4-channel Grass P7 polygraph. Respiration was measured by a strain gauge around the chest.

Procedure

All subjects were individually tested in the developmental psychophysiology laboratory at Michigan State University. After arriving at the laboratory, the subject was seated in a comfortable armchair in a sound-attenuated room. The female experimenter attached the electrodes and briefly explained their purpose.

Each subject was told that a green light located three feet in front of him at eye level would come on periodically. Onset of the green light marked the beginning of the PI; this light remained illuminated for the entire PI. Subjects were told that their job was to press a microswitch as quickly as possible when the green light went off. A white light, located two inches below the green light, served as a rest period stimulus and became illuminated only between blocks of trials.

Each subject participated in a single session which consisted of three blocks of trials and two rest periods. A trial block consisted of 15 trials at one of the three PIs. Only one PI value was used per trial block. For example, a subject assigned to a 4-7-13 second PI combination received the following sequence: 15 RT trials in which the PI was four seconds, a two-minute rest period, 15 RT trials in which the PI was seven seconds, another two-minute rest period, and 15 RT trials in which the PI was thirteen seconds. Subjects were randomly assigned to one of the six possible combinations of the three trial blocks when they appeared at the laboratory. The assignment of order was counterbalanced for each group so that there was an equal number of subjects in each order. The inter-trial interval varied among 10, 15, and 20 seconds.

The subject was alone during the entire experimental session, but could communicate with the experimenter through an intercom system. Five practice trials in which the subject was instructed how to respond appropriately, preceded the first trial block. At the end of practice, all subjects were told that the "real" test would now begin.

Data Quantification

Only the last ten trials in each PI condition were scored for RT and HR. Heart period (HP), the number of milliseconds between successive R waves, was measured from one-second intervals. If more than one R-R interval was completed during any given second, only the first cycle was scored for that second. Four seconds prior to PI onset, all seconds during the PI, and four seconds following PI offset were scored for each PI condition. The HP data were evaluated in separate analyses for each PI condition.

Results

Reaction Time

Analyses of variance of RT scores between groups revealed that retardates had significantly slower RT scores than did normals. There was also a significant PI effect indicating that RT scores were slower for both normals and retardates as the PI increased in length. The group by PI interaction was not significant which indicated that retardates had slower RT scores regardless of the time given to prepare. These results were obtained in analyses of raw RT scores as well as in analyses of log transformed RT scores (Woodworth and Schlosberg, 1954). Details of these and other between-group analyses are presented in a previous publication (Krupski, 1975). These group results are consistent with the majority of studies that have examined RT in retarded and normal subjects (see Baumeister and Kellas, 1968, for a comprehensive review of this work).

As expected, the standard deviations of RT scores for each group showed retarded subjects to be considerably more variable in their performance than normals. In order to examine individual differences within groups, subjects in each group were classified as fast, middle, or slow RT responders on the basis of rank in their group's distribution of mean RT scores for each PI. The consistency of an individual's RT performance over the three PI conditions was tested by the Kendall coefficient of concordance (Siegel, 1950). The coefficient of concordance (W) was .90 for the normal group ($\chi^2 11 = 29.78$, p < .01) and .91 for the retarded group ($\chi^2 11 = 30.18$, p < .01), indicating a high degree of consistency. That is, a subject who had the fastest mean RT score in the 4-second PI condition was likely to have the fastest mean RT score in the 7- and 13-second PI conditions as well.

The RT data for fast, middle, and slow subjects for each group and each PI are presented in Table 3-I. Note that the fast retarded subjects had faster mean RT scores than did slow normals in all three PI conditions. This within-group analysis clearly shows that although retardates as a group had slower mean RT scores than normal subjects as a group, the retardates with the fastest mean RT scores were faster than some of the normal subjects.

In addition to absolute RT score, the consistency of an indi-

TABLE 3-I

MEAN RT SCORES AND STANDARD DEVIATIONS EXPRESSED IN MILLESECONDS FOR 4, 7, AND 13 SECOND PI CONDITIONS FOR FAST, MIDDLE, SLOW NORMALS, FAST, MIDDLE, SLOW RETARDATES; AND FOR NORMAL AND RETARDED GROUPS COMBINED

	Normals				Retardates			
	Fast	*Middle*	*Slow*	*All*	*Fast*	*Middle*	*Slow*	*All*
4-Second PI								
Mean RT	235.8	290.0	354.7	293.6	295.3	370.8	560.0	408.7
Standard Deviation	30.3	16.1	17.8	54.6	37.1	29.4	191.4	155.3
7-Second PI								
Mean RT	232.0	304.7	361.7	299.7	293.3	396.5	662.1	450.7
Standard Deviation	30.8	28.2	32.3	61.9	30.9	36.4	268.6	215.5
13-Second PI								
Mean RT	262.7	337.0	373.4	324.2	330.3	423.0	643.0	465.5
Standard Deviation	20.2	16.4	17.0	50.7	36.5	16.9	215.3	178.4

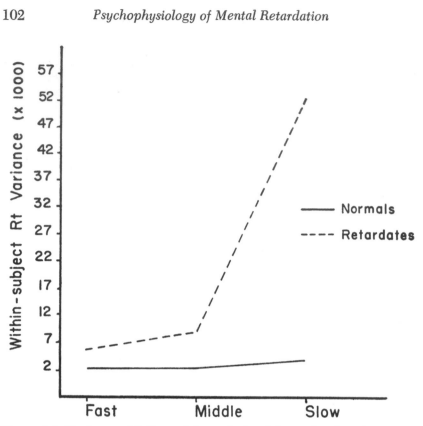

Figure 3-1. Trial-to-trial RT variability calculated for each subject's raw RT scores collapsed across PI conditions for fast, middle, slow normals and fast, middle, slow retardates.

vidual's RT performance across trials was examined in a within-subject variability analysis. The variance of each subject's RT scores in each PI condition was calculated and used as the dependent variable in an analysis of variance. Within each group were fast, middle, and slow classifications as described previously. As expected, the results indicated significant differences between groups with retardates having significantly greater within-subject variance than normals ($F\ 1/18 = 7.53$, $p < .013$). Figure 3-1 illustrates within-subject variance for fast, middle, and slow subjects within each group, collapsed across PI conditions. This figure shows that normal subjects maintained fairly consistent performance throughout the RT task regardless of their mean

RT scores. Retardates as a group had higher variance in their trial-to-trial performance. The greater variability was most dramatic in retarded subjects with the slowest mean RT scores.

Correlations Between Reaction Time Scores and Intelligence Quotients

Pearson Product moment correlations between mean RT and intelligence quotient (IQ) scores were performed for the retarded group; IQ scores were not available for the normal group. Wechsler combined IQ scores were available for all twelve retarded subjects; verbal and performance scores were available for all but one of these subjects. These correlations are presented in Table 3-II. A negative correlation indicates that low IQ is related to a slow RT. As can be seen from the table, significant correlations were found between performance IQ and RT. Although the other correlations were not significant, it is worth noting that the trends were in the appropriate direction (i.e. faster RTs tend to be related to higher IQs in retarded individuals).

Since RT can be viewed as a performance task, it is not surprising that it should be highly related to another performance measure, namely performance IQ. Most other studies reporting significant relationships between intelligence and RT performance have used MA measures rather than IQ and have typically reported somewhat lower correlations (Bensberg and Cantor, 1957; Ellis and Sloan, 1957; Pascal, 1953).

TABLE 3-II

PEARSON PRODUCT MOMENT CORRELATIONS BETWEEN TOTAL IQ, VERBAL IQ, PERFORMANCE WECHSLER IQ SCORES AND MEAN REACTION TIMES FOR 4, 7, AND 13-SECOND PI CONDITIONS FOR THE RETARDED GROUP

PI	Total IQ (df = 10)	Verbal IQ (df = 9)	Performance IQ (df = 9)
4	−.388	−.224	−.707*
7	−.384	−.351	−.782†
13	−.347	−.336	−.750†

* $p < .02$.
† $p < .01$.

Between-Group Heart Rate

The HR data were determined from beat-to-beat measures of heart period. In separate analyses of variance for each PI condition, retardates had significantly slower base level HR than did normals. These differences were about the same magnitude for each condition so that normals maintained a HR of about 78 beats per minute (bpm) and retardates a rate of about 68 bpm throughout the task.

There were also significant group by second interactions in each PI which are illustrated in Figure 3-2. Graphs in this figure depict heart period change from prestimulus mean as a function of seconds past warning light onset for each of the three PI conditions for each group. The significant interaction was found to be due to the differences between groups in the final deceleration occurring simultaneously with the reaction signal. In each PI condition, this deceleration was significantly larger in normal subjects than in retardates. Other components of HR responding such as deceleration after the warning signal or acceleration occurring in about the middle of the PI were not significantly different for groups.

Thus, the between-group HR analyses parallel the between-group RT findings. Retardates, having slower mean RT scores, also exhibited attenuated and/or absent HR decelerations during the second in which the reaction signal occurred. This was true in all three PI conditions, suggesting that retardates were responding inappropriately, compared to normals, regardless of the preparation time. Further, the between-group findings suggest that the retardate's primary deficit is not in the reception of the warning signal as their mean HR response after the warning signal was no different from normals'. Rather the differences between groups appear later in the PI and are apparently related to reaction signal onset.

Within-Group Heart Rate

Second-by-second HR scores were analyzed for fast, middle, and slow subjects in each group. A repeated measures analysis of variance computed for the normal group yielded significant dif-

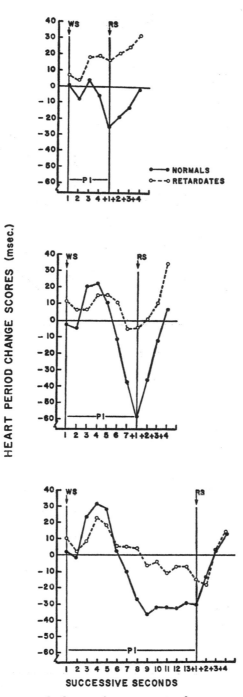

Figure 3-2. Heart period change from pre-stimulus mean as a function of successive seconds during 4- (top), 7- (mid), and 13-second (bottom) PI conditions in normals and retardates. WS = warning signal, RS = response signal.

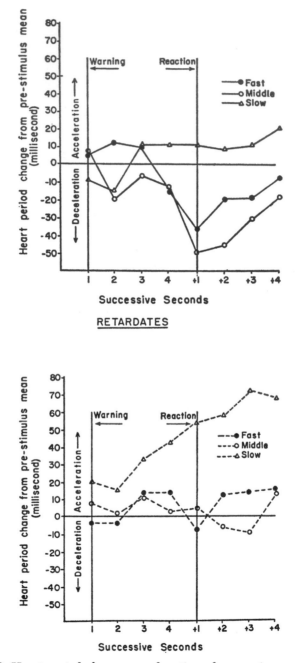

Figure 3-3. Heart period change as a function of successive seconds during the 4-second PI condition in (a, above) fast, middle, slow normals, and (b, below) fast, middle, slow retardates.

ferences between fast and slow responders in all three PI conditions, while in the retarded group there were significant differences between fast and slow responders only in the 4- and 7-second PI conditions.

Four-second PI. Second-by-second HR scores during the 4-second PI condition for fast, middle, and slow subjects in the normal group are illustrated in Figure 3-3a. Fast and slow normal subjects had significantly different HR scores (F 11/66 = 2.55, p < .009). Middle and slow normals were also significantly different from each other (F 11/66 = 3.85, p < .001) while there were no significant differences between fast and middle normals. The primary difference between fast, middle, and slow subjects in this PI occurred during second +1, or the second in which the reaction signal occurred. At this point fast and middle subjects showed HR deceleration while slow subjects showed HR acceleration throughout the PI. In slow subjects there was a very small deceleration which occurred one second after the reaction signal.

There were also significant differences between the HR scores of fast and slow retarded subjects (F 11/66 = 3.71, p < .001), and middle and slow retarded subjects (F 11/66 = 4.62, p < .001) in the 4-second PI condition. These data are illustrated in Figure 3-3b. Fast retardates showed a small HR deceleration during second +1, middle retardates showed their greatest HR deceleration two seconds following the reaction signal, while slow retardates showed HR acceleration throughout the entire PI.

In the 4-second PI condition, then, the most obvious difference between fast, middle, and slow responders parallels the RT results. Those subjects with the fastest RT scores (fast normals, middle normals, and fast retardates) showed HR deceleration concomitant with the reaction signal whereas slow responders (slow normals, middle, and slow retardates) showed either absent or delayed HR deceleration in this condition.

Seven-second PI. In the 7-second PI condition fast and slow normals were significantly different from each other (F 14/84 = 1.86, p < .04). These data are illustrated in Figure 3-4a. As in the 4-second PI condition, the obvious difference between these

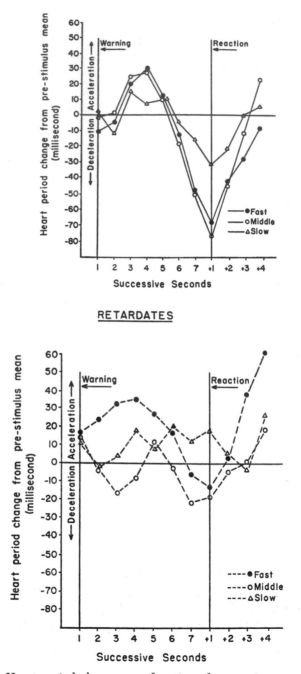

Figure 3-4. Heart period change as a function of successive seconds during the 7-second PI condition in (a, above) fast, middle, slow normals, and (b, below) fast, middle, slow retardates.

groups is in the degree of HR deceleration during second +1, with faster subjects showing greater decelerations at this point.

The HR scores of fast and slow retarded subjects were also significantly different in this PI ($F \ 14/84 = 1.98$, $p < .029$). The HR patterns of fast, middle, and slow retarded subjects are illustrated in Figure 3-4b. Fast and middle retarded subjects showed HR deceleration during second +1, whereas slow subjects did not show HR deceleration until second +3, or two seconds after the reaction signal. In middle retarded subjects, a slight HR deceleration can be observed one second prior to the reaction signal.

The HR patterns observed in the 7-second PI, then, are similar to those reported for the 4-second PI condition. Faster RT subjects, regardless of group, exhibited HR deceleration during second +1, while the slowest subjects exhibited a HR deceleration that was of different latency.

THIRTEEN-SECOND PI. The HR responses of fast and slow normal subjects were significantly different from each other in the 13-second PI condition ($F \ 20/120 = 2.12$, $p < .007$). These data are presented in Figure 3-5. As in the previous conditions, the most obvious difference between the HR patterns of these groups was in the degree of HR deceleration occurring at second + 1. Corresponding to the RT differences, magnitude of HR deceleration was greatest for fast subjects, somewhat less for middle subjects, while HR accelerated for slow normal subjects. In middle and slow normal subjects, the largest magnitude HR deceleration in the PI occurred six seconds before the reaction signal.

There were no significant differences in the HR patterns of fast, middle, or slow retarded subjects in this PI.

SUMMARY. Thus, in all three conditions (except for retardates in the 13-second PI condition), greater HR decelerations concomitant with the reaction signal were observed in those subjects with the fastest RT scores regardless of group. Slower subjects, on the other hand, displayed decelerations which were not only smaller in magnitude, but also of different latency. For example, in the 4-second PI middle retardates showed their greatest HR

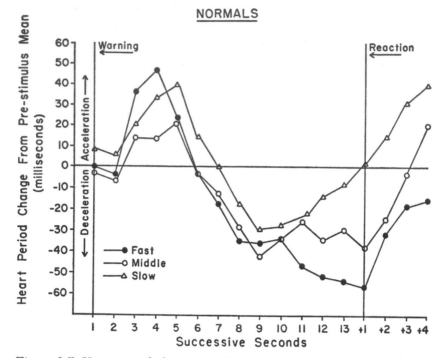

Figure 3-5. Heart period change as a function of successive seconds during the 13-second PI condition in fast, middle, slow normals.

deceleration two seconds after the reaction signal, whereas slow retardates showed a purely accelerative response throughout the PI. In the 7-second PI, middle retardates showed a slight HR deceleration one second before the RT signal while slow retardates showed greatest deceleration two seconds after the reaction signal. Finally, in the 13-second PI both middle and slow normals showed greatest deceleration six seconds prior to the reaction signal, and in the retarded group eight of twelve subjects responded with their greatest deceleration one second after the reaction signal. These observations suggest that subjects with slow RT scores are characterized by HR decelerations which are not only of lesser magnitude when compared to faster subjects, but of considerably more variability in latency than their faster counterparts. This finding has a number of implications which will be discussed in detail later in this chapter.

The HR results discussed up to this point apply to all groups and conditions with the exception of the retardate performance in the 13-second PI. In this exceptional case, there were no second-by-second differences in the HR responses of fast, middle, or slow retarded subjects. The absence of a relationship between RT performance and HR changes in this long, 13-second PI condition probably is due to the greater demands for sustained attention during this interval—a task which might be very difficult for subjects in the retarded group. Thus, it appears as though the retardate's attention deficit becomes more dramatic during tasks that require a relatively long duration of sustained attention.

Respiration

The effects of respiration were assessed by counting the frequency of initiations and terminations of inspirations during the four seconds preceding the warning signal, during the entire PI, and during the four seconds following the reaction signal, for each trial. These analyses were based on only ten subjects per group because of unscorable records for two retardates. Analyses of variance for each PI revealed a significant group by trial interaction in the 4-second PI (F $9/162 = 1.99$, $p < .043$). In this PI condition, normals and retardates showed about the same level of respiration activity until trial seven (ten total). At this point the normal group's respiration decreased slightly and was sustained for the remaining trials. The retarded group, on the other hand, showed a tendency to increased respiration in later trials. The 7-second PI analysis only revealed significant trial effects (F $9/162 = 2.05$, $p < .037$); respiration frequency decreased across trials for both groups. The 13-second PI analysis revealed no significant effects.

The only significant group difference in respiration frequency, then, occurred in the 4-second PI condition. This isolated and rather specific group by trial interaction along with no group differences in respiration frequency in the other PI conditions implies that the respiration variables were not strongly related to the more dramatic group differences observed in other measures. Perhaps a more sensitive measure of respiration would have resulted in more significant group differences.

Discussion

Results of the RT analyses in this study were consistent with the majority of studies that have examined RT performance in retardates and normals. Retardates had significantly slower RT scores, were more variable in their trial-to-trial performance, and were more variable as a group than were normal subjects.

When intraindividual RT variability scores were subjected to within-group analyses, retarded subjects with the slowest mean RT scores had dramatically greater variability than any other subgroup. Berkson and Baumeister (1967) point out that mean RT score for any given subject is a function of both an upper limit of speed and intraindividual variability of scores in a series of trials. They hypothesize that in extremely slow subjects this relationship does not hold as very slow subjects are probably not approaching their upper limit of speed. The question of *why* these subjects do not approach their upper limit and/or are so extremely deviant deserves further investigation.

One of Berkson and Baumeister's suggestions for such future studies is to examine patterns of RT responding within retarded groups. A more detailed version of this idea is presented by Berkson (1973) and will serve as the model for the discussion to follow.

It certainly seems possible that the different patterns of responding exhibited by retarded subjects in fast, middle, and slow groups are related to differences in specific defects in each of the subgroups. For example, fast retardates, as identified in this study, were well within the range of normal RT scores and exhibited HR changes similar to normals in all but the admittedly difficult 13-second PI condition. It seems reasonable to conclude that retarded subjects falling in the fast range of RT scores are not defective in RT performance. Middle retardates were clearly slower than normals in RT and showed HR patterns that were more variable than the faster groups. Perhaps these subjects simply have a lower limit of speed and more than average difficulty in maintaining consistent performance. Experiments with incentives or use of pacing cues might be helpful in clarifying the specific deficits observed at this range of RT speed. Slow retardates, on the other hand, are quantitatively and qualitatively different performers when compared to any of the other subgroups. Their RT performance is slower and more variable than any of the other subgroups and their HR responses are extremely deviant in 4- and 7-second PI conditions. With this group, it is possible that remedial training would be of a different nature than that taken with subjects who fall within the middle ranges.

A discussion of these observed trends, although speculative in nature, suggests that future research on specific deficits in retarded individuals can be productive if individual differences within the retarded group are taken into account. Retardates are not a homogeneous group, even with IQ taken into account. However, if one looks for specific patterns within the diagnostic category of retardation, it seems reasonable that greater understanding of specific defects as well as treatment for these defects can be accomplished in a rational fashion. This approach also implies that there is merit in studying retardates who are at different levels of performance on the specific task under study, as opposed to studying one experimental group of retardates at specific IQ levels with normal subjects as a control.

Heart Rate and Short Preparatory Sets

In measures of heart rate, retardates and normals did not differ in response to the warning signal in any PI condition. This finding presents a discrepancy with a number of other studies that reported lower magnitude autonomic responding in retarded subjects to stimuli of mild or moderate intensity (see Karrer, 1966). It is not likely that the signal value of the warning light used in this study was subjectively intense to either group of subjects. Rather, it appears that the retardate's poor RT performance is not related to reception of the warning signal (see Chaps. 4 and 5 on orienting to signal stimuli).

More clearly, the retardate's poor RT performance is reflected in the temporal relationship between the HR deceleration and the reaction signal. This relationship is obscured in the between-group analyses and graphs in that retarded subjects simply appear to be exhibiting attenuated HR responses during the second in which the reaction signal occurred. When each group is divided into fast, middle, and slow responders, though, it becomes apparent that magnitude of deceleration is compounded with the latency of this response in 4- and 7-second PI conditions. For example, subjects with faster RT scores showed HR deceleration that reached a nadir precisely and reliably during the second in which the reaction signal occurred. Slower RT subjects, on the other hand, exhibited HR decelerations that were considerably more variable in their temporal relations with the reaction signal. In some cases this response preceded the reaction signal by two or more seconds or did not occur until after the reaction signal. This observation suggests that perhaps absolute magnitude of HR deceleration is less important than its latency with respect to the reaction signal when dealing with defective populations.

Ignoring the question of whether HR decelerations directly facilitate RT performance (see Elliott, 1972, and Hahn, 1973, for a discussion of this currently debated issue), it seems reasonable to view HR deceleration as a reflection of maximum subjective preparedness to respond. Such an interpretation appears possible in view of the nature of the fixed RT situation. A number of investigators (Fitzgerald and Porges, 1970; Johnson and May, 1969; Porges, 1972) have pointed out the similarity between fixed RT and temporal conditioning or time estimation. All of these tasks require subjects to make use of temporal cues and the dependent variable is always a latency measure. Since retardates are known to be poor time estimators (McNutt and Melvin, 1968), it is possible that the greater variability in slow RT subjects' HR decelerations reported in the present study indicate that these subjects are simply misjudging the length of the PI. Such inaccurate perceptions of the temporal cues could clearly interfere with the ability to make a fast motor response. Assuming that this is the case, a promising remedial technique might be to train slower RT subjects to pace themselves throughout the PI. Such techniques have recently been reported by Shapiro (1973).

Heart Rate and Long Preparatory Sets.

Most of the discussion up to this point applied to performance in the shorter 4- and 7-second PI conditions. During the 13-second PI different patterns were apparent for the retarded group. First, there were no significant HR differences between fast, middle, and slow retarded RT groups indicating no relation between RT scores and HR changes during this PI. These retarded adults also displayed a HR deceleration during the second *after* the reaction signal, which might be interpreted as a response to the stimulus offset. This is a very reliable response as eight of twelve retarded subjects displayed such responding whereas none of the normal subjects did. Stern (1968) found clear developmental trends for such a response using the galvanic skin response. He found rapid habituation of GSR responses to offset of a 6-second tone in twelve-year-old children but no habituation in six-year-old children. Presumably, the younger children's inability to sustain attention throughout the 6-second stimulus is responsible for their continued response to the tone offset. It is possible that the retarded adult subjects in the present study, like young children in Stern's task, were not attending to the entire PI, hence the delayed HR deceleration. Such inattentive behavior throughout the PI would also explain the absence of a relationship between HR deceleration during the second in which the reaction signal occurred and RT speed. Thus, if retardates were not paying attention, they could not exhibit preparatory responses such as anticipatory HR deceleration during the reaction signal.

Clearly, attending or maintaining an appropriate preparatory set during extended PIs is a more difficult task than maintaining attention during shorter intervals. And, as Elliott (1970), Stern (1968), and Sroufe's (1971) work suggests, the ability to maintain attention for extended periods is a function of development. Thus, it is not surprising that mentally retarded individuals, defined on the basis of developmental defects, should respond like young children in this situation. One method for improving RT performance of young children was demonstrated by Elliott (1970). He found incentives to be successful in improving RT scores, particularly in long fixed PIs (i.e. 8 and 16 seconds). Such an approach might prove useful in attempts to improve RT performance in retardates as well.

In any case, future studies of sustained attention performance in both young children and retarded individuals appear to be of importance in understanding the basic mechanisms involved in sustained attention and how this situation differs from tasks that require short-term attention. Answers to this theoretical question have wide-reaching implications as many real-life situations demand sustained attention. Learning, in or out of the classroom, most jobs, as well as many recreational activities all require some degree of sustained attention for good performance.

CONCLUDING REMARKS

The study reported here attests to the potential value of using the simple RT task and autonomic responses for greater understanding of poor RT performance and attention problems typically displayed by retarded individuals. Hopefully, future studies where motivational variables and external pacing are employed will provide information which can then be applied to educational settings and other realistic situations where improved attention would be of direct benefit to retarded and other individuals handicapped by attention problems.

REFERENCES

Baumeister, A. A., and Kellas, G.: Reaction time and mental retardation. In Ellis, N. R. (Ed.): *International Review of Research in Mental Retardation*, Vol. 3. New York, Academic Press, 1968.

Bensberg, G. J., and Cantor, G. N.: Reaction time in mental defectives with organic and familial etiology. *Am J Ment Defic, 62*:534-537, 1957.

Berkson, G.: An analysis of reaction time in normal and mentally deficient young men. II. Variation of complexity in reaction time tasks. *J Ment Defic Res, 4*:59-67, 1960.

Berkson, G.: When exceptions obscure the rule. *Ment Retard, 4*:24-27, 1966.

Berkson, G.: Behavior. In Wortis, J. (Ed.): *Mental Retardation*, Vol. 5. New York, Grune and Stratton, 1973.

Berkson, G., and Baumeister, A.: Reaction time variability of mental defectives and normals. *Am J Ment Defic, 72*:262-266, 1967.

Chase, W. G., Graham, F. K., and Graham, D. T.: Components of HR response in anticipation of reaction time and exercise tasks. *J Exper Psychol, 76*:642-648, 1968.

Cohen, N. J., and Douglas, V. I.: Characteristics of the orienting response in hyperactive and normal children. *Psychophysiology, 9*:238-245, 1972.

Coquery, J. M., and Lacey, J. I: The effect of foreperiod duration on the components of the cardiac response during the foreperiod of a reaction-time experiment. Paper delivered at the Annual Meeting of the Society for Psychophysiological Research, 1966.

Czudner, G., and Marshall, M.: Simple reaction time in schizophrenic, retarded, and normal children under regular and irregular preparatory interval conditions. *J Can Psychol, 21*:369-380, 1967.

Denny, M. R.: Research in learning and performance. In Stevens, H. A. and Heber, R. (Eds.): *Mental Retardation: A Review of Research*. Chicago, University of Chicago Press, 1964.

Elliott, R.: Simple reaction time: Effects associated with age, preparatory interval, incentive-shift, and mode of presentation. *J Exp Child Psychol, 9*:86-107, 1970.

Elliott, R.: The significance of heart rate for behavior: A critique of Lacey's hypothesis. *J of Pers Soc Psychol, 22*:398-409, 1972.

Ellis, N. R., and Sloan, W.: Relationship between intelligence and simple reaction time in mental defectives. *Perceptual and Motor Skills, 7*:65-67, 1957.

Fitzgerald, H. F., and Porges, S. W.: Cardiovascular effects of paced respiration and selective attention. *Psychon Sci, 19*:65-66, 1970.

Grim, P. F.: A sustained attention comparison of children and adults using reaction time set and the GSR. *J Exp Child Psychol, 5*:26-38, 1967.

Hahn, W. M.: Attention and heart rate: A critical appraisal of the hypothesis of Lacey and Lacey. *Psychol Bull, 79*:59-70, 1973.

Heal, L. W., and Johnson, J. T., Jr.: Inhibition deficits in retardate learning and attention. In Ellis, N. R. (Ed.): *International Review of Research in Mental Retardation*, Volume 4, 1970.

Jennings, J. R., Averill, J. R., Opton, E. M., and Lazarus, R. S.: Some parameters of heart rate change: Perceptual versus motor task requirements, noxiousness, and uncertainty. *Psychophysiology, 7*:194-212, 1971.

Johnson, H. J., and May, J. R.: Phasic heart rate changes in reaction time and time estimation. *Psychophysiology, 6*:351-357, 1969.

Karrer, R.: Autonomic nervous system functions and behavior: A review of experimental studies with mental defectives. In Ellis, N. R. (Ed.): *In-*

ternational Review of Research in Mental Retardation, Vol. 2. New York, Academic Press, 1966.

Krupski, A.: Heart rate changes during a fixed reaction time task in normal and retarded adult males. *Psychophysiology,* in press, 1975,

Lacey, B. C., and Lacey, J. I.: Change in cardiac response and reaction time as a function of motivation. Paper delivered at the Annual Meeting of the Society for Psychophysiological Research, 1966.

Lacey, J. I.: Somatic response patterning and stress: Some revisions of activation theory. In Appley, M. H. and Trumbull, R. (Eds.): *Psychological Stress: Issues in Research.* New York, Appleton-Century-Crofts, 1967.

Liebert, A. M., and Baumeister, A. A.: Behavioral variability among retardates, children, and college students. *J Psychol, 83:*57-65, 1973.

McNutt, T. H., and Melvin, K. B.: Time estimation in normal and retarded subjects. *Am J Ment Defic, 72:*584-589,1968.

Obrist, P. A., Webb, R. A., and Sutterer, J. R.: Heart rate and somatic changes during aversive conditioning and a simple reaction time task. *Psychophysiology, 5:*696-723, 1969.

Obrist, P. A., Webb, R. A., Sutterer, J. R., and Howard, J. L.: The cardiac-somatic relationship: Some reformulations. *Psychophysiology, 6:*569-587, 1970.

Pascal, G. R.: The effect of a disturbing noise on the reaction time of mental defectives. *Am J Ment Defic, 57:*691-699, 1953.

Porges, S. W.: Heart rate variability and deceleration as indexes of reaction time. *J of Exp Psychol, 92:*103-110, 1972.

Shapiro, A. H.: Verbalization during the preparatory interval of a reaction-time task and development of motor control. *Child Dev, 44:*137-142, 1973.

Siegel, S.: *Nonparametric Statistics for the Behavioral Sciences.* New York, McGraw-Hill, 1956.

Sroufe, L. A.: Age changes in cardiac deceleration within a fixed foreperiod reaction-time task: An index of attention. *Devl Psychol, 5:*338-343, 1971.

Sroufe, L. A., Sonies, B. C., West, W. D., and Wright, F. S.: Anticipatory heart rate deceleration and reaction time in children with and without referral for learning disability. *Child Dev, 44:*267-273, 1973.

Stern, J.: Toward a developmental psychophysiology: My look into the crystal ball. *Psychophysiology, 4:*403-420, 1968.

Tizard, J., and Venables, P. H.: Reaction time responses by schizophrenics, mental defectives, and normal adults. *Am J Psych, 112:*803-807, 1956.

Wallace, R. M., and Fehr, F. S.: Heart rate, skin resistance, and reaction time of mongoloid and normal children under baseline and distraction conditions. *Psychophysiology, 6:*722-731, 1970.

Woodworth, S. S., and Schlosberg, H.: *Experimental Psychology.* New York, Henry Holt, 1954.

CHAPTER 4

THE ORIENTING REFLEX AND MENTAL RETARDATION

JOHN T. JOHNSON*

T HE INTEREST OF THIS CHAPTER is focused on the process by which individuals developmentally adapt themselves to the world. In particular, the focus is the concept of attention and the role that it plays in this process. Attention is a concept that smacks of mentalism because historically the term has been used freely with few efforts to objectify and quantify it. It is the opportunity to objectify and quantify attention that led to the use of physiological responses in this research. The utilization of physiological techniques to study psychological phenomena is not without conceptual hazards. We should be very careful to avoid

* The author wishes to acknowledge the contributions of his teacher and colleague, Laird Heal and his students and colleagues, Bob Freeman, Luke Elliott and Morris Powazek to the research discussed in and the writing of this chapter.

119

implicit or explicit value judgments concerning the importance of physiological versus psychological data for understanding attention. It is apparent that there is much room for both physiological and behavioral data relevant to attention. We must be careful to evaluate data in the context of the purpose for which they are obtained and avoid the entanglement of the reductionistic trap (Cantor and Cromwell, 1957; Jessor, 1958).

RATIONALE FOR A THEORIZED RELATIONSHIP BETWEEN MR AND THE OR

The orienting reflex (OR) has been a favorite topic of investigation in Russia in recent years (Cole and Maltzman, 1969). As defined by Sokolov (1963a, 1963b), who has been responsible for much of the research and theory, the OR is the organism's first reaction to any change in the stimulus situation. In effect, it is the organism's normal reaction to a novel stimulus.

The reaction appears to be a preparatory one, a focusing of attention, a getting ready to respond. It apparently tunes the organism to insure optimal reception of stimuli. The ultimate aim of the OR is an increase in receptor sensitivity which allows the organism a more advantageous state from which to receive and evaluate additional stimuli.

Lynn (1966) lists the several components of the OR which have been differentiated. The components include the following: increase in receptor sensitivity; bodily orientation toward the stimulus; arrest of ongoing activity; increase in ongoing electromyographic activity; electroencephalogram (EEG) activation; a divergent vasomotor response, cerebral vasodilation accompanied by peripheral vasoconstriction; decrease in skin resistance as measured by the galvanic skin response (GSR); decrease in respiration rate; and a decrease in heart rate (HR).

The implementation of the OR is theorized by Sokolov to occur in the following manner. With repetition a multidimensional neuronal model of a stimulus is established in the cortex. The dimensions include quality, intensity, frequency and duration as well as more abstract and less well-defined aspects of the stimulus. Once the model is established, all succeeding stimuli are compared to it. If the stimulus is consonant with the model, the cortex does not emit the impulses which evoke an OR. If the stimulus is discrepant from the model, an OR occurs. The magnitude of the OR is directly proportional to the degree of stimulus discrepancy from the model.

Habituation occurs with repetition as the model develops to match all dimensions of the stimulus. The lessening discrepancy of the model from the stimulus is reflected in the decreased magnitude of the OR until the stimulus and model are consonant and no OR occurs. As in the case of extinction of a conditional response, the inhibited OR can be disinhibited by the presentation of a novel stimulus. The findings that decorticated animals do not show habituation of the OR and animals higher in the phylogenetic order habituate faster are the main support for the role of the cortex in the stimulus model (Sokolov, 1963; Razran, 1961).

The Russians have also been interested in the relationship between the OR and mental retardation. Luria has been responsible for much of the research in this area and has drawn several conclusions based on his work (Luria, 1963). Luria found that stimuli which elicited an OR in normal children did so only infrequently in retarded children of the same chronological age. If an OR was evoked, it extinguished much more rapidly than in the normal child. In normal children verbal instructions could be used to make a relevant stimulus a signal stimulus that elicited a strong OR which was resistant to extinction. Such an OR held the child's attention, insuring against distraction by irrelevant stimuli. With the retarded child, however, this method of OR insurance did not occur, and he remained distractable. These conclusions, however, were questioned by Heal and Johnson (1970). In their review of the American literature concerning the relationship between the OR and mental retardation, they found that research has not consistently supported the hypothesis of a weak OR in retarded individuals.

In collaboration with students and colleagues, a series of investigations was designed to clarify the relationship between mental retardation and the OR. It is the data from this series of studies that is reviewed here. The studies are reviewed in a logical order that does not in all cases correspond to their chronological order.

INTELLIGENCE, INHIBITION AND THE OR

It has been demonstrated in the literature that extinction of the classically conditioned eyelid response is a function of the recognition of the change in stimulus conditions from acquisition to extinction occasioned by deletion of the unconditioned stimulus (Spence and Platt, 1967). In addition, it has been shown that retarded subjects extinguish a classically conditioned eyelid response more slowly than normal subjects (Ross, Koski and Yaeger, 1964). On these grounds it may be that the retarded subject's weak OR might be correlated with a deficit in recognition of the stimulus change from acquisition to extinction and his subsequent slow extinction of the conditioned response (Johnson, 1968).

An initial study was designed to investigate the relation of OR to intelligence. The subjects for this study consisted of sixty-four children of fifth-grade age (mean CA = 11.3 years) who were enrolled in regular and special classes in the public schools. The IQ's of the sample ranged from 71 to 117.

The subjects received fifty trials of classical eyelid conditioning, half on a partial and half on a continuous schedule of reinforcement, followed by thirty extinction trials. The blood volume of the subject's finger and his forehead was monitored continuously by photoplethysmography. The data were taken from the last ten acquisition trials and the thirty extinction trials. For each trial the average amplitude of the first fifteen poststimulus heights, the distance from the valley to the peak of the pulse, was computed as a percentage of the average of the last three prestimulus pulse heights.

The final ten trials of acquisition were characterized by the divergent blood volume response that is characteristic of an OR; vasoconstriction in the finger and vasodilation in the forehead. The change from acquisition to extinction was reflected in a pronounced change in the forehead response. While the nature of this change was vasoconstriction and not characteristic of an

OR, it did indicate that forehead blood volume was responsive to the stimulus change occasioned by extinction. However, no correlation was found between this change and the IQ of the subject. It was this study, even though it was open to several criticisms and interpretations, that raised the initial question regarding the generality of the Russian finding of a weak OR in retarded subjects and set the tone for subsequent research.

OR HABITUATION

The Russian literature suggests that the weak OR in retarded subjects is evidenced by faster habituation of the OR. However, according to another interpretation of Sokolov's model (Lewis, Goldberg, and Campbell, 1970) the opposite prediction of slower habituation in retarded subjects would appear feasible. According to their view, with each stimulus presentation information about the stimulus is processed and stored in the model until the model is consonant with the stimulus. It seems likely that retarded subjects would be less efficient in processing stimulus information, that is add less information to the model per stimulus presentation, than normal subjects. The result should be slower habituation. Following the same reasoning one might suspect that the retarded individual's model following a set number of presentations would be less complete than that of a normal subject. A second study (Johnson and Heal, unpublished manuscript) provided a test of these hypotheses.

Sixteen institutionalized retarded (mean CA = 14-0 years; mean IQ = 43) and six normal (mean CA = 16-4 years) subjects who attended a private summer school were presented sequences of auditory and visual stimuli. Each stimulus sequence contained sixteen trials in the following order: seven presentations of the repetitious stimulus followed by a single presentation of the discrepant stimulus; seven more trials of the repetitious stimulus followed by a single presentation of the discrepant stimulus. Each subject was given both an auditory sequence and a visual sequence. The sequence order, as well as the repetitious and discrepant stimulus, was counterbalanced. The visual stimuli consisted of two projected forms, a white cross on a green background and a white square on an amber background. The auditory stimuli consisted of two tones of differing frequency, one 650 Hz and the other 1,300 Hz.

The dependent variable was the heart rate response analyzed in the following manner: a prestimulus measure in beats-per-minute was calculated from the mean of the last three prestimulus interbeat latencies; the poststimulus analysis period covered the first fifteen poststimulus inter-beat latencies. These latencies were grouped into five blocks of three and the mean of each block was converted into beats-per-minute.

The analyses revealed that a momentary deceleration occurred on the first poststimulus block in response to all four stimuli. This deceleration was significant, but small, and did not habituate over trials as an OR should. In addition there was no difference between the normal and retarded groups on this response. Other characteristics of the response were shown by the main analysis to interact with stimuli; therefore individual analyses were carried out for each stimulus. Because of the massive amount of data involved, trials 1, 4 and 7 were selected for analysis. Only the response to the 650 Hz tone appeared to have the properties of an OR, a deceleratory response that began on the first poststimulus block of beats, increased in magnitude over the second block and began recovery on the third block. This response habituated over trials and also was significantly different in normal and retarded subjects.

The nature of this difference may be seen in Figure 4-1 which represents the results from an analysis of covariance with the covariate being prestimulus heart rate. On trial 1 the analysis showed significantly greater deceleration in the retarded than in the normal group for poststimulus blocks 2 (F $1/23$ = 32.84; $p < .001$) and 3 (F $1/23$ = 7.41; $p < .001$). By trial 4, the response of the retarded group had habituated, showed slight acceleration on poststimulus blocks 2 (F $1/23$ = 6.26; $p < .05$) and 3 (F $1/360$ = 9.71; $p < .01$) and was not significantly different from the normal group. As can be seen there was little change in the responses of the two groups from trials four to

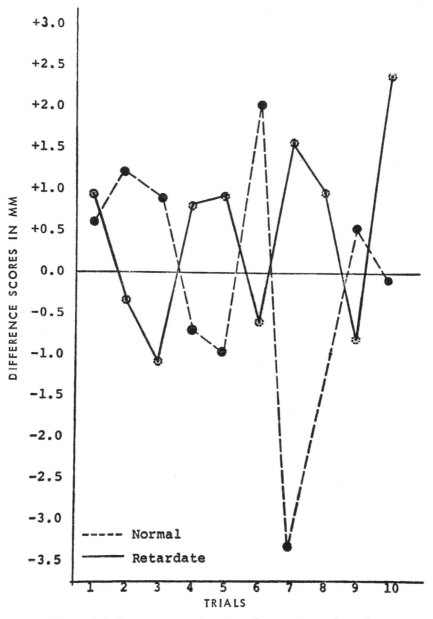

Figure 4-1. Heart rate as a function of repetition and novelty.

trial seven. The previously reported nonhabituating deceleration on poststimulus block one is evident in this figure.

A final analysis on the responses to the 650 Hz tone was conducted on trials seven and eight assess differential response to novelty. While the analysis revealed a main effect due to IQ over all poststimulus blocks except the first, there was no differential response between the groups to the discrepant stimulus.

These results seem to indicate that differences in orienting between normal and retarded subjects are not as general as had been previously supposed. The findings of differences between the normal and retarded groups to only one of four stimuli offers little support for the hypothesized OR weakness in retarded individuals.

DISTRACTABILITY AND THE OR

Elliott and Johnson (1971) investigated the relationship between the OR and distractability in retarded individuals. According to Luria (1963), when both normal and retarded subjects were involved in a task requiring concentration, extraneous events such as someone at the door, or a bird at the window elicited the attention of the retarded but not the normal subjects. The implication was that strong orienting to one stimulus event effectively prevented other stimulus events from impinging on the attention of the organism. Therefore, if retarded individuals have weak ORs, they should also have a defective filtering mechanism as is evidenced by distractibility.

The subjects for this study consisted of fifteen retarded males (mean CA = 11-1; mean IQ = 69.0) and fifteen normal males (mean CA = 11-8; mean IQ = 100). All subjects were enrolled in public schools. The OR was measured by digital blood volume detected by the method described in the first study. The data analyzed consisted of the difference between the means of the three lowest consecutive pulse heights within ten seconds preceding and following the stimulus presentation.

The study consisted of two phases. During the first phase, a small red light was presented in the periphery of the subject's vision while he was circling all occurrences of a specific letter on a sheet of letters. During the second phase of the study, the sub-

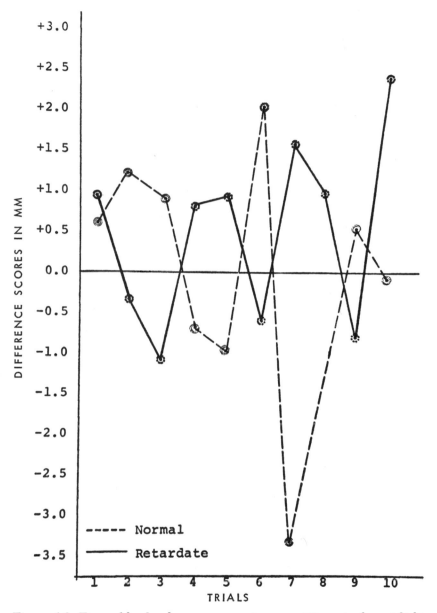

Figure 4-2. Finger blood volume response to a repetitious, irrelevant light.

ject was simply instructed to sit still and listen to a tone (600 Hz presented at 40 db). The phases were counterbalanced and the stimulus in each phase was presented ten times.

Results of the study may be seen in Figure 4-2. No differences between the groups were found in the initial magnitude or rate of habituation of the blood volume response to the tone stimulus. An interesting result was obtained in response to the light stimulus. While there appeared to be nothing systematic associated with the responses of either group, the responses of the two groups over trials were mirror images of each other.

STIMULUS INTENSITY

At this point in time it was becoming apparent that the results being produced in our lab were no more consistent than those already in the literature. The remainder of the studies in the series were designed to investigate some of the stimulus parameters that we felt might be responsible for the inconsistency.

The role of stimulus intensity was investigated as a source of variance by Elliott and Johnson (unpublished manuscript). The subjects consisted of seven trainable mentally retarded (mean CA = 8-6; mean IQ = 39.4), seven educable mentally retarded (mean CA = 7-9; mean IQ = 64.8), seven learning disability (mean CA = 8-3; mean IQ = 97.0) and seven normal (mean CA = 6-1) subjects who were enrolled in public schools.

The subjects were given ten presentations of a 1,000 Hz tone at each of the following intensities: 50, 60, 70, 80 and 90 db. The tones were presented in a random order.

The heart rate response to each of the stimuli was analyzed by comparing the mean of the last six prestimulus interbeat latencies and the first six poststimulus interbeat latencies. The responses as plotted by difference scores (prestimulus measure minus poststimulus measure) may be seen in Figure 4-3. An analysis of variance showed that there was differential responsiveness by the groups to two of the five tones, 70 db and 90 db. To the 70 db tone only the responses of the normal and educable mentally retarded groups were different ($F_{1/96} = 7.83$;

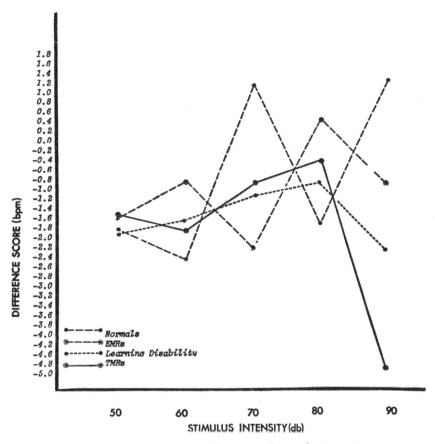

Figure 4-3. Heart rate as a function of stimulus intensity.

p < .01). To the 90 db tone the response of the normal group was significantly different from the responses of both the learning disability (F 1/96 = 7.20; p < .01) and the trainable mentally retarded (F 1/96 = 17.25; p < .01), groups. In addition the educable mentally retarded and trainable mentally retarded groups were significantly different (F 1/96 = 6.61; p < .05). These results indicate that if one is comparing the OR of normal and retarded subjects, then which group demonstrates the stronger OR depends on the intensity of the chosen stimulus and the IQ of the retarded subjects.

SIGNAL VALUE

Powazek and Johnson (1973) investigated the effects of instilling a stimulus with signal value and the relationship between signal value, intelligence and the OR. The subjects consisted of thirty-two retarded (mean CA = 9 years, 10 months; mean IQ = 66.5) and thirty-two normal (mean CA = 10 years, 7 months; mean IQ = 105.3) students who were enrolled in public schools. The retarded subjects had no history of an abnormal EEG or convulsions. The dependent variable was heart rate as measured by the mean of the last six prestimulus interbeat latencies and the mean of the first six poststimulus interbeat latencies. The measures were reported in beats-per-minute.

Half of the subjects in each group were instructed to simply pay attention to the presentation of a tone (1,000 Hz; 73 db). The other half of each group were instructed to press a bar upon presentation of the tone. A barpress was rewarded with an M&M®, a procedure designed to give the tone signal value. Both the signal and nonsignal groups received thirty-two presentations of the tone. For the nonsignal group, the stimulus conditions were identical for all the thirty-two trials. For the signal group the M&M reward was available for the first sixteen trials and withheld for the second sixteen.

The results for the acquisition and extinction trials were very similar and are combined in Figure 4-4. To aid in their visual presentation the sixteen trials are presented in four blocks of four trials each.

Over the sixteen acquisition trials no difference was found in the heart rate response of the normal and retarded subjects to the novel tone. A significant difference was found between the two groups' response to the signal tone (F 1/120 = 17.47; p < .01). The response of the retarded group to the signal tone was an acceleration in heart rate that was different from the retarded-novel, normal-novel, and normal-signal groups which did not differ. The analysis of the extinction trials was very similar and did not add any additional information. These results suggest then that a signal, but not a nonsignal, tone elicits a differ-

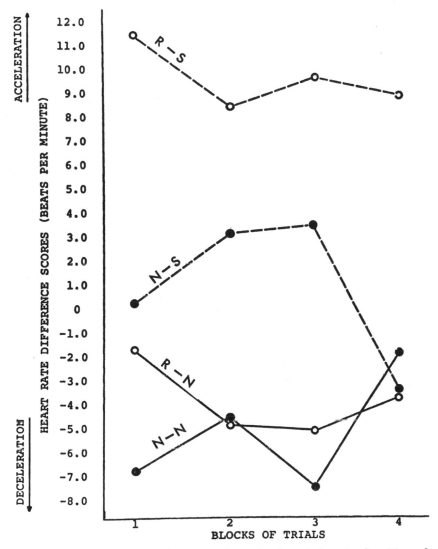

Figure 4-4. Heart rate as a function of signal value of the stimulus. Normal-novel stimulus = N-N; Normal-signal stimulus = N-S; Retarded-novel stimulus = R-N; Retarded-signal stimulus = R-S.

ential HR response in normal and retarded subjects. The next study, however, adds a qualification to this statement.

SIGNAL VALUE AND BRAIN DAMAGED RETARDATES

The Russian definition of mental retardation confounds mental retardation and brain damage in their research. It is not clear, therefore, whether the reported OR weakness is a function of either or both. Freeman (1972) sought to examine the separate influences of brain damage and mental retardation on the OR.

The subjects for the study consisted of fifteen individuals with normal intelligence and no diagnosed brain damage (mean CA = 10-10; mean IQ = 98); fifteen individuals with normal intelligence and diagnosed brain damage (mean CA = 10-5; mean IQ = 99); fifteen mildly retarded individuals with no diagnosed brain damage (mean CA = 10-6; mean IQ = 62); and fifteen mildly retarded individuals with diagnosed brain damage (mean CA = 10-7; mean IQ =65). The operational definition of brain damage for this study was an abnormal EEG or a history of convulsions.

In an effort to duplicate the design of Luria and Vinogradova (1959) the stimuli consisted of four words (cap, hat, map, tree) which were presented auditorily. The dependent variable was heart rate as measured by the difference between the mean of the last six prestimulus interbeat latencies and the mean of the first six poststimulus interbeat latencies.

Following a series of habituation trials during which each word was presented ten times, the stimulus word "cap" was invested with signal value by instructing the subject to press a button each time he heard it, a procedure demonstrated to instill signal value (Freeman, Johnson, and Long, 1972). The stimulus words were presented ten times each in a random order. The analysis indicated that no significant variance was associated with brain damage or the interaction of brain damage with IQ. The remainder of the discussion of the analysis refers to the normal and retarded groups collapsed over the variable of brain damage. As may be seen in Figure 4-5, the results indicated that the signal word, "cap," elicited a similar, strong decelerative response in both the normal and retarded groups. The responses of the

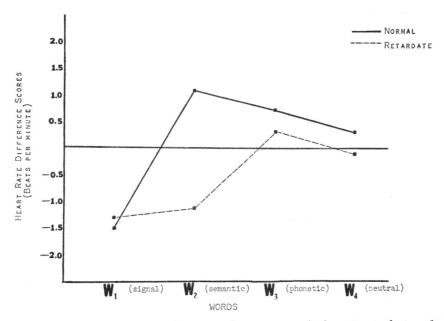

Figure 4-5. Heart rate as a function of semantic and phonetic similarity of words.

two groups to the phonetically similar and the neutral words were slight acceleration and were not significantly different from each other. The only difference between the normal and retarded groups was in their response to the semantically similar word, "hat." The response of the retarded group was significant deceleration (F $1/300$ = 5.19; p < .01) which was not different in magnitude from their response to the signal word. In contrast, the normal group responded to the semantically similar word with significant acceleration (F $1/300$ = 7.21; p < .01). These results suggest two conclusions: (1) the presence or absence of brain damage seems unlikely to be responsible for inconsistencies in the literature; (2) the differences being detected by measures of the OR may be cognitive rather than attentional.

SUMMARY AND DISCUSSION

The major conclusion that may be drawn from this series of studies is simply this: stimuli make a difference. On the basis of these results it appears impossible to make the general statement implied by the Russians that retarded subjects have a weak OR. As concluded in Heal and Johnson's (1970) review and demonstrated again here, depending on the stimulus presented, retarded subjects can be shown to have ORs that are weaker, stronger, or no different from those of normal subjects.

These studies also suggest two other variables which may account for some of the inconsistencies: the measure of the OR and the characteristics of the subjects.

As Stern and Plapp (1969) suggested, the concept of a unitary OR may have little utility since there may be as many ORs as there are dependent measures of the construct. In our own research, we shifted midway in our series of studies from the use of the blood volume measure to heart rate. We intend to stick with heart rate for two major reasons. According to the Russian literature an OR is defined by a divergent response between the head and finger blood volume measures. The head measure, however, is extremely difficult to obtain, especially with the movement artifacts encountered in young children and retarded individuals. Finger blood volume alone gives a limited amount of information since the response is largely unidirectional and an OR cannot be distinguished from a defensive reflex (Sokolov, 1963). Secondly, there is a growing body of literature on heart rate which serves as normative data for obtained results.

The importance of subject characteristics for the retarded sample was demonstrated by what appeared to be systematic differences in the ORs of mildly and moderately retarded individuals. It was not a coincidence that only one of the studies contained retarded subjects who were institutionalized. Even though there were no differences in the OR in the brain damaged and non-brain damaged groups, the strong possibility exists that institutionalized and noninstitutionalized subjects comprise different populations. Because of our interest in generalizing back to normal developmental processes, we have tried to avoid introducing the additional variable of institutionalization to the differences between our "retarded" and "normal" groups. It should also be mentioned that more care should be taken in defining the characteristics of the "normal" groups.

THE OR AND MR: A REEVALUATION

Even though a general statement about a weak OR in retarded individuals appears untenable there does seem to be some basis for the expectation of systematic differences in the OR of normal and retarded subjects. These expectations are based on an integration of the theories of Piaget (Ginsburg and Opper, 1969), and Eleanor Gibson (1969) and the work of Lewis, Goldberg, Campbell (1968) and Jeffrey (1968).

The orienting reflex is better conceptualized as a response correlated with input of information rather than a response correlated to input of novelty. As suggested by Lewis (1970) this means that a stimulus is novel because it provides information which is "relevant" to the organism rather than because it has some unique physical properties. Therefore, a given stimulus might not evoke an OR for two reasons: (1) it contains minimal information; (2) the information that it contains is not relevant to the organism.

Let us consider first a possible relationship between information processing and the orienting reflex. Orienting to a stimulus occurs (to the extent that the stimulus contains unprocessed or unassimilated information which is processed and stored) until there is complete consonance between the information contained in the subject's schema, or model of the stimulus and the information contained in the stimulus itself. The magnitude of the orienting reflex, then, is a function of the discrepancy between the information contained in a schema of a stimulus and the information contained in the stimulus itself. Likewise, the increasing amount of assimilated information in a repetitive stimulus is correlated with habituation of the OR. If we accept these assumptions it allows us to investigate two interrelated topics: (1) information processing; (2) analysis of schema.

Certainly there exists a continuum of efficiency in information processing. There are efficient processors and inefficient processors. It seems reasonable to assume that among the most inefficient information processors are young children and retarded individuals. Characteristic of these inefficient information processors would be inabilities to select that information which is the defining characteristic of a stimulus, to filter out information which is irrelevant, and to maximize the amount of information processed per stimulus presentation.

The most data available is relevant to this latter prediction concerning the rate of information processing. In the model discussed here, information processing is directly correlated with habituation of the OR. It would be expected that the OR of young children would habituate more slowly than that of older ones and that the OR of retardates would habituate more slowly than that of normals. There is ample data to confirm the first prediction, but data relevant to the second prediction is inconsistent.

Lewis, Goldberg and Campbell (1968), convincingly demonstrated in a series of studies that habituation to a redundant visual stimulus is directly correlated with development during the first three years of life; the younger the child, the slower the habituation, i.e. the more inefficient the information processing.

Why then have we not been able to demonstrate reliably that the retarded habituate more slowly than normals? The data obtained in the studies reviewed here indicate the difficulty lies in the nature of the stimulus being used. In going back through the American literature on the orienting reflex and mental retardation, every study without exception, used either a simple tone, light flash, buzzer, white noise or temperature for the stimulus. It is difficult to conceive that these stimuli would contain much information for an individual with a mental age over three and that is the minimum MA used in the studies reviewed. According to the theory discussed here, the inconsistent results are not only not surprising but are to be expected. Furthermore, the theory would predict, and the data reviewed here tend to support the prediction, that reliable and consistent differences would be demonstrated in the habituation of normal and retarded subjects by using stimuli with more information value, i.e. words or signal stimuli.

The second area that this view of the OR opens for investigation is the analysis of schema development. There are at least two broad classes of stimuli which are relevant to the organism. The first class is that of the signal stimulus. This is a stimulus which either through instinct (i.e. the rustling of leaves to a rabbit; the sight of a cat to an owl, Luria, 1963) or through acquisition (your name, the cry of her own baby to a mother) reliably elicits an OR that is extremely difficult to habituate.

The two studies which used signal stimuli found differences between normal and retarded subjects. The nature of the difference appeared to be related to whether the subject had to make a discrimination to respond to one of several stimuli or simply to respond to a discrete stimulus. When these results are compared to the others which generally showed no difference between normal and retarded subjects, they suggest that the retarded individual's deficit may be in responding to the relevancy of the stimulus rather than to its physical characteristics; relevancy in this case being determined by the signal value of the stimulus.

The second class of stimuli that are relevant to the organism is that which we have been discussing here, that class of stimuli that contains information. The developing child goes through stages which are characterized by an ability to process certain kinds of information. During these stages the child will be maximally sensitive, that is more likely to orient, to stimuli containing a certain kind of information. The relevancy of information, then is determined by the developmental level of the subject. If left at this point of explanation the concept of relevancy is meaningless because of its circularity. The concept takes on meaning, however, when it becomes apparent that by judicious selection of stimuli we can analyze schema development.

It is this analysis of schema development that leads toward the goal of this research, understanding the relationship between attention, and/or information processing and the individual's adaptation to his environment. If it is possible to construct developmental norms of information processing, then one can investigate what implications being ahead or behind schedule have for concurrent and future adaptive behavior. It is in the direction of the construction of norms that our current research is being directed.

REFERENCES

Elliott, L. S., and Johnson, J. T.: The orienting reflex in intellectually average and retarded children to a relevant and an irrelevant stimulus. *Am J Ment Defic, 76*:332-336, 1971.

Cantor, G. N., and Cromwell, R. L.: The principle of reductionism and mental deficiency. *Am J Ment Defic, 61*:461-466, 1957.

Cole, M., and Maltzman, I.: *A handbook of contemporary Soviet psychology.* New York, Basic Bks, 1969.

Freeman, B. L.: The relationship of brain damage and intelligence to the orienting response. Unpublished doctoral dissertation. Memphis State University, 1972.

Freeman, B. L., Johnson, J. T., and Long, C. L.: Semantic generalization of orienting response. *J Ex Res in Person, 6*:39-43, 1972.

Ginsburg, H., and Opper, S.: *Piaget's Theory of Intellectual Development.* New Jersey, Prentice-Hall, 1969.

Gibson, E. J.: *Principles of Perceptual Learning and Development.* New York, Appleton-Century-Crofts, 1969.

Heal, L. W., and Johnson, J. T.: Inhibition deficits in retardate learning and attention. In Ellis, N. R. (Ed.): *International Review of Mental Retardation.* Vol. 4, New York, Academic, 1970.

Jeffrey, W. E.: The orienting reflex and attention in cognitive development. *Psychol Rev, 75*:232-334, 1968.

Jessor, R.: The problem of reductionism in psychology. *Psychol Rev, 65*: 170-178, 1958.

Johnson, J. T.: Intelligence, inhibition and the orienting reflex. Unpublished dissertation. George Peabody College, 1968.

Lewis, L.: Attention and verbal labeling behavior: a study in the measurement of internal representations. *Research Bulletin.* Princeton, Educational Testing Service, 1970.

Lewis, M., Goldberg, S., and Campbell, R.: A developmental study of information processing within the first three years of life: response decrement to a redundant signal. *Child Dev Mon, 33*:No. 133, 1968.

Luria, A. R.: *The Mentally Retarded Child.* New York, Macmillan, 1963.

Luria, A. R., and Vinogradova, O. S.: An objective investigation of the dynamics of semantic systems. *Br J Psychol, 30*:89-105, 1959.

Lynn, R.: *Attention, Arousal, and the Orientation Reaction.* New York, Pergamon, 1966.

Powazek, M., and Johnson, J. T.: Acquisition and extinction of the orienting response in normals and retardates to novel and signal stimuli. *Am J Ment Defic,* 78:286-291, 1973.

Razran, G.: The observable unconscious and the inferable conscious in current Soviet psychology: interoceptive conditioning, semantic conditioning, and the orienting reflex. *Psychol Rev, 68:*109-140, 1961.

Ross, L. E., Koski, C. H., and Yaegar, J.: Classical eyelid conditioning of the severely retarded: partial reinforcement effects. *Psychon Sci, 1:*253-254, 1964.

Sokolov, E. N.: Higher nervous systems: The orienting reflex. *An Rev Physiol, 25:*545-580, 1963a.

Sokolov, E. N.: *Perception and Conditioned Reflex.* New York, Macmillan, 1963b.

Spence, K. W., and Platt, J. R.: Effects of partial reinforcement on acquisition and extinction of the conditioned eyeblink in a masking situation. *J Exp Psychol, 74:*259-263, 1967.

Stern, J. A., and Plapp, J. M.: Psychophysiology and clinical psychology. In *Current Issues of Clinical and Community Psychology.* New York, Academic, 1969.

CHAPTER 5

ORIENTING RESPONSES OF NORMAL AND RETARDED CHILDREN TO VERBAL STIMULI

J. P. DAS*

SOME FREQUENTLY USED PROCEDURES for studying attention in humans have been dichotic listening, vigilance, and the orienting response (Worden, 1966; Swets and Kristofferson, 1970). Of these, we have used the orienting response (OR) as a procedure to examine the attention of the retardate to verbal stimuli. By focusing on verbal stimuli, we wish to combine two major types of attention: attention to external objects and attention to

* The experiments reported here were done in collaboration with Dr. A. C. Bower. Dr. G. M. Kysela often acted as a consultant. The author gratefully acknowledges their assistance.

internal events such as memory and thought. Probably both types of attention share the same neural mechanism, although how neural processes are transformed to attention and perception is far from clear.

There is little doubt that we attend to central events (Worden, 1966). Ontogenetically, a child first learns to focus his attention on an external object through his sensory apparatus, then subsequently, he can attend to the idea of the object. According to Schachtel (1959), the focal attention to thought may develop in the second year together with the learning of language. Schachtel distinguishes between autocentric perception which is confined to pleasure, pain, heat, cold, and smell, and allocentric perception which enables the child to have a grasp of the real world. Allocentric perception is representational, and depends on attending to conceptual schemata.

Attention is directional. It is described by Neisser (1967) as an active, reconstructive, general cognitive function. One gets the same impression about OR in Sokolov's and Maltzman's description of the process (Sokolov, 1969; Maltzman, Langdon, and Feeney, 1970). The OR is not merely reactive, but may reflect active search and thinking. Most experiments on OR, however, have tended to concentrate on its reactive nature, treating it as an unspecific response to a novel stimulus. In some of the experiments reported in this chapter, one can detect evidence of OR being evoked when the subject is searching to resolve stimulus ambiguity.

The research to be discussed used verbal stimuli in the form of words and nonsense syllables. It was felt that "attention" to stimuli whose semantic characteristics could be manipulated has an obvious importance in an educational context. Thus it is hoped that the research findings may be easily integrated with practice in remedial education.

Evocation of OR, its conditionability and reversal, habituation and disinhibition are examined below in a series of experiments. How far a study of these phenomena has implications for a general theory of attentional deficit as proposed by Zeaman and House (1963) is at best unclear. The latter use attentional deficit as an explanatory construct for the retardate's discrimination learning. As such, learning involves the hypothesized ability to attend to the salient dimension in a conglomeration of stimulus objects. It is not a typical procedure for studying attention in itself. Our objective is to analyze one of the basic indices of attention, OR, and determine if normal-retardate differences can be obtained in the various measures of the OR. We assume that the OR is an integral if not the sole manifestation of attention. For instance, attention is sometimes described to be contingent on an OR: the subject does not pay attention to a novel stimulus because it fails to evoke an OR (Lynn, 1966). Thus, our results are quite specific in that they delineate the characteristics of OR in the retardate.

Luria (1963) refers to deficits in the retardate's OR. Retardates give fewer ORs to stimuli of medium and low intensity. Since their verbal system is weak in maintaining self-instructed behavior, their OR to stimuli in a learning situation cannot be sustained by asking them to attend to the stimuli. According to Luria, overall weak cortical processes characterize the retardate. This would explain why retardates cannot maintain an instructional set and fail to concentrate and attend to irrelevant stimuli.

However, as the retarded child grows up, some of these defects are minimized. The verbal system, for example, increasingly regulates the child's behavior. His deficiencies in attention and learning can be further reduced through the use of appropriate instructions. Luria, following Vygotskii (1962), emphasizes the role of instruction for learning and problem solving. In our research we have used instructions for reducing the effect of pre-experimental learning in which the normal child naturally has an advantage over the retardate. Our subjects were also older than those studied by Luria, generally over the mental age (MA) of six. At this stage the dissociation between speech and motor response has been overcome. Speech begins to regulate simple motor acts by the age of five and one-half years, according to Luria (1961). Thus, gross differences between normal and retardate samples in our experiments were reduced by using children above MA 6 who were deliberately instructed in all tasks to minimize the role of spontaneously acquired experiences.

OR: EVOCATION, HABITUATION AND CONDITIONABILITY

We distinguish here between two kinds of OR: (1) ORs that are evoked by stimuli which have not been assigned a signal value in the experiment and (2) ORs that are evoked by stimuli which have acquired signal value. Sokolov (1965, p. 151) has named these unconditioned and conditioned ORs, respectively. A signal stimulus produces a stable OR which resists extinction, maintaining its strength through the system of corticoreticular connections. On the other hand, a neutral stimulus evokes an OR "by means of conductance of the excitation along the collateral pathways into the reticular system." This unconditioned OR is easily extinguished upon repeated stimulus presentation.

The frequency with which OR is evoked and its magnitude may depend on stimulus characteristics such as the intensity of stimulus (Berkson, Hermelin, and O'Connor, 1961; Wolfensberger and O'Connor, 1965; Fenz and McCabe, 1971). In all of these studies nonverbal stimuli, tones and light flashes, were used. When these are substituted by words and nonsense syllables (CVCs), stimulus intensity becomes less salient. Novelty of the verbal item and/or its meaningfulness may become more salient for the strength of OR and its rate of habituation.

The habituation of unconditioned OR has been the subject of several investigations as reviewed by Karrer (1966). Habituation was found to be faster in the retardate in some but not all studies. The lack of agreement seems to be due to variation in tasks, subject groups and experimental conditions. As mentioned before, in most of those studies ORs to simple stimuli such as tones and light flashes were examined. Only a few looked at responses to complex stimuli.

Complex stimuli, such as words or (CVCs) should habituate more slowly than simple ones. This follows from Sokolov's (1969) theory of a comparatory model facilitating and inhibiting OR evocation. Specifically, in the mentally retarded a number of repetitions of a complex stimulus may be required to form an adequate model from which comparisons can be made between the model and the repetitive stimulus to produce OR decrement. In contrast, simple stimuli such as pure tones require far fewer repetitions for a model to be formed for comparison with the stimulus. This process in the retarded was assumed in the following study where tone, work and CVC were used as stimuli for GSR evocation and habituation. Procedures to produce habituation were different from the usual. Instead of presenting the stimulus repeatedly over a number of trials with appropriate intertrial intervals for observing autonomic changes, a satiation procedure was adopted (Das, 1969).

OR Habituation and Stimulus Class

This study compared the GSRs to three classes of stimuli following massed (40) presentations and discrete (2) presentations. Each stimulus class had one item for 40, and another for two presentations. Thus, two tones (600 cps and 1,000 cps), two words (love and friend) and two CVCs (Yuf and Zuk) were selected. The words had comparable association values, as also the CVCs.

Subjects were twenty retarded children (IQ 40-65) from a special school. Their age range was twelve to fourteen years. For one half of the subjects the 600 cps tone, love and yuf were repeated forty times, whereas the other item in the stimulus pairs was repeated only two times. This was counterbalanced for the rest of the subjects. Repetition interval was 0.5 sec and the duration of a stimulus was approximately one sec. Following the massed or discrete repetitions of a stimulus, five presentations (test trials) of each were made to examine habituation. The intertrial interval was varied between 15 and 20 sec. The same interval operated between the end of repetition and the first of the five test trials.

Several tapes with different random orders of stimulus sequences were made, and each subject was assigned one of the tapes arbitrarily. They were merely asked to listen to whatever came through an overhead speaker. No response was required. The following taped instructions were given: Now I just want you to sit quietly and listen to some words and tones. You will hear the words love, friend, yuf, and zuk. Sometimes they will be said more than once, like—love, love, love, love, love . . . or yuf, yuf, yuf, yuf . . . O.K. Just listen to them.

The indexes of OR were GSR frequency and magnitude which were continuously recorded on a polygraph under standard procedures. Stimuli were auditorily presented by magnetic tape; each stimulus occurrence was recorded on one of the polygraph channels.

An overall comparison of GSRs between the two counterbalanced groups was made and no difference was established. Therefore, the two were combined for all subsequent analyses.

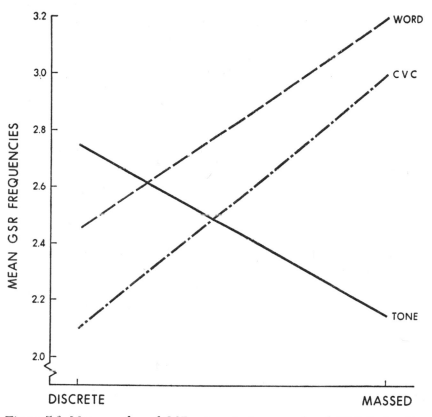

Figure 5-1. Mean number of GSRs given to tone, word and CVC during the five test trials following two (discrete) and 40 (massed) presentations.

GSR frequencies were summed for the five test trials, and examined in a 2 (Massed/Discrete) × 3 (tone, word, CVC) analysis of variance. Only the interaction was significant: F 2/38 = 3.58, P < .05. This is clearly seen in Figure 5-1. Tones in the massed condition evoked a mean GSR frequency of 2.15 compared to 3.20 for words and 3.00 for CVCs (maximum GSR frequency score is five; one GSR response on each of the five test trials). The tones, after two repetitions, evoked greater GSRs than after 40; the reverse was true for word and CVC. We are inclined to suggest that tones, being unambiguous, tend to lose their signal value upon massed repetition. In contrast, the words and CVCs are relatively complex and ambiguous stimuli for the mildly to severely retarded. Hence, repetitions increase their signal value or simply clear up their meaning.

A similar analysis was carried out on GSR magnitude. Magnitude scores were computed by determining the log conductance of the mean of the amplitude changes from prestimulus levels for the five test trials. Prokasy and Ebel (1967) recommend the use of magnitude rather than amplitude scores when a GSR is not always elicited on every trial. The results confirmed the trend for GSR frequency. Tones had the lowest (0.052) conductance compared to words (0.104) and CVCs (0.082). In Figure 5-2 the magnitudes of the five consecutive test trials following 40 or two repetitions have been plotted. The magnitudes were small because of the nonthreatening neutral stimuli used and the fact that the subjects were retarded. This was expected from previous research (Karrer, 1966). Nevertheless, the main effect for trials and the interaction between massed/discrete and the three stimulus classes were significant as revealed by a 2 (massed/discrete) × 3 (stimulus) × 5 (trials) analysis of variance. The trials effect (F 4/76 = 4.40, P < .01) and the interaction between repetitions and stimuli (F 2/38 = 3.28, P < .05) were significant The graphs shows that for word and CVC the magnitudes on the first test trial following massed presentation were higher than the magnitude for tone. This was maintained for the next four trials for word and three trials for CVC. In contrast, magnitude following the condition of discrete presentations gradually declined

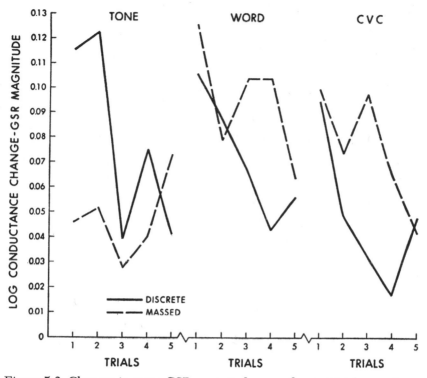

Figure 5-2. Changes in mean GSR magnitudes over five test trials as a function of discrete or massed presentation.

over trials except for the last trial which showed a very slight increase. The interaction was partly due to this as well as the contrast between reaction to tone on the one hand and to word and CVC on the other.

These results suggest that habituation of OR to meaningful stimuli proceeds differently compared to habituation to a simple nonverbal stimulus. A major factor here is whether or not repetitions are necessary for the verbal stimuli to be comprehended. With subjects of average IQ, one suspects that the same results would not be obtained. Words such as friend and love may be instantly comprehensible, and elicit reactions more similar to tone than to CVC. An experiment which considers this possibility is now underway.

A word that is used as an imperative signal for a motor response continues to evoke an OR much longer than a nonsignal word. A warning signal which precedes the imperative signal also resists OR habituation. These are familiar methods of ensuring sustained OR to a signal although, eventually, the OR habituates. Luria (1971) makes the following observation regarding OR: "It is well known that the appearance of any stimulus evokes in a normal person a series of somatic reactions, which are actually symptoms of arousal or components of an *orienting reflex*. . . . The somatic reactions persist for some time and are extinguished when the subject becomes habituated to the stimuli; they can be increased and prolonged if a special instruction is given, . . . in other words, when the stimulus assumes a 'signalling meaning'" (p. 45).

OR to Signal Words

A summary of the procedure and results of the experiment is given here. Details appear in a previously published paper (Das and Bower, 1971).

The twenty-five retarded subjects employed in this study had the same IQ and age characteristics as in study 1. They were compared with twenty-five CA-matched nonretarded subjects from Grade 8 of public schools.

The task involved listening for 30 min to a series of six familiar words, auditorily presented through the tape recorder as in the previous study. Subjects were asked to detect the occurrence of the word *man* which was an imperative signal for button pressing. A preparatory signal word *box* always preceded the imperative signal *man*. The sequence occurred once every min for 30 min. Standard procedures were followed for recording GSRs.

GSRs between one and ten sec after *box* or *man* were counted. If the response occurred within one and five sec after a word, it was scored as a phase I GSR; between five and ten sec it was a phase II GSR. This distinction was made following the work of Grings, et al. (1962) and Prokasy and Ebel (1967). A GSR occurring in phase I is an OR to the word; the phase II GSRs are delayed responses. But in the case of *box,* these would include anticipatory responses to the imperative signal. Recently, Grings and Sukoneck (1971) have labelled the response to a CS as an OR, followed by an anticipatory response (AR) to the UCS, and the response to the UCS as UCR. Although the UCS in their study was a noxious stimulus, unlike our present study, their labels may be appropriate here: phase I GSR to *box* is an OR, phase II GSR is an AR, and phase I GSR to *man,* confounded with response to button pressing, is an UCR.

An analysis of variance for GSR frequencies was performed with Groups (normal/retardate) as an independent measure, and Words (box/man), Phase (I/II) and Blocks (six five-min blocks) as repeated measures. The main findings of interest are presented in Figure 5-3. The retardates gave fewer GSRs to the preparatory signal *box* than the normals, but this was reversed when GSRs to the imperative signal *man* were considered. This

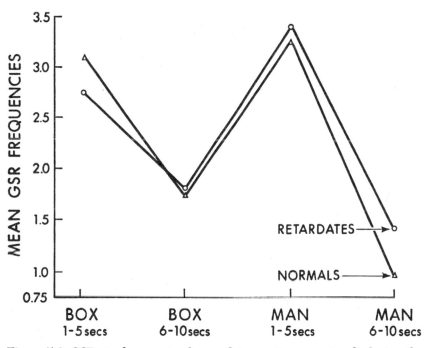

Figure 5-3. GSRs to the warning box and imperative man signals during the first and second five sec periods following signal presentation.

Groups × Word Interaction ($F\ 1/48 = 12.19$, $P < .01$) was significant. The main effect for groups was not significant. The normals were more "attentive" to the preparatory signal. But why did the imperative signal evoke more frequent GSRs for the retarded group? It has been observed that the less firmly established the response, the greater would be the GSR (Sokolov, 1963). In our study the retardates missed the key press response more often than the normals, which would support the notion that the motor habit was not firmly established. More recently, Struikov (1970) has found that a larger GSR during the foreperiod corresponds with a shorter reaction time, whereas a larger GSR to the imperative stimulus is inversely related to response speed. It seems reasonable to hold that when the subject expects the imperative stimulus at a certain time, and is prepared for the response, he will exhibit greater responsivity to the warning signal than to the imperative one. Formation of a strong expectancy would be a characteristic of the normal rather than of retarded subjects in our study. Incidentally, even though the retardates missed the button pressing more often than normals, it did not have an effect on the GSR frequency. GSRs were obtained with the same probability whether or not the subject gave a motor response. Thus, we agree with Sokolov (1963) that GSR does not seem to be an artifact of the motor response itself. It does not develop only as a conditioned response to motor reinforcement.

The GSR to the two signal words showed marked habituation over the testing period of 30 min. This was determined from the significant main effect for the six blocks over which total GSRs for *box* and *man* were counted ($F\ 5/240 = 6.80$, $P < .01$). The rate of habituation was similar for normals and retardates, thus failing to support those who have found faster habituation in the retardates (cf. Karrer, 1966).

The GSRs to the nonsignal words were also counted for the six blocks of five min each. Although in both groups the number of GSRs decreased over blocks, a group main effect along with that for blocks was obtained ($F\ 1/43 = 12.75$, $P < .01$ for groups; $F\ 5/240 = 7.30$, $P < .01$ for blocks). This was due to a higher mean number of GSRs of the retarded subjects to the nonsignal stimuli, showing a greater autonomic reactivity.

ACQUISITION AND REVERSAL OF SIGNAL VALUE
THROUGH INSTRUCTIONS

A stimulus ceases to evoke an OR within a few presentations. Subsequently, if it is given a signal value a conditioned OR is elicited by it. Sokolov (1963) has noticed many instances of this for nonverbal stimuli. Recently, McCubbin and Katkin (1971) contrasted a nonverbal tone with a human voice saying *anything* and found OR habituation to both kinds of stimuli. The human voice, however, evoked a larger GSR than the tone. This is consistent with the notion that perceived signal values influence the strength of the unconditioned OR.

As instructions may impart signal meaning to a stimulus, so also they may cancel the meaning of a signal. The OR to a signal whose meaning has been cancelled decreases. The OR decrement to a repeated neutral stimulus should be distinguished from decrement to a stimulus whose signal meaning has been cancelled. The former, typically, is an instance of habituation. But the latter involves inhibition of the OR (Sokolov, 1965, p. 146). It is conceivable that retarded subjects do not differ from normals in habituation of the OR, but do differ when selective inhibition of the OR to certain stimuli is required. In the next two experiments this question is examined.

Habituation of OR and Reinstatement by Instructions

In this study, data were obtained for OR habituation and disinhibition. The habituation part will be discussed here, whereas the disinhibition data will be presented in a later section.

Subjects were twenty-one students from the same special school as in the two previous studies, with IQs ranging from 40 to 65. The task consisted of listening to four stimuli, *boy, chair, wug, gex,* presented at intervals of 18 to 25 sec through a tape recorder in a random order for a period of six min. Any word or CVC had a probability of occurring once in every 90 sec. The subject was asked to just listen to the stimuli. At the end of this six-min habituation period, subjects were asked to listen to the stimuli again, but to press a button whenever they heard *boy* or *gex.* This condition was introduced to study the effect of ascribing signal meaning. Thus, *boy* and *gex* were signal stimuli requiring a specific response, while *chair* and *wug* did not require a response (Press and No Press stimuli).

The instructions to press marked the acquisition phase of the task. The total period was 12 min in this phase compared to six min in the habituation phase of the task. The first three min of acquisition (eight trial-block) was used to indicate the effect of instruction. Finally, the disinhibition phase followed acquisition. Disinhibition was introduced simply by reducing the loudness of all stimuli from 82 db to 68 db, and by presenting only six min of trials. There was no interruption between the acquisition and disinhibition phase. Each subject was brought back the next day and the habituation and acquisition phases were repeated without any change. For disinhibition, however, the loudness of the stimuli was increased from 82 db to 95 db rather than lowered as before. The GSR was recorded using standard procedures and frequency and magnitude scores were computed as before.

In Figure 5-4, mean GSR frequencies are plotted for the stimuli before and after instruction. There were four Press *(P)* responses required and four No Press *(NP)* responses in each trial block. On the first day, prior to instruction, *P* and *NP* should not be differentiated, which was borne out by the data. An analysis of variance (P/NP × Blocks) indicated that habituation was fast for both sets of stimuli (F $1/20 = 11/72$, P $< .01$). The effect of instruction is also clearly seen as greater GSR frequency on both sets of stimuli, consistent with Sokolov's (1963) observation that any change in signal value temporarily elevated the OR to both positive and neutral stimuli. Magnitude data supported the trend in frequencies, but also revealed a significantly lower value for *NP* than *P* following instruction, as should be expected. The interaction between *P/NP* × pre/post instruction magnitude was significant (F $1/20 = 4.35$, P $< .05$).

On the second day, the *NP* stimuli showed a marked habituation from the outset, but the *P* stimuli had the same initial position as on the first day. The analysis of variance revealed a

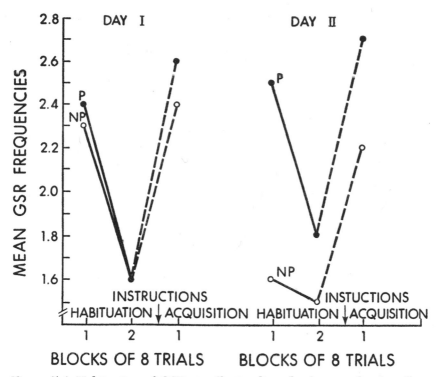

Figure 5-4. Habituation of GSRs to all stimuli, and subsequently, the effect of instruction to press only for P stimuli.

strong P/NP effect (F 1/20 = 12.60, P < .01). Habituation over blocks was also observed, mainly due to the decrement of GSR to P stimuli (F 1/20 = 6.37, P < .01). Instruction raised the GSR frequencies for both sets of stimuli as seen in the graph, but there was no interaction.

Habituation of the OR to neutral stimuli and its recovery through instruction, as well as the carry-over effect seen for NP stimuli on the second day, indicate that the retardate's attentional process involved is selective and lawful as it was in study 2. It is encouraging to see this in the present sample of retarded children who were considered to have too low an ability to be accepted in the classes for the educable mentally retarded.

Acquisition and Selective Inhibition of OR

The use of instructions for establishing as well as reversing signal meaning so that the ORs are selectively evoked or inhibited was the focus of a further study.

Twenty-seven retarded subjects from the school system and the same number of MA- and CA-matched nonretarded subjects participated in this study. Mean CAs of the groups were 114 months (MA Control) and 169 months (CA and retarded), while mean IQs were 107, 113 and 73, respectively. It may be noted that the retarded subjects in this study had higher IQs than those used in the three previous studies. Subjects were asked to listen to a tape which presented them with four words interspersed with four CVCs of low association value. They were required to press a button to the four words. Following six complete presentations of words and CVCs, subjects were asked to press for only two of the four words. Both the first phase (acquisition) and the second phase (reversal) had the same number of trials. Mean inter-trial interval was 12.5 sec varying between 10 and 15 sec. Thus, one complete presentation of all eight stimuli took 100 sec. Acquisition and reversal phases were separated by 2 min of instructing subjects on the words requiring the motor response. The GSR and heart rate (HR) were monitored by a Hewlett-Packard polygraph. Standard procedures were adopted for recording. A cardiotachometer output integrated beats per min HR.

The results are summarized here as details are available in a previous publication (Bower and Das, 1972). Mean GSR frequencies have been plotted in Figures 5-5 and 5-6 for retarded and MA and retarded and CA controls in blocks of 200 sec. The following trends apparent in the graphs were supported by appropriate analysis of variance. MA Controls, on the whole, gave more GSRs than the retarded subjects, but the latter did not differ from CA controls in this respect. This indicates a higher reactivity of the younger children ($F\ 1/52 = 4.51$, $P < .05$). The words evoked a greater number of GSRs than CVCs ($F\ 1/52 = 245.7$, $P < .001$ for MA/ retarded, $F\ 1/52 = 263.3$, $P < .001$

for CA/retarded comparisons). Higher GSR magnitudes were also obtained for words as expected. Words, in contrast to CVCs, were imperative signals for button pressing. Hence, they evoked stronger GSRs. When two of the words ceased to be imperative signals in the reversal phase, the GSR frequencies and magni-

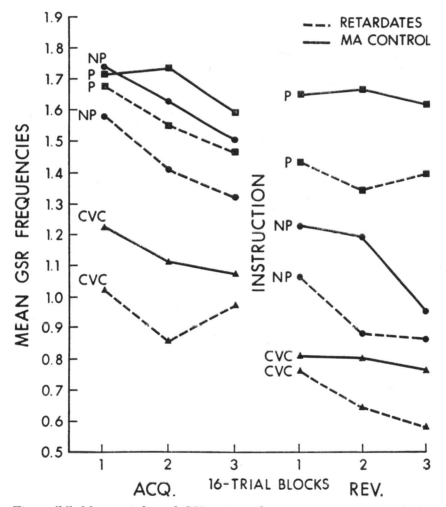

Figure 5-5. Mean number of GSRs given during acquisition to words (P and NP), and to CVCs (with no response requirement). In the reversal phase, half of the words (NP) did not require button pressing. Retarded and nonretarded MA matched subjects.

tudes evoked by them dropped substantially, which resulted in significant interactions between Acquisition/Reversal and *P/NP* words.

In Figures 5-5 and 5-6, the *P* (Press) and *NP* (No Press) labels are not required for the acquisition phase, since the subject had to press for all the words. But the words are labelled to show that there was no intrinsic response preference for either

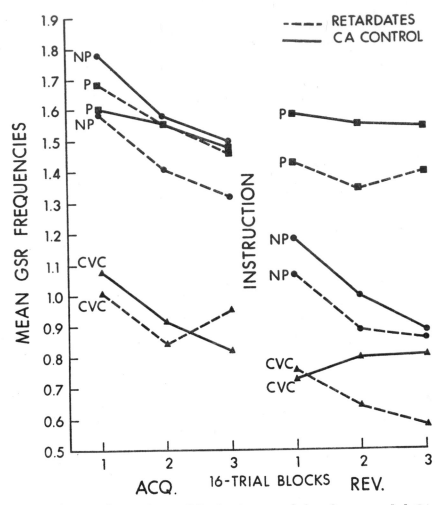

Figure 5-6. Similar to Figure 5-5, showing retarded and nonretarded CA comparisons.

the *P* or *NP* set before reversal. The two figures provide clear evidence that instructions which cancelled the signal value of the two words in reversal acted immediately and produced an inhibition of GSRs, whereas the other two words continued to evoke GSRs at the same level. The results suggest that the retardate's OR, as measured by GSRs, was sensitive to instructions and followed the same lawful process of decrement as the OR of equivalent age normals to words and CVCs.

The heart rate data are markedly different from the GSR in some important aspects. The analysis of the HR scores and results will be described first; these will then be compared with the GSR data.

Two major analyses were carried out: (1) an analysis of sec by sec heart rate data, which had one prestimulus and eight poststimulus scores. This was undertaken for the retardates vs. MA normals and for retardates vs. CA normals. Within this design the *P* words were compared with *NP* words and with CVCs separately, as were the *NP* words with the CVCs. Thus, the general analysis of variance was of a 2 (groups) × 2 (acquisition/reversal) × 2 (word vs. CVC or *P* vs. *NP* words) × 9 (sec) type with all but the first factor repeated. (2) The other major group of analyses was of change in HR as a result of stimulus occurrence. Deceleration and acceleration in HR was calculated from the lowest beat following the stimulus application and the highest beat subsequent to this trough. This measure is more informative than a simple maximum and minimum HR during the interval scanned after stimulus occurrence. A percentage measure for change was used to equate the prestimulus levels and provide a common scale for change. Thus, deceleration was the difference between prestimulus HR and the trough as a percentage of the trough value. Acceleration was similarly scored as the difference between the highest HR following the trough and the trough value as a percentage of the latter.

It should be pointed out here that such a scoring procedure reduces but does not eliminate the influence of differences in prestimulus level. In our procedure the trough in HR was reached within five sec following stimulus presentation, and the highest point following the trough thereafter within eight sec. The sec by sec changes were averaged and plotted in Figures 5-7 and 5-8. Having observed this, the procedure of computing percentage change described in the previous paragraph was adopted. Thus, we did not randomly select fastest beats or slowest beats. The acceleration was scored only after the lowest HR had been identified following stimulus occurrence. This procedure does not seem to be open to the pitfalls discussed by Graham and Jackson (1970). We suggest that the percentage change score merely sharpened the trend noticed in the averaged HR curve and lent itself for statistical treatment. The results of statistical analyses involving these scores were meaningful. If these were spurious scores, meaningful interpretations would be less probable.

The overall analysis of variance of percentage acceleration and deceleration scores was a factorial one with 2 (groups) × 2

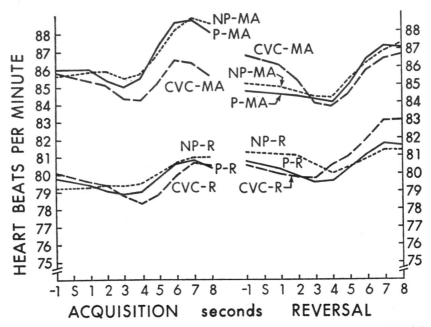

Figure 5-7. Second by second changes in heart beats for retarded (R) and nonretarded MA matched controls. The point-1 on the abscissa represents the average HR for two secs prior to the stimulus (S).

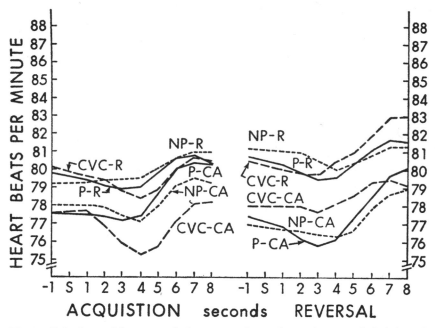

Figure 5-8. Second by second changes in heart beats for retarded (R) and CA matched nonretarded.

(acquisition/reversal) × 3 (blocks of 200 sec) × 2 (decceleration/acceleration) × 2 (*P/NP* words or word vs. CVC) with all except the first factor repeated.

The results of the sec by sec change are presented in Figures 5-7 and 5-8. First, let us consider the acquisition phase of normals and MA retardates (Fig. 5-7). It is clear that the CVC shows consistent deceleration in both groups. The two word categories evoke similar reactions. Acceleration is seen in both groups for the words. Deceleration is prominent for CVCs. During reversal, the CVCs preserved their acquisition characteristics only in the MA normal group. The two types of words should have different patterns in reversal, since the Press words retained their signal value where the No Press words were made neutral through instruction. However, they behaved similarly.

The analyses of variance reflected all these tendencies. Significant F ratios indicated that the sec by sec change was reliable, and the total HR response evoked by CVCs was less than for words. This was perhaps because of larger deceleration and sometimes smaller acceleration evoked by CVCs. This will be seen clearly in the subsequent analysis of the deceleration and acceleration scores. As seen in the graph, no interactions with acquisition and reversal were significant.

Figure 5-8 compares the retardates with CA normals. The CVCs again produced marked deceleration during acquisition. This tendency seems to have disappeared during reversal, suggesting an inhibition of the decelerative component. In a later analysis of extent of change in HR, this will be specifically tested. All other results of analysis of variance were similar to the preceding analysis.

Incidentally, the prestimulus levels were highest for MA Controls (85.38), lowest for CA Controls (77.50), with the retardates in between (80.26). Only the difference between the MA and CA groups was statistically significant. The three scores may reflect maturational levels.

One would expect that the Press and No Press words would produce different heart rate responses during reversal. This is not apparent from the graphs: the No Press words do not show any marked habituation of either the decelerative or the accelerative component. Analyses of variance, therefore, did not show any significant effect involving Press and No Press words. The analysis of percent change scores should reflect the deceleration and acceleration trends more accurately than those in the previous graphs. A summary of the analysis of variance is given in Table 5-1. MA-matched young children showed a greater deceleration and acceleration than the retardates. This was true for both acquisition and reversal phases. The nonsense syllables aroused greater changes in the heart rate than the meaningful words. Heart rate changes should habituate over the three consecutive 200 sec blocks. However, a nonlinear tendency emerged —change at block 1 was higher than that at block 2, but in the final block the change was greater than in the second block.

Deceleration and acceleration responses were sizeable in all groups. The mean acceleration was about twice as large as the

TABLE 5-I

SUMMARY OF ANALYSES OF VARIANCE OF DECELERATION
AND ACCELERATION SCORES

	Retardates and MA	Retardates and CA	MA and CA
Analysis I Press vs. CVC	MA < Ret.* in total change Decl. < Accl.† Press < CVC†	Decl. < Accl.† Blocks* (Smallest decl. and accl. in middle block.)	Decl. < Accl.† Press/CVC × Decl./Accl.* (Decl. for CVC > Press words, accl. was equal.)
Analysis II No-Press vs. CVC	No-Press < CVC Decl. < Accl.	Decl. < Accl.† No-Press < CVC† Acq./Rev. × No-Press/CVC* (Change greater in No-Press rev., but smaller in CVC rev. compared to acq.)	Decl. < Accl.† No-Press < CVC† Blocks × Decl./Accl.† (Decl. smallest in middle block, Accl. largest.)
		Blocks × Decl./Accl. × Groups* (Decl. Smallest in middle block for both groups, accl. changes do not agree between groups)	Acq./Rev. × Decl./Accl. × Groups* (Decl. increases during reversal for MA, decreases for CA compared to acquisition.)
Analysis III Press vs. No-Press	Press vs. No-Press no diff.	Press vs. No-Press no diff.	Press > No-Press*

* p < .05.
† p < .01.

mean deceleration, implying that HR increased beyond the pre-stimulus level for all groups. In reversal, the Press words did not evoke a greater change in heart rate than the No Press words. In order to highlight the heart rate changes to words, the decrease and subsequent increase in heart rate was plotted in Figure 5-9. It can be seen that irrespective of diagnostic groups and other experimental conditions, the CVCs evoked greater deceleration than words.

The results of the HR analyses suggest that words and nonsense syllables evoke heart rate changes and that the nonsense syllables generally evoke greater changes. HR showed little ha-

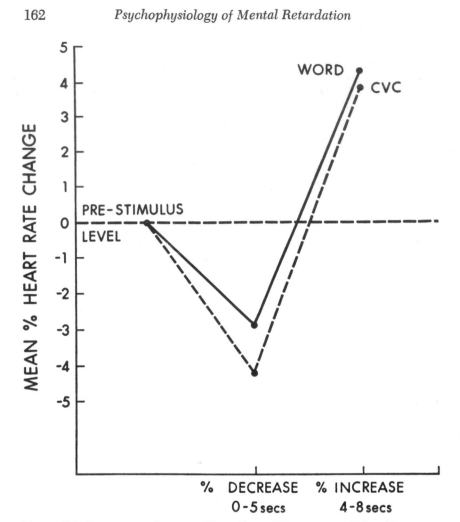

Figure 5-9. Percentage change in Heart Rate. % Decrease = 100 × (Prestimulus bpm − lowest bpm in next five seconds) / Per-stimulus bpm. % Increase = 100 × (highest bpm between fourth and eighth second following stimulus − prestimulus bpm) / prestimulus bpm.

bituation as a function of repeated presentation of the nonsense syllables, and did not habituate when the word became a nonsignal. All these results were contrary to expectation. Among the three subject samples, the young normal children reacted more strongly than either the older normals or the retardates. The retardates cannot be distinguished from the normals of the same chronological age in their reactions to words and nonsense syllables.

The HR and GSR data uniformly show no interaction between the diagnostic groups and the experimental variables. The only group difference is in reactivity. The MA Controls appear to have somewhat higher scores in GSR and HR than the CA controls. Therefore, the retardates appear to be as selective as the normals in their ORs, and their ORs are sensitive to instructional changes.

The disparity between GSR and HR needs some discussion. HR measures in this study did not habituate, unlike the GSRs. HR deceleration is a stable index of OR (Graham and Clifton, 1966; Meyers, 1969; Meyers and Gullickson, 1967). HR acceleration, on the other hand, reflects attention to internal stimuli and need not indicate a defensive response in studies such as the present one where none of the stimuli were aversive. Neither can it be a response to anxiety which is the conditioned expectation of a noxious agent (Brown, 1967, pp. 234-283). The original suggestion of Lacey (1959, 1967) that HR acceleration accompanies cognitive activity has been amply supported (Porges and Raskin, 1969; Tursky, Schwartz, and Crider, 1970).

In the light of our study, it appears that GSR is an index of autonomic arousal confounded with OR, whereas HR deceleration is a purer measure of attention to an external stimulus. GSRs are evoked as long as there is a challenge; a demand for an immediate motor response following the word. Once this is not required, the GSR decreases. HR responses, on the other hand, are evoked by CVCs which have no response requirement. The deceleration, and subsequent acceleration, seem to reflect attention to an unfamiliar stimulus and internal cognitive activity. The subject continues to be intrigued by the CVCs after attending to them. Such a position is consonant with Sokolov's account of the modeling properties of the central nervous system (Cole and Maltzman, 1969, pp. 680-687).

DISINHIBITION OF THE OR

We have shown that ORs can be evoked by verbal stimuli which acquire their signal value through instructions. These sta-

ble ORs also habituate, but much more slowly than unconditioned ORs. Like any other conditioned response, they should also be susceptible to disinhibition. There are many agents which
cause disinhibition of an inhibited conditioned response—loud
sound, light or any unexpected and novel stimulus. Pavlov
(1941) observed that a novel stimulus produces an OR whose effect in the cortex is a spread of excitation. As excitation irradi-
ates, it removes the inhibition associated with extinction, delay,
etc. and reinstates the conditioned response to some extent.
Thus, disinhibition effects appear when an OR destroys the inhibition of the CR. We shall present a study in which change in
the stimulus leads to the disinhibition of both conditioned and
unconditioned ORs in a complex and intriguing manner.

The disinhibition data are taken from part of the experiment
described in the previous section on Acquisition and Reversal of
Signal Value. Subject characteristics and experimental procedures are to be found in that study. Retarded subjects with IQs
between 40 and 65 were used.

In the previous studies, it was noticed that the attentional process of the retarded was lawful and sensitive to experimental
manipulations. One wonders if the same efficiency would be noticed when the task demands relatively more complex adjust-
ments. The disinhibition study and a subsequent study on probability guessing were designed to test this.

Signal Value and Disinhibition of OR

The main findings are presented in Figure 5-10, which should
be looked at in conjunction with Figure 5-4. Acquisition block
1 is common to both figures. GSR frequencies for P and NP
stimuli show habituation on the first day before disinhibition.
On the second day, NP habituated very fast and reached a low
level of response evocation. The effect of learning on the first
day was carried over and seen in the preacquisition habituation
of NP in Figure 5-4 and the low level of GSR prior to disinhibition treatment in Figure 5-10.

An analysis of variance for habituation during the acquisition
phase was carried out and supported the trends in Figure 5-10.

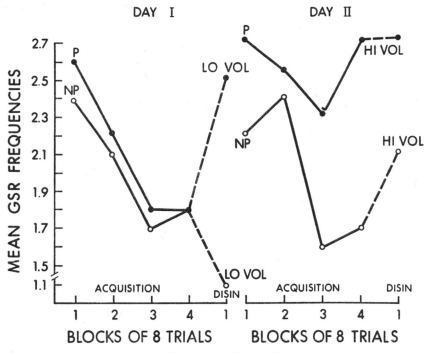

Figure 5-10. Selective disinhibition of GSRs following decrement in voice level on day one, and increment on day two.

Days × *P/NP* × Trial Blocks analysis yielded significance for Blocks (F 3/60 = 5.10, P < .05), for *P/NP* (F 1/20 = 9.78, P < .05) and for Days × *P/NP* (F 1/20 = 9.88, P < .05). The magnitude scores essentially agreed with frequencies.

In order to examine the effect of the disinhibition treatments, a 2 (*P/NP*) × 2 (pre/post disinhibition) analysis of variance was carried out for each day. Pre/post refers to the trial blocks immediately preceding and following the disinhibition treatment. The effect of lowering the voice level (first day) was significant (*P/NP*: F 1/20 = 10.31, P < .01 *P/NP* × pre/post interaction: F 1/20 = 21.90, P < .01). These were due to a large increase in mean GSRs to *P* and decrease to *NP* stimuli. The magnitude data, again, were consistent with frequencies. The effect of increasing loudness of the voice on the second day was similarly analyzed. The GSR frequency analysis demonstrated a *P/NP* difference (F 1/20 = 12.59, P < .01). Although a pre/post difference and the interaction were not significant for frequency scores, the magnitude scores revealed significance for pre/post and the *P/NP* × pre/post interaction (Fs 1/20 = 4.80, 4.69, P < .05 for both, respectively). This was accounted for by a large increase in the conductance for *NP* stimuli, but a negligible change in the already high conductance level for *P* stimuli.

On the whole, the disinhibition phase of the experiment showed a reciprocal effect for *P* and *NP* on the first day. Raising the voice on the second day had no effect on *P*, but increased the response to *NP*. The graphs show that on the second day GSRs to *P* were as strong on the first trial as on the last, before disinhibition, implying the absence of inhibition. Hence, disinhibition treatment could not be expected to remove inhibition for *P* stimuli.

The results of the first day disinhibition treatment need some discussion. Lowering of the voice produced facilitation of the *P* and inhibition of *NP* ORs on the first day. This was different from a typical disinhibition effect as Pavlov had originally noted. One would anticipate that a disinhibiting stimulus of low or medium strength, as used in this experiment, should evoke an OR which displaces the ongoing inhibition of the conditioned response and facilitates CR recovery (Pavlov, 1941). Perhaps we cannot compare a typical disinhibition paradigm in classical conditioning with the design here that included two competing stimuli, *P* and *NP*, which required discrimination and differential responding.

Rather, the situation is similar to those mentioned by Broadbent (1971) on selective perception under stress. Using noise as stress, he observed an improvement of reactions to the probable, familiar or easy signals at the expense of the less probable or irrelevant signals. Introduction of stress, by decreasing auditory intensity of the verbal signals, in our study would conceivably have an effect on filtering. In terms of filtering (Broadbent, 1958, 1971), the subject in our experiment recognizes the stimulus and codes it as a signal that requires a response or rejects it. Since the stimuli were verbal, having a characteristic beginning, a partial recognition of the *NP* stimulus could easily occur before it was filtered out. This would support Treisman's (1960) contention that filtering is a matter of attenuating signals rather than acting as an all-or-none barrier. The filter mechanism is not absolute, as Broadbent (1971) has now observed. Further, filtering is accomplished during the recognition of the stimulus rather than before or after it.

The question which one should ask in relation to our experiment is whether or not partial recognition results in an OR. If the present findings are reliable, it seems that the rejected stimulus (No Press) items were filtered out before they could evoke ORs. Perhaps this reflects a preattentional screening analogous to what Eriksen and Spencer (1969) have proposed in perception. From a purely adaptive point of view, it is quite logical that the retarded subjects concentrate on reacting to the signal stimuli and inhibit their reactions to nonsignal stimuli in a stressful condition which strained their attentional capacity. Unlike the lowering of the voice on the first day, raising the voice did not bring about any such load on their capacity. Hence, we find the typical disinhibition effect on the second day. Therefore, the results of the disinhibition phase on the first day strongly suggest the existence of a preattentive filtering process that rejects the irrelevant stimuli and allows the relevant stimuli to be encoded. The OR becomes a consequence of the encoding process.

There remains the necessity of testing the generality of the hypothesis that load on attentional capacity is a salient variable in a vigilance type task where disinhibition is effected by reducing signal intensity. Nonretarded subjects may be used in a future study, and the task complexity should be increased to introduce stress. In addition, the effect of reversing the disinhibition treatment on the first and second day should be examined. One suspects that if stimulus volume is *increased* on the first day, and *decreased* on the second, the reciprocal facilitation and inhibition effect will disappear.

OR DURING PROBABILITY LEARNING

In probabilistic predictions, the subject is actively engaged in cognitive processing and decision making, and modifies his response strategy upon receiving the feedback (Jones, 1971). Stimulus uncertainty has been varied in two studies on OR (Grings and Sukoneck, 1971; Higgins, 1971), but none of these employed a probability learning design to examine the effects of uncertainty. In the two-choice situation, the frequent as well as the infrequent events need a response. This allows one to compare autonomic changes under different experimental conditions with the response requirement factor held constant. Further, in varying probability levels, a noxious stimulus need not be included. Although, if the stimuli were noxious, these would evoke strong autonomic responses as in the Grings and Sukoneck (1971) experiment. It is hardly appropriate to study the cognitive processes involved in confirmation and violation of a subject's prediction using noxious stimuli. The effects of positive or negative feedback is confounded by the aftereffects of the noxious stimulus.

A two-choice learning situation was studied next in our research program. This task allowed one to observe the autonomic changes during the anticipation of the outcome and after the outcome or feedback. In the particular design used here, the subject had to guess immediately, on cue, which of two events would occur. He then waited five sec before receiving the feedback. GSR and HR were continuously monitored during the five sec anticipation period and during an eight sec period following feedback. It is assumed that during anticipation the subject is attending to internal events, whereas in the feedback period his attention is to external events. Hence, following Lacey (1959) and Graham and Clifton (1966), the anticipation period will be marked by HR acceleration, while HR deceleration will accompany feedback. In either case, the HR change is not an artifact of motor response which may be demanded by the task (Higgins, 1971). In an experiment on normal adults it was shown that instructions to *write* or *think* in solving mental arithmetic evoked the same kind of GSR and HR changes (Tursky, Schwartz, and Crider, 1970). Neither an overt response nor verbalization was required in the present study. The study was a test of the generality of autonomic responses during anticipation and feedback found in nonretarded samples such as college students (Tursky, et al., 1970).

Subjects were mentally retarded adolescents from a special school for the educable mentally retarded. Their mean IQ was 70.59 ($\pm$ SD 8.12) and their chronological age was 15.92 ($\pm$ SD .74). The subject was required to anticipate X or Y following the presentation of a cue word *man*. Probability for X was P, for Y, 1 − P. Probabilities of events were 0.90 for event one (X) and 0.10 for event two (Y) for one group. For another group, probabilities were 0.70 and 0.30. These were reversed in counterbalanced conditions. The feedback was in terms of a match between the subject's anticipation (X or Y) and the randomly predetermined order of occurrence of X or Y. Hits or misses were reinforced five sec after the subject's guess by the experimenter saying "right" or "wrong." The next presentation of *man* followed 10 to 18 sec after feedback. Autonomic changes during the five sec period after the motor response were considered to be anticipatory responses, and those following the feedback "right" or "wrong" as responses to feedback. A trial ending with "right" was further labelled as a confirmation trial and one with "wrong" as a violation of expectation trial.

Separate groups of twelve subjects were assigned to the four conditions: two probability levels and, within each, two counterbalanced conditions. The probabilities were valid for blocks of ten presentations of *man*. Each subject received one block of ten trials in which the frequent event had 100 percent probability; this was followed by six ten-trial blocks where the frequent event had a probability of 90 percent or 70 percent depending on the experimental condition. Adjacent trialblocks did not have the same order of X and Y. There was at least one run of three frequent events in each block.

Each subject was prepared for GSR and HR recordings by appropriate placement of electrodes and was given three min of rest to stabilize his autonomic responses before the instructions. A practice period followed, in which the subject was told to listen carefully and to notice the panels marked X and Y. He was required to press one of the panels as soon as he heard *man* and informed that he would be told if his response was right or wrong. The practice period was prolonged if a subject did not learn to press the panel on hearing the cue word.

The experimental trials were then started. The subject was instructed as follows: "You did fine. Now I want you to press the button a few more times. When you hear *man*, press X or Y. X (or Y) will go with *man* almost all the time. I will tell you if you are right or wrong, O.K.?"

The first ten trials were designed to build up an expectation for the frequent event (X or Y); then in the next 60 trials X or Y anticipation was correct, depending on a predetermined sequence used for the experimental condition to which the subject was arbitrarily assigned.

Certain preliminary decisions were made for analysis of the GSR and HR measures. Since one of our purposes was to compare the effect of violation with that of confirmation of expectation, we had to assure a buildup of expectation prior to the violation trial. Therefore, blocks of trials in which each subject had a confirmation on at least three successive occasions but a violation on the following trial were considered. The length of the confirmatory trial runs varied between three and seven. In subsequent analyses, variation in run length was not found to have any effect on GSR or HR; hence, it was treated as three.

As in previous studies, GSR frequencies and magnitudes were obtained during anticipation and feedback. The HR measure was a simple beats per min computed for each sec. Mean HR of two sec prior to the stimulus provided a prestimulus level against which poststimulus HR scores were compared.

Analyses of variance were carried out for GSR frequency and magnitude scores. The general format was Probability levels (0.90:0.10/0.70:0.30) × Previolation/Violation trials × Anticipation/Feedback. Mean GSR frequencies and magnitudes were found to be higher during anticipation than during feedback.

Both F ratios were significant ($P < .01$). Magnitude scores also showed a significant interaction ($P < .01$) between Previolation/Violation and Anticipation/Feedback. The data appear in Figure 5-11. Since the previolation trial preceded the violation trial, GSR magnitudes should be lower for the latter because of habituation than during anticipation. The relationship is reversed for feedback, indicating that the violation experience caused conductance to increase during this interval.

The data for heart rate changes appear in Figure 5-12. A sec by sec analysis was thought to be most appropriate for examining the effects of the variables mentioned above. The overall analysis of variance yielded a significant main effect for the change in HR over 13 sec ($F\ 12/432 = 3.58$, $P < .01$). The only other significant effect was the interaction between change over 13 sec and probability levels ($F\ 12/432 = 1.921$, $P < .05$).

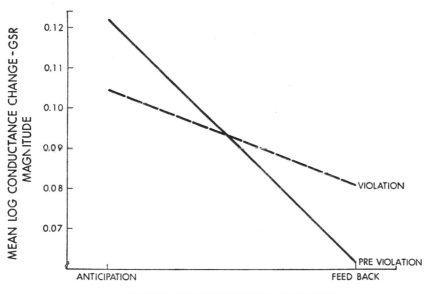

EFFECTS OF EXPECTANCY VIOLATION

Figure 5-11. Mean magnitudes of GSRs evoked during anticipation and feedback periods of the test for trials on which the subject's expectation was violated, and the immediately preceding trial on which expectation was invariably confirmed.

Both effects are clearly seen in the graphs of Figure 5-12. Separate analyses for anticipation and feedback portions of the graph confirmed the acceleration in the former and the deceleration followed by acceleration in the latter. It is clear from the graphs that in 0.70:0.30 event probabilities, the outcome was perceived to be more uncertain than under 0.90:0.10; hence the acceleration was greater. As a consequence, the feedback resulted in a greater OR deceleration in the 0.70:0.30 condition. There was no clear-cut difference between HR deceleration to feedback in violation and previolation trials.

In discussing the results of this study, we focus on Figure 5-12 which bears a close resemblance to the data (Fig. 5-13) of Tursky, Schwartz, and Crider (1970). The portion covered by the seventh to nineteenth sec in Figure 5-13 is relevant here. In their experiment, college students were given a series of four digits on the fourth, fifth, sixth and seventh sec and then waited until the twelfth sec when they were told to add zero, three or

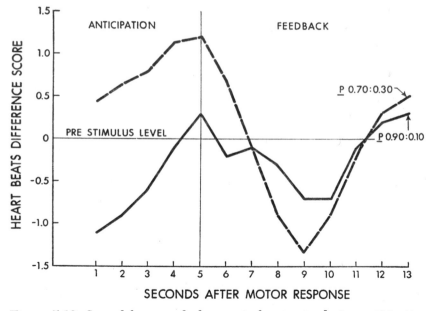

Figure 5-12. Second by second changes in heart rate during anticipation and feedback for the two probability conditions.

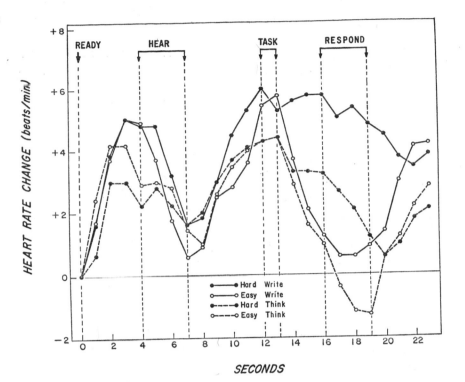

Figure 5-13. Heart rate changes during mental effort of college students. (Reproduced from Tursky, et al. (1970). Copyright by the American Psychology Association. Reproduced by permission.)

four to the previously presented digits. The instruction was given on the twelfth and thirteenth sec. Subjects were required to respond (write or think) following this period. HR deceleration is clearly seen for the "easy" groups who were asked to add zero. We suggest that since no mental processing was required for these groups, the deceleration was a reaction to the feedback as in our experiment. For the "hard" groups, however, who had to add three or four, the task demanded internal attention. Hence, deceleration was not obtained for the "write" condition and was attenuated for the "think" condition. If we follow graphs for the "easy" groups, the HR deceleration reaches its lowest point four to six sec following feedback, and then HR begins to recover, probably reaching its prestimulus level, as in our study (Fig. 5-12).

The same dimension of internal-external attention demand in the two phases of our graph adequately accounts for the difference between the two probability levels. A greater uncertainty should lead to a more serious reflection on the outcome of prediction and, subsequently, a greater attention to the outcome. This produces the interaction observed between anticipation and feedback conditions with the two probability levels.

Of course, in both of these graphs the phasic characteristic of HR is confounded with the effects of the experimental condition (Epstein, 1971). The initial point in the two anticipation curves of Figure 5-12 is determined to a certain extent by the HR to button pressing, although there was no difference in the pretrial HR for the two probability conditions. The deceleration which follows acceleration in anticipation is also expected. But the greater deceleration for the 0.70:0.30 curve than for the 0.90:0.10 cannot be expected from the phasic property of HR. The HR changes are due to the manipulation of experimental conditions.

Several assumptions were not supported by this experiment. The two probability conditions had no differential effect on conductance, but some effect on HR. The effect of violation of expectancy was not distinguishable from confirmation in terms of HR changes, but was for GSR. Therefore, a series of experiments on probability learning is necessary to determine (1) the effect of varying probability levels from 0.50 to 0.90, (2) the effects of the temporal relationship between prediction and feedback, (3) the effect of run length on response to violation of expectation, and (4) the effects of mental and chronological age.

RETROSPECT AND PROSPECT

We had initiated this series of experiments with two objectives in mind: (1) to detect normal-retardate differences in elaboration of OR and (2) to contribute to an understanding of the nature of the OR. In comparing normals with retardates, however, our experimental arrangement and selection of subjects assured that factors such as the level of pre-experimental learning and the ability of the retardate group to follow simple instructions did not interact with experimental factors which were sought to be manipulated. The group comparisons suggested no gross differences in the evocation, maintenance or extinction of OR in instructed learning situations; but where learning had to occur without instruction, the normals were superior.

Habituation and disinhibition of OR to verbal stimuli were studied using only the retardates. The results showed the retardate's remarkable sensitivity to the demands of the experimental conditions. The OR to nonsignals habituated quickly, reappeared immediately following the attribution of signal value to the stimuli, and was facilitated or inhibited in a complex manner depending on the importance of the signals.

The disinhibition study encouraged speculation regarding the nature of the OR. If one assumes that any change in the experimental condition such as lowering the loudness of auditory stimuli should disinhibit ORs to both signals and nonsignals, then our results are difficult to interpret. The effect of signal stimuli was one of facilitating OR evocation, whereas the opposite effect was obtained for nonsignal stimuli. It is probable that OR evocation depends both on a mismatch between the stimulus and the model as Sokolov (1963) advocates, and on the importance weighting that the stimulus has. Since any change in the environment does not evoke OR, we assume that those which are potentially significant elicit OR.

The concept of a preattentional filter system can explain how facilitation of signals and inhibition of nonsignals might occur. A logical extension of this line of thinking would be to monitor OR during the selective attentional tasks of Broadbent (1958). For example, in dichotic listening, does an important message through the irrelevant channel elicit an OR? Would OR size or frequency be modified by conditions which induce a stimulus set vs. a response set (Broadbent, 1970)? Does requiring the subject to make a motor response to a stimulus augment GSR more than heart rate, giving the disparity we found? As Higgins (1971) and Tursky, et al. (1970) mention, response requirement may increase the autonomic changes. These changes become prominent when habitual modes of behavior cannot cope with demands of the environmental conditions. However, the OR is clearly not a correlate of motor response demanded by the tasks. It is not an artifact of overt preparatory response. In selective attention tasks, stimulus or response sets can be varied by asking the subject to merely recognize rather than react to a significant stimulus in the irrelevant channel.

Finally, in the probability learning study, HR acceleration was observed during anticipation of an outcome of prediction, and deceleration as a consequence of both favorable and unfavorable outcomes. Although acceleration during anticipation neatly fits in with expectations from Lacey's work, it can also be looked at as an arousal response. Higher uncertainty in the outcome maintained a faster HR level. However, the difference due to level of uncertainty was not substantial. Subjects also did not react differently to confirmation and violation of their predictions. Therefore, the experiment should be repeated with CA and MA controls to sort out the effects of IQ and maturation on HR changes during two-choice learning. Bower (1974) has now done so.

We would like to consider briefly some neurophysiological observations regarding attention and distraction with a view to understanding the attentional processes of the retarded. Hernández-Peón (1964) demonstrated that distraction was accompanied by sensory facilitation. He recorded evoked potentials from the eye, ear, and skin to the appropriate sensory stimulus (flashes, clicks or electric shock). With human subjects, cortical evoked potentials were found to be increased or reduced by verbal suggestions alone, without changing the stimulus intensity. Attentional changes at the sensory level were shown to be manipulated by instructions or ideas.

It is interesting to note that Hernández-Peón gave as much importance to attention focused on ideas as to attention focused on external objects. Schachtel (1959), a metaphysical-developmental psychologist, considered both kinds of attention and placed the attention to ideas at a higher stage of development. The recent work on autonomic changes accompanying mental effort, mentioned in the last study, thus appears to have both a metaphysical and a neurophysiological base. Hernández-Peón and his colleagues examined the changes in sensory transmission when the subject was engaged in conversation or solving arithmetical problems. During these cognitive activities, light flashes to the eye produced considerably reduced evoked potentials. Perhaps an analogy may be drawn between this and Lacey's finding that during internal attention the subject rejects interference by outside stimuli. It would have been informative if HR were recorded along with evoked potentials in the experiments described by Hernández-Peón. One would expect that during anticipation, for instance, reduced evoked potentials will coincide with HR acceleration. In the feedback period when the subject is relaxed, will their strength be restored?

Luria (1963) has stated repeatedly that the mentally retarded child cannot maintain an OR and that habituation of an OR is much faster when compared to the nonretarded child. He also has stated that the usual procedures to prevent OR habituation (such as counting the stimuli as they are presented) are not effective in the retarded. The retarded child comprehends instructions that increase the signal value of the stimuli, but still cannot resist OR habituation. A major explanation offered by Luria is the weakness of the cortical connections, or as Ellis (1963) labels it, loose CNS integration. It is a Pavlovian notion that is invoked in conditions of brain damage. Mental retardation is characterized by Luria as a condition of diffused brain damage. Therefore, the pathologically changed brain of the retarded child is incapable of prolonged activity. The same idea is expressed in Meldman's (1970) book on *Diseases of Attention and Perception* where mental deficiency is described as mental hypo-attentionism, a characteristic shared in common with acute and chronic brain disorders. According to Meldman, the retarded exhibit a low arousal level and low selectivity in attention. Neither Luria nor Meldman specify the range of IQ of their retarded subjects. The same is true of the experiments on tactile evoked potentials recorded from retarded subjects in the studies by Hernández-Peón (1964, pp. 204-206). He gave a tactile stimulus of low intensity shock and observed that the retardate's evoked potentials were small in the initial trials but increased in magnitude on subsequent trials. The opposite trend was noticed in nonretarded children. He concluded that the retarded have defective corticoreticular mechanisms which are involved in triggering and maintenance of attention.

None of our studies reported in this chapter suggests such general defects in OR in the retarded. It is quite possible that the samples used by us were different from those used by others. Our samples were probably superior in MA to those selected by Luria. Besides, all children in the present studies were in school and had IQs above 40. It is quite probable that the school experience makes the children attentive to regulations and instructions. At the special school for the so-called trainable retardates in our sample, children are expected to abide by the rules of the school and their classrooms. All subjects were included in academic programs at school. Therefore, in relatively simple tasks under a noise-free laboratory condition, their attention was found to be quite adequate. This does not mean that they were functioning as efficiently as nonretarded children in the classroom. Casual observation of these children in their classes would show that their concentration was poor, rates of learning slow, and the level of academic skills substantially lower than those of the normal child.

One may offer some suggestions arising out of our experiments for classroom education. First, if distraction was not a problem in our laboratory only because of a bland noise-free environment, it follows that the classroom for the retarded children should have as few distractors as possible. In current practice, however, the walls in a classroom, for example, are filled with the hand-work of the children, and the physical arrangement in a classroom for retarded children does not differ from one for nonretarded children. Second, our studies used simple tasks involving words and verbal instructions. At the mental age of school-going retarded children, many researchers have noticed that verbal mediations are used and are useful for learning (Luria, 1961, 1963; O'Connor and Hermelin, 1963). The verbal system is more flexible and docile than the direct, first signal system. It acquires regulatory function over motor responses by mental age of six. Thus, simple and direct instructions may be profitably used to draw the attention of the retarded children to the salient features in a task and to guide their behavior even in nonacademic classes such as crafts. Third, most of our tasks in the laboratory had a duration of 20 to 25 min, used familiar stimuli and involved minimal learning. Under these conditions, the attention of the retarded could be selective and was efficiently maintained. If the difficulty level of stimulus material was raised, the task duration should be reduced to maintain the same level of attention. In ordinary classroom learning, the material to be learned should not only be presented in graduated steps having a high probability of eliciting correct responses, but the duration of a lesson should be shorter than 20 min. The teaching sessions can be interspersed with adequate relaxing activity periods. The above suggestions are admittedly speculative until their efficacy is empirically validated.

In conclusion, it should be pointed out that the present studies contributed to an understanding of the nature of the OR in the retardate, but did not reveal any characteristics that typically set the ORs of the retarded apart from those of the nonretarded. This is at variance with what Luria reported in 1963, but not with his more recent writings (Luria, 1971). He observed that habituation of the OR can be resisted by verbal instructions to pay attention to the stimulus, or to execute a response; both of these are instances of giving the stimulus signalling meaning. All of our studies fall into this category. Luria aptly describes this category as regulation of vigilance, for which the frontal lobes are specifically responsible. Lesions in parts of the brain other than the frontal lobes do not affect this function. In subjects with frontal lobe damage, "the verbal instruction we have mentioned does not evoke any stabilization of the vascular symptoms of the orienting reflex" (Luria, 1971, p. 45). He concludes by stating "All these data obtained by E. D. Homskaya and her co-workers show that the frontal lobes play a significant part in the regulation of the active states started by a verbal instruction" (p. 46). In our studies, subjects were not suspected to have frontal lobe damage. They did not show a general inability to follow verbal instructions in their schools, and certainly not in our laboratory. Their ability to regulate vigilance, therefore, should not be grossly defective. The results of the several investigations reported in this chapter show that the retarded were selective and efficient in maintaining ORs under a wide range of vigilance conditions created through verbal instructions.

REFERENCES

Berkson, G., Hermelin, B., and O'Connor, N.: Physiological responses of normals and institutionalized mental defectives to repeated stimuli. *J Ment Defic Res*, 5:30-39, 1961.

Bower, A. C.: Autonomic correlates of anticipation and feedback in retarded adolescents. *J Ment Defic Res*, 18:31-39, 1974.

Bower, A. C., and Das, J. P.: Acquisition and reversal of orienting responses to word signals. *Br J Psychol*, 63:195-203, 1972.

Broadbent, D. E.: *Perception and Communication*. New York, Pergamon Press, 1958.

————: Stimulus set and response set: Two kinds of selective attention. In Mostofsky, D. I. (Ed.): *Attention: Contemporary Theory and Analyses*. New York, Appleton-Century-Crofts, 1970.

————: *Decision and Stress*. London, Academic Press, 1971.

Brown, C. (Ed.): *Methods in Psychophysiology*. Baltimore, Williams and Wilkins, 1967.

Cole, M. and Maltzman, I. (Eds.): *A Handbook of Contemporary Soviet Psychology*. New York, Basic Books, 1969.

Das, J. P.: *Verbal Conditioning and Behavior*. Oxford, Pergamon Press, 1969.

Das, J. P., and Bower, A. C.: Orienting responses of mentally retarded and normal children to word signals. *Br J Psychol*, 62:89-96, 1971.

Ellis, N. R. (Ed.): *Handbook of Mental Deficiency*. New York, McGraw-Hill, 1963.

Epstein, S.: Heart rate, skin conductance, and intensity ratings during experimentally induced anxiety: habituation within and among days. *Psychophysiology*, 8:319-331, 1971.

Eriksen, C. W., and Spencer, T.: Rate of information processing in visual perception: Some results and methodological considerations. *J Exp Psychol Mono*, 79:No. 2, Part 2, 1969.

Fenz, W. D., and McCabe, M. N.: Habituation of the GSR to tones in retarded children and nonretarded subjects. *Am J Ment Defic, 75:*470-473, 1971.

Graham, F. K., and Clifton, R. K.: Heart rate change as a component of the orienting response. *Psychol Bull, 65:*305-320, 1966.

Graham, F. K., and Jackson, J. C.: Arousal systems and infant heart rate responses. In H. W. Reese and L. P. Lipsitt (Eds.): *Advances in Child Development and Behavior.* Vol. 5. New York, Academic Press, 1970.

Grings, W. W.; Lockhart, R. A., and Dameron, L. E.: Conditioning autonomic responses of mentally subnormal individuals. *Psychol Monogr, 76:* No. 39, 1962.

Grings, W. W., and Sukoneck, H. I.: Prediction probability as a determiner of anticipatory and preparatory electrodermal behavior. *J Exp Psychol, 91:*310-317, 1971.

Hernández-Peón, R.: Attention, Sleep, Motivation and Behavior. In R. G. Health (Ed.): *The Role of Pleasure in Behavior.* New York, Harper and Row, 1964.

Higgins, J. D.: Set and uncertainty as factors influencing anticipatory cardiovascular responding in humans. *J Comp Physiol Psychol, 74:*272-283, 1971.

Jones, M. R.: From probability learning to sequential processing. *Psychol Bull, 76:*153-185, 1971.

Karrer, R.: Autonomic nervous system functions and behavior: A review of experimental studies with mental defectives. In N. R. Ellis (Ed.): *International Review of Research in Mental Retardation.* Vol. 2. New York, Academic Press, 1966.

Kendler, T. S.: Development of mediating responses in children. In J. C. Wright and J. Kagan (Eds.): *Basic Cognitive Processes in Children. Monogr Soc Res Child Develop, 28:*(86) 33-52, 1963.

Lacey, J.: Psychophysiological approaches to the evaluation of psychotherapeutic process and outcome. In E. Rubinstein and M. Parloff (Eds.): *Research in Psychotherapy.* Vol. 1, Washington, D.C., American Psychological Association, 1959.

Lacey, J. I.: Somatic response patterning and stress: Some revisions of activation theory. In M. H. Appley and R. Trumbull (Eds.): *Psychological Stress.* New York, Appleton-Century-Crofts, 1967.

Luria, A. R.: *The Role of Speech in the Regulation of Normal and Abnormal Behavior.* New York, Pergamon Press, 1961.

Luria, A. R.: *The Mentally Retarded Child.* Oxford, Pergamon Press, 1963.

Luria, A. R.: The origin and cerebral organization of man's conscious action. *Proceedings of 19th International Congress of Psychology.* London: British Psychological Society, 1971.

Lynn, R.: *Attention, Arousal, and the Orientation Reaction.* Oxford, Pergamon Press, 1966.

Maltzman, I.; Langdon, B., and Feeney, D.: Semantic generalization without prior conditioning. *J Exp Psychol, 83:*73-75, 1970.

McCubbin, R. T., and Katkin, E. S.: Magnitude of the orienting response as a function of extent and quality of stimulus change. *J Exp Psychol, 88:*182-188, 1971.

Meldman, M. J.: *Diseases of Attention and Perception.* London, Pergamon Press, 1970.

Myers, W. J.: The influence of stimulus intensity and repetition on the mean evoked heart rate response. *Psychophysiology, 6:*310-316, 1969.

Myers, W. J., and Gullickson, G. R.: The evoked heart rate response: the influence of auditory stimulus repetition, pattern reversal, and autonomic arousal level. *Psychophysiology, 4:*56-66, 1967.

Neisser, U.: *Cognitive Psychology.* New York, Appleton-Century-Crofts, 1967.

O'Connor, N., and Hermelin, B.: *Speech and Thought in Severe Subnormality.* New York, Pergamon Press, 1963.

Pavlov, I. P.: *Lectures on Conditioned Reflexes.* Vol. 2. New York, International Publishers, 1941.

Porges, S. W., and Raskin, D. C.: Respiratory and heart rate components of attention. *J Exp Psychol, 81:*497-503, 1969.

Prokasy, W. F., and Ebel, H. C.: Three components of the classically conditioned GSR in human subjects. *J Exp Psychol, 73:*247-256, 1967.

Schachtel, E. G.: *Metamorphosis.* New York, Basic Books, 1959.

Sokolov, E. N.: Neuronal models and the orienting reflex. In M. A. Brazier (Ed.): *Central Nervous System and Behavior.* New York, Josiah Macy Foundation, 1960.

Sokolov, E. N.: *Perception and the Conditioned Reflex.* New York, Macmillan, 1963.

Sokolov, E. N.: The orienting reflex, its structure and mechanisms. In L. G. Voronin; A. N. Leontiev; A. R. Luria; E. N. Sokolov and O. S. Vinogradova (Eds.): *Orienting Reflex and Exploratory Behavior.* Moscow, Academy of Pedagogical Sciences of RSFSR, 1958. Washington, D.C., American Psychological Association, 1965.

Sokolov, E. N.: The modeling properties of the nervous system. In M. Cole, and I. Maltzman (Eds.): *A Handbook of Contemporary Soviet Psychology.* New York, Basic Books, 1969.

Struikov, G. A.: On the relationship between skin galvanic responses and expectancy and readiness for the forthcoming action. *Voprosy Psichologie, 5:*110, 1970.

Swets, J., and Kristofferson, A. B.: Attention. *An Rev Psych, 21:*339-366, 1970.

Treisman, A. M.: Contextual cues in selective listening. *Q J Exp Psychol, 12:*242-248, 1960.

Tursky, B.; Schwartz, G. E., and Crider, A.: Differential patterns of heart rate and skin resistance during a digit-transformation task. *J Exp Psychol, 83:*451-457, 1970.

Vygotskii, L. S.: *Thought and Language.* Cambridge, Mass., MIT Press, 1962.

Wolfensberger, W., and O'Connor, N.: Stimulus intensity and duration effects on EEG and GSR responses of normals and retardates. *Am J Ment Defic, 70:*21-37, 1965.

Wolff, J. L.: Concept shift and discrimination-reversal learning in humans. *Psychol Bull, 68:*369-408, 1967.

Worden, F. G.: Attention and auditory neurophysiology. In E. Stellar and J. M. Sprague (Eds.): *Progress in Physiological Psychology,* Vol. 1, New York, Academic Press, 1966.

Zeaman, D., and House, B. J.: The role of attention in retardate discrimination learning. In N. R. Ellis (Ed.): *Handbook of Mental Deficiency.* New York, McGraw-Hill, 1963.

CHAPTER 6

AUTONOMIC RESPONSES AND CLASSICAL CONDITIONING IN THE MENTALLY RETARDED

RUSSELL A. LOCKHART[*]

R EVIEWERS OF CONDITIONING and learning phenomena in the mentally retarded (e.g. Lipman, 1963; Denny, 1964; Ross, 1966; Sersen, 1970) have observed and criticized the paucity of research in the area of classical conditioning. The long history of conditioning, the central role conditioning-type models play

* Preparation of this chapter was supported by USPHS Grant MH 19414.

in contemporary learning theories, and the increasing scientific interest in human mental retardation, would lead one to expect that study of such a basic learning process as classical conditioning would be quite prominent. Why, then, such neglect?

Of course, conditioning research has largely occupied the academic psychologist whose ready populations are college students and various laboratory animals. With rare exception, interest in the relationship between conditioning and human retardation or human development in general, has been lacking. Of those responsible for the care and training of mentally retarded individuals and who daily come in contact with learning deficiencies, few have the time, inclination, training or facilities for the type of contemporary research required in the area of conditioning. This is no small point, for as the investigator focuses on ever smaller units of behavior (e.g. eyeblinks, heart rate, brain waves) and less so on the more molar behavior (e.g. choice of objects, approach or avoidance movements, verbal associations), the technical difficulty and cost of research increases dramatically.

Classical conditioning research almost invariably involves observation and measurement of relatively inaccessible responses requiring sophisticated recording equipment, technical competence, and severe control over environmental variables. The task is made even more difficult when working with populations not so ready to cooperate as is the college sophomore.

But these factors, although forbidding, cannot alone account for the lack of research interest. A crucial factor in the neglect of classical conditioning would appear to be the observation that when retardation occurs, it is the more complex and subtle learning processes—particularly those involving language and language mediated processes—which are most severely disrupted. The conditioned response (CR) seems only marginally affected, if at all. For example, Robinson and Robinson (1965) write:

> . . . mentally retarded persons with organic damage are somewhat slower to acquire a conditioned response and significantly slower to extinguish it than are normal or other retarded subjects of equal CA. Moreover, the evidence indicates that there is probably relatively little if any deficit in the conditioning behavior of mildly retarded

nonorganic subjects when they are compared with normal subjects of the same CA; there is almost certainly no deficit when the groups are matched for MA.

This idea complements the view of classical conditioning as a simple, almost automatic and mechanical acquisition of behavior, dependent only upon the adequacy of conditional (CS) and unconditional (US) stimuli and their temporal relations. The CR is said to be characteristic of even the simplest nervous systems. In the human, the neural mechanisms underlying the simple CR apparently function almost normally in mental retardation. Deficiencies in CR seem to be highly correlated with identifiable brain damage.

Thus, if the classical CR is relatively unaffected by retardation, disinterest is understandable. There must be a feeling that performance in higher level learning tasks will prove more useful in diagnosis, assessment, and treatment of retarded mental functioning. Certainly the amount of research in complex forms of learning far surpasses the meager offerings to be found in the classical conditioning literature of mental retardation.

The aim of the present chapter is to examine a specific area of classical conditioning in order to outline the potential fruitfulness of investigating classical conditioning phenomena for understanding both conditioning and mental retardation. Ross (1966), with much the same goal, has previously reviewed the problems of research and theoretical importance of eyelid conditioning of the mentally retarded. Here, we focus on *autonomic response phenomena* in the classical conditioning of mentally retarded individuals.

PREVIOUS REVIEWS OF CLASSICAL CONDITIONING

As a background of discussion of autonomic response phenomena in the classical conditioning of the mentally retarded (MR), it will be useful to review previous attempts to place classical conditioning and mental retardation in perspective.

Denny (1964) focused separately on appetitive and aversive classical conditioning paradigms. After reviewing the early studies of appetitive conditioning (Mateer, 1918; Cornil and Goldenfoun, 1928; Marineesco and Kreindler, 1933; Krasnagorski, 1933; Melhado, 1949; and Luria, 1932, 1959), Denny concludes:

> As long as the US is positive the results of conditioning in the mentally retarded are nicely consistent. The CR is not too difficult to establish, and inhibition, except for external inhibition is impaired: extinction is retarded, differential conditioning is poor, delayed CRs and conditioned inhibition cannot be established or only with great difficulty, and disinhibition occurs very readily.

It must be emphasized that the studies cited in support of such conclusions are from the early history of classical conditioning and suffer in comparison with modern conditioning work in terms of design, instrumentation, subject specification and analysis of data. In addition, the work on appetitive conditioning has *not* been followed up in recent years—at least in the West. There is essentially no modern data on appetitive classical conditioning in mental retardation. Denny's conclusions must be tempered by these observations.

In the area of aversive classical conditioning, Denny cites the work of Osipova (1933); Cornil and Goldenfoun (1928); Marinesco and Kriendler (1933); Berger (1954); Cromwell, Palk and Foshee (1961); Gakkel, Mololkova and Trofimov (1957); and Franks and Franks (1960). Curiously, he does not cite the important autonomic conditioning study of Birch and Demb (1959). Denny finds the aversive conditioning literature inconsistent, with results sometimes contradicting those found with appetitive conditioning (e.g. Osipova's finding that MRs conditioned significantly faster than normals on a finger withdrawal task). In spite of the few existing studies, Denny concluded on an optimistic note by referring to a number of "promising leads." Perhaps the most important such lead was his interpretation that when *verbal processes* are involved (e.g. conditioning to a verbal cue or command, or verbal/voluntary control over the response system being conditioned), conditioning performance will be deficient in the MR. He says "that the mentally retarded may condition poorly to verbal stimuli and may fail to inhibit because of lack of verbal control, appears to strike at the heart of the mental retardation problem."

Lipman (1963) also reviewed appetitive and aversive conditioning paradigms and while expressing satisfaction over the clarity of the data, he was not happy with the state of their interpretation. He outlined the different and often conflicting interpretations of CR deficiencies involving (a) defective central neural function, (b) attentional deficit, (c) deficient verbal control of motor functions, and (d) the manifest history in retardates of low reward contingency which reduces expectation of reward and thereby decreases CR performance.

Lipman called for better instrumented and controlled studies with particular attention paid to the classification of retarded subjects. He pointed to the need for attention to equal-CA deficits as well as equal-MA deficits. He suggests that equal-CA deficits in conditioning are particularly sensitive indicators of organic processes underlying mental retardation.

Lipman also suggested the use of the *interoceptive paradigm* in classical conditioning research with the mentally retarded. This suggestion followed from Razran's (1961) assumption that interoceptive conditioning controls for the possibility that classical conditioning may be "wholly a function of cognitive-perceptual expectancies." It is now twelve years since Lipman's suggestion was made in a widely available source—the *Handbook of Mental Deficiency* (Ellis, 1963)—yet, to the writer's knowledge, no one has utilized the interoceptive paradigm with retarded individuals. This technique is perhaps even more critical now since classical conditioning research, particularly in the area of autonomic responses, has taken a decided cognitive turn, with several investigators supporting the contention that human classical conditioning may be essentially a cognitive phenomenon. (For a possible interoceptive conditioning technique that could be readily employed with the mentally retarded, see Uno, 1970.)

Ross (1966) reviewed eyelid conditioning and discrimination learning in the mentally retarded. His discussion of the purpose and value of classical conditioning research with MRs is particularly valuable. He emphasized that because of extensive classical conditioning research in general learning theory, it is possible to meaningfully interpret normal-retardate conditioning differences in terms of deficits in basic learning processes. To integrate retarded research into the mainstream of learning research is seen as the only way research will productively lead to applied benefits for retardate learning problems. Ross' discussion of methodological issues (e.g. comparison groups, retardates as experimental subjects, etiological classification, controls, etc.) should be considered basic reading for the researcher interested in conditioning and retardation.

The most detailed review of classical conditioning phenomena in mental retardation has been provided by Astrup, Sersen and Wortis (1967). These authors expanded and updated Denny's (1964) review and, more importantly, provided at least an indication of the nature of Russian research in this area. The authors organized their review in the context of Pavlovian conditioning, emphasizing the three central principles of conditional reflex dynamics: *excitation, inhibition,* and *mobility.* Salivary reflexes, defensive reflexes, motor reflexes, and cognitive processes (or, in Pavlovian terminology, *second signal system* processes involving such phenomena as semantic conditioning, word association, command conditioning, etc.) were reviewed.

These authors concluded (1) simple conditional reflexes are not particularly affected by mental retardation; (2) retardates exhibit deficiencies particularly in the area of mobility (e.g. inability to reverse conditional connections); (3) the more conditioning involves or requires the verbal process of the second signal system, the more retardate conditioning performance will be deficient in comparison with normals; and (4) verbal-verbal (e.g. word association) conditioning is particularly sensitive to MR deficits.

The authors present the case for an MR typology based on conditional reflex behavior. They feel that such a typology is clinically relevant and "could provide a basis for training, education, or drug treatment, designed to restore the equilibrium of nervous processes and to facilitate the adequate elaboration of new conditioning connections." There are few, if any, signs that such an approach is taking root in Western treatment or training of the mentally retarded.

Sersen (1970) has provided a review of the most recent studies in classical conditioning of eyelid and autonomic responses in the mentally retarded. His four conclusions are very perceptive: (1) the simplicity of the classical conditioning paradigm is "relative, if not illusory"; (2) more parametric studies are required to work out the characteristics of the basic phenomena of conditioning in the mentally retarded; (3) more than a single response system should be studied at the same time to test the generality of conditioning phenomena across response systems; and, (4) Western researchers would do well to test the conditioning-based typology of mental retardation espoused in Russian research.

CHARACTERISTICS OF RECENT STUDIES OF AUTONOMIC CONDITIONING IN THE MENTALLY RETARDED

Recent studies of autonomic conditioning of mentally retarded populations are briefly summarized in Tables 6-I, 6-II, and 6-III. Included is a brief indication of the type of retarded population, number and sex of subjects, age, MA, and IQ, type of conditioning paradigm, type and duration of CSs and USs employed, interstimulus interval, responses measured, specification of phases of the experiment in terms of adaptation, acquisition (including percent reinforcement), and extinction, and information unique to each study.

In a period of eleven years, only seven experimental reports have appeared in the Western literature (to the writer's knowledge). With variations in subject populations, types of paradigms, and other procedures it is questionable whether any generalizations regarding autonomic conditioning in the mentally retarded can be adequately supported. For the present, the genuine lack of information would seem to be the main characteristic of autonomic conditioning literature in the mentally retarded.

A serious methodological problem is the wide variability in specification of populations employed. Some investigators have carefully indicated the nature of subjects used (e.g. Birch and Demb's behavioral criterion to distinguish between excitable and nonexcitable brain damaged retarded), while others (e.g. Baumeister, Beedle, and Urquhart) specify only that "the retarded

TABLE 6-I

POPULATION CHARACTERISTICS OF STUDIES OF AUTONOMIC
CONDITIONING IN THE MENTALLY RETARDED

Study No.	Population	Number	Sex	Age	MA	IQ
1. Birch and Demb (1959)	Hyperexcit.	10	6 F, 4 M	9.9	5.9	59.2
	Nonhyperexcit.	8	1 F, 7 M	13.5	7.7	57.4
	Mongoloid	8	6 F, 2 M	9.6	4.6	47.4
	Normals	4	?	?	?	?
2. Grings, Lockhart and Dameron (1962)	"Low" IQ	20	?	14.2	4.8	34.1
	"High" IQ	20	?	14.7	9.3	63.1
3. Grings, Lockhart, Zeiner and Uno (1964)	"Low" IQ	19	?	?	?	20-45
	"High" IQ	19	?	?	?	53-78
4. Baumeister, Beedle and Urquhart (1964)	Retardates	40	40 M	42.4	?	48.7
	Normals	29	13 F, 16 M	29.2	?	?
5. Lobb and Nugent (1966)	Retardates	42	18 F, 24 M	18-25	?	25-65
	Normals	42	18 F, 24 M	18-25	?	?
6A. Lobb (1968)	Retardates	160	80 F, 80 M	18-30	?	?
	Normals	160	80 F, 80 M	18-30	?	?
6B. Lobb (1970)	Reanalysis of Lobb (1968)					
7. Block, Sersen and Wortis (1970)	1) Mongoloid	10	?	4-6	2.2	?
	2) Mongoloid	14	?	6-11	3.2	?
	3) Encephal.	29	?	6-11	4.6	?
	4) Normals	22	?	2-4	3.0	?
	5) Normals	17	?	4-6	5.0	?
	6) Normals	38	?	6-11	8.5	?

group was selected from the population of a residential institution for retarded." Before much can be learned from the comparison of various studies in this area, it will be necessary to more adequately specify the nature of the subject population (including normals).

Despite difficulties in working with retardates in the classical conditioning situation, particularly when aversive stimulation is involved, it is encouraging to find that a sizeable number of subjects have been employed. For the seven experiments, a total of 400 retardates and 322 normals have been studied. These values are obviously influenced by Lobb's massive study involving 160 retardates. Use of large numbers of subjects, however, should not cloud the possibility of learning a great deal from the careful study of small but well defined numbers of retarded subjects—particularly if the conditioning phenomena can be studied on a within-subject basis (e.g. differential conditioning).

Table 6-I reveals that Birch and Demb (1959), Grings, Lockhart and Dameron (1962), Grings, Lockhart, Zeiner and Uno (1964), and Block, Sersen and Wortis (1970) studied conditioning in children and young adolescents, while Baumeister, Beedle and Urquhart (1964), Lobb and Nugent (1966), and Lobb (1968) conditioned adults. It is difficult, if not impossible, to directly compare the results of these two groups of studies without knowing something of the developmental characteristics of conditioning in the retarded. What is required, of course, is the application of a standard paradigm across different age groups. No such studies exist.

The mean IQ or MA have not been specified in every study. The relation between the variable of IQ or MA and degree or speed of autonomic conditioning has been of concern in two studies (Grings, Lockhart, and Dameron, 1962; Grings, Lockhart, Zeiner, Uno, 1964) in terms of comparing different levels of retardation as an independent variable, and specified as a correlation in two other studies (Birch and Demb, 1959; Block, Sersen, and Wortis, 1970). All other studies have focused principally on differences between the retardates and normal. It is necessary to specify MA and IQ if studies are to be adequately compared and questions concerning the relation between conditioning and deficient mental function adequately researched.

Various conditioning paradigms have been employed with MRs (Table 6-II). Both simple and differential and delay and trace paradigms have been studied. However, there exist no published reports of generalization, transfer, temporal conditioning, effects of instructions or interoceptive conditioning. Only one study has reported data on reversal (Block, Sersen and Wortis, 1970) and in that study, the contingency reversal followed a period of reinforcement on both CS+ and CS−.

CSs in autonomic conditioning studies have been limited to tones and lights. The only US to be employed other than electric shock has been an autohorn (Block, Sersen and Wortis, 1970).

The only variable to be systematically studied in autonomic

TABLE 6-II

PARADIGM CHARACTERISTICS OF STUDIES OF AUTONOMIC
CONDITIONING IN THE MENTALLY RETARDED

Study No.	Paradigm Type	CS*	US*	ISI*	Response Measured
1.	Simple: delay	Light (1.5)	Shock (?)	.5	GSR (freq)
2.	Differential: delay	Light, tone (5)	Shock (.6)	.5 5.0	GSR ($\sqrt{\Delta}$ C) HR (unreported)
3.	Differential: delay and trace	Light, tone (5)	Shock (.6)	5.0	GSR ($\sqrt{\Delta}$ C) HR (b/m)
4.	Simple: trace	Tone (1)	Shock (.5)	1.0 1.5 2.0	GSR (freq)
5.	Simple: trace	Tone (1)	Shock (.5)	1.25 2.00 16-61	GSR ($\log_{10} + 2 \times \Delta$C)
6A.	Simple: trace	Tone (.1)	Shock (.5)	.25, .50, 1.0, 2.0, +15.0	GSR (logΔOhms)
6B.	Simple: trace	Tone (.1)	Shock (.5)	.25, .50, 1.0, 2.0, +15.0	GSR Amp and Freq
7.	Differential, Delay, Reinforced extinction, Reversal	Tone (5)	Autohorn (1)	5.0	HR (heart period)

* Duration in sec.

conditioning of mentally retarded has been the interstimulus interval (ISI). Grings, et al. (1962) compared .5 and 5 sec ISIs; Baumeister, et al. (1964) compared 1.0, 1.5, and 3.0 sec ISIs; Lobb and Nugent compared 1.25, 2.00, and 16-61 sec (variable) ISIs; and Lobb (1968) compared .25, .50, 1.00, and 2.00 sec ISIs.

The most popular response system studied has been the GSR. Grings, et al. (1962, 1964) also measured heart rate (HR) but, although reported (Grings, et al. 1964), these data have not been published. The recent study by Block, et al. (1970) measured HR. There has been no published report in the literature directly comparing the conditioning effects in different response systems simultaneously. For this reason, as Sersen (1970) noted, there are no data to bear on the question of conditioning effects

TABLE 6-III

PROCEDURAL CHARACTERISTICS OF STUDIES OF AUTONOMIC
CONDITIONING IN THE MENTALLY RETARDED

Study No.	Adaptation	Acquisition	Extinction	Other
1.	To criterion	50% To criterion	To criterion	
2.	6 CS+	60% 20 CS+	5 CS+	Generalization, disparity, transfer, and extinction data unreported
3.	6 CS+, 6 CS–	20 CS+, 20 CS–	None	Trace and delay extensions, in steps, to 6, 7, 8, 10 and 20 sec following initial 5 sec ISI
4.	10 trials	100%, 20 trials	10 trials	Extinction data only
5.	To criterion	50%, 32 trials	None	
6. A and B	10 trials	32 trials	20 trials	Includes all conditions replicated under drug condition (Benzedrine)
7.	No	1) (100%) 10 CS+, 10 CS– 2) CS+ and CS– both reinforced 10 trials each 3) Reversal; 10 trials each stimulus	None	

across response systems. It is essential that inferences about classical conditioning in mental retardation be based on as wide a sample of response systems as possible.

With the exception of the Block, et al. study, all experiments have included an adaptation period for presentations of CSs without reinforcement prior to acquisition (Table 6-III). During acquisition, most experiments have employed a partial reinforcement schedule making possible the test for development of CR via data from test or probe trials. The experiment reported by Baumeister, et al. (1964) employed 100 percent reinforcement and all data reported are from extinction. Most all experiments have utilized an extinction phase following acquisition although these data are not always analyzed or reported (e.g. Grings, et al., 1962).

AN OVERVIEW OF AUTONOMIC CONDITIONING IN THE MENTALLY RETARDED

Given the paucity of research, what can be concluded about autonomic conditioning in the mentally retarded? We will approach this problem by overviewing the results of recent studies outlined in Table 6-I followed by more detailed analysis of selected studies and consideration of specific research issues.

The Single-Cue Paradigm

The general picture of classical conditioning and mental retardation, as indicated earlier, is that mental retardation does not substantially interfere with the development of the simple conditioned response. Of the studies reviewed in Tables 6-I, 6-II, and 6-III, those of Birch and Demb (1959), Baumeister, Beedle and Urquhart (1964), Lobb and Nugent (1966) and Lobb (1968) utilized the single-cue conditioning paradigm in which one CS is paired with the US with no other stimuli involved. Conditioning is usually assessed by comparing a paired group (CS + US) with an unpaired group (CS, US).

Birch and Demb Study

Birch and Demb (1959) studied conditioning in four groups: (1) hyperexcitable and distractible brain-damage, (2) nonhyperexcitable and nondistractible brain-damaged, (3) mongoloid, and (4) normal. Birch and Demb employed a within-subject trials-to-criterion procedure for both acquisition and extinction. The CR was defined as three successive trials in which the amplitude of the GSR exceeded a pre-set amplitude (90% greater than spontaneous response amplitude). In terms of this measure of conditioning, Birch and Demb found that (1) hyperexcitable/distractible brain-damaged children required significantly more trials to criterion than nonhyperexcitable/nondistractible brain-damaged children; (2) nonhyperexcitable/nondistractible brain-damaged children did not differ from normals; (3) mongoloids required significantly more trials than all other groups (Birch and Demb attribute this group performance as being due to the three youngest, under age seven, mongoloids, since when they were eliminated from the data, the remaining mongoloids conditioned significantly faster than the hyperexcitable/distractible brain-damaged children); (4) the correlation between measured IQ and trials-to-criterion was −.07 (Pearson r); (5) despite differences in acquisition rate, groups did *not* differ in number of trials to extinction criterion (three consecutive zero responses).

The authors attribute poor CR acquisition in the hyperexcitable group to undifferentiated attention to the critical stimuli (CS and US) and believe that this "lack of selectivity in attention may be interpreted as a manifestation of a defective process of inhibition, with the relevant stimulus incapable of achieving dominance and so reducing the effectiveness of explicit sensory arousals." To further support this interpretation, Birch and Demb described the *qualitative* difference between the groups in both acquisition and extinction phases. The hyperexcitable/distractible subjects exhibited marked restlessness throughout with high sensitivity to extraneous stimuli and motor behavior increasing over the acquisition and extinction periods. In marked contrast, the mongoloids, normals, and nonhyperexcitable/nondistractible brain-damaged did not show unusual degrees of restlessness, and during extinction, several subjects fell asleep.

These results suggest that brain damage resulting in hyper-excitability and distractibility interferes not so much with in-hibitory processes underlying extinction, but with the inhibitory/excitatory interaction that underlies selective attention. Differ-ences between hyperexcitable and nonhyperexcitable groups in acquisition suggests that brain damage is not a unitary factor and points to the utility of a conditioning approach in differen-tiating brain damage and as a support for behavioral differentia-tions. In addition, the lack of a correlation between IQ and trials-to-criterion indicates that conditioning behavior adds in-formation independent of that given by IQ scores alone. Indi-viduals with similar IQs who might be otherwise treated in a similar manner could be treated differently if conditioning per-formance were assessed. As the authors point out, their results "have independent implications for the management and train-ing of hyperactive and nonhyperactive brain-injured retarded children." These results support the conclusion that at least some portion of the mentally retarded can acquire a conditional au-tonomic response as rapidly as normals and that deficiencies are correlated with specific types of mental retardation (mongolism) or specific brain damage (hyperexcitable type).

There are factors in the experimental design, however, which should caution overgeneralization. The CS + US pairs were pre-sented in alternating trials with CS alone and at a constant tem-poral interval (90 sec). Thus, there was a high degree of stimu-lus and temporal patterning which might serve to facilitate CR acquisition in the brain-injured groups. Differences between nor-mals and nonhyperexcitable/nondistractible brain-damaged might be accentuated if CS + US and CS alone trials are presented randomly and at a varying temporal interval.

Baumeister, Beedle, and Urquhart Study

Baumeister, et al. (1964) compared retarded (CA = 42.4 yrs) and normal (CA = 29.2 yrs) adults in a simple trace condition-ing paradigm in which the trace interval was 0.0, .5, or 1.0 sec be-tween CS offset and US onset. The CS duration was 1.0 sec mak-ing the interstimulus interval among the groups 1.0, 1.5, and 2.0

sec. Since all acquisition trials were reinforced (CS + US), and the CS-US interval was too brief to measure GSR, all evidence for conditioning necessarily came from extinction trials. This is a serious methodological weakness. For example, had Birch and Demb (1959) based their observations solely on extinction data all groups would have been quantitatively equal in number of trials to extinction. Results concerning acquisition based on extinction data are obviously confounded with extinction processes as well as possible disparity responses arising from perception of changed conditions.

The primary dependent variable was number of GSRs to extinction CSs which had a latency less than 5.0 sec and an amplitude exceeding the last three habituation trial responses. The results for frequency data indicated that (1) there was no difference in number of CRs during extinction for the retardates and normals; (2) the number of extinction CRs decreased significantly as a function of trace interval length; and (3) there was no interaction between level of intelligence and trace interval. Results for the second dependent variable—amplitude of first extinction CR divided by mean amplitude of last three acquisition trial GSRs—led to the same conclusions.

The authors suggest that when a conditioning experiment is made simple enough retardates will perform as adequately as normals. They suggest that classical conditioning procedures—because of their simplicity—be utilized more in the training of retarded individuals. Baumeister, et al. regard their results (i.e. lack of an interaction between trace interval and intelligence) as not supporting Ellis' stimulus trace theory (1963) in which it is predicted that retardate performance, because of defective trace processes, will become increasingly defective in comparison with normals as the trace interval is increased.

Lobb and Nugent Study

Lobb and Nugent (1966) also tested Ellis' trace theory, reasoning that a test for statistical interaction between intelligence and trace interval would constitute a strong test of the "defective trace in retardation" concept. Normal and retarded adults were compared in three trace interval groups: .25, 1.00, and 15-60 sec (variable). The latter group constituted a sensitization and pseudoconditioning control group. The CS was 1.0 sec in duration. Thus, the ISIs for the two experimental groups were 1.25 and 2.00 sec. A 50 percent reinforcement schedule was used in which paired trials and CS alone trials were presented in a predetermined nonalternating pattern. The intertrial interval varied between 20 and 60 sec. (This is the opposite of Birch and Demb's procedure and eliminates the temporal and alternating stimulus patterning.)

The results supported Ellis' theoretical expectation. Both defectives and normals conditioned at the shorter trace interval (.25 sec) but only normals showed conditioning at the longer trace interval (1.0 sec). The interaction between intelligence and trace interval was highly significant. Interestingly, Lobb and Nugent found that in the 1.0 sec condition, female subjects (in both retarded and normal groups) responded with significantly larger responses than males. Another important result was that the unconditioned response (UR) in retardates was significantly less than in normals. This finding supports Berkson's (1961) data suggesting that most physiological responses are reduced in amplitude in retardate populations. Lobb and Nugent point to a serious methodological point when they note that unless this difference in responsivity is taken into account absolute magnitude comparisons might lead to erroneous conclusions—particularly when the data from normal and retarded populations are compared solely on a between-groups basis. The authors suggest use of analysis of covariance as a statistical method to control for differential responsivity between populations. An experimental approach to the same problem would be to use the within-subject design, i.e. differential conditioning. Studies of this type are discussed in the following section.

Lobb Study

Lobb again compared normal and retarded adults in a trace conditioning paradigm with ISIs of .25, .50, 1.00, 2.00 sec, and a +15.00 sec control condition. In this experiment, the CS duration was only .10 sec (in contrast to the 1.0 sec duration in the previous study). Trace intervals were thus .15, .40, .90, and 1.90 sec. In addition to trace variation, the possible facilitating effect of Benzedrine (dl-amphetamine sulphate) on acquisition of the trace CR was studied. A total of 160 retarded and 160 normals were used. Each of the trace subgroups was divided into drug and placebo conditions and sex was balanced across all conditions. Lobb again employed the 50 percent reinforcement schedule during acquisition. Extinction trials (with shock electrode removed) were administered on the day after acquisition.

A $2 \times 2 \times 2 \times 5$ analysis of variance of adaptation response amplitude (intelligence, drug, sex, trace interval) indicated only the difference between normal and defective groups was significant, with the latter being characterized by smaller amplitude GSRs. The rate of habituation during the adaptation phase was the same for both groups. Benzedrine had no effect on the adaptation response of either group and there were no sex differences.

In acquisition, Lobb found that in only one of eight retarded groups (the .50 sec trace placebo group) did the amplitude of the GSR exceed the amplitude of the control group, while five of eight normal groups conditioned significantly. For normals, conditioning was absent in the 2.0 sec trace groups and in the .25 sec trace nondrug condition. In addition, no interactions between intelligence level and trace interval were significant.

During extinction, there was a rapid decrement in responding in the normal groups and during the first block of extinction trials no significant difference between conditioning and control groups was found. In contrast, the mentally retarded groups showed more signs of conditioning during the extinction phase than they did during the acquisition phase: three of eight groups (both .5 sec groups and the 1.0 sec placebo group) exhibited larger amplitude GSRs than the control group.

Lobb's failure to find the intelligence by trace interval interaction contradicts his earlier study and fails to support Ellis' theory of stimulus trace. However, Lobb indicates that the shorter duration CS (.1 vs. 1.0 sec) may have decreased the effective trace too much for the retarded, thus accounting for the lack of conditioning during the acquisition phase. Yet, the MRs showed significant signs of CR during extinction. Lobb attributes this to consolidation and hypothesizes that the essential CR decrement in the mentally retarded is one of rate of CR acquisition. He suggests that rate can be facilitated either by increasing the intensity and/or the duration of the CS. In this sense, then, the data are consistent with the earlier study and do support Ellis' theory in that retardates are more susceptible to trace degeneration than are normals. In addition, the retarded seemed to be more vulnerable to the disrupting effects of the Benzedrine. In contrast to earlier findings, Benzedrine in this study consistently lowered CR performance. Lobb's suggestion that previous positive studies have utilized adrenergically mediated responses (salivary, eyeblink, etc.), while his negative result comes from the cholinergically mediated GSR remains to be tested.

In a follow-up analysis, Lobb (1970) tested the hypothesis "that frequency and amplitude would reveal opposite difference between intellectually average and low-IQ groups." His analysis failed to support the amplitude-frequency differential. In general, frequency data simply replicated the amplitude findings. Lobb suggests that *magnitude* frequency (weighted amplitude) is the best single measure for comparison purposes between retardates and normals.

The results of these studies are not entirely consistent but do support the following generalizations regarding simple conditioning of GSR. When measured *during* acquisition, mentally retarded adults, hyperexcitable brain-damaged children, and young mongoloid children *do not* condition as well as normal controls. This is particularly true in the trace conditioning paradigm if the trace extends beyond .25 sec. Thus, the conclusion that the mentally retarded acquire a simple CR as readily as normals is not supported by autonomic conditioning data. During extinction, mentally retarded CR performance is maintained at an equal or higher level than normal controls, that is, normal subjects extinguish more quickly than retardates. This was particularly clear in the Lobb study. The electrodes had been removed and all subjects had been told that no shocks would be given. We would expect a rapid decrement in CR performance among normals following such instructions (e.g. Grings and Lockhart, 1963). If retardates are not as capable of controlling autonomic responding via the cognitive registration of "no more shock" this fact could play a large part in the maintained performance of retardates during extinction. It is not clear from the Baumeister, et al. study whether subjects were told about extinction or whether the electrodes had been removed. If they were not told and the electrodes were kept in place (extinction followed acquisition immediately) we would expect less rapid extinction of GSR in normals. Thus, the apparent paradox of better or equal CR performance during extinction is most likely a combination of the greater ability of normals to control autonomic responding by means of verbal-cognitive processes and the relatively deficient inhibitory processes in the MR.

The Differential Conditioning Paradigm

In the studies just reviewed, a single CS and a brief inter-stimulus interval (2.0 sec or less) were employed. The term simple CR is applied to responses observed in such single cue, brief ISI paradigms because only one response occurs to the CS. Conditioning is usually inferred from a comparison with an appropriate control group in which CS and US are explicitly unpaired. If, however, the CS-US interval is extended, classical conditioning becomes an extraordinarily complex phenomenon. This is so because when the ISI exceeds the latency of the autonomic response system several discrete responses may occur during the CS-US interval. To complicate the situation further, when the US is withheld, as on test trials or during extinction, one or more responses will occur in the interval of US omission. The fact of several discrete autonomic responses occurring in the longer interval conditioning paradigm has been termed the *multiple response phenomenon* (Lockhart, 1966a). The occurrence of multiple responses raises the question of their status as conditioned responses and the further possibility that such responses may reflect the operation of different processes in the extended interval classical conditioning paradigm.

Before analyzing these questions further, the studies of differential and long ISI conditioning in the mentally retarded will be reviewed. The studies in question are those of Grings, Lockhart, and Dameron (1962), Grings, Lockhart, Zeiner and Uno (1964), and Block, Sersen, and Wortis (1970).

Grings, Lockhart and Dameron Study

In this study (1962), two groups of mentally retarded adolescents (mean IQ of 34 and 63) were conditioned in a differential delay paradigm. ISIs of .5 and 5 sec were compared orthogonally to IQ variation. Figure 6-1a illustrates the mean magnitude of differential responding (difference between CS+ and CS−) over trials for the .5 sec condition. Differential responding began near zero and increased gradually over trials. No difference in rate or magnitude of differential responding was found between the two IQ groups even though they differed widely in terms of intelligence and conceptual-verbal capacity. Thus, when the ISI is

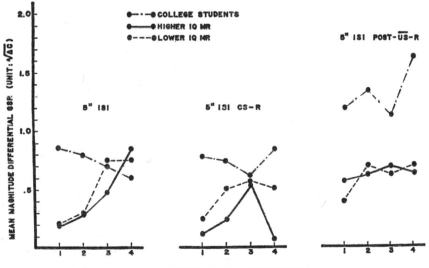

Figure 6-1. Mean magnitude of differential GSR for Lower IQ, Higher IQ, and college student subjects under ISI conditions of .5-sec (A) and 5-sec (B and C). (Redrawn from Grings, Lockhart, and Dameron, 1962, and Lockhart and Grings, 1964.)

quite brief, intelligence within the MR range sampled does not influence the degree of differential autonomic conditioning.

In duplicating this experiment with a college population (Lockhart and Grings, 1964), it was found that .5 sec differential conditioning developed suddenly, almost maximally with the first one or two differential reinforcements and without an increase during the remainder of the training. From Figure 6-1a, it can be seen that with the brief ISI, normal subjects exhibit differential responding more quickly and to a greater degree than do the mentally retarded. This difference between normals and MRs seems to be more accentuated in the differential paradigm than in the simple paradigms discussed earlier. The performance difference between normals and MRs evident in Figure 6-1a suggests a qualitatively different factor operating in the college student rather than a simple difference in rate of CR acquisition as proposed by Lobb (1968). That is, MRs may not be particularly deficient in conditioning per se, but deficient in those processes (presumably cognitive in nature) which underlie the rapid and abrupt conditioning performance in nonretarded populations. This point will be examined further in the following section.

When the CS-US interval is increased to 5 sec, the multiple response phenomenon occurs and differential conditioning becomes more complex. Figure 6-2 pictures one pattern of multiple responding found on acquisition test trials when the US is omitted. Lockhart (1966) suggests a terminology for referring to these responses in which the response closely tied to the onset of the stimulus is termed the *CS-R*, the response occurring just prior to the onset of the US is termed the *Pre-US-R*, and the response occurring in the normal UR interval when the US is omitted is termed the *Post-$\overline{US}$-R* (with the bar over US indicating US omission).

The multiple response phenomenon raises troublesome questions. Which response is the CR? Is each response a CR? How are these responses interrelated? Do the responses reflect different processes? These questions are by no means resolved and the issue of multiple responding is currently a center of focus in classical conditioning research. In connection with mental re-

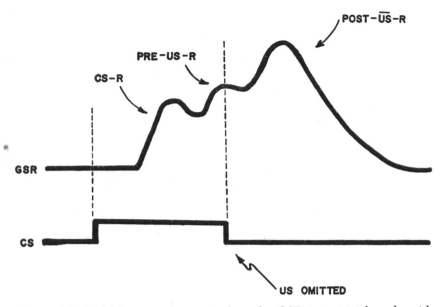

Figure 6-2. Multiple response terminology for GSR in test trial mode with US omitted.

tardation interest focuses naturally on how cognitive deficiency affects these different responses.

The Grings, et al. study provides the first evidence on this question. Figure 6-1b illustrates the mean differential response for the Lower IQ group, Higher IQ group, and a college student group (Lockhart and Grings, 1964) in terms of the CS-R (the initial response in CS+ and CS−) in the 5 sec ISI condition. As in the .5 sec case, the college student differentiates abruptly, while the retarded exhibit more gradual differentiation. Within the MR population, the Lower IQ group showed a consistently greater degree of differentiation than the Higher IQ group. The reason for this was the difference in responding to the CS−. The Lower IQ group did not respond on 55 percent of the CS− trials, while this was true of 38 percent of CS− trials in the Higher IQ group. In addition, responses to CS− were of smaller amplitude in the Lower IQ group. Both groups responded at the same level to CS+.

If nonresponding or lowered responding to CS− is taken as an indication of an inhibitory process, this study provides evidence that this type of inhibition is superior at lower levels of intelligence—a finding which contrasts with the popular inhibition-deficit notion of mental retardation. Grings, et al. interpreted this greater responsiveness on the nonreinforced cue in higher IQ subjects as "suggesting that the high IQ group indulges in more 'questioning' behavior, or more investigative concern for the cue which has never been associated with shock, than does the low IQ group." That is, higher level IQ subjects engage in a kind of primitive hypothesis testing and such activity, no doubt mediated by verbal and symbolic processes, expresses itself autonomically in more frequent and larger amplitude responses to CS−.

Perhaps the most important observation to be made in connection with these results is that differences between levels of intelligence within an MR population begin to appear with long ISIs, differences which are not evident when the ISI is very brief. Thus, the relationship between mental retardation and autonomic classical conditioning must necessarily take into account the temporal parameter. Systematic analysis of differences between levels of MR intelligence as a function of the ISI should yield considerable information concerning the interaction between intelligence and the kind of processes involved in long ISI situations.

Comparison of Figure 6-1a and 6-1b indicate that the final level of differentiation in the mentally retarded groups was higher when the CS-US interval was .5 sec, while early in acquisition, the longer interval condition produced more rapid and superior differentiation—particularly in the Lower IQ group. It should also be noted that the results for college subjects under the two conditions were nearly identical. In any case, it is obvious that satisfactory differential conditioning may be obtained even in profoundly retarded subjects when the ISI is relatively long. This contrasts sharply with the results of Lobb and Nugent (1966) and Lobb (1968) who found that MRs failed to condition in a trace paradigm when the trace interval exceeded 1.0 sec. The results of Grings, et al. should caution investigators from generalizing too broadly on the basis of results obtained only with brief ISIs.

Figure 6-1c illustrates differential responding occurring during the normal UR interval on test trials when US was omitted (Post-$\overline{US}$-R). Surprisingly, the earliest signs of differential responding occur in this interval. That is, before differential responding develops in the ISI, there is evidence of differential responding following the ISI at the point of normal US occurrence. Such a Post-$\overline{US}$-R might be interpreted as a response to the "omission" of the US. This idea is complicated by the failure to find signs of differential responding prior to the US. Presumably a differential set to perceive the US (a prerequisite to perceiving its absence) should be accompanied by differential autonomic responding. Grings, et al. consider the Post-$\overline{US}$-R as requiring a "reinterpretation of the nature of autonomic classical conditioning." Certainly conditioning research has always focused on responding during the ISI; the Post-$\overline{US}$-R, if nothing else, calls attention to a neglected but obviously significant characteristic of classical conditioning.

The Post-$\overline{US}$-R in the two retardate populations was more similar to the performance of the college subjects than was the CS-R. That is, differentiation was abrupt with little change during acquisition. Although the difference in performance between higher and lower IQ subjects was not significant, there was a tendency for the higher level subjects to exhibit more Post-$\overline{US}$-R differentiation than lower level subjects, the reverse of findings for the CS-R.

Magnitude data for the Pre-$\overline{US}$-R in this study are not available. However if the *frequency* of Pre-US-R is plotted as a function of differing levels of intelligence, an interesting relationship emerges. The data are shown in Figure 6-3. Data for CS+ and CS− are plotted for the MR groups reported in Grings, et al., and for college subjects reported in Lockhart and Grings. As is evident, the frequency of Pre-US-R during CS− is approximately equal for each group, while the frequency of Pre-US-R during CS+ increases as level of intelligence increases. In addition, it is clear that the differential frequency of such responses

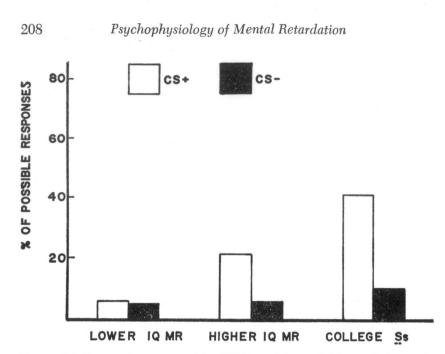

Figure 6-3. Percent frequency of Pre-US-R on CS+ and CS— trials for Higher and Lower IQ mentally retarded (Grings, Lockhart and Dameron, 1962) and college students (Lockhart and Grings, 1964).

increases indicating that Pre-US-R cannot be attributed solely to a responsitivity factor. *No other response exhibits this particular relationship to intelligence.* Lockhart (1966b) has commented on this finding in the following way:

> The Pre-US-R may prove to be the most sensitive indicator of second signal system functioning. This response may reflect the operation of perceptual-verbal relating processes by which the subject becomes aware of or expresses his awareness of CS-US contingencies.

This potential relationship between Pre-US-R and the hypothesized perceptual-verbal relating processes will be discussed further in the following section.

The results of the Grings, et al. experiment indicate that classical conditioning of autonomic responses is not a simple phenomenon even in the case of the mentally retarded. Not only is there a complex relationship between mental retardation and simple and differential conditioning paradigms, but when the

ISI is relatively long, conditioning seems to involve qualitatively different factors which express themselves in the form of multiple response phenomena.

Grings, Lockhart, Zoinor and Uno Study

In a study reported but not published, Grings, et al. (1964) repeated their earlier study with the additional feature of extending the ISI through various steps from 5 to 20 sec. Half the subjects were given *trace* extensions and the other half *delay* extensions. A differential conditioning paradigm was employed with an initial acquisition series given to all subjects at an ISI of 5 sec. Some subjects used in this study were also subjects in the previous study. GSR results with new subjects replicated those of the earlier study. Results with repeat subjects indicated an interference in conditioning performance only if the interstimulus interval represented a *change* from the first to the second experiment.

The main result of the experiment appears to be the finding that when ISI is extended differential conditioning persists more readily in the delay than in the trace mode. This was true both for Post-$\overline{\text{US}}$-R and responses occurring during the ISI. An important observation was that Higher IQ subjects exhibited more ISI responses during the extension trials than did Lower IQ subjects.

In this study, heart rate (HR) measures were also taken. The only analysis reported indicated that HR exhibited significant CS-R and Post-$\overline{\text{US}}$-R differential conditioning. Thus, the multiple response pattern, at least in terms of CS-R and Post-$\overline{\text{US}}$-R, was found to be significant both for GSR and HR.

Block, Sersen, and Wortis Study.

Block, et al. (1970) have provided the first systematic study of HR differential conditioning in the mentally retarded. In addition, the authors provided a reversal condition to assess the Russian hypothesis that mentally retarded are deficient in "mobility," that is, the ease of reversing a conditioned discrimination. Three main groups were studied: *normals* (subdivided into three age ranges of 2-4, 4-6, and 6-11 years); *mongoloids* (divided into two age ranges of 4-6 with mean IQ of 41.0; and 6-11 with mean

IQ of 41.7); and *encephalopathics* (one group ages 6-11 with mean IQ of 51.5). The diagnosis of encephalopathy emphasized that these patients were characterized by a type of *biological* retardation of uncertain cause.

The CSs were a 400 and 1,000 Hz pure tone with a duration of 5 sec. The US was an autohorn. The ISI was 5 sec. For all subjects, the 400 Hz tone was CS+ and the 1,000 Hz tone was CS−. No adaptation sequence was employed. The CS+ and CS− were *alternated* during the experiment and the intertrial interval apparently was nearly constant at 20 sec. After ten presentations of CS+ and CS−, both tones were reinforced for an additional ten trials each (a procedure the authors term "reinforced extinction"). The experiment was completed with 10 presentations of the CS+ and CS− with the US now paired with the previous CS− and the former CS+ now unreinforced.

The CR was interpreted as a higher HR during CS+ than during CS−. The only group showing significant differential responding during initial acquisition was the oldest (6-11 years) normal group. During the reinforced extinction phase, no group evidenced differential responding. During reversal, significant reversal responding was found in the two oldest normal groups. The mongoloids failed to show any evidence of differentiation at any time during the experiment. Paradoxically, the encephalopathy group responded significantly more during reversal phase to the formally reinforced stimulus than to the stimulus currently reinforced.

The authors compared degree of differential responding for each phase of the experiment with mental age. Correlations between mental age and performance scores ranged between +.11 (during discrimination) to −.11 (during reversal). These correlations were not significant.

In the normal group, the authors report an orderly increase in CR differentiation as a function of age, a result emphasizing the importance of developmental information in the interpretation of autonomic conditioning.

The authors interpreted the paradoxical reversal behavior of the encephalopathics as due to "a slowed conditioning ability" and "marked slowness to extinguish." In other words, the original differential CR was not as great as the normal but not as affected by reinforced extinction and thus persisted into the reversal phase with a tendency to respond more to the current CS— (former CS+) than to the current CS+ (former CS—).

The lack of correlation between performance and mental age supports the view that the critical variable in relating mental retardation to conditioning is presence or absence of brain damage (e.g. Franks and Franks, 1960). In interpreting these correlations, however, it must be kept in mind that the patient groups did not show significant differential conditioning.

Comparison of the Block, et al. failure to obtain differential autonomic conditioning conflicts with the relative ease of autonomic differentiation reported by Grings, et al. (1962) for GSR and heart rate (Grings, et al., 1964).

That age may be a factor is suggested by Block's, et al. failure to find significant differentiation in normal children younger than six years of age. If differentiation is a developmental phenomenon it might be expected to be slowed in the mentally retarded. That is, differential conditioning may not appear in the retarded until perhaps twelve years of age, i.e. near the age of subjects studied by Grings, et al. It should be remembered, however, that single-cue conditioning was found to occur in very young mentally retarded (Birch and Demb, 1959). It appears that an interaction between paradigm type and age may exist.

Another possibility is that GSR conditioning is affected differently than HR conditioning. Although Grings, et al. (1964) report overall HR conditioning, data are not available on a trial-by-trial comparison basis. That is, differential GSR conditioning may be more rapid than differential HR conditioning.

A third possibility is that Grings, et al. tended to study nonorganic retardates while Block, et al. specifically included organic pathology (although of unknown etiology). Autonomic differentiation in familial retardation may be superior to that in organic retardation. What is required is direct study of the effects of different types of organic and nonorganic retardation on conditioning.

CONCLUSIONS

In previous sections the existing experimental literature concerning classical conditioning of autonomic responses in the mentally retarded has been examined in terms of general characteristics of this research and the types of results obtained. Single-cue and differential conditioning paradigms have been considered separately. In the single-cue paradigm, trace conditioning was difficult to achieve in MRs at intervals exceeding a fraction of a second. Yet, in the differential paradigm, quite adequate and even rapid conditioning was found in profoundly retarded subjects at an ISI of several seconds. Obviously, the relation between retardation and classical conditioning of autonomic responses cannot be assessed without attention to the type of paradigm employed. However, based only on the results of existing studies, it is difficult to attribute the difference between single and multiple cue paradigm results solely to the paradigm difference. All but one of the single cue studies employed a *trace* procedure, while all differential paradigms have used a *delay* procedure. What is required is study of both paradigm types using trace and delay procedures under conditions of long and short ISI variation.

In connection with the importance of paradigm type, it should be mentioned that in the case of the eyeblink response, differential conditioning is more difficult to achieve than single cue conditioning (Ross, 1971). Ross believes that the single cue paradigm is primarily a *detection* task. The primary requirement for successful conditioning is a mechanism sensitive to stimulus occurrence, since each occurrence of CS invariably cues the US. In the differential paradigm, Ross finds two processes involved—*detection* and *recognition*. Not only must stimulus occurrences be detected, but stimuli must be recognized in terms of their history of pairing or nonpairing with US if the subject is to properly prepare for and anticipate the occurrence of US. Ross believes that it is the recognition processes that are more likely to be sensitive to cognitive functioning than are detection processes. Since mental retardation consists in large part of deficient cognitive functioning, it is reasonable to expect slower differential than simple conditioning in retardates.

At first glance this notion of deficient recognition processes is not supported by the autonomic conditioning data. The very rapid differential conditioning of the Post-US-R GSR in very low IQ retardates (Grings, et al., 1962) is hardly evidence of deficient recognition. However, at least two problems of interpretation must be considered. First, there exist no studies directly comparing single and multiple cue autonomic conditioning in the same population (or in the same subject). Such an experiment is absolutely necessary before differences between eyeblink and autonomic response data can become theoretically important. Second, the rapid autonomic conditioning of MRs in the differential paradigm was found only when the CS-US interval was rather long—intervals at which eyelid conditioning no longer occurs. As Ross emphasized, strict comparison of eyeblink and GSR topography is not possible. Which aspect of the multiple response pattern in GSR conditioning is to be compared with the single component eyeblink CR? If the Pre-US-R is taken as the comparison response to the anticipatory eyelid CR, then the autonomic data would seem to be consistent with the eyelid data. Although direct comparison has not been made, the relationship between Pre-US-R and level of intelligence pictured in Figure 6-3 suggests that Pre-US-R differentiation would be more difficult to achieve than simple acquisition of that response. However, answers to these questions obviously await future research.

Although the Post-$\overline{\text{US}}$-R exhibits very rapid differentiation in the MR, it is questionable whether this response involves cognitive mediation. The difference found between higher and lower IQ subjects with regard to the Pre-US-R CR has been found in studies where subjects are unaware of stimulus contingencies (as assessed by verbal report) (Lockhart, 1965), and is more common in lower animals than is the Pre-US-R (as distinct from CS-R). It is possible that Post-$\overline{\text{US}}$-R may occur without cognitive involvement and represent some basic characteristic of classical conditioning. Further study of such responding in MRs deficient in cognitive function should throw considerable light on the nature of this response and its relation to other responses of the multiple response pattern.

The data reviewed in previous sections also point to the critical importance of the temporal factor (ISI) in relating mental retardation and autonomic conditioning. The studies of long ISI conditioning have shown that it is not possible to directly compare short and long intervals as if there were a single, simple temporal continuum. The longer interval situations evoke qualitatively different phenomena than the shorter interval conditions. And, at least in the case of differential conditioning, it is in the longer interval conditions that differences between levels of retardation are accentuated. In particular, the occurrence of the Pre-US-R can be tentatively associated with the degree of deficiency, being quite common in the college student, less so in higher level retardates, and virtually absent in the lower level retardate. Of course this relationship must be more adequately verified than is the case at the present time, yet, if mental retardation is conceptualized as a deficiency in cognitive processing, particularly in terms of the mediating function of language, it is quite possible that the Pre-US-R represents a direct correlate of cognitive capacity. This notion receives empirical support from other areas as well. For example, there is no evidence of an early and distinct Pre-US-R in autonomic conditioning of animals although the response may appear after extensive training (Lockhart, 1970), the Pre-US-R is absent when the subject fails to verbalize the stimulus contingencies (Lockhart, 1965); the Pre-US-R is prominent when the subject verbalizes the contingencies (Fuhrer and Baer, 1965); and the Pre-US-R is more easily modified by verbal instructions than is any other response (Lockhart, 1968). Thus, the possibility exists that the Pre-US-R represents something unique to language capable subjects. In relation to mental retardation, the relative occurrence of such responding could be taken as a possible objective indicator of cognitive functioning.

The CS-R is often conceptualized as an *orienting* response occasioned by the subject's detection and attention to stimulus occurrence. Differential conditioning of this response reflects the involvement of recognition processes as well. Some authors speak of such differential CRs as *conditioned* orienting responses. This so-called conditioned orienting response is achieved rapidly in college students but more gradually in MRs. The relation between the differentially conditioned CS-R and degree of deficiency is complex. In the Grings, et al. (1962) study, higher level retardates were found to be responding more often and in larger degree to CS−, a result the authors attributed to the subjects' active perceptual involvement in the paradigm, rather than to deficient inhibitory processes. If degree of mental retardation was simply manifested in degree of inhibitory deficiency then the lower IQ subjects in that study should have been inferior in differential conditioning to the higher IQ subjects. If, however, autonomic responses are sensitive to verbal and cognitive processes, then as a retardate develops these functions he may respond to these factors in addition to or in contrast with the stimulus paradigm. In other words, the autonomic responding we see in a conditioning experiment may represent a type of interaction between the paradigm characteristics and the subject's perceptual-verbal response to the situation. If so, autonomic responding in lower levels of retardation should be more "paradigm bound," while higher levels of retardation should begin to exhibit the type of responding characteristic of cognitive involvement (e.g. abrupt acquisition and extinction, control of responding via instructions, etc.).

Perhaps the major research focus in the area of autonomic conditioning and mental retardation should be the determination of the extent to which mental retardation disrupts basic conditioning mechanisms and/or the cognitive mechanisms which are so prominently involved in autonomic behavior of normal subjects in classical conditioning situations.

The phenomenon of multiple responding and the relationship of mental deficiency to each component of the multiple response pattern are only hinted at in the studies available to the present time. However, it is not difficult to see that study of deficient cognitive processes can be a valuable means of understanding the mechanisms of attention, anticipation, and preparation which must underlie the phenomenon of multiple responding. Nor is it difficult to conceive that by understanding these mechanisms we might reach a point where autonomic responding in conditioning situations could be helpful both in finer assessment of cognitive deficiency and in designing techniques for improving deficient processes.

REFERENCES

Astrup, C., Sersen, E. A., and Wortis, J.: Conditioned reflex studies in mental retardation. A review. *Am J Ment Defic, 71*:513-530, 1967.

Baumeister, A. A., Beedle, R., and Urquhart, D.: GSR conditioning in normals and retardates. *Am J of Ment Defic, 69*:114-120, 1964.

Berger, A.: Inhibition of the eyelid reflex in three etiologic groups of mentally retarded boys as compared with normals. *Train Sch Bull, 51*:146-152, 1954.

Berkson, G.: Responsiveness of the mentally deficient. *Am J Ment Defic, 66*:277-286, 1961.

Birch, H. G., and Demb, H.: The formation and extinction of conditioned reflexes in "brain-damaged" and mongoloid children. *J Nerv Ment Dis, 129*:162-170, 1959.

Block, J. D., Sersen, E. A., and Wortis, J.: Cardiac classical conditioning and reversal in the mongoloid, encephalopathic and normal child. *Child Devel, 41*:771-785, 1970.

Cornil, L., and Goldenfoun, F.: Sur les reflexes associatifs chez les enfants anormaux. *C R Soc Biol, 99*:406-409, 1928.

Cromwell, R. L., Palk, B. F., and Foshee, J. G.: Studies in activity levels: V. Relationship of eyelid conditioning to intelligence and activity level. *Am J Ment Defic, 65*:744-748, 1961.

Denny, M. R.: Research in learning and performance. In Stevens, H. A. and Heber, R. (Eds.): *Mental Retardation, A Review of Research*. Chicago, University of Chicago, 1964.

Ellis, N. R. (Ed.): *Handbook of Mental Deficiency*. New York, McGraw-Hill, 1963.

———: The stimulus trace and behavioral inadequacy. In Ellis, N. R. (Ed.): *Handbook of Mental Deficiency*. New York, McGraw-Hill, 1963.

Franks, C., and Franks, V.: Conditionability in defectives and in normals as related to intelligence and organic deficit: The application of a learning theory model to a study of the learning process in mental defectives. *Proc London Conference Sci Studies Ment Defic, 2*:577-583, 1962.

Fuhrer, M. J., and Baer, P. E.: Differential classical conditioning: Verbalization of stimulus contingencies. *Science, 150*:1479-1481, 1965.

Gakkel, L. B., Mololkova, I. A., and Trofimov, N. M.: Experimental study of nervous processes in oligophrenics. *Zhurnal Visshei Nervnoi Deyatelmosti, 7:*495, 1957. *Psychol Abs, 32:*5649, 1958.

Grings, W. W., Lockhart, R. A., and Dameron, L. E.: Conditioning autonomic responses of mentally subnormal individuals. *Psychol Monogr, 76:* 39, whole No. 558:1-35, 1962.

———: Effects of "anxiety lessening" instructions and differential set development on the extinction of the GSR. *J Exp Psychol, 66:*292-299, 1963.

Grings, W. W., Lockhart, R. A., Zeiner, A., and Uno, T.: Delay and trace conditioning of mentally subnormal individuals. Paper presented at the Annual Convention of the American Psychological Association, September 7, 1964.

Krasnagorsky, N. I.: Uber die Grundmechanismus der Arbeit der Grosshirnrinde bei Kindern. *Jarhbuch fur Kinderheilkunde, 78:*374-398, 1913. (Described in Razran, 1933.)

Lipman, R. S.: Learning: verbal perceptual-motor, and classical conditioning. In Ellis, N. R. (Ed.): *Handbook of Mental Deficiency.* New York, McGraw-Hill, 1963.

Lobb, H.: Trace GSR conditioning with Benzedrine in mentally defective and normal adults. *Am J Ment Defic, 73:*329-346, 1968.

———: Frequency vs. magnitude of GSR in comparisons of retarded and nonretarded groups. *Am J Ment Defic, 75:*336-340, 1970.

Lobb, H., and Nugent, C. M.: Interaction between intelligence level and interstimulus trace interval in electrodermal conditioning. *Am J Ment Defic, 70:*549-555, 1966.

Lockhart, R. A., and Grings, W. W.: Interstimulus interval effects on GSR discrimination conditioning. *J Exp Psychol, 67:*209-214, 1964.

Lockhart, R. A.: Dominance and contiguity as interactive determinants of automatic conditioning. Ph.D. Dissertation, University of Southern California, 1965.

———: Comments regarding multiple response phenomena in long interstimulus interval conditioning. *Psychophysiology, 3:*108-114, 1966.

———: Recent developments in the classical conditioning of autonomic responses. Paper presented at the Symposium on Higher Nervous Activity, IV World Congress of Psychiatry, September 9, 1966, Madrid, Spain.

———: Distinguishing component processes reflected in autonomic behavior of human subjects during classical conditioning. Paper presented at the First International Symposium on Higher Nervous Activity, Milan, October, 1968.

Lockhart, R. A., and Steinbrecher, D. C.: Differential heart-rate conditioning in the rabit: Failure to find a specific pre-US response. *Psychon Sci, 19:*175-177, 1970.

Luria, A. R.: *The Nature of Human Conflicts.* New York, Liveright, 1932.

————: Experimental study of the higher nervous activity of the abnormal child. *J Ment Defic Res*, 3:1-22, 1959.

Marinesco, G., and Kreindler, A.: Des reflexes conditionnels. *J Psychol, 30:* 855-886, 1933.

Mateer, F.: *Child Behavior*. Boston, The Gorham Press, 1918.

Melhado, J.: Irradiation and Generalization in Aments. Unpublished Master's Thesis, University of New Hampshire, 1949.

Osipova, V. N.: Speed of formation of the associated reflex in school children. *Novoye v Reflexologii i Fiziologii Nervnoy System*, 2:218-234, 1926 (described in Razran, 1933).

Razran, G. H.: Conditioned responses in children—a behavioral and quantitative critical review of experimental studies. *Arch Psychol*, No. 148, 1933.

Razran, G.: The observable unconscious and the inferable conscious in current Soviet psychophysiology: Introceptive conditioning, semantic conditioning, and the orienting reflex. *Psycholog Rev*, 68:81-147, 1961.

Robinson, H. B., and Robinson, N. M.: *The Mentally Retarded Child, A Psychological Approach*. New York, McGraw-Hill, 1965.

Ross, L.: Classical conditioning and discrimination learning research with the mentally retarded. In Ellis, N. R. (Ed.): *International Review of Research in Mental Retardation*. Volume 1, New York, Academic Press, 1966.

Ross, L. E.: The role of awareness in differential conditioning. Paper presented at a symposium: Classical Conditioning and the Cognitive Processes. Annual Meeting of the Society for Psychophysiological Research, St. Louis, October 1971.

Sersen, E.: Conditioning and learning. In Wortis (Ed.): *Mental Retardation 1*, New York, Grune and Stratton, 1970.

Uno, T.: The effects of awareness and successive inhibition on interoceptive and exteroceptive conditioning of the Galvanic Skin Response. *Psychophysiology*, 7:27-43, 1970.

CHAPTER *7*

PSYCHOPHYSIOLOGICAL STUDIES OF DOWN'S SYNDROME CHILDREN AND THE EFFECTS OF ENVIRONMENTAL ENRICHMENT

FRED S. FEHR*

* This research was supported in part by Public Health Research Grant MH-07346 from the National Institute of Mental Health. I am especially indebted to Dr. Chalfant and Dr. Silikovitz of the University of Illinois at Urbana-Champaign for their willingness to share the language and IQ findings of their research, which was supported by grant OEG 0-8-001025-1777(032), Bureau of Research No. 7-1025 (Chalfant, 1970). Also I wish to express my appreciation to R. M. Wallace and C. A. Warren who collaborated with me in collecting some of the data reported in the latter part of this chapter.

219

THE STUDY OF DOWN'S SYNDROME may be viewed from numerous technical perspectives. The research aims related to this important child problem may be subdivided into three broad categories. These include (1) the delineation of characteristics which more completely and objectively distinguish this syndrome both from other retarded and also normal functioning children; (2) research efforts to determine the specific predisposing and/or causative etiological conditions of this syndrome and subsequent methods of prevention; and (3) the study of psychophysiological, psychological, pharmacological, and other parameters to alleviate disruptive symptoms and facilitate the relative readjustment of children already disposed to this disorder.

As with many research endeavors related to the study of this syndrome, psychophysiological investigations have first involved comparative studies of "normal" and Down's syndrome children to establish relevant findings and initiate the development of a theoretical model for a more comprehensive conceptualization of this retarded child problem. While these psychophysiological findings and theoretical assertions may indirectly influence the study of more specific etiological conditions of Down's syndrome, the emphasis of the present discourse is both to describe these comparative physiological findings and theoretical assertions in relation to behavioral adjustment, and also detail a longitudinal study of social and psychophysiological changes of Down's syndrome children as a function of environmental enrichment.

THEORETICAL CONSIDERATIONS

The rationale for the psychophysiological study of Down's syndrome children may be cast within at least two frames of reference. Traditionally, and suggested by clinical observations as well as experimental demonstration, peripheral autonomic variables, such as cardiovascular, plethysmographic, respiratory, skin resistance responses, and other autonomic changes, have been related to verbal and behavioral manifestations of arousal. Thus, in combination with verbal and skeletal motor responses, these autonomically innervated responses are particularly manifest in the organism's total reaction to simple sensory stimuli as well as to stimuli which have been either viewed as harmful, injurious, or associated with some form of stress within the past history of the organism. The literature supporting and elaborating this viewpoint is reviewed in a recent publication (Fehr and Stern, 1970).

A question may be raised as to the utility of this physiological approach as compared to other behavioral means of studying retarded children. The reasons for this approach are threefold. First, peripheral physiological responses are sensitive indices of environmental influences which may not be readily manifested either in the verbal expressions or general skeletal motor behavior of the young, disturbed and often uncommunicative retarded child. Second, peripheral physiological activity may function as interoceptive stimuli which feed back to the central nervous system and influence the child's perceptions and transactions with his environment. Third, interoceptive stimulation resulting from peripheral autonomic activity may be subject to different principles and have significance for the adjustment of the retarded child apart from that either demonstrated or inferred from findings in which exteroceptive stimulation and measures of skeletal motor responses are the primary independent and dependent variables, respectively.

Furthermore, autonomic responses have been hypothesized to be functionally related to levels of arousal and alertness. For example, Lacey and Lacey (1958) have theoretically related spontaneous fluctuations of autonomic responses, cortical activity, and skeletal motor functions. Accordingly, autonomically labile subjects are reported to demonstrate faster reaction time, greater impulsivity, and are characteristically hyperactive. On the other hand, individuals showing relatively few spontaneous fluctua-

tions tend to be low in hyperkinesis and are described as "phlegmatic, repressed, and lacking affect." These spontaneous fluctuations of peripheral physiological response systems are also proposed as "energizers" of central nervous system activity. Stern
(1966) has also provided findings and reviewed evidence to suggest that spontaneous fluctuations of peripheral systems may be
important for maintaining levels of central nervous system activity which are necessary for the organism to attend and respond to the environment. Consistent with this hypothesis, Stern,
Stewart, and Winokur (1961) have demonstrated a significant
positive relationship between spontaneous fluctuations and orienting responses to simple sensory stimuli. Furthermore, Corah
and Stern (1963) suggest that spontaneous fluctuations can be
experimentally influenced and related to alertness as described
in the work of Burch and Greiner (1960).

Findings from a number of studies suggest that Down's children may be appropriately considered within the context of the
aforementioned general experimental findings and theoretical
systems. These findings and hypothesized relationships will be reviewed and subsequently extended in a report of the longitudinal effects of enrichment procedures on the physiological and
behavioral functioning of Down's syndrome children.

The literature dealing with autonomic activity of Down's syndrome children is quite meager. When Down's syndrome children have been studied at all, they have usually been combined
with other classes of mental defectives (Karrer, 1966).

Generalizations that can be gleaned from the work with mental defectives as a whole seem to follow a pattern. The defectives usually demonstrate fewer spontaneous heart rate fluctuations and skin resistance fluctuations, some showing no fluctuations at all. To the onset of novel stimuli they often show less
reactivity than normals on skin resistance, heart rate, and a number of other physiological response systems. Furthermore, longer
reaction times are generally found with defectives than with
normals. These specific methodological operations and findings
will be detailed in the following sections.

REVIEW OF EXPERIMENTAL FINDINGS

Skin Resistance (SR)

Resting Levels

As compared to SR changes in response to stimulation, the findings regarding resting SR are apparently contrary. Collman (1931, 1959) consistently reported that defective groups demonstrated greater SR levels than normals. On the other hand, numerous other investigators (O'Connor and Venables, 1956; Ellis and Sloan, 1958; Berkson, Hermelin and O'Connor, 1961; Karrer and Clausen, 1964) have reported lower SR levels for defective groups as compared to normals. These latter findings suggest that in terms of resting levels the defective groups are more highly aroused and alerted than the normal control groups. While these findings generally suggest that defectives demonstrate higher levels of arousal as defined by resting SR measurements, the findings more specifically related to Down's syndrome children show that they have higher SR levels than other defectives, even when matched for IQ (O'Connor and Hermelin, 1963; see also Chap. 2). Also, they are not significantly different from normal control children in resting SR levels (Berkson, et al., 1961; O'Connor and Hermelin, 1963). Berkson, et al. (1961) speculate along with Tredgold (1956) that this difference between Down's syndrome children, and other defectives relative to normal controls, may be due to peripheral mechanisms related to the coarseness of Down's syndrome children's skin rather than differences in arousal. However, differences in skin coarseness would also influence measures of reactivity. As detailed below, retarded subgroups have not been so distinguished.

Responses to Programmed Stimuli

In Collman's (1931) review of the earlier literature, defective children with but one exception (Gregor and Gorn, 1913) were found to demonstrate minimal SR changes, especially to "ideational stimuli." Prideaux (1922) also found a similar insensitivity to simple sensory stimuli (e.g. threat of pin prick, a whistle, motor horn, and a Dalby's clacker) among twelve of seventeen "idiot" and four of fourteen "imbecile" groupings. In an extensive study with approximately equally large ($n = 100$) groups, Collman (1931) found defectives relative to normals exhibited less SR responsiveness to all forms of stimuli, but both gifted and defective children were less responsive to "concrete" simple sensory stimuli. Collman (1959) reported similar findings regarding gifted defective, and normal children to "simple words" (e.g. chocolate, toothache, ghost), simple addition, and pictures of the Royal Family of England. An inverted-U function between intelligence and SR responsiveness was suggested to best describe these findings. That is, while the retarded were relatively unattentive to the stimuli and thus autonomically unresponsive, the "bright" children by means of a "superior analysis of the elements of the situation" (p. 631) showed more efficient adaptation and thus were equally unresponsive. On the other hand, "dull" and normal children are suggested to be interposed between these extremes with increases in SR responsiveness proportional to assessed intelligence. Karrer and Clausen (1964) report similar trends for defectives in response to a 55 db buzzer. Moreover, Berkson, et al. (1961) report corresponding differences for skin potential measures of adult defectives in response to a brief flash of a 60 watt bulb. The intensity of this latter stimulus may reasonably well conform in part to conditions in a study by Wolfensberger and O'Connor (1965, 1967). They manipulated combinations of two light intensities and three durations to provide "six different types of stimuli." Contrary to previous findings (Collman, 1931, 1959; Berkson, et al., 1961; O'Connor and Hermelin, 1963), they report retardates as compared to normals to be *more* responsive to these simple stimulus conditions.

A number of possible explanations for these disparate findings may be considered. One explanation is suggested in the apparently overlooked findings of Collman (1931) regarding the SR response of highly anxious defective children. As distinguished by "two competent judges," fourteen of fifteen defectives characterized by "marked emotional instability" were noted to demonstrate a *greater* SR response than the median of a normal control group. Given that "many retardates . . . tend to be anxious and fearful" and required special pre-experimental setting instructions and treatment in the Wolfensberger and O'Connor study (1965, 1967), their findings may not be incompatible with earlier ones. Rather, their findings may qualify and emphasize the importance of anxiety as a variable often confounding the study of the relationship between intelligence and physiological reactivity. Ringness (1959, 1962), using more participatory active tasks (counting and stacking pennies and simple addition) with defective, normal, and high IQ children, found no differences on SR resting levels, variability, and reactivity.

Whereas Down's syndrome and other defective groups have been distinguished on resting SR measures, no differences between Down's syndrome and other defective groupings have been demonstrated as a function of mildly intense light flashes (Berkson, et al., 1961). Thus, in common with other retarded children, Down's syndrome children seemingly demonstrate reduced SR responsiveness which may be interpreted to suggest difficulties in obtaining and sustaining attention. As indicated by Moskowitz and Lohman (1970), some theorists (Zeaman and House, 1963) have suggested an attention deficit as the major factor in the learning disability of Down's syndrome children. Following the lead of Luria (1963) and Sokolov (1960), Moskowitz and Lohmann determined that Down's syndrome adults as compared to aged-matched normals required a 32 db greater intensity 1,000 Hertz tone to elicit an orienting SR response of 2,000 ohms or greater. Thus, thresholds for evoking a response were considerably greater than normal controls. Kimmel, Pendergrass, and Kimmel (1967) also report differences of orienting responses in defective groups as compared to normal controls. Moreover, when SR changes are instrumentally modified, these authors report that retardates demonstrate corresponding increases in attention and performance on relatively complex tasks.

This failure of attention may also account for the significant deficiency of conditioning of the SR responses of Down's syndrome children. Pairing a 7½ watt light CS with mild shock, Birch and Demb (1959) found that Down's syndrome children conditioned slower than either normal controls or brain-damaged groups of children with somewhat higher intelligence levels. Of great importance for conditioning studies is the need for determining the equivalence of CS and UCS intensities for normal and retarded groups so that differences in attention, conditioning, and learning are not confounded with the efficiency of sensory processes. If substantiated, the findings of Birch and Demb (1959) may suggest that Down's syndrome children are more resistent to SR conditioning procedures as compared to other defective groupings. Grings, Lockhart, and Dameron (1962) found no differences between two defective groups with mean IQ's of 34 and 63 respectively. Also, Baumeister, Beedle, and Urquhart (1964) found no skin resistance conditioning differences between defectives and normals (see Chap. 6).

Cardiovascular System

As described by Benda (1960), Down's syndrome children frequently have heart defects and thus, psychophysiological studies using this measure may be complicated. Beyond the first decade of life, approximately 25 percent of Down's syndrome children have suggestive evidence of a septum defect of the heart and other peculiarities of the vascular and capillary systems. According to Benda (1960), the entire system is inadequate, narrow, and thin, and the peripheral capillaries are underdeveloped. Similarly, the vessels of the brain are thin and less numerous than in controls. Consistent in part with the SR findings reviewed previously, Berkson, et al. (1961) and Karrer and Clausen (1964) report no differences in the resting HR levels of Down's syndrome children as compared to normals. Block, Sersen, and Wortis (1970) conclude that the significantly elevated prestimulus levels of their Down's syndrome samples relative to normals is contrary to these aforementioned findings.

This apparent discrepancy may be due to the fact that resting measures, obtained either while older more mature subjects are quietly reclining (Berkson, et al. 1961) or at the end of a fifteen-minute resting period (Karrer and Clausen, 1964), may not be expected to compare with prestimulus levels throughout an experiment in which the child is provided with play materials and periodically stimulated with a 95 db auto horn (Block, et al., 1970). In fact, this latter finding may be viewed more consistently with those of Carrier, Malpass, and Orton (1961) who found that *during the performance* of learning tasks institutionalized and noninstitutionalized retarded children were generally more aroused on a number of autonomic measures. They also had higher scores on the Children's Manifest Anxiety Scale. As noted by Karrer (1966) regarding these latter findings, the retarded children generally indicated little difference in arousal on the various tasks. According to him, this may be interpreted to suggest that retarded children demonstrate a more generalized nondiscriminative approach while performing various active learning tasks.

Consistent with the reviewed skin resistance findings of defectives generally, Down's syndrome children are reportedly less reactive than normals in response to stimulation in pulse rate (Vogel, 1961) and vascular responses (Razran, 1961). Karrer and Clausen (1964) have also found that defectives generally are less responsive in HR and HR variability than normal control subjects. Vogel (1961) has found no differences between Down's syndrome children and normals for blood pressure and finger volume measures.

Contrary findings are reported by Block, et al. (1970) in a cardiac classical conditioning experiment with Down's syndrome and normal controls. They found no differences in heart period variability, nor in response to a 400 and 1,000 hertz CS and auto horn UCS. In addition, Down's syndrome children indicated no evidence of cardiac discrimination. They concluded that the cardiac response of the four-to-eleven-year-old Down's syndrome children was similar to comparable MA two-to-four-year-old normal children.

If these positive heart rate findings between normal controls and Down's syndrome children are found to be valid, they, together with the known anatomical and physiological impairments referred to above by Benda (1960), may be especially important because of the role blood plays in the adequate intellectual and behavioral functions of the organism. A restricted supply of blood to skeletal motor and brain systems may be very primary in the inefficient functioning of the Down's syndrome child. For example, McIntire and Dutch (1964) report a generalized hypotonia in all major muscle groups of the Down's syndrome child, especially in the resting state. The relation of cerebral blood flow, metabolism, and the electroencephalogram (Himwich, 1943, 1951; Meyer, Sakamoto, Akiyama, Yoshida and Yoshitake, 1967) also provide findings which support this general conclusion. Moreover, autonomic responses may feed back to the central nervous system and influence levels of alertness as reflected in measures of the electroencephalogram.

Spontaneous Fluctuations of Autonomic Systems

Although spontaneous fluctuations as compared to reactivity to stimuli may have different behavioral and theoretical implications for the Down's syndrome child, there is some dispute as to the nature of these differences in physiological response systems. Compared to Lacey and Lacey's (1958) hypothesis that spontaneous fluctuations are intrinsic manifestations of cellular activity, Stern (1966) contends that spontaneous fluctuations are responses to stimuli that are not under the experimenter's control, such as extraneous noises, ideas, thoughts, hallucinations, daydreams, etc. Thus, according to Stern, the relationship between activity and spontaneous fluctuations may suggest that a system responsive to stimuli programmed by the experimenter is also responsive to extraneous kinds of stimuli. This latter hypothesis has some support in the studies of Corah and Stern (1963), Johnson (1962), and Martin (1963).

In spite of Collman's (1931) early report that defectives showed minimal interstimulus changes, relatively few investigators have attended to this variable of spontaneous fluctuation. Designated as "disconnected GSR" Collman (1959) in a later study again reported fewer fluctuations for retarded children but no differences between dull and normal groupings. Peculiar-ly, "bright" children demonstrated few if any spontaneous fluctuations in this same study. Karrer and Clausen (1964) found more defectives than normals who demonstrated fewer SR fluctuations and a tendency for fewer heart rate fluctuations. In the latter study, fluctuations of systolic blood pressure and finger volume measures did not distinguish these groups.

Electroencephalography (EEG)

Himwich (1943, 1951) has provided a comprehensive work in this area. He not only has demonstrated a relationship between EEG responses and cerebral rates of metabolism, but also has reviewed research on cerebral metabolism and mental deficiency. From his work, he concluded that in relation to cerebral metabolism there are two types of mental deficiency: one with normal cerebral metabolism and the other with a reduced rate of metabolism. He suggested that the cerebral metabolic rate is normal in the undifferentiated mental defective, but is below normal in patients with Down's syndrome, cretinism, phenylpyruvic-oligophrenia, advanced hydrocephalus, and microcephalus. With more elaborate techniques, Kennedy (1967) has provided some data to suggest that undifferentiated mental defectives also may have significantly lower rates of cerebral blood flow and cerebral oxygen rates.

Parallel to the peripheral autonomic findings reviewed to this point are the findings of the EEG of Down's syndrome children. That is, Down's syndrome children, and other defective children are often reported by investigators to demonstrate relatively more diffuse slowing of the EEG than normal controls. Hermelin and O'Connor (1968) excluded six of the sixteen Down's syndrome children as compared to two of ten normals from their study of alpha rhythms because of prominent 4 to 7 Hz theta rhythms in the recordings. Moreover, according to Seppalainen and Kivalo (1967), most investigators report "low-frequency waves" especially in the youngest age Down's syndrome groups. In their own study of ninety-two Down's syndrome subjects, these authors report negative EEGs in only 12 percent of their cases (the nature of these are not well specified). Possibly because of only brief periods between stimulus presentations (30 seconds between light flashes), Berkson, et al. (1961), however, did not find these differences contrasting Down's syndrome, defective, and normal children. Slowing of EEG rhythms as indicative of lower levels of arousal together with the finding that the EEG of their remaining Down's syndrome children were less aroused during the resting conditions, is consistent with the peripheral autonomic functions indicating reduced arousal.

High frequency activity (16 to 26 Hertz) is also a fairly common finding in Down's syndrome individuals (Godinova, 1963; Nakagawa, 1963; Gibbs, 1964). Thus, the contrary findings noted for peripheral functions are also well represented in the EEG literature of defective and Down's syndrome children. Again, as with the studies of autonomic functions, a consideration of instructions, set, and other variables involving the more subjective emotional reactions of the Down's syndrome individual might help to disentangle these seemingly diverse findings. Correlational findings within defective and normal classifications have been even more contrary in attempting to substantiate the hypothesized relationship between behavioral, intellectual functions, and the EEG. These will not be pursued here.

Finally and briefly, Berkson, et al. (1961) found that Down's syndrome children and other defectives showed less persistent alpha blocking to visual stimuli. However, Hermelin and O'Connor (1968) were unable to confirm this finding with either visual or auditory stimuli. Moreover, Hermelin and Venables (1964) report more persistent alpha blocking in Down's syndrome than in equivalent IQ defective groups to a complex of light-sound stimuli.

Reaction Time (RT)

Attempts to determine the behavorial implications of these psychophysiological parameters have most often involved simple reaction time studies. The hypothesized relation to alpha rhythms of the EEG has been suggested particularly from activation theory as depicted by Lindsley (1960) and supported in part by research of normal subjects. In these studies with normal samples (Lansing, Schwartz and Lindsley, 1959; Fedio, Mirsky,

Smith and Parry, 1961), an auditory warning signal resulting in alpha blocking was found to be positively related to reaction time. In a similar study, but with a visual warning signal, Hermelin and Venables (1964) were not able to confirm this hypothesis with either normal or Down's syndrome and defective children.

There are a number of studies demonstrating that defective children generally have longer reaction time than normals (Berkson, 1960a; Hermelin, 1964; Hermelin and Venables, 1964; Semmel, 1965). More complex tasks elicited slower responses than simpler tasks (Berkson, 1960b) and Down's syndrome children are generally found to have even longer latencies of response than other retarded children of the same IQ (Berkson, 1960; Hermelin, 1964; Hermelin and Venables, 1964).

Deprivation and Enrichment

Numerous studies have demonstrated that institutional experience has deleterious effects on psychological function (Lyle, 1959, 1960; Centerwell, 1960; Kugel and Reque, 1961; Kaufman, 1963, 1967). Relatively few studies have attempted in a very ambitious way to develop and evaluate the success of planned treatment programs on behavioral and physiological functions of retarded children. While the evidence reviewed and the theories alluded to previously are by no means parsimonious and entirely consistent across diverse conditions and general experimental settings, retarded children have been differentiated from normals on a number of variables. Hypotheses derived from these findings will subsequently be reiterated in an introduction to a detailed study of Down's syndrome children. First, brief mention may be made of some findings which provide some glimmer of hope for facilitating the development of the retarded child.

Benda (1960) reviews findings and advocates administration of vitamins and the use of thyroid and pituitary hormones. In one study (Benda, 1960), Down's syndrome children treated by these means demonstrated some improvement in mental age as compared to untreated controls. Reportedly, these infants often became more "active," "alert," and "responsive" to environmental stimuli.

Heber (1963) has reviewed a number of studies suggesting the facilitory effects of enrichment procedures on the development of retarded children. Clarke and Clarke (1954) and Clarke, Clarke, and Reiman (1958) have concluded from their research that retarded children may demonstrate significant increases in intelligence when removed from very impoverished environments and placed into more enriched ones. Kirk (1958) has demonstrated that retarded children receiving preschool education undergo significantly greater changes in intelligence and adjustment on the Binet, Kuhlmann, and Vineland measures. Finally, Vogel, Kun, and Meshorer (1967) reported that after four years of special educational classes, retarded children demonstrated rather minimal increases in intelligence as compared to the significant decrements observed for untreated retarded control children. Although Vogel, et al. (1967) concluded that the differences noted were thus related to further impairments in the latter as compared to the possible facilitory effects of the enriched children, certainly one must recognize that to sustain the IQ levels of retarded children actually means the mental age has been significantly increased over the four chronological ages of the study relative to previous development. Their findings would seem quite remarkable in suggesting that relative to normal controls the mental and chronological age of the treated retardates increased in a "normally" proportionate manner over these four enriched years. The studies reviewed thus far in this section have dealt with retarded children quite generally. Our research investigates the effects of enrichment on behavioral and physiological variables of Down's syndrome children. The study was designed to determine behavioral and physiological changes which accompany intensive training and general enrichment of the environment of Down's syndrome children. The physiological changes noted to accompany such a program might then be more directly conditioned and related to subsequent learning variables as suggested in Miller's recent review article (1969) and represented in the report of Kimmel, et al. (1967).

Hypotheses of the present study were derived in part from Lacey's theoretical system relating spontaneous fluctuations of autonomic responses, cortical activity, and skeletal-motor functions (Lacey and Lacey, 1958).

As indicated previously, autonomically labile subjects are reported to demonstrate faster reaction time, greater impulsivity, and are characteristically hyperactive. On the other hand, individuals showing relatively few spontaneous fluctuations tend to be low in hyperkinesis and are described as "phlegmatic, repressed, and lacking affect."

Findings reviewed above suggest that Down's syndrome children may be appropriately considered within the context of these theoretical systems. Together with other retarded children, they are often reported to show fewer spontaneous fluctuations of physiological systems than normal controls. Moreover, they are less physiologically responsive to novel stimulation and demonstrate a longer latency of reaction time. The relationship between spontaneous fluctuations and skeletal-motor responses was supported in an initial study by Wallace and Fehr (1970). In this latter study, reaction time, body movement, heart rate, and skin resistance of Down's syndrome and normal control children were evaluated under baseline and distraction conditions. Relative to controls, Down's syndrome children demonstrated slower reaction time under both conditions, a reduced skin resistance response and fewer heart rate fluctuations during the baseline period, and fewer skin resistance fluctuations during the distraction condition. Furthermore, skin resistance fluctuations were negatively correlated with reaction time. Heart rate fluctuations, although not significant, were in the same direction. These findings offered some support for the theoretical assertions of Lacey and Lacey (1958) that spontaneous activity is related to motor impulsivity, cortical activity, and general skeletal-motor functions. Body movement was negatively related to these measures of spontaneous activity and thus could be invoked as an explanation for the findings.

A STUDY WITH DOWN'S SYNDROME CHILDREN

To extend these earlier comparisons of Down's syndrome children and a matched group of normal controls following gen-

eral enrichment of the environment of Down's syndrome children was our specific intent. We reasoned that physiological responses of Down's syndrome children would be sensitive indices
of the effects of the environmental enrichment procedures. Assuming these intervening training and educational procedures to
be successful, one may observe, together with the development
of both greater language and intellectual skills, corresponding
changes in physiological responsiveness associated with increasing
levels of "alertness" and responsiveness to environmental stimulation. More specifically, it was predicted that the Down's syndrome children would show a shorter latency of RT, increased
spontaneous fluctuations, and enhanced responsiveness to simple
sensory stimulation following the enrichment program.

Intervening Enrichment

During the course of the initial and follow-up study, these
Down's syndrome children participated in a systematic intensive
enrichment program. This program was carried out during a
twelve-month period especially under the direction of James C.
Chalfant (1970; Chalfant, Silikovitz and Tawney, 1973). These
children resided in the Herman Adler Zone Center. Curricula included the development of self-help skills, a receptive and expressive language program, and recreational and motor-perform-
ance activities. While a wealth of idiographic data was collected
and reported in their project, only mental-age (Stanford-Binet,
Form L-M) and the number of intelligible verbalizations are to
be related to the behavioral and physiological measures of the
present study.

Method

Subjects

The sample consisted of six female and four male Down's
syndrome children (mean age—six years, one month, S.D. = 9.13
months; IQ ranged from 5 to 50), and an equal number of normal controls individually matched for sex and chronological age.

Apparatus and Procedure

Physiological and behavioral response were recorded simultaneously with a Grass Model 7P4A tachograph, skin resistance with

a model 7P1A DC preamplifier. Skin electrodes were attached to the left index and ring fingers, and HR electrodes were attached to the upper arm and left lower leg. Each subject was briefly retrained to press a telegraph key to terminate a mildly aversive buzzer (70 ± 5 db). Because we questioned the ability of the Down's syndrome children to understand the instructions to press a telegraph key "rapidly" or "as quickly as possible," verbal instructions were minimized and the pressing of the telegraph key was instead demonstrated and imitated. Thus, "fast" reaction time was not emphasized for either the Down's syndrome or the control children.

After approximately five minutes of retraining and five minutes of rest, the subjects received seven presentations of the mildly aversive auditory stimulus on a variable interval schedule of 25 to 50 seconds. Each stimulus presentation was terminated by the subject depressing a telegraph key attached to the arm of the chair. The onset and duration of the auditory stimulus was recorded on the polygraph, and this provided the measure of RT during this base condition. Subsequently, subjects viewed a motion picture sound cartoon, "Peter and the Wolf," while performing the RT Task for seven additional trials (distraction condition). As in the initial study, the competing stimulation of the film was assumed to complicate the task and delay the reaction to the primary auditory stimulus.

Data Analysis

Three measures of SR were scored. (1) Resting levels were determined at the beginning and end of the experiment. (2) Spontaneous fluctuations were scored by dividing each inter-trial interval period into ten-second segments (these periods did not include and/or overlap the evoked response periods). In each segment the maximum *change* in resistance level was scored. The variance of each subject's scores was defined as his measure of spontaneous SR fluctuations. (3) Evoked responses were defined by substracting the maximum resistance change during an equal period prior to buzzer stimulation from the maximum change from baseline during stimulation. These evoked physiological responses did not overlap the RT response period.

Three analogous measures were computed for heart rate (basal level, spontaneous fluctuations, and evoked responses). For each ten-second period during the intertrial interval, the shortest interbeat interval was recorded in beats per minute. The mean of all these intervals was taken as an index of basal level heart rate. The variance of these shortest interbeat intervals became our index of spontaneous fluctuations. Evoked heart rate responses were scored as the shortest interbeat interval during stimulation minus the shortest interval before stimulation. These difference scores were based upon periods of equal duration.

These measures were collected prior to the enrichment (Wallace and Fehr, 1970) and after the twelve-month enrichment.

Results

Mental Age and Verbalization

From our own within-group analysis of Chalfant (1970) data, the Down's syndrome children demonstrated a significant increase in mental age (mean increase = 6.3 months, $t = 6.66$ $p < .001$) during this twelve-month period. As a rough estimate, and assuming a linear relationship between mental age and chronological age, this change relative to their past average yearly development indicated a facilitation of their measured abilities of 33.79 percent ($t = 1.99$, $p < .05$). Similarly, enhancement of their language abilities was suggested by the number of intelligible verbalizations ($t = 3.164$, $p < .01$). These within-group comparisons of change are consistent with the hypothesis that language and intellectual functions may be influenced by enrichment procedures. That is, while still very disparate from normal adequately functioning children, these findings suggest the potential ameliorative effects of intensive training and other educational techniques. We then investigated the change in physiological functioning of these Down's syndrome children relative to a matched normal control group under baseline and distraction conditions and with respect to the behavioral changes.

Reaction Time and Autonomic Response

From inspection of the data of the pre and post studies, the data of the latter study appeared to be generally less variable than the data of the preenrichment period. For the purpose of evaluating group differences and also changes from pre to postenrichment periods, the data of all the dependent measures of this study were logarithmically transformed and analyzed both by an overall repeated measures anova and, subsequently, to determine simple effects, by means of planned t-test comparisons as described by Ferguson (1959).

The overall anova results (F ratios and significance levels) are presented in Table 7-I for each of the dependent variables of this study. A number of main effects and interactions can be noted to attain acceptable levels of significance. Down's syndrome children (B comparison) demonstrated significantly longer latencies of RT and generally fewer SR fluctuations than controls. Reaction time results (C comparisons) are complex as detailed below, but the overall trend was for increased RT from

TABLE 7-I

F RATIOS FOR EACH DEPENDENT VARIABLE (AFTER LOGARITHMIC TRANSFORM) AS A FUNCTION OF GROUPS, FILM, AND PRE-POST CONDITIONS OF THIS EXPERIMENT

Source	df	RT	SR Rest	HR Rest	SR Fluct.	HR Fluct.	SR Response	HR Response
Groups (B) ...	1	18.39‡	.01	.29	6.09†	2.02	1.60	2.13
Subjects (A) ..	15							
Pre-Post (C) ..	1	2.27*	1.07	.94	5.71†	.94	.79	1.32
B × C	1	.01	.09	.01	.06	4.83†	1.12	3.66*
A × C	15							
Film (D)	1	40.71‡	50.21‡	18.06‡	.00	.19	6.24†	3.12*
B × D	1	3.58†	5.14†	.19	.49	3.79†	.86	3.52*
A × D	15							
C × D	1	7.15‡	4.41†	.16	1.00	.07	1.39	.10
B × C × D ...	1	2.98*	1.11	.32	.30	.41	2.99*	.40
A × C × D	15							

* $p < .10$.
† $p < .05$.
‡ $p < .01$.

pre to post measures. Similarly, SR fluctuations generally declined from pre- to post-measurements.

For the nonfilm and film main effects (D comparisons), reaction time latencies were generally increased, resting SR decreased, resting HR decreased, and SR and HR responses to the auditory reaction time stimulus decreased during the film as compared to the nonfilm conditions.

The interaction results of this study may be more readily understood by examining the anova breakdown and simpler comparisons as presented in Table 7-II. In Table 7-II, the mean values are presented for the pre and post conditions. Also, t-values for comparisons of pre to post changes within each group as well as t-values for comparisons between groups for the postenrichment condition (last column) are presented. These postenrichment comparisons indicate significant differences between the Down's and normals on the reaction time and HR fluctuation measures.

TABLE 7-II

COMPARISONS BETWEEN GROUPS AND OF THE CHANGES FROM
PRE TO POST ENRICHMENT FOR BEHAVIORAL AND PHYSIOLOGICAL
RESPONSES OF DOWN'S SYNDROME (DS) AND NORMAL CONTROLS
(C) DURING FILM (F) AND NON-FILM (N) CONDITIONS
(T-TESTS OF SIMPLE EFFECTS AFTER ANOVA, FERGUSON, 1959)

Measure	Condition	DS Means Pre	Post	t	C Means Pre	Post	t	C vs. DS t Post
RT (sec)	1 N	3.45	2.88	1.76†	1.81	1.86	.01	2.34*
	2 F	6.40	9.03	9.41	2.33	2.92	1.79	7.69†
Rest SR	1 N	47.1	61.23	.21	46.3	48.55	.11	.31
(× 1000 ohm)	2 F	48.5	31.56	6.15‡	44.8	38.91	1.04	.51
Rest HR	1 N	105.89	109.60	—	101.72	105.07	—	—
(bpm)	2 F	102.26	106.28	—	100.06	102.70	—	—
SR Fluct.	1 N	2.17	1.58	.12	1.45	.98	.13	1.21
(× 1000 ohm)	2 F	.85	1.30	.14	3.14	.97	5.73‡	1.21
HR Fluct.	1 N	14.63	52.21	3.66‡	31.53	29.39	.02	1.70*
(bpm)	2 F	26.34	36.82	.23	21.26	14.83	1.00	4.83‡
SR Response	1 N	1.24	1.63	.50	4.16	2.43	11.95‡	.71
(× 1000 ohm)	2 F	1.16	1.10	.12	1.50	1.50	.41	.22
HR Response	1 N	−.54	3.23	2.74‡	+2.33	1.93	.01	.1
(bpm)	2 F	+1.35	3.14	.02	+2.06	1.80	.00	.03

* $p < .1$.
† $p < .05$.
‡ $p < .025$.

After enrichment the Down's children demonstrated significantly shorter RT, increased HR fluctuations, and greater HR responsiveness to the auditory signal during the non-film condition. For the film condition, they demonstrated significantly longer RT and a decrease in resting SR after enrichment.

Within the normal group, significant changes from pre to post periods were more generally in the direction of lower levels of arousal. That is, significantly longer RT, and decreased SR fluctuation can be noted for the film condition. Similarly, for the non-film condition, normal children were significantly less responsive on the SR measure from pre to post periods.

Intercorrelations

These dependent variables were also correlated with the changes in intellectual and language functions reported in Chalfant's Down's syndrome project (1970). First, preenrichment mental age (base MA) was correlated with RT, HR, and SR measures of the initial study (the base period for this follow-up). The higher the base MA the greater were the HR fluctuations ($r = .657$, $p < .05$), and the faster the RT during the base nonfilm period ($-.59$, $p < .1$). During the film period, base MA was positively correlated only with HR fluctuations ($.786$, $p < .01$).

Second, changes in MA from pre to postenrichment were correspondingly correlated with changes in the other measures after enrichment. Generally, only during the film condition were changes in MA and number of intelligible verbalizations significantly related to RT changes, and HR and SR fluctuations. Thus, the greater the increase in MA over the twelve-month program period, the greater the decrease in RT ($-.67$, $p < .05$), and the greater the increase in HR and SR fluctuations ($.72$ & $.75$, respectively, $p < .05$). Verbalization results were very similar to these results (i.e. $-.69$, $.61$, $.64$). The consistency of these relationships was particularly marked for the film condition, but not at all evident for the nonfilm condition. Correlations were also computed for the resting and evoked HR and SR data, but none were significant, and most were negligibly related to the abilities measures.

DISCUSSION

As noted in the preenrichment study (Wallace and Fehr, 1970), and consistent with Karrer's review of the literature (1966), Down's syndrome children generally demonstrated a longer RT than normal children. For the nonfilm condition the Down's children had faster RT after enrichment. This faster reaction time during the nonfilm period was also accompanied by significantly increased HR responsiveness, and a greater number of HR fluctuations. While the Down's group tended to sustain the same level of SR responsiveness from pre to post measurements as compared to the habituated response of the normal controls, an untreated Down's control group would be necessary to meaningfully interpret this result. However, Karrer (1966) suggests that the habituation of autonomic responses appear to be similar for normal and exceptional children. Thus, the sustained levels of SR responsiveness of the Down's as compared to the controls, may be of interest to subsequent researchers.

In the preenrichment comparisons (Wallace and Fehr, 1970), Down's children demonstrated a longer latency of RT, fewer HR fluctuations, and less HR and SR responsiveness to auditory stimulation. Thus, the changes noted postenrichment during the nonfilm period suggest reaction time and physiological changes in the direction of the normal group.

The only exceptions to these changes for the nonfilm condition were for resting HR, resting SR, and SR fluctuations which were, however, consistently not differentiated in the preenrichment condition.

Within the framework of Lacey's theoretical system and the findings and theoretical assertions of Stern reviewed above, increased spontaneous fluctuations and responsiveness of physiological systems may enhance CNS activity, increase general responsiveness to the environment, and increase the likelihood that an alerted and attending organism will subsequently be more susceptible to learning procedures. Thus, as a function of concentrated training and educational efforts, Down's syndrome children may become generally more physiologically and behaviorally responsive and "alerted" to environmental stimulation.

The correlational findings between the dependent variables of the present study and the intellectual and language measures recorded by Chalfant (1970) are in part consistent with this analysis. The higher the base MA of Down's children at the beginning of the enrichment program, the faster the reaction time, and the greater were the heart rate fluctuations. Similarly, changes in MA and language functions from the first to the follow-up study were correspondingly related to reaction time change and both HR and SR fluctuations, but only for the distraction condition.

However, while Down's children, as compared to controls, showed a tendency to respond with faster RT during the non-film period, they demonstrated a significant slowing in RT during the distraction condition. This finding is contrary to prediction. Seemingly, they were more distracted by the extraneous and competing aspects of the film than formerly.

The physiological findings for the film condition of the present study, together with those of Cohen, Silverman, and Burch (1956), provide a possible explanation for the apparent deterioration of the simple reaction time performance of these Down's children. Accordingly, Cohen, et al. (1956) suggests that autonomic responses monotonically increase as one progresses from low to high extremes on the arousal continuum. Moreover, while specific physiological responses to stimulation increase from low to moderate arousal levels, these specific responses decrease from moderate to high levels of arousal. At high levels of arousal, as in the distraction condition of the present study, RT performance may also be impaired. The results of the present study are not consistent with this interpretation. Based on an analysis of the SR levels from the beginning to the end of the distraction condition, the Down's children did sustain higher levels of arousal in the post than in the preenrichment study. However, the HR and SR response and fluctuation measures are not consistent with this inverted interpretation between autonomic responses and performance.

The findings have several implications for the further study and possible treatment of Down's children. Most basically, these physiological measures may prove especially helpful as sensitive and very immediate indices of the child's attention and response to training, education, and pharmacological treatment endeavors. Because of language and other problems of communication, attempts to determine relevant stimulus dimensions and problem complexities which may be successfully applied in the study and treatment of Down's children are presently very limited. The findings of the present study, together with the findings and theoretical systems reviewed, may provide a useful alternative.

REFERENCES

Baumeister, A. A., Beedle, R., and Urquhart, D.: GSR conditioning in normals and retardates. *Am J Ment Defic, 69:*114-120, 1964.

Benda, C. E.: *Mongolism and Cretinism.* New York, Grune and Stratton, 1949.

Berkson, G.: An analysis of reaction time in normal and mentally deficient young men. I. Duration threshold experiment. *J Ment Defic Res, 4:*pt. 1, 51-58, 1960(a).

——: An analysis of reaction time in normal and mentally deficient young men. II. Variation of complexity in reaction time task. *J Ment Defic Res, 4:*pt. 1, 59-67, 1960(b).

——: Responsiveness of the mentally deficient. *Am J Ment Defic, 66:* 277-286, 1961.

Berkson, G., Hermelin, B., and O'Connor, N.: Physiological responses of normals and institutionalized mental defectives to repeated stimuli. *J Ment Defic Res, 5:*pt. 1, 30-39, 1961.

Birch, H. G., and Demb, H.: The formation and extinction of conditioned reflexes in "brain-damaged" and mongoloid children. *J Nerv Ment Dis, 129:*162-170, 1959.

Block, J. D., Sersen, E. A., and Wortis, J.: Cardiac classical conditioning and reversal in the mongoloid, encephalopathic, and normal child. *Child Dev, 41:*771-785, 1970.

Boneau, C. A.: The effects of violations of assumptions underlying the *t* test. *Psychol Bull, 57:*49-64, 1960.

——: A comparison of the power of the U and *t* tests. *Psychol Rev, 69:* 246-256, 1962.

Burch, N. R., and Greiner, T. H.: A bioelectric scale of human alertness: Concurrent recordings of the EEG and GSR. *Psychiatric Research Report,* No. 12, 1960.

Carrier, N. A., Malpass, L. F., and Orton, K. D.: *Responses of Bright, Nor-*

mal, and Retarded Children to Learning Tasks. Carbondale, Southern Illinois University, 1961.

Centerwell, S. A., and Centerwell, W. R.: A study of children with mongolism reared in the home compared with those reared away from home. *Pediatrics, 25:*678-685, 1960.

Chalfant, J.: Final report, O. E. Grant 0-8-001025—1777 (032), Bur. Research No. 7-1025. 1970.

Chalfant, J., Silikovitz, R., and Tawney, J.: *Systematic Instruction for Retarded Children: the Illinois Program.* Danville, Interstate, 1973.

Clarke, A. D. B., and Clarke, A. M.: Cognitive changes in the feebleminded. *Brit J Psychol, 45:*173-179, 1954.

Clarke, A. D. B., Clarke, A. M., and Reiman, S.: Cognitive and social changes in the feebleminded—three further studies. *Br J Psychol, 49:* 144-157, 1958.

Cohen, S. I., Silverman, A. J., and Burch, N. R.: A technique for the assessment of affect change. *J Nerv Ment Dis, 124:*352-360, 1956.

Collman, R. D.: The psychogalvanic reactions of exceptional and normal children. *Contributions to Education,* No. 469, New York, Teacher's College, 1931.

———: The galvanic skin responses of mentally retarded and other children in England. *Am J Ment Defic, 63:*626-632, 1959.

Corah, N. L., and Stern, J. A.: Stability and adaption of some measures of electrodermal activity in children. *J Exp Psychol, 65:*80-85, 1963.

Ellis, N. R., and Sloan, W.: The relationship between intelligence and skin conductance. *Am J Ment Defic, 63:*304-306, 1958.

Fedio, P., Mirsky, A. F., Smith, W. J., and Parry, D.: Reaction time and EEG activation in normal and schizophrenic subjects. *Electroencephalog Clin Neurophysiol, 13:*923-926, 1961.

Fehr, F. S., and Stern, J. A.: Peripheral physiological variables and emotion: The James-Lange theory revisited. *Psychol Bull, 74:*411-424, 1970.

Ferguson, G. A.: *Statistical Analysis in Psychology and Education.* New York, McGraw-Hill, 1959.

Gibbs, E. L., Gibbs, F. A., and Hirsch, W.: Rarity of 14- and 6-per-second positive spiking among mongoloids. *Neurol, 14:*581, 1964.

Godinova, M. A.: Electroencephalographic changes in Down's syndrome. *Zb Neuropat Psikhiat, 63:*1058, 1963.

Gregor, A., and Gorn, W.: Zur psychopathologischen Klinischen Bedentung des psychogalvanischen Phänomens. *Z ges Neurol Psychiat, 16:*1-104, 1913.

Grings, W. S., Lockhart, R. A., and Dameron, L. E.: Conditioning autonomic responses of mentally subnormal individuals. *Psychol Monogr, 76:* No. 39, 1962.

Heber, R. F.: The educable mentally retarded. In S. A. Kirk and B. B.

Weiner (Eds.): *Behavioral Research on Exceptional Children.* Washington, D.C., The Council for Exceptional Children, 1963.

Hermelin, B., and O'Connor, N.: Measures of the occipital alpha rhythm in normal, subnormal and autistic children. *Br J Psychiat, 114:*603-610, 1968.

Hermelin, B.: Effects of variation in the warning signal on reaction times of severe subnormals. *Q J Exp Psychol, 16:*241-249, 1964.

Hermelin, B., and O'Connor, N.: Recognition of shapes by normal and subnormal children. *Br J Psychol, 52:*281, 1961.

———: Effects of sensory input and sensory dominance on severely disturbed autistic children and on subnormal controls. *Br J Psychol, 55:* 201-206, 1964.

Hermelin, B., and Venables, P. H.: Reaction time and alpha blocking in normal and severely subnormal subjects. *J Exp Psychol, 67:*365-372, 1964.

Himwich, H. E.: *Brain Metabolism and Cerebral Disorders.* Baltimore, Williams and Wilkins, 1951.

Himwich, H. E., and Fazekas, J. F.: Cerebral arteriovenous oxygen difference: I. Effect of age and mental deficiency. *Arch Neurol Psych, 50:* 546, 1943.

Johnson, L. D.: Spontaneous autonomic activity, autonomic reactivity and adaptation. Report 62-7, U.S. Navy Medical and Neuropsychiatric Research Unit, San Diego, California, 1962.

Karrer, R.: Autonomic nervous system functions and behavior: A review of experimental studies with mental defectives. In N. R. Ellis (ed.): *International Review of Research in Mental Retardation.* Vol. 2. New York, Academic, 1966.

Karrer, R., and Clausen, J.: A comparison of mentally deficient and normal individuals upon four dimensions of autonomic activity. *J Ment Defic Res, 8:*149-163, 1964.

Kaufman, M. E.: The formation of a learning set in institutional and non-institutional children. *Am J Ment Defic, 67:*601-605, 1963.

———: The effects of institutionalization on development of stereotyped and social behaviors in mental defectives. *Am J Ment Defic, 71:*581-585, 1967.

Kennedy, C.: The cerebral metabolic rate in mentally retarded children. *Arch Neurol, 16:*55-58, 1967.

Kimmel, H. D., Pendergrass, V. E., and Kimmel, E. B.: Modifying children's orienting reactions instrumentally. *Cond Refl, 2:*227-228, 1967.

Kirk, S. A.: *Early Education of the Mentally Retarded.* Urbana, University of Illinois Press, 1958.

Knights, R. M., Hyman, J. A., and Wozny, M. A.: Psychomotor abilities of familial, brain-injured and mongoloid retarded children. *Am J Ment Defic, 70:*454-457, 1965.

Knights, R. M., Atkinson, B. R., and Hyman, J. A.: Tactual discrimination and motor skills in mongoloid and non-mongoloid retardates and normal children. *Am J Ment Defic, 71*:984-1000, 1967.

Kugel, R. B., and Reque, D.: A comparison of mongoloid children. *J Am Med Assoc, 175*:959-961, 1961.

Lacey, J. I., and Lacey, B. C.: The relationship of resting autonomic activity to motor impulsivity. *Proc Assoc Res Nerv Ment Dis, 36*:144-209, 1958.

Lansing, R. W., Schwartz, E., and Lindsley, D. B.: Reaction time and EEG activation under alerted and nonalerted conditions. *J Exp Psychol, 58:* 1-7, 1959.

Lindsley, D. B.: Attention, consciousness, sleep, and wakefulness. In J. Field, H. W. Magoun, and V. E. Hall (Eds.): *Handbook of Physiology.* Sec. 1, Vol. 3. Washington, American Physiological Society, 1960.

Luria, A. R. (Ed.): *The Mentally Retarded Child.* Translated and distributed by O. T. S. U.S. Department of Commerce, 1963 (JPRS: 10615, CSO:6692-N).

Lyle, J. G.: The effect of an institution environment upon the verbal development of delinquents. *Am J Psychiat, 3*:121-128, 1959.

————: The effect of an institution environment upon the verbal development of imbecile children. II. Speech and language. *J Ment Defic Res, 4*:1-13, 1960.

McIntire, M. S., and Dutch, S. J.: Mongolism and generalized hypotonia. *Am J Ment Defic, 68*:669-670, 1964.

Martin, I.: A note on reflex sensitivity and formation of conditioned responses. *Behav Res Ther, 64*:185-190, 1963.

Meyer, J. S., Sakamoto, K., Akiyama, M., Yoshida, K., and Yoshitake, S.: Monitoring cerebral blood flow, metabolism and EEC. *Electroenceph Clin Neurophysiol, 23*:497-508, 1967.

Miller, N. E.: Learning of visceral and glandular responses. *Science, 163:* 434-445, 1969.

Moskowitz, H., and Lohmann, W.: Auditory threshold for evoking an orienting reflex in mongoloid patients. *Percept Mot Skills, 31*:879-882, 1970.

Nakagawa, S.: Electroencephalographic studies of mental deficiency. *Jap J Child Psychiat* (Kyota), *4*:40, 1963.

O'Connor, N., and Hermelin, B.: *Speech and Thought in Severe Subnormality.* New York, Macmillan, 1963.

O'Connor, N., and Venables, P. H.: A note on the basal level of skin conductance and Binet IQ. *Br J Psychol, 47*:148-149, 1956.

Prideaux, E.: Expression of emotion in cases of mental disorder as shown by the pyschogalvanic reflex. *Br J Psychol Med, 2*:23-46, 1922.

Razran, G.: The observable unconscious and the inferable conscious in current Soviet psychophysiology: Interoceptive conditioning, semantic conditioning and the orienting reflex. *Psychol Rev, 68*:81-147, 1961.

Ringness, T. A.: GSR during learning activities of children of low, average, and high intelligence. *Child Dev, 33*:879-889, 1962.

Ringness, T. A.: Emotional reactions to learning situations as related to the learning efficiency of mentally retarded children. U. S. Office Educ Proj SAE Univ Wisc 1959.

Semmel, M. I.: Arousal theory and vigilance behavior of educable mentally retarded and average children. *Am J Ment Defic, 70*:38-47, 1965.

Seppäläinen, A. M., and Kivalo, E.: EEG findings and epilepsy in Down's Syndrome. *J Ment Defic Res, 2*:116-125, 1967.

Sokolov, E. N.: Neuronal models and the orienting reflex. In M. A. B. Brazier (Ed.): *The Central Nervous System and Behavior.* New York, Josiah Macy, Jr., Foundation, 1960.

Stern, J. A.: Stability-lability of physiological response systems. *Ann NY Acad Sci, 134*:1018-1027, 1966.

Stern, J. A.; Stewart, M. A., and Winokur, G.: An investigation of some relationships between various measures of galvanic skin response. *J Psychosomat Res, 5*:215-223, 1961.

Tredgold, R. F., and Soddy, K.: *A Textbook of Mental Deficiency.* London, Baillière, 1956.

Vogel, W.: The relationship of age and intelligence to autonomic functioning. *J Comp Physiol Psychol, 54*:133-138, 1961.

Vogel, W., Kun, K. J., and Meshorer, E.: Effects of environmental enrichment and environmental deprivation on cognitive functioning in institutionalized retardates. *J Consult Psychol, 31*:570-576, 1967.

Wallace, R. M., and Fehr, F. S.: Heart rate, skin resistance, and reaction time of mongoloid and normal controls under baseline and distraction conditions. *Psychophysiology, 6*:722-731, 1970.

Wolfensberger, W., and O'Connor, N.: Stimulus intensity and duration effects on EEG and GSR responses of normals and retardates. *Am J Ment Defic, 70*:21-37, 1965.

———: Relative effectiveness of galvanic skin responses latency, amplitude and duration scores as measures of arousal and habituation in normal and retarded adults. *Psychophysiology, 3*:345-350, 1967.

Zeaman, D., and House, B. J.: The role of attention in retardate discrimination learning. In N. R. Ellis (Ed.): *Handbook of Mental Deficiency.* New York, McGraw-Hill, 1963.

CHAPTER 8

THE DEVELOPMENT OF THE EVOKED RESPONSE AS A DIAGNOSTIC AND EVALUATIVE PROCEDURE

ROBERT E. DUSTMAN, THOMAS SCHENKENBERG*
AND EDWARD C. BECK

* Supported in part by National Institute of Child Health and Human Development, Contract PH-43-67-1451. Special thanks is given to Dr. James W. Prescott who administered the contract and gave generously with his ideas and advice.

Acknowledgement is made to Mr. David Ditsworth, senior medical student, University of Utah College of Medicine, for his valuable contribution to the study, The Effects of Socioeconomic Deprivation on Evoked Responses.

Dr. Patrick F. Bray, Professor of Pediatrics and Neurology, University of Utah College of Medicine, and Dr. Walter E. Needham, Clinical and Research Psychologist, West Haven VA Hospital, and Assistant Professor, Department of Neurology, Yale University, were principal investigators in the study: Visual Evoked Potentials of Patients with Centrencephalic Epilepsy: Evidence for a Genetic Etiology.

THE PRESENT STATUS OF BRAIN RESEARCH has far exceeded the expectancies of two decades ago. At that time so little was known about brain function and its relationship to higher mental processes that many psychologists disregarded the brain in their theorizing and experiments, confining themselves mainly to an analysis of the stimulus and the response and ignoring the intervening function of the central nervous system. With recent technical advances the leap from brain to mind appears to be plausible, indeed, "mental processes" are being reduced, albeit rather grossly, to electrical and chemical changes that can be measured and analyzed.

Two approaches or techniques have contributed significantly to this surge of information regarding brain function. One is the advance in biochemistry, particularly in relation to cell physiology. The other involves recent strides in electronics wherein high speed computers have come to be used in the analysis of bioelectrical signals emitted by the brain and sense organs. Experiments that will be described in this chapter derive mainly from the latter approach, e.g. the application of computers in the analysis of electrical patterns or signals emitted by the brain in response to a variety of sensory stimuli. The wave form configuration of these electrical patterns, or averaged evoked responses as they are called, is affected by a variety of conditions. This chapter focuses on changes in evoked responses which occur throughout maturation, during senility, with ingestion of drugs, and with a number of clinical conditions including brain injury or dysfunction.

The evoked response, or evoked potential, is the electrical response of the brain to a brief peripherally applied stimulus such as a pulse of light, a shock or brief touch or a click by way of the respective sensory pathways. Single evoked response recordings have a long history and should not be confused with summed or averaged evoked responses. Single evoked responses were seen on cathode oscilloscopes or directly in the electroencephalogram. From these "older" methods it was concluded for years that the response of the brain to an instantaneous stimulus is a simple biphasic or triphasic wave lasting only a small fraction of a second. With the averaging or summing of evoked responses, methods that will be subsequently described, it was found that the response is much more complex. There are six or more phase shifts rather than two or three, and the response endures, not for a few milliseconds as previously thought, but often for several hundred milliseconds.

The process of averaging or summing eliminates or reduces the ongoing background brain activity that obscures the wave form of the response, thus providing an increase in signal-to-noise ratio and allowing the evoked response to emerge. It is a rather simple technique involving multiple stimuli rather than a single stimulus. With each flash or other stimulus, a series of brain waves occurs that differs from the ongoing background electrical activity in that it is time locked or time related to the stimulus. If one takes a number of samples, generally fifty or more, the random background electrical turbulence of the brain tends to average or to sum algebraically towards zero, while the recurring time locked waves precipitated by the neural volley as it arrives at cortex emerge as a consistent, complex response. Thus, in a sense the computer "extracts" the evoked response from the ongoing brain patterns. The evoked response is generally described in terms of several waves or phase shifts reaching peaks at reliably identifiable points in time after the presentation of the stimulus.

Interestingly, the nature of the evoking stimulus is faithfully reflected in the electrical pattern of the evoked response, i.e. visual, auditory and somatosensory evoked responses have unique patterns which characterize them. The same is true with complex stimuli such as patterned light or light of different spectra. These differ from responses to unpatterned light even though the intensities are identical.

The evoked response technique has several advantages over older recordings of spontaneous electrical activity of the brain, the EEG. In contrast to the EEG, evoked responses are under stimulus control and, thereby, provide additional information about the different sensory systems, functionally different pathways and brain areas involved in the response. Further, evoked responses lend themselves to more quantifiable analysis than does the EEG trace.

A feature of the evoked response that makes it extremely promising as a tool in brain research is that its various components appear to be determined or affected by different cerebral systems or brain structures (Bishop and Clare, 1953; Andersen and Eccles, 1962; Towe, et al., 1964; Towe, 1965; Heath and Galbraith, 1966). Also a high correlation exists between the pattern of a surface recorded evoked response and the firing pattern of certain individual cortical cells (Fox and O'Brien, 1965; Creutzfeldt, et al., 1969).

Most investigators divide the evoked response into two main temporal sequences which have come to be known as the *primary* or short latency response and the postprimary or *secondary* response. The primary response generally includes a short surface positive wave and a subsequent slowly rising surface negative wave. These are the first and generally the smallest components of the evoked response in the human. With human subjects we record from scalp and hence because of the electrical resistance of skull and scalp, the primary responses are small or often missing. These components are large and clearly seen in responses of experimental animals when the recording is directly from the dura or cortex. The primary response is believed to represent activation of cortical elements in lower layers of the cortex, i.e. the arrival of a geniculo-cortical volley initiated by the stimulus, the initial surface positive component representing activation of cortical elements in the lower pyramidal layers and the subsequent surface-negative phase of the primary response representing the antidromic conduction upwards through pyramidal cell apical dendrites (Chang and Kaada, 1950; Bishop and Clare, 1953; Tasaki, et al., 1954; Widen and Ajmone-Marsan, 1960).

As we will not deal with the primary response in the majority of studies that we report, its elaboration may seem academic, however, as we and others speculate that the primary or early short latency components of the evoked response are "sensory receiving" in function as contrasted to the presumed function of "information processing" assigned to later components, some discussion of the nature of the primary response is indicated. Some identifying features of the primary response are that it (1) is confined to primary sensory areas (Jasper, et al., 1955; Cigánek, 1961; Hirsch, et al., 1961; Goff, et al., 1962), (2) remains unchanged under anesthesia, during sleep, and during changes in the psychological state of the organism and (3) has a fairly rapid recovery cycle (Allison, 1962; Torres and Warner, 1962; Abrahamian, et al., 1963; Goff, et al., 1966). The point to be stressed is that a change in the latency or amplitude of the primary response reflects some change along pathways from receptor organ to *specific* thalamic nuclei and thence to a *restricted* primary sensory area of the cortex.

The *secondary* response comprises components generally arriving 70 msec or later after a stimulus and is more directly related to the interests of psychologists. It is characterized by being polysensory in nature, i.e. responses to different stimuli may be elicited from the *same* areas of associational cortex. Secondary responses are markedly sensitive to changes in level of consciousness as well as to anesthesia and sleep, disappearing during these latter conditions and increasing in amplitude with increased levels of attention. They are widely and bilaterally distributed over the cortex and reportedly change with a number of psychological and psychopathological conditions (Davis, 1964; Haider, et al., 1964; Satterfield, 1965; Sutton, et al., 1965; Callaway, 1966; Sakai, et al., 1966; Shagass and Schwartz, 1966). Since the secondary components are affected by conditions related to attention, consciousness and certain behavioral changes, it has been repeatedly speculated that they are affected by, or related to, nerve impulses conducted extralemniscally by way of the reticular formation or the midline thalamic nuclei (French, 1960; Jasper, 1960; Goff, et al., 1962, 1966; Dustman and Beck, 1965a; Bergamini and Bergamasco, 1967). In view of these findings the evoked response technique offers promise in probing the electrophysiological substrate of psychological processes.

We report now on the methods, equipment and experiments we have employed to investigate this relationship.

EQUIPMENT AND PROCEDURE

Figure 8-1 is a block diagram of the equipment used to evoke, record and average responses. Equipment changes have occurred throughout our experiments, but Figure 8-1 describes our most efficient method of data acquisition and storage.

Evoked responses were recorded from most subjects while they were seated in a comfortable padded chair in a sound deadened, darkened room which was electrically shielded. Nonambulatory patients were frequently seated in wheel chairs during recording

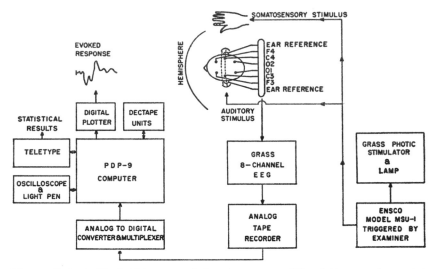

Figure 8-1. A Block Diagram of the Apparatus. Stimulating equipment is on the right, recording equipment in the center, and data reduction equipment on the left of the figure. ENSCO MSU-1 is a locally manufactured shock and sound source device.

procedures, and infants on their mothers' laps. While electrode placements varied slightly from one study to another, the electrodes were usually placed at F_3, F_4, C_3, C_4, O_1 and O_2 according to the International "10-20" System. All recordings were unipolar with both ear lobes combined serving as a reference.

Stimuli (flashes, clicks or shocks) were triggered manually at two to three second intervals during artifact free periods of EEG. The brain waves were amplified by an eight channel Grass EEG machine and, together with pulses accompanying stimuli, were stored on magnetic tape by a seven-channel magnetic data recorder. The stored EEG was then played into either a Computer of Average Transients (CAT) or the analog-digital converter of a Digital Equipment Corporation PDP-9 computer (Figure 8-1). Responses which were averaged by the CAT were plotted on graph paper by an X-Y plotter. When the PDP-9 computer was used, the resulting digital values were stored on digital tape from which they could be retrieved for plotting by a digital plotter. The sampling rate employed was usually 400/sec for the CAT and 500/sec for the PDP-9 computer.

Visual stimuli of 10 microsecond duration were generated by a photic stimulator. With few exceptions the setting on the stimulator was at PS = 2 on a scale of 1-16. The stimulator lamp was enclosed in a fiber glass and foam rubber container to muffle clicks accompanying flashes. The lamp was positioned behind and directly above the subject's head and was aimed at a reflecting hemisphere 70 cm in diameter. The hemisphere was used to ensure a relatively constant level of retinal illumination regardless of the position of the subject's head. The center of the hemisphere was 70 cm from the lamp and 40 cm from the subject's eyes. At a stimulator setting of PS = 2, the measured luminance at the center of the hemisphere was 12.

To obtain auditory evoked responses, clicks of 0.25 msec duration and 80 db intensity with reference to 0.0002 microbars were delivered to subjects binaurally through earphones. These relatively low intensity stimuli were used to decrease the possibility of myogenic contamination of the auditory responses.

Somatosensory responses were evoked by 0.25 msec electrical

pulses. The stimulus intensity for each subject was based on his subjective threshold, which was determined by the method of ascending and descending limits. The stimulus intensities employed in the studies to be reported varied from 1.5 to 3.5 times

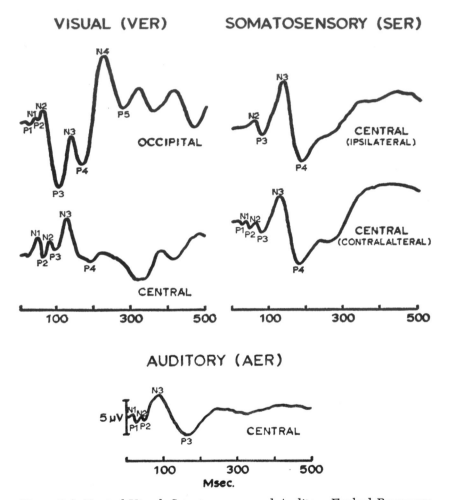

Figure 8-2. Typical Visual, Somatosensory and Auditory Evoked Responses. The difference in wave form of the visual response when recorded from central and occipital areas may be seen in the upper left of the figure. Additional components in the somatosensory response when recorded contralaterally may be seen by comparing somatosensory responses in the upper right of the figure.

the threshold values obtained. The stimuli were delivered to the subject's left or right index finger through two silver clip electrodes. A copper cuff was placed on the forearm to ground the spread of shock artifact. Figure 8-2 illustrates typical visual (VER), somatosensory (SER) and auditory (AER) evoked responses with the various wave components commonly observed. In this and all subsequent figures an upward deflection indicates a negative voltage change.

The results of the studies to be reported will be concerned with three types of measurement: peak delay, wave component amplitude and an overall amplitude measure encompassing a specified time segment of an evoked response. Peak delays were measured in milliseconds from the beginning of an evoked response (time zero) to the peaks shown in Figure 8-2. Wave component amplitudes, measured in microvolts, were determined by measuring the vertical distance between two peaks of opposite polarity. The overall amplitude measure was obtained by tracing the wave form of responses with a map reading wheel which yielded measurements in centimeters, or by using the PDP-9 computer to calculate the actual total voltage change (regardless of the direction, positive or negative) occurring within a time segment of the response.

RELIABILITY

The reliability of the averaged evoked response was an early concern for us and others. Before a measure can be useful, its reliability or reproducibility over time must be established. This is particularly true if diagnostic application is contemplated. To determine evoked response reliability we proceeded as follows. A baseline for each response was established by drawing a horizontal line below the base of the largest positive deflection which occurred within the first 250 msec. One hundred vertical lines, equally spaced within the first 250 msec of the response, were drawn from the baseline to the point of intersection with the response (see Fig. 8-3). The distance in millimeters between the baseline and each intersection was determined for each of the 100 lines. These amplitude values describing the contours of one evoked response could then be correlated (Pearson product-

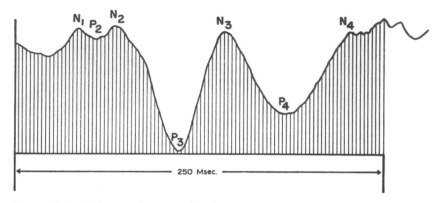

Figure 8-3. A Summed VER. The figure illustrates a method of obtaining evoked response amplitude measures which can be correlated with amplitude measures from a second response.

moment correlation) with similarly derived values from a second response (see Dustman and Beck, 1963).

The reliability data to be reported are from three groups of normal subjects and are concerned with visual and somatosensory responses. The first group participated in five recording sessions while the other two groups participated in two sessions. The interval between sessions was approximately a month.

For a particular recording site, the two or five responses obtained from each subject were intercorrelated, thus yielding ten correlations for each member of Group 1, $\frac{N(N-1)}{2}$, and a single correlation for members of the remaining two groups. The correlations were converted to Fisher Z scores which have a normal sampling distribution prior to computing the group mean reliability coefficients shown in Table 8-I.

In Figure 8-4 three of the five VERs recorded from left occipital scalp of each of four subjects in Group 1 are superimposed to illustrate the marked reproducibility of the evoked responses of most subjects. The mean correlations for subjects W.M., M.R., I.A. and B.B. were .92, .92, .90 and .94, respectively. Also of interest are the individual differences reflected among the four sets of responses. Even though the major waves in the responses of different individuals occur at approximately the

TABLE 8-I

MEAN EVOKED RESPONSE RELIABILITY COEFFICIENTS FOR
THREE GROUPS OF NORMAL SUBJECTS

Group	N	Age	Stimulus	Left Central	Right Central	Left Occipital	Right Occipital
1	10	26-36	Flash	.88	.89	.86	.87
2	20	10-11	Flash	.84	.87	.92	.92
3	24	5-16	Flash	.81	.84	.91	.88
3	24	5-16	Shock	.87	.86	—	—

same time, the overall configurations of the responses are notice-
ably different.

To determine the degree of evoked response similarity (homogeneity) among subjects, the responses from each brain area
of the ten subjects in Group 1 were intercorrelated. The mean
intersubject correlations for left and right central scalp were .58
and .63 and for left and right occipital scalp they were .51 and
.52. These correlations, although much smaller than the reliability coefficients, are fairly respectable positive correlations, again

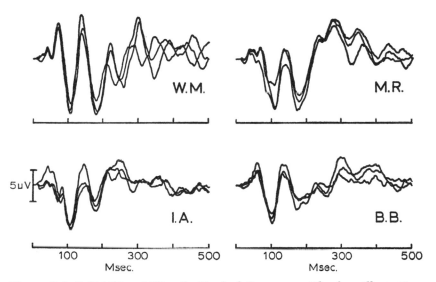

Figure 8-4. Reliability of Visually Evoked Responses. The four illustrations
show the superimposition of averaged visually evoked responses recorded
at monthly intervals for four subjects.

attesting to the fact that there is a reasonable degree of similarity among the evoked response wave forms of different individuals.

To observe gross differences between the evoked responses of two groups of subjects or before and after a treatment has been imposed on a single group, averaged group composites are often useful. These are obtained by averaging all of the responses of all members of a group. Figure 8-5 illustrates overlays of three composites for responses from each of four scalp areas of the ten subjects in Group 1. Thus each tracing represents the responses to 1000 flashes of light, i.e. 100 flashes per subject. The mean month to month reliability coefficient for these responses was .97 indicating that they are extremely stable over time.

With evidence that the averaged evoked response was reliable and unique we moved on to other studies. These were divided into two main groups. The first group was parametric or normative. In this group we studied the evoked responses of twins, and the effects of handedness, age, sex differences, intellectual level

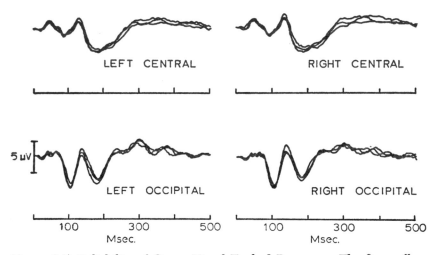

Figure 8-5. Reliability of Group Visual Evoked Responses. The figure illustrates overlays of three group composite responses for each of four scalp areas. The group was composed of 10 subjects. Superimposed group composites are from responses separated by one month.

and attention on the evoked response. The second group of studies was an attempt to evaluate the clinical usefulness of the technique, applying it to a number of abnormal subjects and situations.

NORMATIVE STUDIES

The Evoked Response of Twins

Having demonstrated that the evoked response is a stable measure and that it reflects individual differences, we were interested in studying response similarities in monozygotic and dizygotic twins. Experiments were designed to determine whether the evoked response has an hereditary basis, as had been shown earlier for EEG tracings by Lennox, et al. (1945), who concluded after scrutinizing EEG tracings of seventy-one pairs of twins that the EEG pattern does appear to be an hereditary trait.

We recorded visually evoked responses from twelve pairs of monozygotic twins, eleven pairs of dizygotic twins and twelve pairs of unrelated children age matched with the monozygotic pairs (Dustman and Beck, 1965b). Zygosity was determined by: identity of physical features, similarity of iris pigmentation, presence or absence of hair between the first and second joints of fingers, blood groups, M-N agglutination, Rh factor and ridge count of finger patterns (Rife, 1933a, 1933b).

The first 250 msec of the evoked responses of each pair of subjects were correlated using the methods described above. The correlations were made for responses from left central and left occipital scalp. After the correlations had been converted to Fisher Z scores, an analysis of variance was computed to test for differences between the mean correlations of the three groups. See Table 8-II for a listing of mean correlations. The analysis of variance yielded an F ratio of 8.82, df 2/33, ($p < 0.001$). A Duncan Multiple Range Test (to evaluate differences between means) showed that identical twin correlations were reliably larger than those of the other two groups ($p < 0.01$), while the mean correlations of the nonidentical twins and age-matched controls were not different. An illustration of the striking similarity between the evoked responses of some pairs of identical

TABLE 8-II

A COMPARISON OF COEFFICIENTS OF CORRELATION OF EVOKED RESPONSES AMONG IDENTICAL TWINS,
NONIDENTICAL TWINS AND CHILDREN MATCHED FOR AGE

Group	Number of pairs	Mean age (in years and months)	Age range (in years)	Region of recording	$\bar{X}r$	Range
Identical twins	12	12, 5	5-17	Occipital	0.82	0.41-0.93
				Central	0.74	0.29-0.94
Nonidentical twins	11	15, 3	7-15	Occipital	0.58	-0.05-0.90
				Central	0.48	-0.24-0.75
Children matched for age	12	12, 3	5-17	Occipital	0.61	-0.07-0.78
				Central	0.53	-0.20-0.82

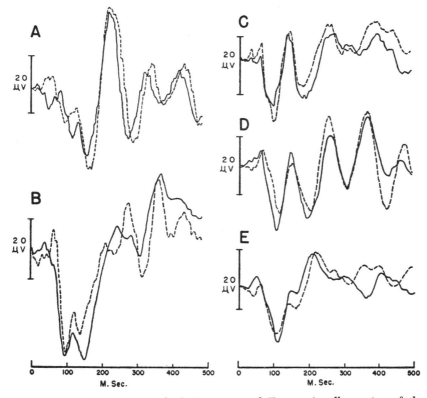

Figure 8-6. The Visual Evoked Responses of Twins. An illustration of the individuality and similarity of visually evoked responses of five sets of identical twins. (A) 11-year-old girls, r = .93; (B) 14-year-old boys, r = .90; (C) 15-year-old boys, r = .92; (D) 7-year-old girls, r = .93; (E) 9-year-old girls, r = .87. (From Dustman & Beck, 1965b, by courtesy of the Editor of *Electroenceph Clin Neurophysiol*)

twins is shown in Figure 8-6. The responses in this figure also demonstrate the unique qualities found in responses of different individuals.

Handedness and the Evoked Response

Asymmetry of functions in man and other mammals has long been recognized. The predominance of right sidedness in man is a salient example. Related to this is the observation that handedness is associated with cerebral dominance for speech, with the left hemisphere almost always dominant among right-handed persons.

A few studies have investigated the relationship between handedness and laterality of EEG background activity. The comparisons have generally been based on the amplitude and frequency of alpha rhythm. Raney (1939) studying alpha rhythm in mirror-image twins, monozygotic twins discordant for handedness, found that right-handed twins had larger hemispheric differences in amount of alpha than did their left-handed counterparts. The tendency for increased alpha was generally towards the right or nondominant hemisphere.

Several investigators report asymmetrical amplitude with photic driving (Cornil and Gastaut, 1951; Kooi, et al., 1957; Hughes and Curtin, 1960; Lansing and Thomas, 1964). The results have been contradictory. While the majority of studies reported greater amplitude from the nondominant or minor hemisphere, Lansing and Thomas (1964) found the opposite, greater amplitude from the dominant hemisphere. Still others (Williams and Reynell, 1945; Glandville and Antonities, 1955) found no asymmetries.

To date no studies have reported on cerebral evoked responses recorded from the dominant and nondominant hemispheres of left- and right-handed subjects. Because the evoked response technique could provide for more precise hemispheric comparisons than the EEG, we decided to pursue the problem.

The subjects were forty college students. Twenty were right-handed and twenty left-handed. Handedness was determined by a written test (Crovitz and Zener, 1962) as well as by a number of physical tests for lateralization including relative coordination, grip strength and reaction time.

Averaged cerebral evoked responses evoked by finger shock and light pulses were obtained from each subject. Somatosensory evoked responses were recorded from left and right central scalp. Stimulus intensity was 2.5 times subjective threshold. Two hundred shocks were delivered to the left or right index finger, selected randomly, followed by 200 to the other, so that from each of the two scalp locations two SERs were obtained, one contralateral and one ipsilateral to the shocked hand. Visual evoked responses to 100 flashes were also recorded from occipital and central scalp as previously described. To preclude any amplitude bias due to possible differences in amplification characteristics associated with the various EEG channels, the channels employed for recording brain potentials were randomly paired with the scalp electrodes of each subject.

A striking result was observed in the somatosensory responses. Amplitudes of the late waves P3-N3 and N3-P4 were much larger in the responses of the right handed subjects, regardless of the scalp area from which records were made, or whether the responses were contralateral or ipsilateral to the stimulated finger. For example the mean N3-P4 amplitudes for contralateral responses from the left- and right-handed groups were 6.2 and 13.8 microvolts respectively, 7.6 and 15.4 microvolts for ipsilateral responses (see Fig. 8-7). The means in both pairs were statistically different ($p < 0.001$). Evoked response wave amplitudes from left central scalp were not significantly different from amplitudes of corresponding waves from right central scalp. Hence, while somatosensory responses showed differences between the right- and left-handed subjects, the differences were not related to asymmetry.

The visually evoked responses yielded still different results. While handedness was not related to VER wave amplitudes, significant differences between left and right VERs recorded from central scalp were found for *both* groups. Waves N2-P3, P3-N3 and N3-P4 were all reliably larger for responses recorded from the right side ($p < 0.01$, 0.001 and 0.01 respectively). Figure 8-8 shows that while these differences were seen in the responses of both right- and left-handed subjects, they were more pronounced for the right-handed group. It should be emphasized that these differences were confined to evoked responses recorded from central scalp leads; no differences were noted from occipital recordings.

From the above findings it was concluded that there are no evoked response hemispheric asymmetries peculiar to handedness. Handedness was, however, reflected in the somatosensory re-

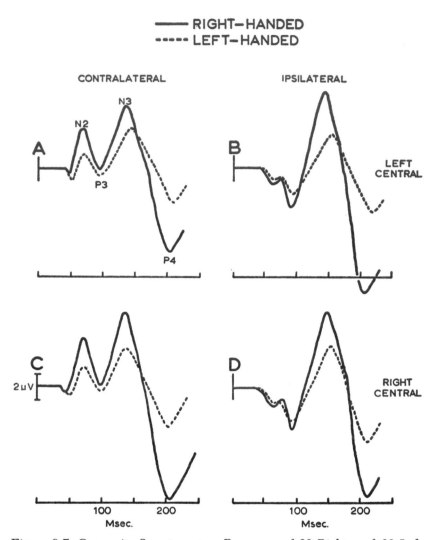

Figure 8-7. Composite Somatosensory Responses of 20 Right- and 20 Left-Handed Subjects. Responses are from left and right (C_3 and C_4) central scalp, contralateral and ipsilateral to shocked finger. The group responses were constructed by plotting the mean peak delays and amplitudes of waves N2 through P4 on graph paper and drawing interconnecting lines through the graphed points. Earlier components, P1-N1, by nature of the somatosensory system occur only in the contralateral response and hence were not included.

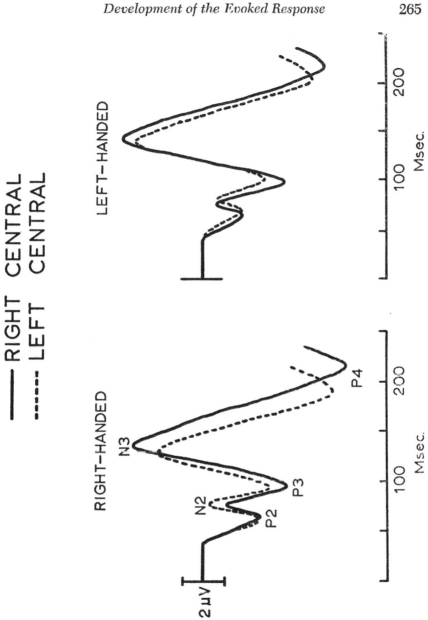

Figure 8-8. Composite Visual Evoked Responses Recorded from Central Scalp. The responses were constructed from the individual responses of 20 right- and 20 left-handed subjects in the same manner as those described in Figure 8-7.

sponse as being related to "whole" brain functioning, left-handed subjects showing, as a group, more variable and smaller somatosensory evoked responses bilaterally. Asymmetry in VERs recorded from central scalp is commonly seen in most normal subjects regardless of handedness, but the hemispheric difference is not as pronounced in left-handed subjects as it is in right-handed subjects.

The Evoked Response and Intelligence

For years investigators have looked for some relationship between brain wave patterns and level of intelligence. While some have reported significant correlations between various parameters of the EEG and intelligence test scores, others have been unable to demonstrate such a relationship. In recent years these contradictory findings have been interestingly summarized and debated by Vogel and Broverman (1964, 1966) and Ellingson (1966). While Ellingson argues that the evidence concerning the relationship between EEG waves and intelligence is contradictory and inconclusive, Vogel and Broverman stress that there is reliable evidence to support the existence of such a relationship.

The evoked response appeared to offer a promising approach to the problem, since its wave configuration is more easily measured than that of spontaneous EEG waves.

A population of approximately eight hundred school children was screened. From among them two groups of ten- and eleven-year-old children were selected. The first group was composed of twenty bright children who had Full Scale Wechsler Intelligence Scale for Children (WISC) IQ scores that ranged from 120 to 140, mean 130, while the second group consisted of twenty dull children, age and sex matched with the brightest group. The latter group had Full Scale WISC IQ scores which ranged from 70 to 90, mean 79. All of the low IQ children were adapting satisfactorily to school and none had any known history of brain damage or emotional disturbance. See Rhodes, et al. (1969) for a complete description of the study.

Visually evoked responses to 100 flashes of light were recorded from each subject as previously described. There were two recording sessions separated by about one month. Flash intensity

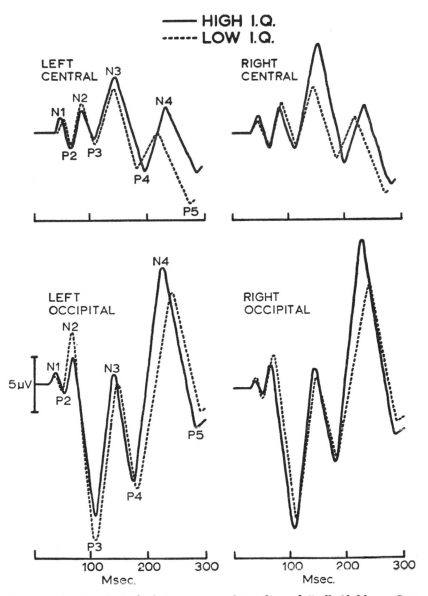

Figure 8-9. Visual Evoked Responses of Bright and Dull Children. Composite VERs recorded from left and right central and occipital scalp of 20 high IQ and 20 low IQ children illustrating amplitude differences between groups.

was set at PS = 2 for the first session, while two additional intensities were used in the second session, one dimmer (PS = 1 + filter), the other brighter (PS = 8).

Peak delays and amplitudes of all major waves occurring within the first 300 msec were scored. The mean peak delays and amplitudes of waves N2 through P5 may be seen in Figure 8-9. Amplitude excursions of late waves were measured for all subjects with a map reading wheel.

Only one peak delay differentiated the two groups. Peak N4 in responses recorded from occipital scalp occurred significantly later in the VERs of low IQ children ($p < 0.01$). Interestingly, this wave, when recorded from central leads, arrived earlier in the responses of the low IQ group.

The excursion measures of the late waves (approximately 100-250 msec) from both central and occipital VERs were reliably

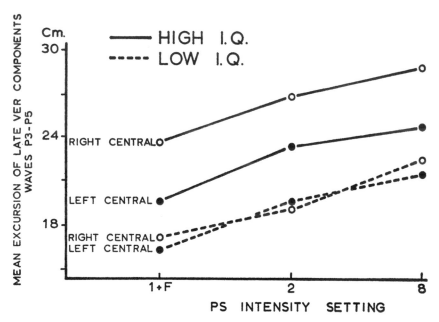

Figure 8-10. Hemispheric Differences of High and Low IQ Children. Mean hemispheric amplitudes of VERs of high IQ and low IQ children at three levels of stimulus intensity showing interhemispheric asymmetry for the high IQ children only.

GROUP-1 (N=57)

	AGE	I.Q.
RANGE	4.3-15.0	70-131
MEAN	9.8	109.8
S.D.	3.3	11.6

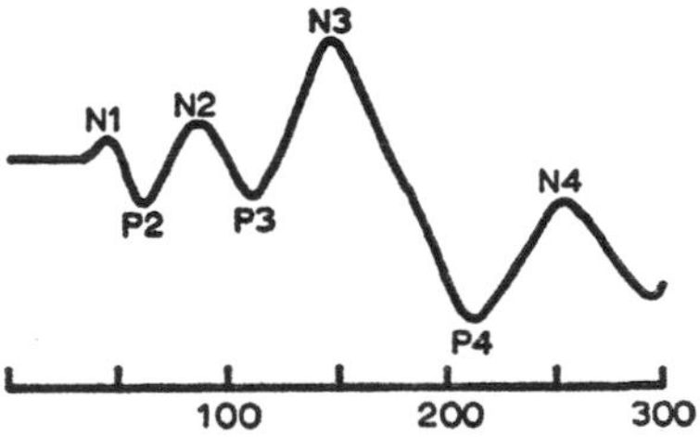

AMPLITUDE

PEAK	CENTRAL		OCCIPITAL	
	LEFT	RIGHT	LEFT	RIGHT
N1	.20	.15	.03	.14
P2	.08	.08	.00	-.10
N2	.12	-.19	.05	.13
P3	.11	.12	-.21	-.17
N3	-.12	.04	-.08	-.40‡
P4	-.13	-.05	-.22	-.41‡
N4	.01	.04	-.13	-.20

PEAK DELAY

PEAK	CENTRAL		OCCIPITAL	
	LEFT	RIGHT	LEFT	RIGHT
N1	.15	.05	-.11	-.06
P2	.06	.21	-.03	.02
N2	-.12	-.20	.13	.11
P3	.02	-.10	-.08	.03
N3	.01	.09	-.05	-.10
P4	.23	.28*	-.13	-.12
N4	.37‡	.38‡	-.08	.06

* P=<.05
‡ p=<.01

Figure 8-11. Correlations of IQ with Amplitude and Peak Delay of Visual Evoked Response Components. Children in this group had a mean IQ of 110.

larger in the responses from the high IQ children ($p < 0.05$ central; $p < 0.01$ occipital). The amplitude differences can be seen in Figure 8-9 in which the composite VERs of the two groups are superimposed.

The high IQ group also differed from the low IQ group with respect to amplitude asymmetry in VERs recorded from central leads (Fig. 8-10). The graph in Figure 8-10 is based on VER wave excursion measures which encompassed waves P3 through P5 in responses evoked by three different flash intensities. At each intensity setting late waves in the right central VERs of the high IQ group were reliably larger than they were in responses from left central scalp. The responses of the low IQ children did not show an amplitude asymmetry.

Consistent with the findings mentioned above, the responses of the bright children were significantly larger than those of the low IQ children across all three intensities.

A correlational study was undertaken with two additional groups of children to determine the relationship of IQ to VER wave amplitude and peak delay in subjects whose ages and IQs spanned a continuum. Group 1 was composed of fifty-seven normal children whose IQ scores were between 70 and 131, mean IQ = 110. Group 2 included 114 children whose parents were either on welfare rolls or were economically qualified to receive welfare assistance. The IQs of this group ranged from 62 to 133 with a mean IQ of 88. Subjects in both groups ranged in age from four to fifteen years. Full Scale WISC intelligence tests were administered to all children except those in Group 1 who were twelve years of age or older (17 children). The older chil-

GROUP-2   (N=114)

	AGE	I.Q.
RANGE	4.0-15.0	62-133
MEAN	9.6	87.8
S.D.	3.1	13.5

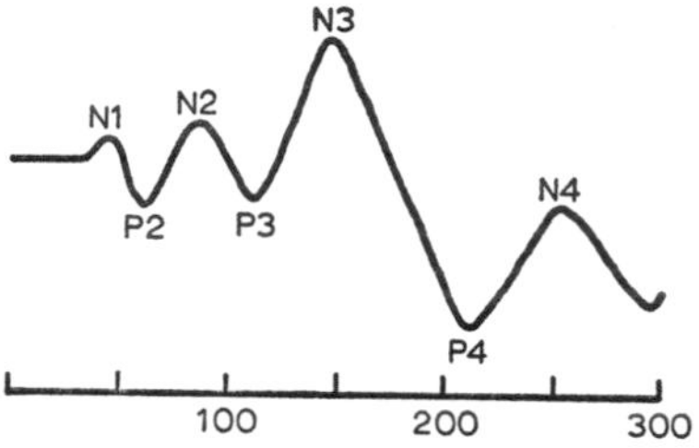

AMPLITUDE

	CENTRAL		OCCIPITAL	
PEAK	LEFT	RIGHT	LEFT	RIGHT
N1	.00	.04	.04	.06
P2	.00	.02	-.08	-.04
N2	-.10	-.04	-.25‡	-.13
P3	.00	.04	-.04	.00
N3	-.06	.11	.18	.19
P4	-.10	.04	.18	.13
N4	-.14	-.12	.11	.10

PEAK DELAY

	CENTRAL		OCCIPITAL	
PEAK	LEFT	RIGHT	LEFT	RIGHT
N1	.09	.04	-.02	.06
P2	.09	.04	-.01	-.04
N2	.08	.05	-.06	-.06
P3	.02	.07	-.02	-.03
N3	-.09	.04	.00	-.01
P4	.05	.08	.02	-.01
N4	.02	.07	-.11	.00

‡ P=< .01

Figure 8-12. Correlations of IQ with Amplitude and Peak Delay of Visual Evoked Response Components. Children in this group came from an impoverished environment and had a mean IQ of 88.

dren in Group 1 were tested with the Culture Fair Intelligence Test (Cattell and Cattell, 1960).

Visually evoked responses to 100 flashes of light (PS = 2) were recorded from C_3, C_4, O_1 and O_2 of each subject. After the responses were plotted, the peak delays and amplitudes of waves N1 through N4 were measured. For each group the peak delays and amplitudes of each of the seven waves were correlated with IQ using the Pearson product-moment correlation technique. This procedure was followed for VERs from each scalp area, yielding 28 correlations of IQ with wave amplitude and an equal number with peak delay.

As can be observed in Figures 8-11 and 8-12 few correlations, only 6 of 112, were significantly different from zero and these were relatively small and showed no consistent trends.

We conclude that while intelligence appears to be related to visually evoked response amplitude, the relationship is small and can only be observed when carefully selected groups are studied, in which age related amplitude changes are minimized and the intelligence levels of the groups are quite different.

Changes in the Evoked Response During Periods of Increased Attention

The following study was conducted to investigate the effect of varying levels of attention on the evoked response. Ten normal young adult males served as subjects. Visually evoked responses, each to 250 flashes, were recorded from C_3, C_4, O_1 and O_2. Five conditions were investigated (a) two control sessions, (b) a period during which the subject was fitted with earphones conducting white noise at an 80-100 db intensity, (c) a period during which the subject was instructed to count flashes, and (d) a "conditioning" period during which the subject was shocked on the right index finger at a twice threshold intensity, if he failed to flex his finger in response to each flash. It was presumed that the latter two conditions would raise attention level while the "white noise" would be distracting. With the exception of one control session which was always first, the order in which the conditions were presented was randomly determined. Only data from the central leads will be reported as differences from these areas were most obvious.

The peak delays and amplitudes of prominent waves, N1 through P4, were measured. Analyses of variance computed on these data clearly showed that, while peak delays of these waves were not related to the five conditions, amplitudes of four of the waves were significantly related. Amplitudes of all waves except P2-N2 were reliably larger ($p < 0.05$) in responses recorded during the "conditioning" period than during the other four periods. The last three VER waves recorded during the "counting" period were larger than those recorded during the control and "white noise" periods. Responses recorded during the "white noise" period were not different from the control responses. Table 8-III lists the mean amplitudes of the waves recorded from left central scalp during the five conditions while Figure 8-13 illustrates the amplitude changes that occurred during periods of heightened attention.

In previous studies we found that late waves in the VERs recorded from left and right central scalp were asymmetric, the waves being larger in responses from the right hemisphere. Analysis of the data gathered from the ten subjects in the present study also yielded this type of asymmetry.

For each of the five conditions, wave amplitudes of VERs recorded from C_3 and C_4 were compared. Wave N3-P4 was significantly larger in responses from the right hemisphere ($p < 0.01$, "conditioning"; $p < 0.05$, other four conditions). While wave

TABLE 8-III

MEAN AMPLITUDES (μV) OF FIVE WAVE COMPONENTS OF VISUALLY EVOKED RESPONSES RECORDED FROM LEFT CENTRAL SCALP DURING FIVE TREATMENT CONDITIONS

	Components				
	N1-P2	P2-N2	N2-P3	P3-N3	N3-P4
First Control	0.5	1.1	2.2	3.5	5.1
Randomized Control	0.5	1.1	2.2	3.6	4.7
White Noise	0.6	1.4	2.0	3.3	4.7
Counting	0.6	1.3	2.6	4.2	5.6
Conditioning	0.8	1.4	3.2	5.9	6.9

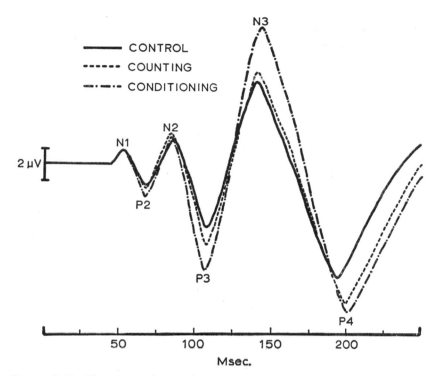

Figure 8-13. Changes in the Evoked Response with Increased Levels of Attention. Composite visual evoked responses of 10 individuals during three levels of attention. The evoked responses were recorded from left central scalp.

P3-N3 was larger in right hemisphere responses for all conditions the differences did not reach statistical significance.

To determine whether the asymmetry increased during periods of increased attention, the following procedure was used. Asymmetry measures for all subjects under each of the five conditions were obtained by subtracting the N3-P4 amplitude in responses recorded from C_3 from the N3-P4 amplitude of C_4 responses. An analysis of variance computed on these differences and a Duncan Multiple Range Test showed that the asymmetry was accentuated during the periods of increased attention. The mean asymmetry difference for the "conditioning" period was significantly larger than the differences for the control and "white

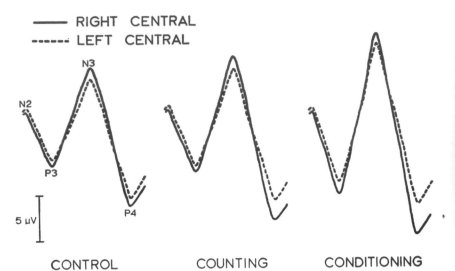

Figure 8-14. Effects of Attention on Asymmetry. The figure illustrates changes in hemispheric amplitude differences with increasing levels of attention. The evoked response components are from composites as described in the text and as illustrated in Figure 8-13.

noise" periods ($p < 0.01$) and for the "counting" period ($p < 0.05$). The asymmetry for the "counting" period was larger than the first control and "white noise" periods ($p < 0.01$).

Figure 8-14 illustrates the larger asymmetries associated with increased attention. The mean amplitude differences shown in the figure for the N3-P4 wave were 1.9, 3.3 and 4.4 microvolts for the control, "counting" and "conditioning" responses.

Changes in the Averaged Evoked Response During Maturation and Aging

Developmental changes in the EEG were an early interest of clinical neurophysiologists. A number of first generation electro-encephalographers studying the ontogeny of the human EEG reported that, generally, the younger the child the larger and slower the brain potentials (Smith, 1937, 1938; Lindsley, 1938, 1939). While a common observation was the extreme variability within each age group, there was a consensus that, in a majority of children, most rhythms and amplitudes of brain waves had reached a stabilized adult pattern by age thirteen to fifteen.

Studies of electrocortical changes at the other end of the developmental continuum, i.e. changes during senescence, were possibly delayed by the general concern regarding covariance of age with health status. Nevertheless, as early as 1941, Davis reported the presence of delta waves and slower alpha rhythms in older psychiatric patients. Definite changes in the EEG of the aged psychiatric patient and the healthy normal adult have been repeatedly demonstrated by a number of investigators (Mundy-Castle, et al., 1954; Obrist, 1954, 1963; Otomo and Tsubaki, 1966).

It is surprising that the same trend has not been followed with the evoked response technique. While the evoked response of infants has been adequately described (Ellingson, 1958, 1960; Engel and Butler, 1963; Barnet and Goodwin, 1965; Ferriss, et al., 1967), any thorough description of evoked response changes and their relation to increasing age during the formative years is lacking. Similarly little is known about changes in the evoked response during later life. To study these changes and to investigate further the developing nervous system this laboratory has conducted two studies. The first step was a study of the visual evoked responses of 215 normal subjects whose age distribution spanned eighty years (Dustman and Beck, 1966, 1969).

Amplitude of several waves in the first 250 msec of the visual evoked response changed markedly with age. In responses recorded from the occiput there was a rapid increase in amplitude of later waves reaching a maximum in five- to eight-year-old children. The mean amplitude of the visual evoked response at this age was about twice as large as the response amplitudes of some older age groups. With older children there was a decline in amplitude until ages thirteen to fourteen, when an abrupt increase in amplitude appeared. Amplitude appeared to stabilize at about age sixteen. With older subjects, mean age sixty-seven years, earlier components (those appearing in the first 100 msec) were consistently larger and arrived significantly later than those of younger subjects. A comparison of responses of different brain areas as well as the degree of homogeneity of the visual evoked response between age levels showed a gradually changing relationship with increasing age.

To study these changes more carefully and extensively a second study was initiated in which the visual, auditory and somatosensory evoked responses of eighty male and eighty female subjects between the ages of four and eighty-six years were obtained (Schenkenberg, 1970). Responses were recorded from electrodes placed bilaterally over frontal, central, and occipital scalp as previously described. All subjects were given IQ tests to ensure that those included in the study were not below the normal range of intelligence. Age, hemisphere and sex comparisons were made on the basis of response amplitudes and peak delays. The study yielded a number of interesting findings, but for the sake of brevity we mention only a few. VER and SER amplitude, particularly of the later components, increased markedly from childhood to adolescence, followed by a similar dramatic decrease through senescence. This is illustrated in Figure 8-15 which provides examples of typical visual evoked responses from subjects at three age levels. Attention is directed to the size of the evoked responses in the formative years, those in A of the figure as compared to those during adolescence and young adulthood, B in the figure. It should be noted that earlier components, N1-P2-N2, are somewhat larger and appear later in the responses of the older subjects.

Trends for age changes in visual, auditory and somatosensory evoked responses are illustrated in Figures 8-16 and 8-17. Figure 8-16 compares the changes in the responses as a function of age using group composites. It will be noted that visual and somatosensory responses showed trends with aging that auditory responses did not. It also should be noted in Figure 8-16 that, in contrast to the EEG, reliable changes may be seen in the amplitudes of the visual and somatosensory evoked responses beginning at an early age. By age forty-one there is marked diminution in the late components of these evoked responses; such dramatic changes are not seen in the EEG.

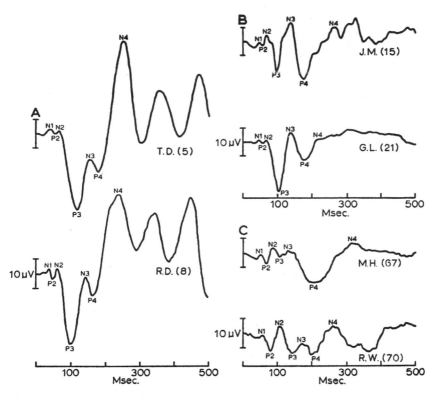

Figure 8-15. Visual Evoked Responses of Subjects at Different Ages. VERs of six subjects at three age levels, illustrating typical responses during (A) childhood, (B) adolescence and young adulthood, and (C) senescence. The large amplitude of the evoked response during formative years and the decrease in amplitude in later years are illustrated in these individual records.

Figure 8-17, a graph of voltage changes occurring within the first 300 msec of visual responses recorded from right frontal, central and occipital scalp as a function of age, demonstrates that the major age related amplitude changes are restricted to responses from occipital scalp. Since the large amplitude responses associated with childhood were not found in the more anterior scalp areas, it appears unlikely that they are a result of increased eye blinking as suggested by Eisengart and Symmes (1971).

From behavioral observations there are obvious developmental

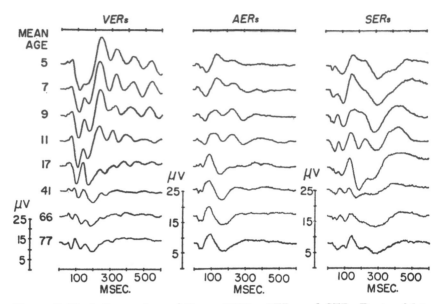

Figure 8-16. A Comparison of Group VERs, AERs and SERs During Maturation and Aging. Each trace was obtained by averaging the evoked responses of the 20 subjects, 10 males and 10 females, in each group. VERs are from O_1; AERs and SERs are from C_3. The mean age of each group is shown at the left of the figure.

transitions at different age levels. Whether the changes we have noted in the evoked response at these same age levels reflect electrophysiological correlates of these processes is presently a speculation, but these data seem to suggest that it is a reasonable one.

It was also noted in this study that the amplitude of the visual evoked response recorded from right central area was greater at all age levels than that from the left. These hemispheric differences were more pronounced in recordings from central scalp; they were not noted with the auditory response and were confounded in evaluation of the somatosensory evoked response, since the wave configuration of responses contralateral to the stimulated finger are more complex, include more waves, and hence make amplitude comparisons difficult. Sex related differences were noted and will be described in the following section.

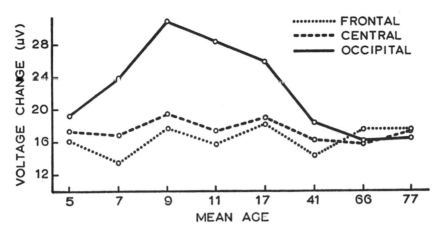

Figure 8-17. Changes in VER Amplitude During Maturation and Aging. The total amplitude change of the various components of the visual evoked response during a time epoch of 0-300 msec. It may be seen that amplitude of the occipital VERs increases markedly during the formative years, stabilizes to some degree, then shows a marked reduction in later life. VERs from frontal and central areas do not follow this trend.

Sex Differences in the Evoked Response

A number of investigators (Shagass and Schwartz, 1964, 1965; Rodin, et al., 1965; Shagass, et al., 1966; Rhodes, et al., 1969) have studied sex differences in the averaged evoked response. Consistent results, especially in regard to response amplitude, have not been reported. However, when one reviews these seemingly contradictory findings, it appears that those who found the evoked responses of males to be larger than the evoked responses of females used children as subjects. Those who found that females had larger responses used adults as subjects.

Data for our evaluation of sex differences were derived from subjects in the study just described. In that study 160 normal subjects were divided into eight age groups, each group being composed of ten males and ten females. This design allowed assessment of the effect of the sex of the subject on the evoked response in relation to the age of the subject, albeit cross-sectionally. A *t* test for independent means was used to compare the re-

TABLE 8-IV

PERCENT OF VISUAL, AUDITORY AND SOMATOSENSORY EVOKED
RESPONSE EXCURSION AMPLITUDE COMPARISONS IN WHICH THE
AMPLITUDE OF THE RESPONSES OF FEMALES WAS LARGER THAN
THE AMPLITUDE OF RESPONSES OF MALES*

	Number of Comparisons	5	7	9	Mean Age 11	17	41	66	77
VER	25	12	8	68	60	100	100	96	84
AER	15	0	33	20	40	100	92	86	40
SER	20	30	55	35	40	100	65	100	100

* These comparisons involved frontal, central and occipital responses and a variety of time segments during the interval from 0 to 500 msec.

sponse amplitudes and peak delays of males and females within each age group. These comparisons were made for responses from F_4, C_3, C_4, O_1 and O_2. F_3 was used to monitor responses and was not included in the analysis.

Table 8-IV presents the percentage of these comparisons in which the excursion amplitudes of responses of females were greater than those for responses of males.

The table indicates that during childhood the responses of males were generally larger than those of females. The reverse characterized those responses recorded during adolescence and adulthood, i.e. the females' responses were larger. Peak delay comparisons yielded a consistent trend in which the peak delays for responses of males were consistently longer than those for responses of females, regardless of age.

These amplitude and peak delay differences were not specific to any particular stimulus, electrode placement or component.

It may be seen that these results explain some of the apparent contradictions observed in earlier studies. Rhodes, et al. (1969) studying children reported larger evoked responses in boys, while Rodin, et al. (1965) and Shagass, et al. (1966) studying adults, reported the opposite, i.e. larger responses in women. Our data indicate that in the formative years the evoked response is larger in males while with maturation the opposite is true.

CLINICAL STUDIES

Evoked Responses from Down's Syndrome Children

It will be recalled that we emphasized earlier the unique quality of the evoked response, pointing out that the wave form configuration of a person's evoked response is individualized. Pertinent to this was the observation that the evoked responses of monozygotic twins were often nearly identical, suggesting that individuals with similar sensory systems and similar brains have similar evoked responses. In a number of instances an identical twin's visually evoked response was more like that of his twin than his own response recorded at a different time. In view of the unique characteristics of several forms of mental retardation it would be reasonable to expect that the electrical activity of the brains of such persons would reflect some specific manifestation of the disorder.

Of all the groups considered, those afflicted with Down's Syndrome appeared to be the most promising for such an experiment. Down's children are a relatively homogeneous group exhibiting unique physical and psychological features. Neuroanatomical studies have reported consistently that the Down's brain is not only different from the normal brain but is different in unique ways (Meyer and Jones, 1939; Crome, 1954; Benda, 1960; Crome, et al., 1966).

The above considerations led us to compare the visual and somatosensory evoked responses of twenty-four Down's children with those of twenty-four normal children who were matched with the Down's group for sex, handedness and age. Each group contained fifteen girls and nine boys and ranged in age from six to sixteen years. All of the Down's children were enrolled in a day school for trainable, mentally handicapped children (Bigum, et al., 1970).

Recording electrodes were attached to the scalp as previously described. All subjects participated in two recording sessions separated by about one month. In the first session responses were obtained from two sets of flashes and two sets of shocks. Shock intensity was 2.5 times each subject's threshold. During the second session, in addition to one set of flashes, three sets of shocks, each set at a different intensity (1.5, 2.5 and 3.5 times threshold), were presented in a randomly determined order. One hundred stimuli were used for each set of VERs and SERs.

Visual Evoked Responses

While the VER wave form of the Down's and normal children was basically similar (see Fig. 8-18), several differences were observed. In centrally derived responses wave P2 occurred earlier ($p < 0.01$) and P4 appeared later ($p < 0.001$) in responses from the normal group (see Table 8-V for mean peak delays and amplitudes). Two significant amplitude differences were found.

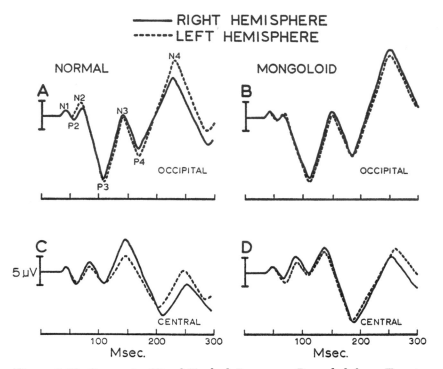

Figure 8-18. Composite Visual Evoked Responses Recorded from Twenty-four Normal and Twenty-four Down's Children. Note that the central responses of the normal children show an amplitude asymmetry which is absent in the responses of the Down's children.

TABLE 8-V

MEANS AND p VALUES COMPUTED FROM THE PEAK DELAYS (msec) AND AMPLITUDES (µV) OF VER COMPONENTS RECORDED FROM LEFT AND RIGHT CENTRAL (C₃ AND C₄) AND OCCIPITAL (O₁ AND O₂) SCALP OF 24 DOWN'S AND 24 NORMAL CHILDREN

Peak	Peak Delay					Component	Amplitude				
	Down's		Normal		p*		Down's		Normal		p*
	C_3	C_4	C_3	C_4			C_3	C_4	C_3	C_4	
P2	69	68	63	62	< 0.01	P2-N2	3.9	4.2	3.3	4.3	
N2	89	87	84	82		N2-P3	2.6	3.1	3.4	4.1	
P3	110	110	109	109		P3-N3	4.4	4.9	5.5	8.0	< 0.05
N3	137	138	145	145	< 0.001	N3-P4	12.3	13.4	9.1	13.1	
P4	184	188	204	212		P4-N4	12.9	11.9	6.6	5.8	< 0.001
N4	260	252	264	251							
	O_1	O_1	O_1	O_1	O_1		O_1	O_1	O_1	O_1	O_1
P2	52	53	50	54		P2-N2	1.4	1.2	3.2	3.0	
N2	66	65	67	70		N2-P3	12.2	11.3	14.3	13.1	
P3	109	109	108	106	< 0.05	P3-N3	12.4	12.0	11.8	11.6	
N3	147	148	139	139	< 0.01	N3-P4	7.6	7.8	7.2	6.3	
P4	182	182	168	167		P4-N4	17.5	18.3	16.7	12.9	< 0.001
N4	247	247	227	225	< 0.001						

* p values were computed from the average of both hemispheres and thus indicate a significant difference between groups.

Wave P3-N3 was larger in the responses of the normal group while P4-N4 was larger in the Down's VERs. Once again an amplitude asymmetry was found in responses from the central areas but only for the normal group. Waves P3-N3 and N3-P4 were reliably larger ($p < 0.01$) in responses from right central scalp. In C and D of Figure 8-18 the asymmetry of normal VERs and the lack of asymmetry in the VERs of the Down's children are illustrated.

Visually evoked responses from occipital scalp differentiated the two groups primarily on the basis of peak delay. The three latest waves shown in Figure 8-18, N3, P4 and N4, occurred significantly later in the Down's VERs (see bottom of Table 8-V).

Somatosensory Responses

The somatosensory responses of the two groups were quite different in appearance. The SERs of the Down's were characterized by two late waves (P4-N4 and N4-P5 in Figure 8-19) which were approximately three times the amplitude of those of the normal children. An illustration of the magnitude of these differences is shown in Figure 8-19 while Table 8-VI lists the mean peak delays, amplitudes and significant differences. Although the shock thresholds of the Down's group were higher than those of the normal children (12.4 and 9.5 volts respectively), this cannot be the explanation for the differences in amplitude. Waves P4-N4 and N4-P5 were considerably larger in Down's SERs to low intensity shock than they were in the normals' SERs to high intensity shock, despite the fact that the normals received nearly twice as much voltage. As can be seen in Figures 8-19 and Table 8-VI the P4-N4-P5 wave complex was not only larger but was of longer duration in the responses of the Down's children.

Since recording sessions were separated by a month, it was possible to determine the reliability, or stability, of the two groups' evoked responses over time. With the procedure described in EQUIPMENT AND PROCEDURE reliability coefficients were computed for VERs and SERs from each scalp area of the sub-

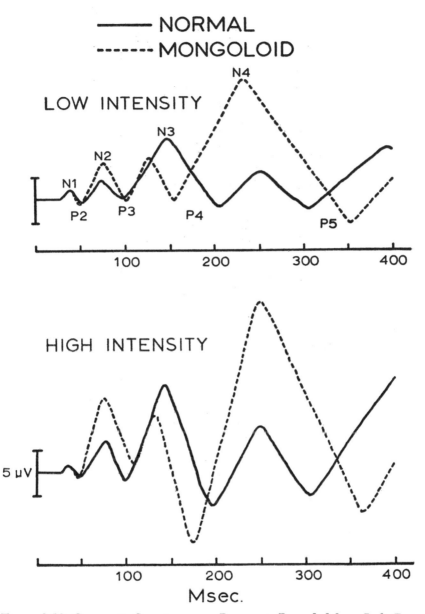

Figure 8-19. Composite Somatosensory Responses Recorded from Left Central (Contralateral) Scalp of Twenty-four Normal and Twenty-four Down's Children. Low and high intensity refers to shock stimuli which were 1.5 and 3.5 times subjective threshold.

TABLE 8-VI

MEANS AND p VALUES COMPUTED FROM THE PEAK DELAYS (msec) AND AMPLITUDES (μV) OF SER COMPONENTS RECORDED FROM LEFT AND RIGHT CENTRAL SCALP OF 24 DOWN'S AND 24 NORMAL CHILDREN*

| | Peak Delay | | | | | | Amplitude | | | | |
| | Down's | | Normal | | | | Down's | | Normal | | |
Peak	C_3	C_4	C_3	C_4	$p^\dagger$	Component	C_3	C_4	C_3	C_4	$p^\dagger$
P2	50	60	53	62		P2-N2	5.0	1.6	2.7	1.4	< 0.05
N2	76	78	74	81		N2-P3	4.6	1.7	2.5	2.5	
P3	101	101	98	111	< 0.001	P3-N3	5.2	5.6	7.3	6.5	
N3	127	136	148	157	< 0.001	N3-P4	5.1	7.1	8.1	8.9	
P4	155	189	206	214		P4-N4	14.1	8.9	4.2	5.0	< 0.001
N4	232	260	250	261		N4-P5	16.8	12.6	4.5	3.4	< 0.001
P5	352	366	305	308	< 0.001						

* A low intensity (1.5 × Threshold) shock stimulus was used.
† p values were computed from the average of both hemispheres and thus indicate a significant difference between groups.

TABLE 8-VII

MEAN PEARSON PRODUCT-MOMENT CORRELATIONS COMPUTED
FROM THE VERs AND SERs OF 24 DOWN'S AND 24 NORMAL
CHILDREN SHOWING (1) RELIABILITY OVER A MONTH'S TIME
AND (2) INTERSUBJECT SIMILARITY (HOMOGENEITY)
OF EVOKED RESPONSE WAVE FORM

	VERs				SERs	
	C_3	C_4	O_1	O_2	C_3	C_4
Reliability						
Down's	.86	.84	.91	.90	.89	.83
Normal	.81	.84	.91	.88	.87	.86
Homogeneity						
Down's	.45	.43	.61	.61	.74	.63
Normal	.41	.43	.52	.47	.48	.49

jects in each group. The mean correlations of the Down's and
normals were relatively high, ranging from about .80 to .90 (see
Table 8-VII), but they did not show group differences.

To determine the similarity of evoked responses within a
group, a response from one scalp area of each subject within
each group was intercorrelated with the responses from the same
scalp area of the remaining twenty-three subjects. A mean of the
intercorrelations obtained for each scalp area was then computed. These means, reflecting homogeneity of responses, are listed
in Table 8-VII. The occipital VERs of the Down's were more
homogeneous than those of the normals ($p < 0.001$).

In general then, the evoked responses of Down's children
(both VERs and SERs) like their physical features, appear to
be unique and characteristic of the group.

The Effects of Socio-Economic
Deprivation on Evoked Responses

As early environment and critical periods modify or fix later
behavioral patterns, they are topics which have elicited the investigative interests of a wide spectrum of scientific specialities.
The pervasiveness of early environmental stimulation or deprivation has been shown by the studies of the Berkeley group
(Bennett, et al., 1964) in their analyses of weight and chemical
composition of rat brain after the animals were subjected to

various environmental conditions. The stimulatory needs of human infants have been fairly well established by Spitz (1958), and Harlow's well-known studies (1962) brought experimental quantification to maternal and other social deprivation effects on monkeys.

For a variety of reasons, not the least of which are social and political implications, there has been increasing concern regarding the effects, both immediate and long term, of an impoverished environment on children. That such concern may be well founded is seen in the results of such studies as one recently published (Naeye, et al., 1969) in which the authors measured the weight of several organs, including the brains of stillborn babies and infants who died shortly after birth. These were separated into two groups on the basis of the economic level of the families from which they came. It was found that the average weight of all organs sampled was less in the "poor" group than in the other.

The relationship between early social environment and brain development is poorly understood at present. A clearer understanding of the effect of early nutrition does seem to be emerging. One might well infer a nutritional factor in the results of Naeye, et al. (1969) cited above. In addition both postnatal physical development and intellectual functioning have been shown to be impaired as a consequence of malnutrition (Stock

TABLE 8-VIII

THE NUMBER, AGE RANGE, MEAN AGE, IQ RANGE AND MEAN IQ
OF THREE GROUPS OF CHILDREN FROM ECONOMICALLY
DEPRIVED FAMILIES*

| Group | N | Age (Years) | | IQ | |
		Range	Mean	Range	Mean
Never	27	4.4-15.0	9.9	62-119	85
Intermittent	51	4.2-14.9	10.2	62-117	89
Always	36	4.0-13.6	8.8	62-113	89

* Groupings were based on the welfare history of each child's parents since the child's birth as follows: The parents (1) had *never* received welfare assistance; (2) had received welfare assistance on an *intermittent* basis; and (3) had *always* been receiving welfare assistance.

TABLE 8-IX

MEAN AMPLITUDES (μV), HEMISPHERIC DIFFERENCES AND
PROBABILITY VALUES COMPUTED FOR TWO LATE VER WAVES
RECORDED FROM SCALP AREAS C_3 AND C_4 OF THREE GROUPS
OF CHILDREN WHOSE PARENTS WERE ECONOMICALLY DEPRIVED[*]

Group		Wave P3-N3				Wave N3-P4		
	C_3	C_4	*Diff.*	p[†]	C_3	C_4	*Diff.*	p[†]
Never	8.2	8.4	0.2		10.8	10.0	0.8	
Intermittent	7.9	10.3	2.4	< 0.001	11.0	12.7	1.7	< 0.05
Always	10.8	14.5	3.7	< 0.001	15.5	18.7	3.2	< 0.01
p[‡]	< 0.05	< 0.001			< 0.05	< 0.001		

[*] Groupings were based on the welfare history of each child's parents since the child's birth as follows: (1) had *never* received welfare assistance; (2) had received welfare assistance on an *intermittent* basis; and (3) had *always* been receiving welfare assistance.
[†] p values refer to differences between *hemispheres*.
[‡] p values refer to differences between *groups*.

and Smythe, 1963; Cabek and Najdanvic, 1965). Changes in EEG activity have also been seen in cases of malnutrition, e.g. Kwashiorkor syndrome (Engel, 1956). Preliminary investigation with cerebral evoked response analysis suggests that this measure may also be sensitive to specific early nutritional deficits in both humans (Mizuno, et al., 1969) and animals (Mourek, et al., 1967).

The study to be reported was undertaken to determine whether socioeconomic deprivation is reflected in altered brain function as measured by the evoked response.

Subjects for the investigation were 114 children selected from various economically depressed sections of Salt Lake City. They were principally identified through their participation in various government sponsored poverty related programs such as Head Start, OEO Title I Program, or as recipients of state government "welfare" assistance. Through these agencies and personal interviews information regarding each child's economic and health status was obtained.

Each child was assigned to one of three groups based on the welfare history of his parents as follows: (1) The parents had *never* received welfare assistance since the child's birth; they were "poor but proud" families, definitely deprived. (2) The parents had received welfare assistance on an *intermittent* basis since the child's birth. (3) The parents had *always* been receiving welfare assistance since the child's birth. The number of subjects in each group, as well as age and IQ information, are

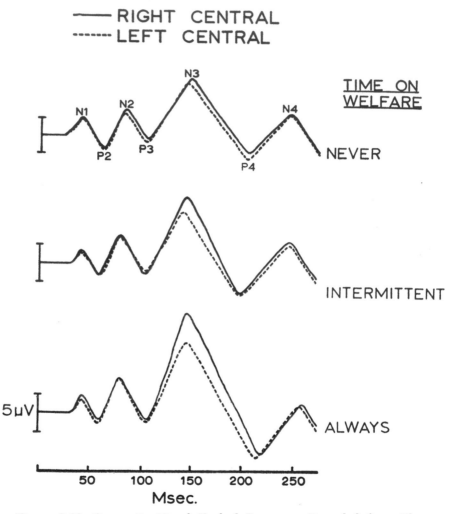

Figure 8-20. Composite Visual Evoked Responses Recorded from Three Groups of Economically Deprived Children. Note that the amplitude asymmetry is most marked in the responses of children who have continuously received welfare benefits and is absent in the responses of those whose parents were never on welfare.

shown in Table 8-VIII. Analysis of variance indicated that neither the mean ages nor the IQs of the groups were reliably different.

For the sake of brevity we report only the amplitude data from the *central* scalp areas. The amplitudes of two late waves, P3-N3 and N3-P4, from both scalp areas (C_3 and C_4) were significantly larger in the VERs of the group whose parents had always been on welfare during the child's development. The mean amplitudes of these waves in the VERs of the remaining two groups were not different. Table 8-IX lists the mean amplitudes for the three groups and shows significant probability values. The mean differences between the *always* and the other two groups were largest for responses recorded from right central scalp. For example, while the largest difference for N3-P4 in C_3 responses was 4.7 μV, the difference was 8.7 μV for C_4 VERs.

Interestingly we found that the VERs of two of the three groups showed an amplitude asymmetry favoring the right hemisphere (see Table 8-IX). Waves P3-N3 and N3-P4 in the responses of children whose parents had received welfare assistance were reliably larger from the right hemisphere than from the left. As can be seen in Table 8-IX and Figure 8-20, the asymmetry was most pronounced in the *always* group. Thus, in terms of amplitude asymmetry, the VERs of the two groups who had benefitted from a welfare program were more like the responses of normal subjects reported in our earlier studies than were those of the children whose parents had not participated in a welfare program.

Visual Evoked Responses of Children with Centrencephalic Epilepsy: Evidence for A Genetic Etiology

Visual evoked responses were used in an effort to answer the question of whether or not certain forms of epilepsy may be determined in part by hereditary factors. While a common cause of epilepsy is brain injury in some form, numerous epilepsies appear to follow a developmental trend. These often come on full force in childhood only to abate or disappear in late adolescence or early adulthood. Such cases are so numerous and the etiology so obscure that hereditary and developmental factors seem to be the most logical explanation.

While EEG is generally used in any evaluative study of epilepsy, the evoked response technique can provide *quantitative* information which is not available in the usual EEG tracings. A number of evoked response investigators have reported reliable differences in amplitude between the responses of epileptic patients and normal subjects, but there is little agreement as to which of the wave components differ and as to the exact nature of these differences. Some of the controversy derives from the neurological characteristics of the patients studied, the various types and severity of epilepsy included in different samples, and such variables as age, medication and recording techniques. To avoid these difficulties we studied a relatively homogeneous group of epileptic patients, those with centrencephalic epilepsy. We compared this group with a control group matched for age and sex.

Metrakos and Metrakos (1961) suggested a genetic basis for this type of seizure disorder, noting that relatives of centrencephalic epileptics have a higher incidence of epileptiform EEGs than do controls. In view of this observation we decided to extend the study to include close relatives, siblings and parents of the epileptic patients. These we divided into two groups, those with epileptiform EEGs but no clinical signs of a seizure disorder and those judged to be free of any signs of abnormality, EEG and otherwise. These groups were also carefully matched with controls.

Thus the study had two goals. The first was to note the nature of the visual evoked responses of patients with centrencephalic epilepsy. The second was to compare evoked responses of close relatives of epileptics with matched controls and epileptic patients. Would such responses be more like those of normal subjects or epileptic patients?

Results indicated that epileptic patients had significantly larger visual response amplitudes than did matched control subjects. The differences were most obvious in recordings from central areas. Visual evoked response components, P3-N3-P4 (see Fig. 8-2 for designation of these components) were larger and more pronounced in patients with epilepsy and differentiated epileptic patients from both close relatives and controls. Close relatives of the seizure patients also possessed many of these same large amplitude characteristics. They too differed from controls, occupying an intermediate rank in evoked response amplitude between the patients and the matched controls. As both epileptic patients and their nonepileptic relatives were found to have centrally derived visual evoked responses of higher amplitude than the controls, a genetic basis for centrencephalic epilepsy might be argued.

The Effects of Alcohol on Visual and Somatosensory Evoked Responses

A point of interest has been our repeated observation of hemispheric asymmetry in the amplitude of evoked responses recorded from central areas. It will be recalled that in normal subjects, bright youngsters and various control groups, the amplitude of responses from the right hemisphere was greater than that from the left. This asymmetry was lacking in mongoloid and low IQ children. It appeared to change with level of attentiveness, increasing in amplitude with an increase in attention. Since alcohol presumably affects the nervous system and level of consciousness, how would ingestion of alcohol affect evoked response asymmetry? Would alcohol affect the amplitude and asymmetry of the evoked response so that it appeared like that of the retarded individual?

It has been repeatedly demonstrated that drugs, most often barbiturates, alter the cerebral evoked response in animals and man (French, et al., 1953; Brazier, 1963; Domino, et al., 1963; Wilson, et al., 1964; Kugler and Doenicke, 1965). These are only a few of many studies indicating that intoxication with a variety of drugs will affect the amplitude of the evoked response. Moderate doses of alcohol have also been reported to alter the amplitude of the evoked response (Gross, et al., 1966; DiPerri, et al., 1968). As we believe that the early components of the evoked response may be related to impulses arriving at the cortex from specific thalamic pathways, whereas later components, those appearing after approximately 70 msec, derive from collaterals from the reticular formation and thence through diffuse thalamic projections to the cortex, we set out to note what components of the evoked response would be most affected by the ingestion of alcohol (Lewis, et al., 1970).

We selected nine subjects, all moderate drinkers, who imbibed various amounts of alcohol or placebo, after which visual and somatosensory evoked responses were recorded in a manner previously described. The subjects were given 95 percent alcohol at two dose levels, .41 g and 1.23 g/kg of body weight, the equivalent of 1 and 3 ounces of alcohol respectively for a 160 pound man.

Results indicated that after ingestion of 3 ounces of alcohol the amplitude of a number of late waves for both visual and somatosensory evoked responses recorded from central areas attenuated significantly. Evoked responses recorded from occipital areas showed no such changes. The hemispheric asymmetry of amplitude, generally noted with recordings from central areas

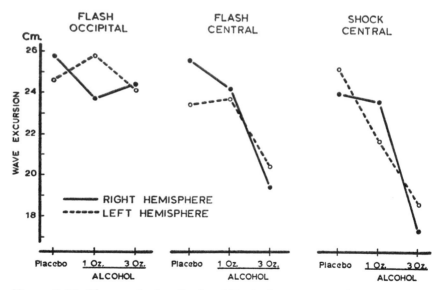

Figure 8-21. Changes in Amplitude of Evoked Response Following the Ingestion of Alcohol. Amplitude of waves (in cm) recorded from occipital and central areas at 0, 0.03 and 0.09% blood alcohol concentration.

to visual stimuli tended to disappear following the ingestion of 3 ounces of alcohol. The reduction in response amplitude and changes in hemispheric asymmetry following ingestion of alcohol are illustrated in Figure 8-21. As late components of the evoked response were attenuated, particularly those recorded from association or polysensory areas, i.e. central scalp recordings, the results suggest that one site of action of alcohol is the reticular formation.

DISCUSSION

The foregoing studies, we believe, clearly indicate that the evoked response is useful, both as a research tool and as a diagnostic procedure.

It should be pointed out that the evoked response technique has enjoyed widespread acceptance in areas other than those we have described. For example, several laboratories and clinics use the evoked response technique to measure sensory capacities. The evoked response has been useful in evaluating hearing loss, particularly with pre-speech and mentally defective children (Barnet and Lodge, 1966; Rapin and Graziani, 1967; Davis, 1968; Rapin, et al., 1970). Visual evoked responses show promise in the evaluation of visual disorders (Vaughn and Katzman, 1964; Walsh, et al., 1966). Peripheral and spinal cord lesions have been evaluated and localized by the use of somatosensory evoked responses (Bergamini and Bergamasco, 1967). Locus and extent of cerebral lesions have also been investigated with the technique. These reflected their presence in the evoked response by hemispheric asymmetries and reduction in amplitude of the components of the response (Williamson, et al., 1970). Interestingly, all components were reduced or disappeared on the side of the lesion. The technique has also been helpful in distinguishing central from peripheral lesions. In this instance, lesions in the optic pathway distal to the optic nerve reduce both the electroretinogram (ERG) and the evoked response, while more central lesions leave the ERG intact and abolish or diminish only the evoked response (Callaway, 1969).

Despite these and other diagnostic developments it must be remembered that the exact source and nature of the components of the evoked response are still being debated. A critical reader might argue, indeed a number have, that this would severely limit the usefulness of the technique. It is interesting that similar criticism was leveled at those working with the EEG some forty years ago. Parenthetically much of this criticism is still valid. While such issues will require time and considerable research before discovery and agreement yield a reliable degree of certainty, it still remains without question that evoked response components do change differentially and reliably under a variety of conditions. As the response is reliable and stable over long periods of time, careful descriptive and correlative inquiry into those treatments and conditions that change the response seems to us, and to others, justified. Such descriptive research may well lead to inferential information about the functional systems of the brain and how they relate to the evoked response. Such research has traditionally shed as much light on the origin and nature of the brain's electrical activity as have some more esoteric approaches.

We return now to comments about some of our findings. It will be recalled that visually evoked responses of the majority of identical twins were strikingly similar. Although these data suggest an hereditary basis for the brain's electrical patterns, alternate explanations must be considered. Head shape and size may be a determinant. This becomes a critical question in the case of identical twins, as head lengths and widths of twins are known to correlate highly, $r = .91$ (Lenz, 1961). In an effort to settle this problem the evoked responses of thirteen subjects of varying head sizes, cephalic indices (CI) from 71 to 84, were intercorrelated. No relationship was found between evoked response correlations and cephalic index, $r = .04$. Interestingly, two of the subjects had strikingly similar evoked responses, $r = .82$, but one was a dolichocephalic, CI $= 71$, and the other a brachycephalic, CI $= 84$.

In our study of the evoked response and intelligence, the response differentiated bright from dull children in two ways. The bright children had reliably larger amplitudes in the late components of their evoked responses in both central and occipital recordings and they also demonstrated a hemispheric asymmetry, with larger responses in the right hemisphere, which lower IQ children did not. It may be that the organization of the central nervous system in lower IQ children is less mature than that of intellectually superior children and that such a difference is reflected in the wave form or amplitude of the evoked response as we have noted. However, the possibility of differences in level of attention cannot be ignored. It will be recalled from one of our studies that, with increased levels of attention, there was an enhancement of late components of the evoked response. Similarly, increased asymmetry with higher amplitude responses occurring in the right hemisphere was noted during those periods of heightened attentiveness. As higher IQ children are more alert and generally operate at a higher level of attention, this could account for some of the group differences.

Chalke and Ertl (1965) reported large latency differences between evoked responses of high and low IQ subjects. Some of these were as large as 60 msec. As may be seen in Figures 8-11 and 8-12, our results did not confirm their findings. Latency differences were few and small and showed no consistent trend.

The marked changes in amplitude and configuration of the evoked responses, particularly to visual stimulation, that take place during maturation and aging have been repeatedly observed in this laboratory. While necessity dictated a cross-sectional approach rather than the preferred longitudinal method, we are convinced that gross changes in evoked responses occur at both ends of the developmental continuum, both during maturation and throughout senility. Such changes must be seriously considered whenever the response is used clinically or in an evaluative procedure.

Initially there was concern that these changes could reflect extracerebral factors, e.g. skull thickness, scalp impedance, refractory or pupillary differences, etc. Skull differences cannot explain why evoked responses were not larger in the extremely young children or why the responses diminished in amplitude in late adolescence and again in later life. Interelectrode resistances were measured for the majority of subjects and as these were consistently small, scalp impedance can hardly account for the large differences among various age groups. Finally, extracerebral factors should affect *all* components rather than certain waves at different age levels. Consequently, we feel reasonably certain that the changes we see are of cerebral origin. A number of findings from these studies are deserving of elaboration, but we will dwell only on a few.

The first is the marked increase in amplitude of the evoked response, particularly the late components, during the formative years (see Fig. 8-17). Assuming that the evoked response differences at different ages are due to intracerebral, anatomical and electrophysiological variation, let us look at brain development during these years. Decided developmental changes in the brain continue after infancy, especially throughout the formative years, stabilizing only after adolescence. If we look to the morphology of brain changes during development, we find that those areas of the cortex that continue their development throughout childhood are the large "silent" or association areas (Turner, 1948; Yakovlev, 1962). Closely related to this is the growth of collaterals to the brain stem reticular formation with continued myelination of these, as well as the pathways to unspecific or diffuse nuclei of the thalamus (Yakovlev and Lecours, 1967). Current neurophysiological theory contends that all of these structures, i.e. brain stem reticular formation (ascending), diffuse thalamic nuclei and association cortices are intricately and reciprocally intercorrelated (Jasper, 1960). It may be that changes in these structures contribute significantly to changes in late components of the evoked response seen so clearly during formative years. There are, of course, interesting behavioral changes at this same age in language development, concept formation, perception and mental abilities. The observation that corticoelectrical activity, neuroanatomical changes and behavioral development are all changing rapidly at this time leads to interesting speculation regarding the anatomical and physiological substrates of certain psychological processes.

Bear in mind that the associational cortices are polysensory, responding to a variety of stimuli as contrasted to the specific or primary cortical areas which are relatively specific in their responses, responding only to visual stimuli in the case of the visual cortex, auditory stimuli in the case of the auditory cortex, etc. Polysensory convergence in association areas of the cortex allows two or more stimuli to interact in a variety of ways, and the manner in which they interact may change with the situation or the mental state of the subject. Critical to this notion is the point of view that reticular formation and its extension through the diffuse thalamic system and thence to the association cortex may provide both generalized and localized activation at the cortex. States of hyperexcitability and possibly inhibition at various restricted cortical areas could be produced by such a mechanism. This hypothesis (Jasper, 1960) describes how the brain could selectively tune in or out various stimuli as well as provide the necessary interconnections at a subcortical level for such processes as conditioning and learning. This situation has been regarded for some time with great interest by those searching for the anatomical and physiological basis of selective attention, conditioning and learning.

In Figures 8-15 and 8-16 it may be seen that the overall amplitude of the late or postprimary portions of the evoked response, P3 through N4, is markedly reduced, beginning in middle and continuing throughout old age. Peak delays of these same components arrive later in middle age and continue to increase in latency throughout senescence. Late components, as we have emphasized, are believed to be associated with the alerting, activating and integrative functions of the brain.

This observation fits interestingly with certain behavioral changes associated with aging. A general slowing of all voluntary responses to peripheral stimulation has been widely observed, and increased thresholds for perception of visual, auditory and somatic stimuli have been consistently found in subjects of advanced age.

Several attempts have been made to determine whether changes with increasing age in peripheral sense mechanisms could account for the slowing of voluntary responses (Critchley, 1956; Birren, et al., 1959; Magladery, 1959; Weiss, 1959). The consensus is that changes in peripheral sense organs and in nerve conduction that occur with increasing age do not account to any appreciable degree for the loss of speed or the slowing of voluntary response with age. The logical alternative is to look to central, integrative processes rather than peripheral mechanisms.

The procedures we have adopted do provide a look at central integrative processes, assuming that these are somehow reflected in the electrical activity of the brain. As has been pointed out, attenuated amplitude and increased latency in those components of the response assumed to be related to central integrative functions suggest that there is a gradual diminution from adulthood to senium in the brain's electrical respondency. This trend appears to involve the same systems as those that change during maturation, but the changes are in an opposite direction. Anatomical correlation of such processes is provided by the observations of Yakovlev and Lecours (1967) who noted that the brain stem and reticular core of senescent individuals are smaller and contain fewer fibers, suggesting some shrinkage with old age.

Two additional observations should be made before leaving this topic. The first is that earlier components, i.e. the so-called primary responses, do not attenuate with age, but increase in amplitude (see Fig. 8-15). The second is that auditory responses (see Fig. 8-16) do not follow the trend described. During maturation and aging changes in the auditory evoked response are quite different and less pronounced than those seen in the visual and somatosensory systems. We may summarize changes in these latter two systems by stating that the part of the brain presumed to function in "information processing" shows the greatest change during both maturation and aging as contrasted to the "information receiving" function generally relegated to sense organs and specific cortical areas.

We turn now to results of our study of evoked responses of Down's children. It will be recalled that Down's children differed from normals in both their visual and somatosensory evoked responses. However, the most striking differences were seen in the somatosensory responses. The somatosensory responses of Down's children were sufficiently unique to be recognized with relatively casual inspection (see Fig. 8-19).

The stability of responses from Down's children was an unexpected result in view of their known abnormal brain structure and disposition toward incidental cerebral lesions (Benda, 1960). This finding suggests that, despite their disorder, Down's cases give a consistent electrical brain response and as a group exhibit marked homogeneity in their cerebral electrical activity (see Table 8-VIII).

The somatosensory responses that typify the Down's child are characteristized primarily by a high amplitude of late waves, mainly components N3-P4-N4 and P4-N4-P5 (see Fig. 8-19). At first it seemed that these were determined by the background frequency of the EEG. Normal children appeared to have a late wave component and EEG frequency of 8-12 c/sec whereas Down's youngsters generally had a frequency of 4-7 c/sec. However, when we made selected comparisons between late wave frequencies and EEG activity of Down's subjects, a low correlation resulted. Correlation of EEG with frequency of wave N3-P4-N4 was −0.12, to wave P4-N4-P5, 0.28. This lessens the likelihood that the average EEG frequency contributes significantly to the frequency or latency of SER waves. This possibility needs further study.

With the majority of children and adults examined in our laboratory, the visual evoked response was found to be greater in the minor or right hemisphere. This difference was most striking in recordings from central scalp. This hemispheric asymmetry increased during mental activity, decreased during periods of relaxation and was diminished or abolished during ingestion of alcohol. It was absent in children afflicted with Down's syndrome and in children with reduced intelligence.

How do we explain these data? We do not have an immediate explanation; we can only speculate. The hemispheric asymmetry of the evoked response may be related to asymmetries found in the spontaneous EEG alpha rhythm as there is evidence that alpha is more common and of greater amplitude in the right hemisphere (Raney, 1939; Rodin, et al., 1965). However, it should be noted that the asymmetry we report is occurring in components that we have found do not correlate with alpha frequency. The very late rhythmic after-activity (usually after 300 msec) in visual evoked responses correlates with alpha frequency; earlier waves do not. Further, alpha is more prominent in occipital areas, less so in central recordings. The asymmetries we report are just the opposite.

The evoked responses of some groups of socioeconomically deprived children were found to differ from those of normal children as may be seen in Table 8-IX and Figure 8-20. In terms of amplitude asymmetry, the VERs of the children who had benefitted from a welfare program were more like the responses of normal subjects reported in our earlier studies than were those of the children whose parents had not received welfare assistance but were decidedly economically deprived. As the groups did not differ in IQ, or to our knowledge in health status, this is a difficult result to explain. A reasonable speculation may be that those families with welfare assistance received more and possibly better medical care, particularly during the mother's pregnancy and during the child's early infancy.

It is interesting that we find asymmetries mainly in the visual evoked response and not in auditory and somatosensory responses. It is generally accepted that the right hemisphere is dominant for visual perception as contrasted to the left for speech and language. Possibly this contributes to the asymmetry we observe, however, this doesn't seem likely.

We note that a common denominator in all of the studies wherein we find changes in asymmetry, with the exception of the economically deprived children, is level of attention. Thus, bright children are by definition more attentive than dull or Down's youngsters; alcohol is a depressant and level of attention is probably reduced after ingestion; during counting or conditioning the level of attention is more probably increased. In all these instances there is a marked change in amplitude and stability of the evoked response recorded from right central scalp and in the same direction as the level of attentiveness.

At this point it should be noted that the psychological state of increased attention or arousal is generally believed to have its neurophysiological substrate in the mesencephalic reticular formation. The original concept of Morruzzi and Magoun (1949) was that this area of the midbrain produced a continuous stream of impulses which ascend to bombard and energize the neuronal networks of the cortex thereby producing a fast electrical pattern in the electroencephalogram and waking behavior in the animal.

Later this view was extended (Jasper, 1960) to include the more rostrally located unspecific thalamocortical projection system composed of closely interconnected multisynaptic network of neurons extending largely through the midline intralaminar nuclei of the anterior thalamus. While the functional significance of this centrencephalic portion of the activating system is not clear a number of experiments indicate that it must play a role in the regulation of spontaneous electrical rhythms of the entire cortex and is capable of directing local or topographical effects. That is, it may cause shifts in thresholds and rhythms of the cortex in discrete areas or possibly in different hemispheres (Starzl and Magoun, 1951; Jasper, et al., 1955; French, 1960; Jasper, 1960; Steriade, 1970). Amplitude and stability as well as hemispheric asymmetry of the evoked response could very well be modulated through this ascending activating system and its reciprocal relationship with the cortex.

It is well known that, as we move from lower to high phyla, there is a concomitant increase in brain size and in encephalization. With the higher mammals there is also an increase in size and in number of convolutions in the telencephalon and hence the association areas are larger and there are more possible connections. We speculate that such encephalization continues with a tendency towards lateralization, one hemisphere serving some functions, the other hemisphere, others. Because of the intimate reciprocal relations of the brain stem with the cortex and particularly the association areas, these lower centers must play some critical role in the cortical asymmetry we have described, particularly with regard to attention and consciousness.

From our studies as well as the observations of others (Raney,

1939), we surmise that there is a functional cerebral asymmetry in human beings insofar as activation is concerned. We propose that the reticular formation may act differentially with each hemisphere. It may be that in a less efficient brain such a hemispheric differentiation is less developed or missing. In this reciprocal relationship between the brain stem and the two hemispheres, the reticular formation can possibly selectively facilitate or inhibit hemispheric electrical activity. Evidently this function is reduced in the less efficient nervous system, whether because of reduced level of consciousness, developmental disorder or CNS depressant.

REFERENCES

Abrahamian, H. A.; Allison, T.; Goff, W. R., and Rosner, B. S.: The effects of thiopental on human cerebral evoked responses. *Anesthesiology, 24:* 650, 1963.

Allison, T.: Recovery functions of somatosensory evoked responses in man. *Electroenceph Clin Neurophysiol, 14:*331, 1962.

Andersen, P., and Eccles, J.: Inhibitory phasing of neuronal discharge. *Nature, 196:*645, 1962.

Barnet, A. B., and Goodwin, R. S.: Averaged evoked electroencephalographic responses to clicks in the human newborn. *Electroenceph Clin Neurophysiol 18:*441, 1965.

Barnet, A. B., and Lodge, A.: Diagnosis of deafness in infants with the use of computer-averaged electroencephalographic responses to sound. *J Pediat, 69:*753, 1966.

Benda, C. E.: *The Child With Mongolism.* New York, Grune and Stratton, 1960.

Bennett, E. L.; Diamond, M. C.; Krech, D., and Rosenzweig, M. R.: Chemical and anatomical plasticity of brain. *Science, 146:*610, 1964.

Bergamini, L., and Bergamasco, B.: *Cortical Evoked Potentials in Man.* Springfield, Thomas, 1967.

Bigum, H. B.; Dustman, R. E., and Beck, E. C.: Visual and somatosensory evoked responses from mongoloid and normal children. *Electroenceph Clin Neurophysiol, 28:*202, 1970.

Birren, J. E.; Imus, H. A., and Windle, W. F.: *The Process of Aging in the Nervous System.* Springfield, Thomas, 1959.

Bishop, G. H., and Clare, M. H.: Responses of cortex to direct electrical stimuli applied at different depths. *J Neurophysiol, 16:*1, 1953.

Brazier, M. A. B.: Role of the limbic system in maintenance of consciousness. *Anesth Analg Curr Res, 42:*748, 1963.

Cabek, V., and Najdanvic, R.: Effect of undernutrition in early life on physical and mental development. *Arch Dis Childhood, 40:*532, 1965.

Callaway, E.: Averaged evoked responses in psychiatry. *J Nerv Ment Dis,* *143:*80, 1966.

———: Diagnostic use of the average evoked potential. In E. Donchin and D. B. Lindsley (Eds.): *Average Evoked Potentials.* Washington, U.S. Govt. Printing Office, 1969.

Cattell, R. B., and Cattell, A. K. S.: *Handbook for Culture Fair Intelligence Test, Scale 2.* Champaign, Institute for Personality and Ability Testing, 1960.

Chalke, F. C., and Ertl, J.: Evoked potentials and intelligence. *Life Sci,* 4:1319, 1965.

Chang, H. T., and Kaada, B. R.: An analysis of primary response of visual cortex to optic stimulation in cats. *J Neurophysiol, 13:*305, 1950.

Cigánek, L.: The EEG response (evoked potential) to light stimulus in man. *Electroenceph Clin Neurophysiol, 13:*165, 1961.

Cornil, L., and Gastaut, H.: Note complémentaire sur l'étude electroencephalographique de la dominance cérébrale (á propos de la gaucherie). *Ext. C. R. Congres des Medecins Alienistes Et Neurologist, 1951.*

Creutzfeldt, O. D.; Rosina, A.; Ito, M., and Probst, W.: Visual evoked response of single cells and of the EEG in primary visual area of the cat. *J Neurophysiol 32:*127, 1969.

Critchley, M.: Neurological changes in the aged. *Res Publ Assn for Res Nerv Ment Dis, 35:*198, 1956.

Crome, L.: Some morbid-anatomical aspects of mental deficiency. *J Ment Sci, 100:*984, 1954.

———; Cowie, V., and Slater, E.: A statistical note on cerebellar and brain stem weight in mongolism. *J Ment Defic Res, 10:*69, 1966.

Crovitz, H. F., and Zener, K.: A group test for assigning hand and eye dominance. *Am J Psychol, 75:*271, 1962.

Davis, H.: Enhancement of evoked cortical potentials in humans related to a task requiring a decision. *Science, 145:*182, 1964.

Davis, H.: Averaged-evoked response EEG audiometry in North America. *Acta Oto-laryngol, 65:*79, 1968.

Davis, P. A.: The electroencephalogram in old age. *Dis Nerv Syst, 2:*77, 1941.

DiPerri, R.; Dravid, A.; Schweigert, A., and Himwich, H.: Effect of alcohol on evoked potentials of various parts of the central nervous system in cat. *Q J Stud Alcohol, 29:*20, 1968.

Domino, E. F.; Corssen, G., and Sweet, R. B.: Effects of various general anesthetics on the visually evoked response in man. *Anesth Analg Curr Res, 42:*745, 1963.

Dustman, R. E., and Beck, E. C.: Long-term stability of visually evoked potentials in man. *Science, 142:*1480, 1963.

———: Phase of alpha brain waves, reaction time and visually evoked potentials. *Electroenceph Clin Neurophysiol, 18:*433, 1965a.

————: The visually evoked potential in twins. *Electroenceph Clin Neurophysiol, 19:*570, 1965b.

————: Visually evoked potentials: Amplitude changes with age. *Science, 151:*1013, 1966.

————: The effects of maturation and aging on the wave form of visually evoked potentials. *Electroenceph Clin Neurophysiol, 26:*2, 1969.

Eisengart, M. A., and Symmes, D.: The effect of eye blink on the visual evoked response in children. *Electroenceph Clin Neurophysiol, 31:*71, 1971.

Ellingson, R. J.: Electroencephalograms of normal, full-term newborns immediately after birth with observations on arousal and visual evoked responses. *Electroenceph Clin Neurophysiol, 10:*31, 1958.

————: Cortical electrical responses to visual stimulation in the human infant. *Electroenceph Clin Neurophysiol, 12:*663, 1960.

————: Relationship between EEG and test intelligence: a commentary. *Psychol Bull, 65:*91, 1966.

Engel, R.: Abnormal brain patterns in Kwashiorkor. *Electroenceph Clin Neurophysiol, 8:*489, 1956.

————, and Butler, B. V.: Appraisal of conceptual age of newborn infants by EEG methods. *J Pediat, 63:*386, 1963.

Ferriss, G. S.; Davis, G. D.; Dorsen, M. McF., and Hackett, E. R.: Changes in latency and form of the photically induced averaged evoked response in human infants. *Electroenceph Clin Neurophysiol, 22:*305, 1967.

Fox, S. S., and O'Brien, J. H.: Duplication of evoked potential wave form by curve of probability of firing of a single cell. *Science, 147:*888, 1965.

French, J. D.: The reticular formation. In J. Field (Ed.): *Handbook of Physiology Sect I.* Washington, Amer. Physiol. Soc., 1960.

French, J. D.; Verzeano, M., and Magoun, H. W.: The neural basis of the anesthetic state. *AMA Arch Neurol Psychiat, 69:*519, 1953.

Glandville, A. D., and Antonities, J. J.: Relationship between occipital alpha activity and laterality. *J Exp Psychol, 49:*249, 1955.

Goff, W. R.; Rosner, B. S., and Allison, T.: Distribution of cerebral somatosensory evoked responses in normal man. *Electroenceph Clin Neurophysiol, 14:*697, 1962.

Goff, W. R.; Allison, T.; Shapiro, A., and Rosner, B. S.: Cerebral somatosensory responses evoked during sleep in man. *Electroenceph Clin Neurophysiol, 21:*1, 1966.

Gross, M. M.; Begleiter, H.; Tobin, M., and Kissin, B.: Changes in auditory evoked response induced by alcohol. *J Nerv Ment Dis, 143:*152, 1966.

Haider, M.; Spong, P., and Lindsley, D. B.: Attention, vigilance, and cortical evoked-potentials in humans. *Science, 145:*180, 1964.

Harlow, H. F., and Harlow, M. K.: Social deprivation in monkeys. *Scient Am, 207:*137, 1962.

Heath, R. G., and Galbraith, G. C.: Sensory evoked responses recorded simultaneously from human cortex and scalp. *Nature, 212*:1535, 1966.

Hirsch, J. F.; Pertuiset, B.; Calvet, J.; Buisson-Ferey, J.; Fischgold, H., et Sherrer, J.: Etude des réponses électricorticales obtenues chez l'homme par des stimulations somesthesiques et visuelles. *Electroenceph Clin Neurophysiol, 13*:411, 1961.

Hughes, J. R., and Curtin, M. J.: Usefulness of photic stimulation in routine clinical electroencephalography. *Neurology, 10*:777, 1960.

Jasper, H. H.: Unspecific thalamocortical relations. In J. Field: *Handbook of Physiology*, Sect. I. Washington, *Amer Physiol Soc*, 1960.

Jasper, H. H.; Naquet, R., and King, E. V.: Thalamocortical recruiting responses in sensory receiving areas of the cat. *Electroenceph Clin Neurophysiol, 7*:99, 1955.

Jasper, H. H.; Senda, R., and Rasmussen, E.: Evoked potentials from exposed somatosensory cortex in man. *J Nerv Ment Dis, 130*:526, 1960.

Kooi, K. A.; Eckman, H. G., and Thomas, M. H.: Observations on the response to photic stimulation in organic cerebral dysfunction. *Electroenceph Clin Neurophysiol, 9*:239, 1957.

Kugler, J., and Doenicke, A.: Amplitudes and evoked responses in the EEG in humans during sleep and anesthesia. *Progr Brain Res, 18*:178, 1965.

Lansing, R. W., and Thomas, H.: Laterality of photic driving in normal adults. *Electroenceph Clin Neurophysiol, 16*:290, 1964.

Lennox, L. G.; Gibbs, E. L., and Gibbs, F. A.: Brain wave patterns: an hereditary trait. *J Hered, 36*:233, 1945.

Lenz, W.: *Medizinische Genetik: eine Einführung in ihre Grundlagen und Probleme*. Stuttgart, Thieme, 1961.

Lewis, E. G.; Dustman, R. E., and Beck, E. C.: The effects of alcohol on visual and somato-sensory evoked responses. *Electroenceph Clin Neurophysiol, 28*:202, 1970.

Lindsley, D. B.: Electrical potentials in the brain of children and adults. *J Genet Psychol, 19*:285, 1938.

———: A longitudinal study of the occipital alpha rhythm in normal children: frequency and amplitude standards. *J Genet Psychol, 55*:197, 1939.

Magladery, J. W.: Neurophysiology of aging. In J. E. Birren (Ed.): *Handbook of Aging and the Individual*. Chicago, University of Chicago, 1959.

Metrakos, K., and Metrakos, J. P.: Genetics of convulsive disorders, II. Genetics and electroencephalographic studies in centrencephalic epilepsy. *Neurology, 11*:474, 1961.

Meyer, A., and Jones, J. B.: Histological changes in the brain in mongolism. *J Ment Sci, 85*:206, 1939.

Mizuno, T.; Chiba, F.; Sakai, M.; Watanabe, S.; Tamura, T.; Arakawa, T.;

Tatsumi, S., and Coursin, D. B.: Frequency analysis of electroencephalograms and latency of photically induced averaged evoked responses in children with Riboflavinosis: Preliminary report. (Presented by D. B. Coursin at Palo Alto NIH Conference, June, 1969.)

Morruzzi, G., and Magoun, H. W.: Brain stem reticular formation and activation of the EEG. *Electroenceph Clin Neurophysiol, 1:*455, 1949.

Mourek, J.; Himwich, W. A.; Myslivecek, J., and Callison, D. A.: The role of nutrition in the development of evoked cortical potentials in the rat. *Brain Res, 6:*241, 1967.

Mundy-Castle, A. C.; Hurst, L. A.; Beerstecher, D. M., and Prinsloo, T.: The electroencephalogram in the senile psychoses. *Electroenceph Clin Neurophysiol, 6:*245, 1954.

Naeye, R. L.; Diener, M.; Dellinger, W. S., and Blanc, W. A.: Urban poverty: Effects on prenatal nutrition. *Science, 166:*1026, 1969.

Obrist, W. D.: The electroencephalogram of normal aged adults. *Electroenceph Clin Neurophysiol, 6:*235, 1954.

———: The electroencephalogram of healthy aged males. In P.H.S. Publ. No. 986, *Human Aging: A Biological and Behavioral Study.* Washington, U.S. Printing Office, 1963.

Otomo, E., and Tsubaki, T.: Electroencephalography in subjects sixty years and over. *Electroenceph Clin Neurophysiol, 20:*77, 1966.

Raney, E. T.: Brain potentials and lateral dominance in identical twins. *J Exp Psychol, 24:*21, 1939.

Rapin, I., and Graziani, L. J.: Auditory-evoked responses in normal, brain-damaged, and deaf infants. *Neurology, 17:*881, 1967.

Rapin, I.; Ruben, R. J., and Lyttle, M.: Diagnosis of hearing loss in infants using auditory evoked responses. Paper read at the meeting of the Eastern Section of the American Laryngological, Rhinological, and Otological Society, Boston, Mass., Jan. 1, 1970.

Rhodes, L. E.; Dustman, R. E., and Beck, E. C.: The visually evoked response: A comparison of bright and dull children. *Electroenceph Clin Neurophysiol, 27:*364, 1969.

Rife, D. C.: Genetic studies of monozygotic twins: Diagnostic formula. *J Hered, 24:*339, 1933a.

———: Genetic studies of monozygotic twins: Finger patterns and eye-color as criteria for monozygosity. *J Hered, 24:*407, 1933b.

Rodin, E. A.; Grisell, J. L.; Gudobba, R. D., and Zachary, G.: Relationship of EEG background rhythms to photic evoked responses. *Electroenceph Clin Neurophysiol, 19:*301, 1965.

Sakai, M.; Gindy, K., and Dustman, R. E.: Amplitude changes of components of the visually evoked response as related to mental states. *Proc Amer Psychol Assoc, 2:*139, 1966.

Satterfield, J. H.: Evoked cortical response enhancement and attention in man. A study of responses to auditory and shock stimuli. *Electroenceph Clin Neurophysiol, 19:470,* 1965.

Schenkenberg, T.: Visual, Auditory, and Somatosensory Evoked Responses of Normal Subjects from Childhood to Senescence. Unpublished doctoral dissertation, University of Utah, 1970.

Shagass, C., and Schwartz, M.: Evoked potential studies in psychiatric patients. *Ann NY Acad Sci, 112:526,* 1964.

——: Age, personality, and somatosensory cerebral evoked responses. *Science, 148:1359,* 1965.

——: Somatosensory cerebral evoked responses in psychotic depression. *Br J Psychiat, 112:799,* 1966.

Shagass, C.; Schwartz, M., and Straumanis, J. J.: Subject factors related to variability of averaged evoked responses. *Electroenceph Clin Neurophysiol, 20:97,* 1966.

Smith, J. R.: The electroencephalogram during infancy and childhood. *Proc Soc Exp Biol Med, 36:384,* 1937.

——: The electroencephalogram during normal infancy and childhood. I. Rhythmic activities present in the neonate and their subsequent development. *J Genet Psychol, 53:431,* 1938.

Spitz, R. A.: An inquiry into the genesis of psychiatric conditions in early childhood. In *The Psychoanalytic Study of the Child,* Vol. I, New York, International Univ., 1958.

Starzl, T. E., and Magoun, H. W.: Organization of the diffuse thalamic projection system. *J Neurophysiol, 14:133,* 1951.

Steriade, M.: Ascending control of thalamic and cortical responsiveness. *Int Rev Neurobiol, 12:87,* 1970.

Stock, M. V., and Smythe, P. M.: Does undernutrition during infancy inhibit brain growth and subsequent intellectual development? *Arch Dis Childhood, 38:546,* 1963.

Sutton, S.; Braren, M., and Zubin, J.: Evoked potential correlates of stimulus uncertainty. *Science, 150:1187,* 1965.

Tasaki, I.; Polley, E. H., and Orrego, F.: Action potentials from individual elements in cat geniculate and striate cortex. *J Neurophysiol, 17:454,* 1954.

Torres, F., and Warner, J. S.: Some characteristics of delayed responses to photic stimuli in the cat. *Electroenceph Clin Neurophysiol, 14:654,* 1962.

Towe, A. L.: Electrophysiology of the cerebral cortex: Consciousness. In T. C. Ruch, and H. D. Patton (Eds.): *Physiology and Biophysics,* Philadelphia, W. B. Saunders, 1965.

Towe, A. L.; Patton, H. D., and Kennedy, T. T.: Response properties of neurons in the pericruciate cortex of the cat following electrical stimulation of the appendages. *Exp Neurol, 10:325,* 1964.

Turner, O. A.: Growth and development of the cerebral cortical pattern in man. *Arch Neurol Psychiat, 59:1,* 1948.

Vaughn, H. G., and Katzman, R.: Evoked response in visual disorder. *Ann NY Acad Sci, 112:305,* 1964.

Vogel, W., and Broverman, D. M.: Relationship between EEG and test intelligence: A critical review. *Psychol Bull, 62:132,* 1964.

————: A reply to "Relationship between EEG and test intelligence: A commentary." *Psychol Bull, 65:99,* 1966.

Walsh, T. J.; Smith, J. L., and Shipley, T.: Blindness in infants. *Amer J Ophthal, 62:546,* 1966.

Weiss, A. D.: Sensory functions. In J. E. Birren (Ed.): *Handbook of Aging and the Individual,* Chicago, Univer. of Chicago, 1959.

Widen, L., and Ajmone-Marsan, C.: Effects of corticipetal and corticofugal impulses upon single elements of the dorsolateral geniculate nucleus. *Exp Neurol, 2:468,* 1960.

Williams, D., and Reynell, J.: Abnormal suppression of cortical frequencies. *Brain, 68:123,* 1945.

Williamson, P. D.; Goff, W. R., and Allison, T.: Somato-sensory evoked responses in patients with unilateral cerebral lesions. *Electroenceph Clin Neurophysiol, 28:566,* 1970.

Wilson, W. P.; Johnson, J. E., and Feist, F. W.: Thyroid hormone and brain function. II. Changes in photically elicited EEG responses following the administration of Triiodothyronine to normal subjects. *Electroenceph Clin Neurophysiol, 16:329,* 1964.

Yakovlev, P. I.: Morphological criteria of growth and maturation of the nervous system in man. In L. C. Kolb; R. L. Masland, and R. E. Cooke (Eds.): *Mental Retardation,* Baltimore, Williams and Wilkins, 1962.

————, and Lecours, A.: The myelogenetic cycles of regional maturation of the brain. In A. Minkowski (Ed.): *Regional Development of the Brain in Early Life,* Philadelphia, F. A. Davis, 1967.

CHAPTER 9

ELECTROPHYSIOLOGICAL STUDIES OF MENTAL RETARDATION

GARY C. GALBRAITH, JACK B. GLIDDON AND JYTTE BUSK*

IN OUR LABORATORY WE ARE STUDYING the electrophysiology of mental retardation using digital computers to compare patterns of the electroencephalogram (EEG) and sensory evoked response (SER) in retarded and nonretarded (normal) individuals. It is our belief, and there is growing supporting evidence, that the mentally retarded nervous system is characterized by unique patterns of electrical activity. The elucidation of such

* This research was supported in part by Public Health Services Research Grant No. MH-08667 from the National Institute of Mental Health, Department of Health, Education and Welfare, and National Institute of Child Health and Human Development Grant Nos. HD-06650, and General Research Support Grant No. FR-05632 from the General Research Support Branch, Division of Research Facilities and Resources, National Institutes of Health. The biofeedback research was carried out by Gary C. Galbraith at the University of Southern California and was supported in part by NASA Multidisciplinary Research Grant No. NGL-05-018-044, and by the Advanced Research Projects Agency of the Department of Defense and was monitored by the Office of Naval Research under contract N00014-70-C-0350 to the San Diego State College Foundation.

patterns should not only be of value in furthering our understanding of how the nervous system functions, but might possibly have practical implications for the treatment of mentally retarded patients.

In the first stages of investigation it is important to establish a catalog of reliable pattern differences between retarded and normal subjects. Such research is necessarily descriptive and correlational in nature, but could be of great value in supplementing existing diagnostic criteria. For example, the literature is quite consistent with regard to larger SER amplitudes in Down's syndrome. Using a paradigm similar to that reported by Schafer and Marcus (1973) we are finding characteristic SER patterns in patients whose retardation is linked to early asphyxia (this work is presently in progress and will be reported elsewhere). Among the many diagnostic categories, one of the most interesting is Uncertain-Functional, a rather amorphous class that quite possibly could yield reliable subgroupings by means of EEG and SER analysis.

Beyond classification, however, it would be desirable to progress to the point where direct manipulation and control of retarded neural activity is possible; as, for example, in EEG biofeedback. In normal subjects there is some evidence that EEG biofeedback can alter performance (Engstrom, London, and Hart, 1970; Beatty, *et al.*, 1974). It is interesting to speculate whether strategies such as EEG biofeedback, in which nonretarded electrical patterns are selectively reinforced, may lead to improvement in performance. This possibility as yet remains completely untapped.

In the present chapter we consider several suggestive relationships between perceptual behavior (including perception of emotional stimuli) and electrophysiological activity in the mentally retarded. In addition, there is a consideration of the possible application of EEG analysis and EEG biofeedback.

A GESTALT MODEL OF PERCEPTION AND THE VISUAL EVOKED RESPONSE

Spitz (1963) has shown that the perception of illusions among the institutionalized retarded differs significantly from the nonretarded. For example, in tests designed to assess visual and kinesthetic aftereffects, retardates typically do not report aftereffects as readily as normals. Once perceived, however, the duration of such aftereffects is longer in the retardate. Spitz concluded from such results that ". . . retardates as a group are characterized by a lowered capacity for (cortical) cellular modification" (p. 27). Working within the framework of Gestalt field theory, Spitz proposed four postulates of neural functioning to account for the observed perceptual behavior in the retardate:

POSTULATE I. "In retardates, it takes longer to induce temporary, as well as permanent, electrical, chemical and physical changes in stimulated cortical cells."

POSTULATE II. "Once stimuli induce temporary chemical and electrical modification of cortical cells, it takes longer for these cells to return to their previous state."

POSTULATE III. "In retardates, once stimuli induce permanent chemical, electrical, and/or physical changes in cortical cells, it will be more difficult and take a longer period of time to switch consequent like, or relatively similar stimuli, away from these particular cell traces or concurrent patterns as to form new, or different, traces or patterns."

POSTULATE IV. "In retardates, there is less spread of electrochemical activity from stimulated cells into the surrounding cortical field."

Although the above postulates are expressed in terminology of neurophysiology it must be remembered that the original data came from behavioral observations. Thus, inferences about actual neural processes are necessarily indirect. Note, however, that Postulates I, II, and IV deal with the transient effects of sensory stimulation upon cortical cells. This is clearly a situation where sensory evoked response analysis can be employed as a more direct test of the postulated neural functioning. Some possible implications of these postulates in terms of the evoked response are as follows: Postulate I—retardates will have longer evoked response latencies; Postulate II—retardates will show greater duration of evoked response components; Postulate IV—the topographic distribution of the sensory evoked response will show reduced amplitudes in recording sites further removed from the primary sensory cortex.

Latency and Topography of the VER

A study was carried out (Galbraith, Gliddon, and Busk, 1970) in which the computer averaged visual evoked response (VER) was recorded in twenty-four retarded and sixteen nonretarded subjects in order to address the questions of cortical cellular modifiability raised by Spitz. The mean chronological age (CA) for the retarded group was 16.3 years (range = 9-27), and the mean IQ was 46.7 (range = 26-66). The mean CA for the non-retarded group was 20.0 years (range = 7-32). Scalp electrodes were positioned over primary visual cortex as well as adjacent associative cortical fields. A posterior-midline electrode was located 2 cm above the inion (this corresponds closely to O_z in the "10-20" system). A reference electrode was then positioned 5 cm anterior to O_z along the midline. All electrodes were referred to this electrode in bipolar derivations. Lateral-left and lateral-right electrodes were positioned 5 cm to the left and right of the reference, respectively. An anterior-midline electrode was positioned 5 cm anterior to the reference along the midline. Anterior-left and anterior-right electrodes were placed 8 cm along a line extending at 45° from the reference electrode. Bipolar VERs were recorded to visual stimuli consisting of triangular geometric forms flashed into left and/or right visual fields (7° lateral to visual fixation).

Analysis of VER patterns showed support for several of the postulates. For example, a VER positive component occurring at 55 msec in nonretarded subjects occurred at 75 msec in retarded subjects, and a late VER component appearing at 279 msec in nonretarded subjects was delayed to 322 msec in retarded subjects. Both differences were statistically significant. Thus, the implication of Postulate I, that VER latencies should occur later in the retardate, was supported. Similar results have been observed by others. Rhodes, Dustman, and Beck (1969) and Chalke and Ertl (1965) reported significantly longer mean latencies for VER components among retardates. In our laboratory, Brown

(1968) studied the P300 component (first described by Sutton, Teuting, Zubin, and John, 1967) which normally appears 300 msec beyond the expected onset of an omitted stimulus. In Down's syndrome subjects the latency was delayed to approximately 400 msec. The occurrence of delayed evoked response components in retarded subjects is thus a consistent finding in a number of different studies. It appears that the mentally retarded nervous system can be characterized as being "sluggish" in response to sensory stimulation.

Support for Postulate II, however, was inconclusive. Certain electrode derivations showed a reduced responsiveness in the retardates, resulting in VER waveforms devoid of small rapid fluctuations and appearing somewhat longer in duration. However, further study will be required to substantiate Postulate II.

Data supporting Postulate IV is summarized in Figure 9-1. Late VER component amplitudes were measured in both groups and expressed as a percentage of the amplitude recorded in the posterior-midline electrode, which appears as 100 percent in Figure 9-1. The results show a marked difference in the topographic pattern of VER amplitudes in the two groups. Nonretarded subjects actually show enhanced amplitudes (values greater than 100 percent) in three recording sites over association cortex. Retardates, on the other hand, show a generalized reduction in all VER amplitudes recorded over association cortex. Thus, the prediction of "less spread of electrochemical activity" in the mentally retarded appears to have been supported by our results.

John (1972) has shown that information processing in the central nervous system depends upon the establishment of widespread patterns of coherent neural activity. In these terms, the pattern of spread of electrical activity observed in nonretarded and retarded subjects has a certain degree of face validity. That is, normal subjects, who are better able to process information, are characterized by enhanced evoked response amplitudes in areas removed from the primary receiving cortex; while mentally retarded subjects, who are less able to process information, are characterized by a reduced spread of electrical activity.

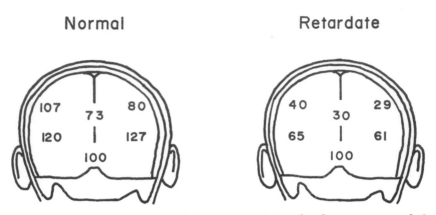

Figure 9-1. Topographic distribution of VER amplitudes in nonretarded and retarded subjects expressed as a percentage of the posterior-midline amplitude.

It seems worthwhile to note that these evoked response results support theoretical postulates derived from an entirely different domain, viz., visual and kinesthetic perception. There is recent evidence for quite good correspondence between evoked response amplitudes and psychophysical thresholds in normal subjects (Campbell and Maffei, 1970). Certainly the relationship between perception and electrophysiology deserves much more study in the field of mental retardation.

RETARDATE RESPONSIVENESS TO PATTERN VISUAL STIMULATION

Just as the above electrophysiological experiment was suggested from behavioral (perceptual) research, it is possible that behavioral research may take some hints from the electrophysiology laboratory. For example, Marcus (1970) demonstrated that Down's syndrome has developmental abnormalities in evoked response patterns to complex (checkerboard) visual stimuli. Essentially, the evoked response to such pattern stimuli is developmentally less mature than the response to nonpatterned, homogenous, light stimulation. Thus, it would appear from an electrophysiological point of view that the Down's nervous system is selectively deficient in its processing of pattern light stimulation. This result suggests a similar deficit in perceptual behavior.

To test this behaviorally we utilized a backward visual masking paradigm (Galbraith and Gliddon, 1972) in which the threshold to a brief test flash (TF) is elevated due to the subsequent presentation of a spatially overlapping masking flash (MF) (see reviews by Kahneman, 1968; Raab, 1963). Masking is increased when the TF-MF interflash interval (IFI) is decreased. Although the exact mechanisms of backward masking are not clearly understood, it is generally agreed that masking is due to neural rather than photochemical factors (Baker, 1963; Boynton, 1961; Sperling, 1965). Moreover, the neural locus of masking depends upon parameters of the MF. Nonpatterned, homogenous, MF stimuli exert their effect early in the visual system, primarily within the retina; whereas patterned MF stimuli affect higher visual centers, presumably the visual cortex (Schiller, 1965). Moreover, Liss and Haith (1970) have shown that the degree of masking is greater in young subjects. Thus, on the basis of developmentally immature evoked responses to pattern stimuli, it seemed reasonable to hypothesize greater masking (a less mature perceptual response) in Down's subjects.

The results are seen in Figure 9-2. For the homogenous masking flash the IFI threshold for retardates was approximately 10 msec greater than for nonretardates. Since masking with a homogenous MF occurs primarily within the retina it would appear that retardates are somewhat slower in their peripheral processing. However, when a patterned MF was used the threshold difference increased to 33 msec. Thus, Down's were more severely impaired in their ability to perceive test flash visual stimuli when followed temporally by a patterned masking stimulus.

Unfortunately, the data does not permit the conclusion that the observed effects of a pattern MF are unique to Down's syndrome, since no other groups were compared. Indeed, increased masking in retardates other than Down's syndrome has been demonstrated by Spitz and Thor (1968), suggesting a general inability to extract information from the TF. Clearly, more re-

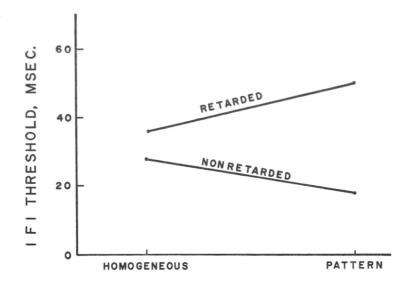

MASKING CONDITION

Figure 9-2. Mean interflash interval (IFI) at which threshold was reached as a function of group and masking condition. Data represent the average of 10 normals and 10 Down's syndrome subjects. Each point graphed is based on a minimum of 60 stimulus presentations for each subject (a minimum of 600 for the average), and for some subjects as many as 100 presentations.

search is required to answer this question. Yet, there does appear to be an encouraging compatability between perceptual and electrophysiological data.

LIGHT INTENSITY AND VER AMPLITUDE

Barnet and Lodge (1967) recorded the auditory evoked response in normal and Down's infants and found significantly larger amplitudes for Down's. Bigum, Dustman, and Beck (1970), in a study involving normals and Down's between the ages of six to sixteen years, found that Down's had larger primary and secondary amplitudes to somesthetic stimulation. However, visual stimulation produced higher amplitudes only for secondary components but lower amplitudes for primary components. An important observation in the Bigum, et al. study was the evoked response amplitude asymmetry found in normals, but not in retardates. Thus, normal VERs showed larger late component amplitudes recorded over the right than over the left central scalp region. Similar asymmetry in the evoked response has been reported by Rhodes, Dustman, and Beck (1969; see Chap. 8).

In our laboratory we tested the effects of light intensity in ten normals and ten Down's (Gliddon, Busk, and Galbraith, in press). Subjects were age matched with a mean CA of 22.8 ± 3.8 years. Unipolar EEG scalp activity was recorded from occipital (O1 and O2) and central (C3 and C4) areas, with linked ears serving as reference. Homogenous light flashes were presented by means of a Grass photo-stimulator and a Ganzfeld reflector. By placing neutral density filters in the light path it was possible to present a 2 log unit range of intensities (0.43, 4.3 and 43 phots); much lower than the unfiltered intensity of the photo-stimulator (approximately 115 phots). The intensity levels used in this experiment were selected primarily in order to extend the range of observations considerably below that reported in earlier research.

VER amplitude was computed by means of a perimeter measure previously described by Dustman and Beck (1969). This method of analysis was chosen since certain peaks of the VER could not be observed reliably for the lowest light intensity condition, and since the analysis could be performed objectively by computer. The technique is analogous to measuring the distance traced out by the various components within certain time intervals. Both "early" (0-125 msec) and "late" (125-300 msec) perimeters were analyzed, as well as the total perimeter (sum of early and late).

The results for the occipital VER are presented in Figure 9-3. It was found that Down's had significantly greater perimeters at all intensities for the late components (Fig. 9-3, middle). However, for the early components, Down's were significantly greater only at the highest intensity (Fig. 9-3, left).

Normal subjects showed an obvious VER asymmetry, consisting of a larger perimeter in the left occipital recording (signifi-

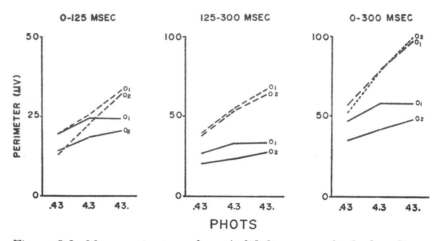

Figure 9-3. Mean perimeter values (solid line—normals, broken line—Down's syndrome) based on 200 stimulus replications for each intensity. Recordings are from O_1 and O_2. Separate results are presented for early (left), late (middle) and total (right) VER components.

cant for both early and late components, at all intensities). Most interesting, however, is the fact that Down's actually show greater asymmetry than normals at the 0.43 phot intensity for the early perimeter.

The results of the present experiment are thus in agreement with previous studies (Barnet and Lodge, 1967; Bigum, et al., 1970) in demonstrating larger evoked response amplitudes in Down's syndrome. However, the results disagree in several important respects. First, evoked response asymmetry favored larger amplitudes over the left hemisphere, rather than over right. Second, assymetry in the present study occurred only in occipital and not in central recordings. Finally, there was clear evidence for evoked response asymmetry in Down's patients, but only at the lowest intensity and for the early perimeter. All of these differences may be due to the lower range of light intensities used in the present experiment. If so, then it is clear that future evoked response studies of mentally retarded subjects must emphasize the widest possible range of stimuli. Moreover, the results suggest that evoked response asymmetry is not uniquely characteristic of the nonretarded nervous system, as previously reported, but rather appears to depend upon the choice of stimulus parameter.

In comparing the slopes of the curves in Figure 9-3, it is apparent that VER amplitude increases for Down's at a much faster rate as a function of light intensity. Since larger evoked response amplitudes are also a consequence of increased stimulus intensity (Vaughan and Hull, 1965), it would appear that Down's may be responding nonveridically, i.e. as if greater stimulus intensities were actually presented. If so, then these results could have possible implications in terms of Down's perception of light intensity. For example, subjective estimates of sensory magnitudes would probably grow at a much faster rate in Down's (the power function exponent would be larger). This has been suggested by Karrer (1966) for all retardates based upon ANS reactivity data. At the time of this writing we are unaware of adequate research dealing with magnitude estimation in Down's (obviously a difficult test). Should such psychophysical experiments agree with the evoked response data reported here, then further support will have been marshalled for meaningful brain-behavior relationships among the mentally retarded.

EVOKED RESPONSE CODING OF EMOTIONAL STIMULI

The search for physiological correlates of emotion has been an ever-present problem in psychology (Lindsley, 1951). Past research in this area has often dealt with the attempt to discover emotion-specific response patterns within the autonomic nervous system. However, several recent studies have demonstrated reliable patterns in the cortical evoked response to stimuli differing in subjective emotional qualities. Using normal subjects, Begleiter, Gross, and Kissin (1967) significantly altered VER amplitudes by pairing a previously neutral visual stimulus with affective works in a semantic conditioning paradigm. Unpleasant conditioned stimuli elicited the smallest VER amplitude, neutral conditioned stimuli the largest, with pleasant conditioned stimuli falling between these extremes. It is a common experience that retardates are capable of a wide range of emotional behavior. In light of the evoked response coding of emotional stimuli found in nonretarded subjects, we sought to determine whether such coding was demonstrable in the mentally retarded (Gliddon, Busk, and Galbraith, 1971).

Institutionalized retardates were shown black-and-white photographic reproductions of a variety of stimulus slides to be used in the study. Subjects were urged to express their likes or dislikes for each stimulus. Two independent observers eliminated all subjects who were (a) not expressive, or (b) inconsistent in their repeated response to the same stimuli. The nine subjects satisfying these criteria had a mean CA of 15.4 years (range = 11-20) and a mean IQ of 53.3 (range = 39-71). For each subject a unique set of stimulus slides was compiled corresponding to his own pleasant, unpleasant and neutral responses to the photographs. As a further control, each slide was presented defocused so as to be unrecognizable. The stimuli were thus divided into the following groups: pleasant focused (PF), pleasant defocused (PD), unpleasant focused (UF), unpleasant defocused (UD), and blank (B) slides completely devoid of form. The PD, UD, and B slides were considered to be relatively neutral stimuli (subjects in this experiment showed very few neutral responses to the photographs). The stimuli were then flashed in known random order to elicit the evoked response.

The results are shown in Figure 9-4. It can be seen that occipital VER amplitudes vary according to the category of affective stimulus. An analysis of variance showed that the F-G component (155-215 msec, see figure insert) was significantly different; the same amplitude pattern is also seen for the E-F component (130-155 msec). Specifically, neutral stimuli elicited the largest VER amplitude, unpleasant stimuli the smallest amplitude, with pleasant stimuli between these two extremes. This pattern of retardate VER amplitudes to emotional stimuli is thus identical to that found in normals by Begleiter, et al.

These results suggest a common feature in the neural coding of emotional information that transcends differences in intellectual ability. Thus, based upon the data at hand, the affective dimension appears to be represented by relatively stable neural pat-

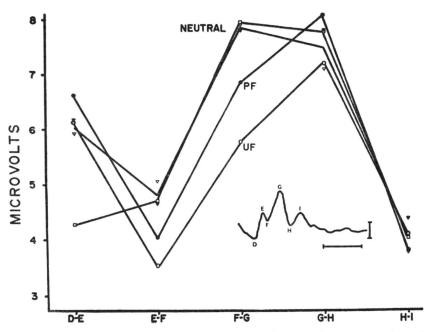

Figure 9-4. VER insert: Occipital group VER (averaged across 9 subjects) for the PF condition. Peaks and troughs labeled D-I have the following latencies (in msec): D = 90, E = 130, F = 155, G = 215, and I = 320. Horizontal and vertical calibrations equal 200 msec and 4 μv, respectively.

Main Figure: Comparison of mean O_2 amplitudes for all affective conditions represented by the following symbols: O, unpleasant focused (UF); ●, pleasant focused (PF); ∇, unpleasant defocused (UD); ▼, pleasant defocused (PD); □, blank (B). Note that a single line graphs the average values for the PD and UD conditions.

terns in both nonretarded and retarded subjects. It is interesting to speculate upon possible uses of such knowledge. For example, it now seems conceivable to determine, by means of evoked response analysis, those stimuli which are pleasant or positively reinforcing in noncommunicative patients. Perhaps such stimuli could then be used to advantage in behavior modification programs.

COMPUTER ANALYSIS OF EEG

In place of manual methods of scoring EEG ink tracings, we have used digital computers to quantify the frequency spectrum of EEG signals (Brazier and Casby, 1952; Walter, 1963; Bingham, Godfrey and Tukey, 1967; Papakostopoulos, Cooper and Walter, 1971). For example, auto-spectral analysis quantifies the amplitude of the various frequencies recorded from a single EEG channel. One important advantage conferred by the computer, in addition to high levels of resolution, is the ability to extract information concerning interactions between channels. Thus, cross-spectral frequency analysis provides useful information concerning shared EEG patterns recorded simultaneously from two electrodes.

We were interested to determine whether such EEG analyses, particularly the assessment of shared EEG patterns, might suggest functional differences in subjects with impaired neural organization. We collected data from a group of selected institutionalized mentally retarded patients and age-matched normal controls ($N = 10$ in each group). The patients had to meet the following selection criteria: (1) no history of seizures; (2) receiving no medication that would affect the EEG; (3) no known vision defects; and (4) known to be cooperative. EEG activity was recorded from left (O_1) and right (O_2) occipital and left (P_3) and right (P_4) parietal leads. All subjects received the following experimental conditions: resting with eyes closed, photic driving at 4, 7, 10, 13, and 16 Hz. EEG activity was recorded on magnetic tape and later analyzed by spectral analysis. Specifically, the analysis involved a determination of weighted-average coherence ($\overline{C}$), which expresses the overall linear relationship between two EEG signals (Galbraith, 1967). $\overline{C}$ is bounded between zero (no linear relationship) and one (perfect linear relationship). $\overline{C}$ analysis was used to assess the magnitude of shared EEG activity between homologous areas of left and right hemisphere O_1-O_2 and P_3-P_4), and the shared activity within hemispheres (O_1-P_3 and O_2-P_4).

Figure 9-5 graphs the mean $\overline{C}$ values averaged over all normal and retarded subjects in the different conditions (two minutes of artifact-free EEG data were analyzed for each subject in each condition). These results show that normals have somewhat higher levels of shared EEG activity, as reflected in larger $\overline{C}$ magnitudes. Normals tended also to show increased EEG coherence as a result of increased frequency of photic driving, particularly in the P_3-P_4 (Fig. 9-5A) and O_2-P_4 (Fig. 9-5C) cross-spectral derivations.

These preliminary results suggest that the level of intellectual functioning is expressed in the pattern of interactions among brain regions. The slight increase in EEG coupling in normals during photic driving may indicate a higher degree of shared information during conditions of dynamic (repetitive) stimulation. The lower $\overline{C}$ values observed among retardates may reflect reduced interactions in a nervous system less able to share and communicate information. Although the effect here is not large, it leads to the identical conclusion reached in the evoked response study reported at the beginning of the present chapter. Moreover, the use of EEG coherence analysis is quite analogous to the types of coherent brain activity which John (1972) has shown to be important in learning and memory.

Along similar lines, we have assumed that the developing nervous system should also be characterized by increasing function-

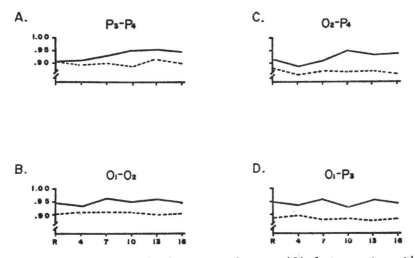

Figure 9-5. Graph of weighted-average coherence (C) during resting with eyes closed (R), and photic driving. Values of $\overline{C}$ are presented for various cross-spectral combinations between (Fig. 9-5A, B) and within (Fig. 9-5C, D) hemispheres. Note truncated ordinate. Solid line = normal, dashed line = retardates.

al neural interactions. To test this assumption, the EEG cross-spectrum was analyzed, in a pilot study, for both retarded and normal subjects of differing ages (4-13 years in normals, 12-17 years in retardates). Auto-spectra were also determined in order to compare the relative value of auto- and cross-spectra as measures of central nervous system development (we assumed further that if one measure was better than another, then it should more closely relate to chronological age). Electrodes were placed over left occipital (O_1) and left central (C_3) scalp. The cross-spectrum thus quantifies shared activity between O_1-C_3. Mean EEG frequency was computed over a fifteen minute sample (individual epochs with obvious artifacts were eliminated).

Figure 9-6 shows increasing EEG frequency as a function of

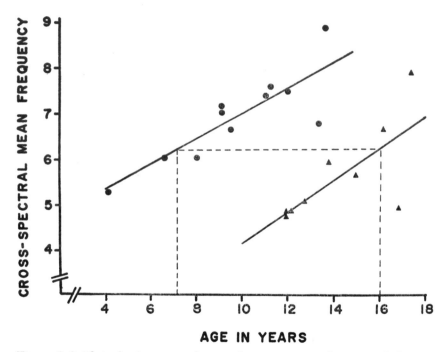

Figure 9-6. Plot of cross-spectral mean frequency as a function of chronological age. Solid circles represent the normal data, triangles represent data for mentally retarded subjects. The computed regression equation for normals is $Y = .275X + 4.181$, for retardates, $Y = .345X + .710$.

TABLE 9-I

VARIABILITY OF EEG MEAN FREQUENCY (IN Hz) ABOUT
CHRONOLOGICAL AGE REGRESSION LINE

Group	Occipital Auto-Spectrum (O_z)	O_z-C_3 Cross-Spectrum	Central Auto-Spectrum (C_3)
Normal	.57	.47	.54
Retarded	1.02	.74	.57

chronological age for both groups. Such a relationship, at least in normal subjects, is to be expected (Lindsley, 1936). Note, however, that the normal and retardate data are virtually non-overlapping. Thus, all retardates show lower mean frequencies for a given chronological age. Variability of the data about the regression line was assessed by computing the standard error of estimate according to the formula:

$$\sigma_{y.x} = \sigma_Y \sqrt{1 - r^2} = \sqrt{\Sigma (y - \hat{y})^2/n},$$

which represents the closeness of fit of the observed data to the predicted data (Guilford, 1965). In other words, $\sigma_{y.x}$ is to be interpreted as the standard deviation of the observed y-values about the ŷ-values predicted from the linear regression.

The results are presented in Table 9-I. For normal subjects the best predictive relationship (smallest standard error) between EEG frequency and chronological age occurred in the O_1-C_3 cross-spectrum (.47 Hz). For retardates the best predictive relationship occurred in the C_3 auto-spectrum (.57 Hz). In every case, however, retarded subjects show more variable relationships between EEG frequency and chronological age.

If we accept the least variable relationship between EEG and age as the best indicator of age-related development within the central nervous system, then for normal subjects it involves patterns of shared interaction between brain sites; while for retarded subjects it involves activity recorded at a single brain locus. Once again, it appears that patterns of shared neural activity may be indicative of the level of intellectual functioning.

BIOFEEDBACK AND THE POSSIBLE ENHANCEMENT OF HUMAN PERFORMANCE

Biofeedback provides immediate information concerning moment-to-moment physiological changes that normally are not available to the subject. Thus, heart rate or skin temperature is registered on a meter, EEG alpha activity is used to modulate a tone, etc. Miller (1969) has described biofeedback experiments with animals in which electrical stimulation of brain reward centers is delivered whenever the desired change in physiological activity occurs. His results show that dramatic changes in physiological functioning are possible. For example, rats can learn to control vasodilation in very limited body regions (only one ear), or to slow heart rate to fatally low levels. With such stimulation from the animal research, the possible application of human biofeedback is receiving increasing attention (Stoyva, et al., 1972; Beatty, et al., 1974). In our laboratory we are teaching subjects to control electrocortical patterns by means of on-line computer analysis. Our results, thus far, suggest that quite complex EEG patterns can be brought under some degree of voluntary control, at least by normal subjects.

The subject is seated in front of a computer graphics terminal, which presents the feedback display. A large-scale digital computer samples EEG activity, computes auto- and cross-spectra, and updates the display every four seconds. The subject is free to select any one of four EEG auto-spectra, or any one of six cross-spectral combinations, for feedback. Although the subject receives feedback for only a single EEG parameter, the computer stores data for all auto- and cross-spectra. Subsequent analyses can thus determine if patterns of control are specific to particular brain regions, or occur simultaneously in all electrodes.

Figure 9-7 illustrates the results of a subject who was attempting to control O_z-C_3 weighted-average coherence (only the COHER data were displayed during feedback). The subject had previously determined that visual plus auditory imagery, with eyes closed, would lower $\overline{C}$. The results show that $\overline{C}$ was lowered from the eyes closed baseline to the period of deepest imagery.

J. B., SECOND SESSION, OZ-C3 CBAR FEEDBACK

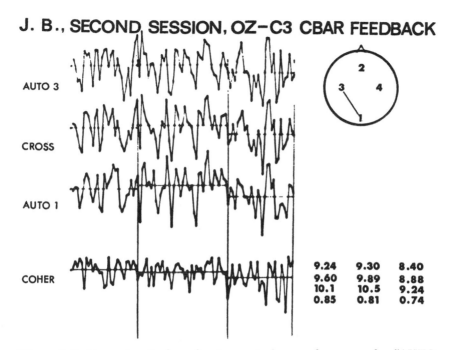

AUTO 3

CROSS

AUTO 1

COHER

9.24	9.30	8.40
9.60	9.89	8.88
10.1	10.5	9.24
0.85	0.81	0.74

Figure 9-7. Computer display of auto-spectral mean frequency for "AUTO 3" (C_3), "AUTO 1" (O_z), "CROSS" (O_z-C_3 cross-spectrum) and "COHER" (weighted-average coherence). Moment-to-moment changes are displayed during eyes closed baseline (left segment), visual plus auditory imagery (middle segment), and deepest imagery (right segment). Computed mean values for EEG frequency and coherence for the three segments are shown in lower right-hand corner.

The results are further summarized in Table 9-II. This table presents values of coherence during baseline and feedback conditions (divided into three segments of increasing depth of imagery) for all electrode combinations. Note that the greatest decline in coherence occurs in the O_z-C_3 combination, which was the combination used in feedback. However, a decline is also seen in the O_z-C_4 combination of nearly the same magnitude. All other electrode combinations, however, show a smaller magnitude of change. Thus, the subject was able to lower the pattern of coherence between occipital and central brain sites. Oth-

TABLE 9-II

BIOFEEDBACK OF O_x-C_3 COHERENCE

Electrode Combination	Baseline	Feedback (Visual and Auditory Imagery)			Difference (Baseline-Deepest)
		(Lightest)	(Intermediate)	(Deepest)	
O_x-C_x	.69	.65	.61	.63	.06
O_x-C_3*	.85	.81	.76	.73	.12
C_x-C_3	.82	.81	.83	.84	−.02
O_x-C_4	.79	.78	.72	.68	.11
C_x-C_4	.83	.81	.83	.83	.00
C_3-C_4	.84	.83	.84	.77	.07

* Electrode Combination Receiving Feedback.

er subjects have been able to increase the coherence level between different brain sites. The point to be emphasized here is that subjects can often bring quite complex electrophysiological patterns under an increased degree of voluntary control.

Although by no means conclusive, there is evidence for altered performance as a consequence of biofeedback training. Thus, Engstrom, et al. (1970) showed a significant increase in scores of hypnotic susceptibility in a group of subjects that learned to increase their alpha activity. A necessary condition of this experiment was the foreknowledge that alpha activity was positively correlated with hypnotic susceptibility (London, et al. 1968). Beatty, et al. (1974) have altered performance on a vigilance task by theta training.

In our experiments we have repeatedly found evidence for differences in EEG and evoked response patterns between retarded and normal subjects. Basically, the recurring theme points to a reduction in spread of "information" between different brain regions in the mentally retarded. The question we raise here, is whether it would be useful, via biofeedback, to selectively reinforce neural patterns involving increased levels of shared activity. This might be accomplished by having patients wear small telemetry systems so that reinforcers could be delivered within such controlled hospital environments as, for example, token economy wards. If such patterns of neural activity are successfully modified, would there be concomitant improvement in behavior or intellectual development? If the results are positive, quite novel and exciting approaches to the direct treatment of at least some forms of mental retardation might be forthcoming.

REFERENCES

Baker, H. D.: Initial stages of light and dark adaptation. *J Opt Soc Am,* 53:98-103, 1963.

Barnet, A. B., and Lodge, A.: Click evoked EEG responses in normal and developmentally retarded infants. *Nature, 124:*252-255, 1967.

Beatty, J.; Greenberg, A.; Deibler, W. P., and O'Hanlon, J. F.: Operant control of occipital theta rhythm affects performance in a radar monitoring task. *Science, 183:*871-873, 1974.

Begleiter, H.; Gross, M. M., and Kissin, B.: Evoked cortical responses to affective stimuli. *Psychophysiology, 3:*336-344, 1967.

Bigum, H. B.; Dustman, R. E., and Beck, E. C.: Visual and somato-sensory evoked responses from mongoloid and normal children. *Electroencephalog Clin Neurophysiol J, 28:*576-585, 1970.

Bingham, E.; Godfrey, M. D., and Tukey, J. W.: Modern techniques of power spectrum estimation. *IEEE Transactions on Biomedical Engineering,* AU 15, 55-56, 1967.

Boynton, R. M.: Some temporal factors in vision. In Rosenblith, W. A. (Ed.): *Sensory Communication.* New York, Wiley, 1961.

Brazier, M. A. B., and Casby, J. U.: Crosscorrelation and autocorrelation studies of electroencephalographic potentials. *Electroencephalog Clin Neurophysiol J, 4:*201-211, 1952.

Brown, W. S., Jr.: Evoked potential correlates of information delivery and responsiveness in mongoloid and normal children. Unpublished Master's Thesis, University of Southern California, 1968.

Campbell, F. W., and Maffei, L.: Electrophysiological evidence for the existence of orientation and size detectors in the human visual system. *J Physiol* (London), 207:635-652, 1970.

Chalke, F. C., and Ertl, J.: Evoked potentials and intelligence. *Life Sci, 4:* 1319-1322, 1965.

Dustman, R. E., and Beck, E. C.: Maturation and visually evoked potential. *Electroencephalog Clin Neurophysiol J, 26:*2-11, 1969.

Engstrom, D. R.; London, P., and Hart, J. T.: Hypnotic susceptibility increased by EEG alpha training. *Nature, 227:*1261-1262, 1970.

Galbraith, G. C.: The effect of prior EEG "coupling" upon the visual evoked response. *IEEE Trans Biomed Eng, 14:*233-239, 1967.

Galbraith, G. C., and Gliddon, J. B.: Backward visual masking with homogeneous and patterned stimuli: Comparison of retarded and nonretarded subjects. *Percept Mot Skills, 34:*903-908, 1972.

Galbraith, G. C.; Gliddon, J. B., and Busk, J.: Visual evoked responses in mentally retarded and nonretarded subjects. *Am J Ment Defic,* 75:341-348, 1970.

Gliddon, J. B.; Busk, J. and Galbraith, G. C.: Visual evoked responses to emotional stimuli in the mentally retarded. *Psychophysiology,* 8:576-580, 1971.

————: Visual evoked responses as a function of light intensity in Down's syndrome and nonretarded subjects. *Psychophysiology,* (in press).

Guilford, J. P.: *Fundamental Statistics in Psychology and Education.* N.Y., McGraw-Hill, 1965.

John, E. R.: Switchboard versus statistical theories of learning and memory. *Science, 177*:850-864, 1972.

Kahneman, D.: Method, findings, and theory in studies of visual masking. *Psychol Bull, 70*:404-425, 1968.

Karrer, R.: Autonomic nervous system functions and behavior: A review of experimental studies with mental defectives. In Ellis, N. R. (Ed.): *International Review of Research in Mental Retardation.* Vol. 2, New York, Academic, 1966.

Lindsley, D. B.: Brain potentials in children and adults. *Science, 84*:354, 1936.

Lindsley, D. B.: Emotion. In Stevens, S. S. (Ed.): *Handbook of Experimental Psychology.* New York, Wiley, 1951.

Liss, P. H., and Haith, M. M.: The speed of visual processing in children and adults: Effects of backward and forward masking. *Percep Psychophy, 8*:396-398, 1970.

London, P.; Hart, J., and Leibovitz, M.: EEG alpha rhythms and susceptibility to hypnosis. *Nature, 219*:71-72, 1968.

Marcus, M. M.: The evoked cortical response: A technique for assessing development. *Calif Ment Health Res Dig, 8*:59-72, 1970.

Miller, N.: Learning of visceral and glandular responses. *Science, 163*:434-445, 1965.

Papakostopoulos, D.; Cooper, R., and Walter, W. G.: A technique for the measurement of phase relations of the EEG. *Electroencephalog Clin Neurophysiol, 30*:562-564, 1971.

Raab, D. H.: Backward masking. *Psychol Bull, 60*:118-129, 1963.

Rhodes, L. E.; Dustman, R. E., and Beck, E. C.: The visual evoked response: A comparison of bright and dull children. *Electroencephalog Clin Neurophysiol J, 27*:364-372, 1969.

Schafer, E. W. P., and Marcus, M. M.: Self-stimulation alters human sensory brain responses. *Science, 181*:175-177, 1973.

Schiller, P. H.: Monoptic and dichoptic visual masking by patterns and flashes. *J Exp Psychol, 69*:193-199, 1965.

Sperling, G.: Temporal and spatial visual masking: I. Masking by impulse flashes. *J Op Soc Am, 55:*541-559, 1965.

Spitz, H. H.: Field theory in mental deficiency. In Ellis, N. R. (Ed.): *Handbook of Mental Deficiency.* New York, McGraw-Hill, 1963.

Spitz, H. H., and Thor, D. H.: Visual backward masking in retardates and normals. *Percep Psychophy, 4:*245-246, 1968.

Stoyva, J.; Barber, T. X.; DiCara, L. V.; Kamiya, J.; Miller, N. E., and Shapiro, D. (Eds.): *Biofeedback and Self-Control, 1971.* Chicago, Aldine-Atherton, 1972.

Sutton, S.; Teuting, P.; Zubin, J., and John, E. R.: Information delivery and the sensory evoked response. *Science, 155:*1436-1439, 1967.

Vaughan, H. G., Jr., and Hull, R. C.: Functional relation between stimulus intensity and photically evoked cerebral responses in man. *Nature* (London), 206:720-722, 1965.

Walter, D. O.: Spectral analysis for the electroencephalograms, mathematical determination of neurophysiological relationships from records of limited duration. *Exp Neurol, 8:*155-181, 1963.

CHAPTER **10**

LEARNING DISABILITIES AND CONDITIONAL BRAIN ACTIVITY

JEROME COHEN

THE EMPHASIS OF THIS CHAPTER is on the applicability of conditional cerebral activity, mainly slow potentials, to diagnostic studies of children with *learning disabilities* (LD) of a general type. Some discussion of the kind of children we are concerned with is in order, and the rationale for this particular psychophysiological approach must be considered.

Children are usually first suspected of having learning problems by parents or professional workers when difficulties in language and the development of communication skills disrupt the normal family relationships or expectations. Five primary conditions result in referrals to any learning center, whether by parents, teachers, or physicians: (1) acute or chronic physical ailment or disease, such as cerebral palsy or systemic lead poisoning, (2) deprivation of social or cultural experiences, as often seen in extreme poverty coupled with broken family life, (3) emotional or severe psychological or behavior problems, (4) inherent or constitutional lack of adequate mental ability, and (5) dysfunction of specific learning processes including communication. Our conception of the children considered as learning disabled will be limited to the last category. We attempted to distinguish children with generalized mental retardation and those with primary emotional or psychiatric disorders from children with a suspected specific disability in the learning function, by differential diagnostic testing methods currently in use. The assumption is that an impairment in some aspect of learning may depend on a subtle difference in brain chemistry, structure or function which may be revealed by our electrophysiological testing methods. Suspected brain differences may be due to many causes, such as a specific injury to a restricted anatomical area or a generalized brain impairment of a cellular or biochemical nature, which may be constitutional or acquired.

Clements (1966) has collected a list of over 100 problems in learning disabled children. Disturbances may be mild, severe, congenital or acquired, generalized or specific. Despite the great diversity, educators, physicians and psychologists have come to identify this group of children with some degree of agreement. McCarthy and McCarthy (1969) cite some of the common elements: "(1) The children are retarded or disordered in school subjects, speech or language, and may have manifest behavior problems. (2) None are assignable to major categories of exceptionality, such as mental retardation or deafness. (3) All have some presumed neurologic basis for their manifest disability" (ibid. p. 8-10).

The presumption of a neurologic basis for the involvement stems from the traditional orientation of the field, but our interpretation is of "brain different" (in a possibly extreme way), rather than "brain damaged" or "dysfunctional" unless other medical evidence for organic damage is presented. The basis for brain difference may be in the hereditary constitutional factors in which a specific, localized, or general biochemical difference in brain activity may impair various functions of learning compared to "normal" children.

Birch (1964) summarized objections to the concept of neurologic etiology by stating two difficulties: (1) the lack of evidence of neurological abnormalities in children with learning disabilities, and conversely, (2) the lack of learning disabilities in some children with clear evidence of neurological abnormalities. Examinations by conventional neurological and electroencephalographic examinations have frequently failed to reveal neurological abnormalities in children with learning disabilities, or to differentiate them from normal children (Paine, 1965; Freeman, 1967; McGrady, 1971). Nevertheless, the relationships between deficiencies in behavioral and intellectual functions and brain injuries have been clearly demonstrated by such authorities as Penfield and Roberts (1959), Sperry (1961), Luria (1964) and Geschwind (1968).

The learning functions involve many steps, any of which may be defective, and some of which are elusive to observe. Information must be perceived or taken in, it must be held in short term memory store, integrated in a meaningful way with other related information and stored appropriately in memory. On recall, it must be retrieved from memory and integrated with new sensory inputs or ideational processes, related to new experiences and organized in integrated action for an effective output from long-term storage. The output may be verbalization, motor action or ideational association, thought or imagination. The output may be fed back into the appropriate system of the brain for partial control of future learning. Obviously the internal integration of the brain processes is more elusive to observation than activity related to perceptual inputs and motor outputs, but the opportunity to study some of these processes by computer analysis of its electrical activity is encouraging in that we may infer some things about associative processes as well.

Learning also involves motivation, selective attention, inhibition of other spontaneous unrelated activity, memory and recall, and directed performance. It is tempting to look at neurophysiological measures which may relate to some of those functions. Very few studies in the past have demonstrated brain impairments in children with learning disabilities using standard clinical EEG recording techniques with its emphasis on wave frequencies and the occurrence of transient abnormalities. The new highly sophisticated neurophysiological techniques based on computer analyses have greater promise of revealing such brain differences in LD children compared to children with normal learning ability and performance. Eventually these laboratory studies may shed light on the neurophysiological processes which actually underlie the functions of learning and memory, as well as furnish a significant diagnostic aid for detecting essential disabilities in the learning area.

THE CONTINGENT NEGATIVE VARIATION AND CEREBRAL EVOKED RESPONSES

When a sense organ is stimulated and the encoded neural message is transmitted to the cerebral cortex, the consequent neural activity in the surface layers of the cortex is measurable as a complex wave form on the scalp. The pattern of the voltage change which is amplified and recorded by the EEG is referred to as the cerebral *evoked response* (ER). The ER to a light flash is of low amplitude (about 10 micv) in the usual vertex scalp monopolar recording to an ear lobe reference.

The characteristics of the ER may be enhanced and made visible for study by increasing the signal to noise ratio (S/N). This is done by "averaging" the potentials which are time locked to the sensory input, that is, by summing the voltages at any instant and dividing by the number of presentations of the stimulus. This method of "averaging" increases the signal to noise ratio proportional to the square root of the number of trials in the average (S/N $= \sqrt{N/1}$). Thus, repeating the same stimulus 100 times increases the visibility of the ER by 10 times and repeating the stimulus only ten times increases the clarity of the ER by 3.2 times over the background of unrelated activity. This is the method generally employed by electrophysiologists to study changes in cerebral activity which relate to the discrete stimulus-response events of behavior. (See Donchin and Lindsley 1969 for a comprehensive account of recent work.)

W. Grey Walter and his colleagues (1964) were using these methods to study the evoked response patterns to a variety of

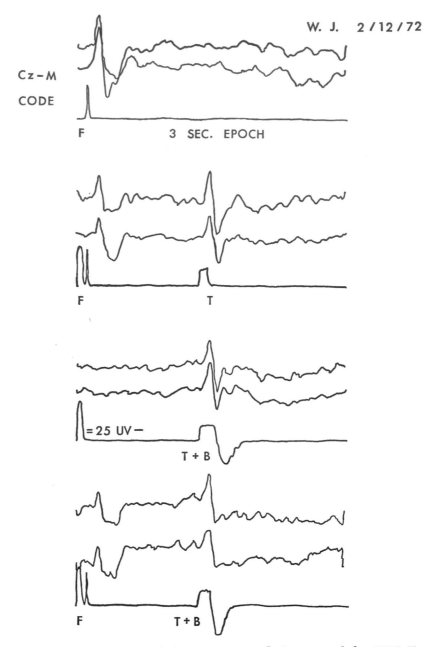

Figure 10-1. Average evoked responses to a flash, tone and the CNV. Each trace is an average of eight epochs, of three seconds each. Two traces are shown for each condition to show reliability of the responses. The CNV is seen in the last pair of traces, larger in the second set, since the first set represents the first conditioning trials in a naive subject. The first rise on the left of the code line is a 25 μv calibration signal. F is flash, T is tone and B is a push button to stop the tone.

stimuli when they discovered the contingent negative variation (CNV) quite by accident. Walter's group was investigating the interaction effects of stimuli presented in pairs. They noticed that a slow negative potential shift occurred between stimuli when the subject had to make an instrumental response to the second stimulus as in a conditioning situation or a reaction time experiment with a "ready" signal. This is illustrated in Figure 10-1. The ER to single and paired stimuli are seen, and the CNV is shown as an upward (negative) deflection of the pen when the person expects to make a response to the second stimulus (S_2). He "gets ready" at the first stimulus (S_1) which results in the negative shift and then makes his motor response after S_2, at which time the negative brain activity goes back to the baseline.

It is as if there were two kinds of electrical activity produced by the brain. The rhythmical activity such as alpha represents alternating current (ac), seen as sine wave oscillations about the baseline. The change in steady potential, such as the CNV, represents a direct current (dc) shift in the voltage level. Because of the technical difficulty of defining the absolute dc baseline over a long period of time during recording, the relative baseline is defined at each trial as the level of stable activity which precedes the first stimulus, averaged over a few hundred msec in order to smooth out transient occurrences.

DEVELOPMENT OF CEREBRAL EVOKED RESPONSES (ER)

Evoked responses in young children tend to be slower and more diffuse than in adults. Most investigators find that the early components of the ER are more affected by stimulus variables and less by subject or attitudinal variables, which affect the later slow components to a greater degree. We believe that two pathways are involved in the projection of the electrical response to a stimulus onto the surface of the brain. A primary or specific sensory system conducts from thalamic nuclei, which are specific for a sensory modality, to cerebral cortical receptor areas, and then to relevant association cortex. A secondary or diffuse system conducts impulses from the mid-line thalamus in the mid-brain to widespread cortical association areas. These two components become mixed and additive when recorded on the surface. The fastest early components may be more specific, but the longer latency responses, over 80-100 msec, are mixtures of both the specific and nonspecific pathways. Lindsley (1969) discussed the importance of disentangling the primary and secondary aspects of the ERs.

Rose and Lindsley (1968) demonstrated primary and secondary systems in studies of the development of visual ERs in kittens. At four days of age only a long latency negative wave was seen to flash. This appeared in all cortical areas and was thought to be a secondary response, since the eyes were not yet open and therefore non-functional for visual information processing, although a flash was a sufficient physiological stimulus. At fifteen days two components were clearly seen, the original long latency negative component and a new short latency positive-negative wave which occurred only in the visual projection area. By thirty days, the long latency negative wave was reduced and mingled with the negative wave of the short latency complex to form the typical response seen in mature animals. The two systems had different latencies, different times of development and distinct distributions over the head. A lesion made in the lateral geniculate nucleus (the direct visual pathway) blocked the short latency complex, but not the long latency negative wave. A lesion in the superior colliculus, on the other hand, blocked the long latency wave, but not the short, specific response complex.

Dustman and Beck (1966) studied the visual ER over the whole range of the human life span (see Chap. 8). The amplitudes develop, from one month to five or six years of age, and then decline to about one half of the peak value until thirteen to fourteen years of age. From fifteen years to the eighties, there were no systematic differences among age groups. The ER in newborn infants was studied by Creutzfeldt and Kuhnt (1967). They found only a long slow low voltage negative-positive complex in the occipital area with no ER in nonspecific cerebral areas. They only found dependable vertex responses in children at five years of age, but then the characteristics of the visual ER matured through adolescence.

The above suggests that the ERs may in some way relate to maturational level. Chalke and Ertl (1965) found that more intelligent subjects exhibit shorter response latencies. Ertl and Schafer (1969) found the latency of ER correlates with intelligence tests in children. They suggested that the speed of information processing could be reflected by response latencies and represent the biological substrate of intelligence level.

Rhodes, et al. (1969) studied ER in bright and dull children to flash. They found that bright children have larger late response components in the posterior region of the right hemisphere. Dull children displayed greater variability of the ERs and were thought not to be similar to a younger group of average intelligence, that is, the difference was not merely maturational.

The influence of psychological parameters on long latency waves in the ER was best shown by Sutton, et al. (1965). They recorded vertex waves in a situation where the subject had to guess which of two stimuli would occur. They reported a large slow positive wave between 300 and 500 msec latency accompanying stimulus uncertainty and called it the "P300 wave."

The P300 wave was studied in a signal detection experiment by Hillyard (1969). He found that the wave was much greater (21.2 micv) when a low level signal was discriminated than when it was not detected (6.0 micv). He concluded that the slow positive components represent a "higher order decision or discrimination process rather than a simple sensory elaboration." Donchin and Cohen (1967) also found the late positive wave to relate to a selective attention process when subjects were asked to discriminate stimuli and respond to only one of them.

Sutton (1969) provides an extensive list of psychological constructs and terms which have been associated with evoked response variability. One of the strongest that emerges is "task relevance" which was tested by Chapman and reported by him in the discussion section of Sutton's paper (Sutton, 1969, pp. 262-275). Chapman studied changes in ERs to identical verbal and numerical stimuli flashed on a screen when they had different relevance to what the subject was doing. The subject was to compare the two numbers presented as first and second stimuli and state which was larger, or to compare two letters, and state which comes later in the alphabetical order. Numbers or letters were frequently interposed between two sets of stimuli on which the subject was doing his simple calculation. Responses were sorted and averaged separately for the two types of trials, and stimuli which were task relevant had larger positive secondary slow components than those which were irrelevant.

Other studies of ERs which could relate to learning disabilities focus on attention and habituation or sensitivity to changes in stimulus situations as relevant psychological variables. Haider, et al. (1964) asked subjects to press a button to a certain stimulus presented in long series with other stimuli over prolonged time periods. Percentage of correct responses was taken as a measure of attention. The amplitude of the ERs decreased in periods in which a large number of missed signals occurred. Spong, et al. (1965) recorded responses to visual or auditory stimuli while the subject was told to attend or to respond to one modality, but not the other. When the subject attended to one modality and ignored the other, the ER for the attended to modality was greater than when that modality was ignored. Black and Walter (1965) found that when two stimuli are presented many times with short delays, the response to the second one habituates rapidly, but that the ER to the first stimulus remains high, since it contains all of the information. It was found by Cohen and Walter (1966) and by Begleiter and Platz (1969) that semantic stimuli result in greater evoked response amplitudes and complexity than blank flash visual stimuli.

Liberson (1966) found a decrease in amplitude of ER on the damaged side of the brain in aphasics. The relationships of cerebral dominance, handedness and dyslexia is controversial, but has led to comparisons of ER between the two hemispheres. Differences in the magnitude of visual responses were found for right and left handed people (Eason, et al., 1967). Also, differences between left and right hemispheres were found when comparing ER to verbal and spatial visual stimuli (Buchsbaum and Fedio, 1969). Conners (1971) studied children with severe reading disability and found that a significant number of the children had a great reduction of amplitude of the late components of the ER specific to the left parietal region. He identifies these children as familial dyslexics since other members of the families tended to have similar brain response patterns.

The late waves are shown to relate to attentiveness (Goff, 1967), and they tend to be more positive in the parietal region (Conners, 1971) in children who are poor readers and test low in verbal ability. Shields (1972) also found an increase in the late positive waves in dyslexic children, and the latencies of most components of the ER in dyslexic children were longer on the average than in normal children. Cohen, et al. (1965) first reported an enhancement of a very slow positive component following semantic stimuli, which is larger in amplitude in some dyslexic children compared to normal children.

VARIABLES RELATED TO THE CNV

The CNV is seen in all normal mature subjects who cooperate in the experiment and it may prove to be the most reliable of the EEG characteristics. The form of the CNV wave may be (1) ramp shaped with a steady rise in negative potential until the peak value is reached, that is, just before the motor response is discharged; or (2) a square wave with a rapid rise after S_1 and a fairly steady peak value; or (3) a shape in between (1) and (2) with a decelerating rise time, producing a convex curve resulting in a peak value also just before the motor response. The ramp shape is the most common form. Variations due to age will be dealt with in the section on the development of the CNV in children. The quantitative measures which may be applied are maximum amplitude, area under the curve between S_1 and S_2, latency to the onset, the rate of increase of potential, and the time of return to the baseline value after S_2. The distribution of amplitudes over the scalp and the symmetry of the CNV and ER in both hemispheres are also of interest, especially in the assessment of specific brain lesions involving localized areas.

Caspers (1961) concluded from his studies in animals that there is a relationship between a dc negative shift and behavioral arousal. He supported Clare and Bishop (1955), concluding that dendritic excitation results in graded potentials rather than conforming to the "all or none" principle of axonal discharge. The appearance at the surface of a dc shift could in fact relate to the summation of synchronous changes in steady potential in large groups of neurons whose dendritic felt-work is spread over the surface of the cerebral cortex. Caspers (1961) demonstrated a cortical negative shift in rats when they engaged in locomotion, exploratory behavior and orienting, and a positive dc shift during grooming, relaxation, and falling asleep. The negative cortical shift may be thought to accompany cerebral activation, alerting or arousal behavior, that is, increased "attention" in psychological terms. The presence of the CNV indicates that the subject is actively responding to stimulus-response sequences and paying attention to the stimuli. In order for activation to be inferred at the beginning of stimulation, there must also be signs of deactivation or relaxation after a period of stimulation, that is, the termination of the CNV by a positive going voltage or return to the baseline.

Cohen and Walter (1966) reported the CNV in anticipation of visual stimuli when no motor response took place. They interpreted the CNV as a correlate of psychological "expectancy" rather than a priming function for a motor discharge as Walter first hypothesized in his original report (1964). Irwin, et al. (1966) stressed motivation as the primary accompaniment of the CNV. Low, et al. (1966) interpreted the CNV as a cerebral conditional response and suggested conation or the perception of relationship in humans as the main psychological factor. Since the first few reports confirming the reality of the CNV, over a hundred articles have appeared emphasizing the great variety of psychological factors which have been studied in relation to it.

The CNV relates to learning and the efficiency of voluntary behavior in that it follows many of the characteristics of a Pavlovian conditional response, increasing with repetition of conditional association and reinforcement, and diminishing during extinction trials in which either the second stimulus or the instrumental response is omitted. It increases in amplitude during acquisition trials, in which performance, as measured by motor reaction time improves, and it continues at a high level as long as motivation toward good performance continues in human subjects. Cant and Bickford (1967) showed a positive relationship between CNV amplitude and motivation and Hillyard and Galambos (1967) showed, in accordance with Walter's original hypothesis, that the amplitude of the average CNV is negatively correlated with reaction time; the larger the CNV, the shorter the reaction time tends to be. Tecce and Scheff (1968) attempted to explain the CNV by relating it to attention. Cohen (1973a) indicated the role of selective attention by reporting a somewhat different scalp distribution of the CNV when the subject anticipates a visual stimulus for recognition instead of a stimulus requiring a motor response as in the reaction time situation. The CNV was found to be a reliable characteristic of the individual by retesting the same subjects, yielding a test-retest reliability coefficient of about .80.

The CNV is an expression of a person's unique makeup, but we do not as yet know which personality or psychological variables are definitely related to different characteristics of the CNV in normal people. There have been several convincing studies relating changes in the CNV to psychopathology (Walter, 1966; Timsit, et al., 1968), mostly limited by reliability of the psychiatric diagnosis. McCallum and Walter (1968) studied the effects of distracting stimuli on patients and normal control subjects. They found that anxious and also schizoid patients who may have fairly normal looking CNVs are drastically affected by extraneous stimuli, which they were told to ignore, and their CNVs were greatly reduced.

Another subject variable which has been studied is anxiety level. Contrary to their expectations, Knott and Irwin (1968) did not find a significant increase in the CNV when anxious subjects were shocked. They attributed the negative results to a ceiling effect, that is, the anxious subjects were already at a peak of arousal with cortical negativity: there was no more room for the expectancy of a shock to increase the level of negativity beyond the ordinary level of their CNV. More recent work (Knott and Peters, 1972) showed that complex interactions with anxiety level may mask main effects. There is an interaction with the sex of the subject and length of the interval between S_1 and S_2. They found a larger average CNV in women with long delay intervals, but a smaller CNV in men with longer delays. Also men tended to have a higher CNV when shocked than not shocked, whereas, in women, the opposite effect was found; that is, shock tended to decrease the amplitude of the CNV. The conclusion is that CNV measures may depend on intrinsic subject variables, such as sex, if the experimental conditions are suitably manipulated, but such specific variables have yet to be determined.

The CNV is difficult to establish in many chronic neurotic or psychotic patients, and Walter (1966) found it not to be present in psychopathic patients. The CNV in chronic anxiety patients developed very slowly and inconsistently, sometimes also being absent. Walter reports the CNV would extinguish very rapidly and take a long time to reappear when S_2 was omitted for many trials and then later restored. In normal subjects under the same conditions of extinction and restoration, the response usually disappears after five or six trials with no S_2, and reappears in the first few trials after restoration of the S_2 signal. Phobic patients, like chronic anxiety patients, tend to extinguish the CNV very rapidly and it takes a long time to restore it, although there may be normal appearing CNVs in the early conditioning stages. Obsessional patients were found by Walter to have unusually high amplitude CNVs, however it may be absent in some patients. Obsessive-compulsive patients were found to have fairly high amplitude CNVs which persist for very many trials during extinction, whereas normal subjects would have extinguished the CNV in only a few trials if S_2 were omitted. Also, in these patients the CNV does not return promptly to the baseline after the motor response to S_2, but it takes a second or two longer. The CNV was rarely seen in autistic or severely disturbed children. Dongier's group (Timsit, et al., 1967) reported prolonged CNVs in schizophrenic patients with a slow return to the neutral baseline after the response to S_2.

Findings in psychotic patients have questionable relevance to learning disabilities, but they do indicate the relationship between the functional neurophysiological responses to conditional situations and the serious disturbances of psychological and emotional functions.

DEVELOPMENT OF THE CNV WITH AGE

Walter (1966) first reported the presence of the CNV in children, noting that it is lower in amplitude, but he did not indicate the course of its development with age. He could not detect it in children under four years of age, and found that persuasion and social facilitation by encouragement of the experimenter was necessary until about seven years of age. He felt that the developmental period lasted through about fifteen years of age, and that the CNV is better if the experimenter urges the child to be competitive in shortening his reaction time to S_2. It was the slow development of the CNV in children, which was the clue that the CNV might be sensitive to psychopathological changes, and be a valuable diagnostic tool for psychiatry.

Low, et al. (1966) in their first replication study of the CNV showed its presence in a few young children who were highly motivated since they belonged to the investigators. However, they did not distinguish significant differences between thirteen to eighteen year olds and adult CNV patterns. Cohen, et al. (1967) reported developmental changes in the CNV from its earliest inception at six through eighteen years of age.

Cohen tested blind children and observed normal CNVs in blind and partially sighted children (ages 11-16) to auditory and tactile stimuli. Blind children with light perception would exhibit CNVs to light as either the first or second stimulus as long as they had sufficient vision to see the light and unimpaired mental ability, even though short latency evoked responses to light were lacking (unpublished report). Guibal and Lairy (1967) studied the CNV along with other EEC variables in eleven- to eighteen-year-old partially sighted and normal children, using visual, auditory and tactile stimuli. Partially sighted children with difficulties in psychomotor performance were often lacking in the CNV in response to visual stimuli. The conclusion from these studies is that a specific sensory defect which does not generally impair psychophysiological functioning does not cause a reduction in the CNV, but a reduced CNV does relate to impaired psychological functioning.

Gullickson (1972) made a methodological contribution showing that the CNV may be studied in younger children by using stimulus-response behaviors which engaged their interest. He used a sliding pitch tone as S_1, lasting for one second until S_2, a colored abstract visual pattern was shown for two seconds, to two and three year olds. A verbal report from this age group is at best unreliable and it is therefore difficult to speculate on the attitudinal variables other than attention, which may play a significant role in the expression of cerebral activity.

Fenelon (1968) reported the difficulty of establishing an "expectancy wave" (CNV) in young dyslexic children, but he tested only three subjects with rather ambiguous results. Low and Stoilen (1972) reported on a large group of children with minimal cerebral dysfunction (MCD), comparing psychological functioning, EEG abnormalities and brain rhythms, and the CNV with a control group of normal children. He found the CNV to be either present or absent, but not a graded phenomenon related to the learning function. The CNV was quantitatively present in children over ten, and absent in children under eight years of age, with no increases in amplitude as a function of age. As Low's group did not include children between eight and ten years of age, the developmental changes from no CNV to a mature CNV are not revealed in that study.

Interhemispheric differences, cortical information processing, and localization of some intellectual functions are beginning to be revealed. So it is likely that integrated studies of the behavioral and electrical properties of brain function in learning disabled children will be fruitful if the proper techniques of recording, experimental situations and analyses are applied. We are just on the threshold of such studies and believe that psychophysiological research will reveal important aspects of brain processes involved in learning, memory, and recall.

A STUDY OF CNV IN LEARNING DISABILITIES

Pupils, aged six to eighteen, in a private coeducation school in the North Shore area of Chicago were selected for testing on the basis of normal distribution of intelligence, no history of chronic physical or emotional illness, and no acute illness at the time of testing. In order to provide developmental normal data, five subjects at each of thirteen yearly intervals were used; a total of sixty-five subjects. We also obtained forty-one children suffering from a developmental disability of learning to such an extent that, although considered in the normal range of intelligence, they were not able to succeed in a normal school program (Cohen, 1972b). Hence, they were all educationally retarded. They were referred to the laboratory by a hospital learning disorders center, a dyslexia clinic, a university learning disabilities center and pediatricians. Most of the children were from the hospital center where they also received complete medical, psychological, and psychiatric examinations as well as the EEG. The normal group provides tentative guidelines against which to compare children with clinical problems, in order to assess the normality of their brain functions. However, the numbers of children are still too small to report adequate normative measures.

An Offner (type TC) EEG machine was modified to provide 8 sec time constants to permit recording very slow potential changes against a fairly stable baseline. Silver-chloride electrodes, matched for impedance were applied to the head with collodion. Seven channels of EEG, eye movements, cardiac rate, and skin potentials (GSR) were recorded on paper. Eye movements and five EEG channels from the vertex, left and right frontal and parietal electrode positions (C_z, F_3, F_4, P_3, P_4) were also recorded on magnetic tape for later analysis.

The topographical characteristics of the CNV were derived from standard ten-twenty electrode placements on both sides of the head and the midline, referred to the linked mastoids as the monopolar reference. Data were obtained only from children who participated cooperatively in the task. Most of them actually enjoyed the challenge of the reaction time experiment.

The mean amplitude of the peak CNV excluding rhythmical or fast ER components to S₂ was taken as the maximum CNV for each child.

The child sat in an easy chair with a loud speaker behind his head and a silver screen in front of his eyes. After a few minutes he was stimulated by a single flash (S₁) from a bright white strobe lamp reflected on the screen every four seconds for 36 trials. Then he was presented with thirty-six trials of single short audible tones of 400 Hz (S₂). This was followed by the presentation of 36 pairs of flashes and tones with a 1¼ second interval and a four second delay between pairs. During this time the child was told only to sit quietly and attended to the stimuli.

Next the child was told to press a thumb button held in his hand, as quickly as possible to the tone (S₂). This turned off the sound. This paradigm looked to the subject like a reaction time experiment, and he could tell how well he was doing by how long the sound lasted. If he did not press the button the sound was turned off automatically after one second, or if he pressed the button too soon, the trial was aborted. The child found that in order to shorten the sound he had to wait until it started before pressing the button. Next, 25 tones were presented at random intervals from four to nine seconds apart to prevent tem-

TABLE 10-I

MEAN CNV AMPLITUDES IN MICRO-VOLTS

Age of Child	Vertex	Frontal		Central		Parietal	
		L.	R.	L.	R.	L.	R.
6	11	6	6	11	10	12	11
7	13	9	8	12	13	12	11
8	13	9	9	12	13	12	12
9	15	11	10	13	12	13	12
10	14	10	11	13	12	12	11
11	16	12	13	13	14	11	11
12	15	12	14	14	13	11	12
13	16	14	12	13	14	11	10
14	17	13	13	15	14	12	12
15	21	15	13	15	16	12	13
16	20	14	15	17	17	13	12
17	21	15	14	17	18	14	13
18	22	16	15	18	19	13	12

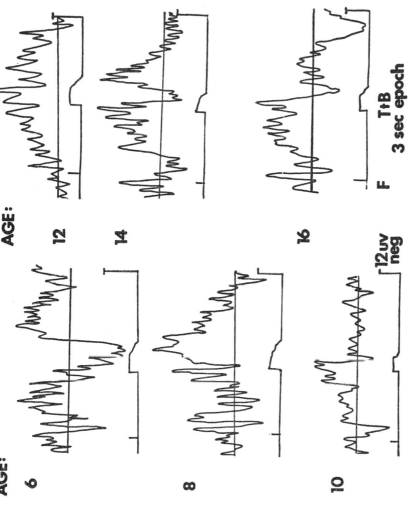

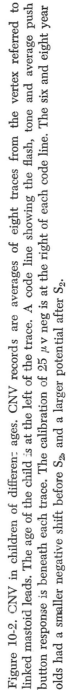

Figure 10-2. CNV in children of different ages. CNV records are averages of eight traces from the vertex referred to linked mastoid leads. The age of the child is at the left of the trace. A code line showing the flash, tone and average push button response is beneath each trace. The calibration of 25 μv neg is at the right of each code line. The six and eight year olds had a smaller negative shift before S_2 and a larger potential after S_2.

poral conditioning and to establish a baseline of reaction time without a "ready" signal. Then about 100 tones were presented after a light flash as a "ready" signal given 1¼ seconds before the tone. This procedure can be viewed as a conditioning situation in which the response is verbally instructed to follow the tone which is the unconditional or imperative stimulus, and light the conditional stimulus. The subject learns to "expect" the tone at a certain time after the light, and "gets ready" to press the button, but delays his response until the tone is heard. This is a surprisingly interesting task for children of all ages studied between six years and adulthood. The conditioning trials were fol-

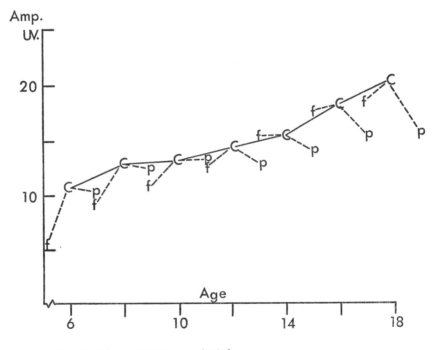

A—P Dist. CNV in Children

Figure 10-3. Anterior-posterior distribution of the average CNV in normal children. The ordinate of the solid line is the CNV amplitude in micv (neg) and the abscissa is the age of the child. Each point represents five children. C is the vertex lead, "f" is the mid-frontal lead and "p" is the parietal lead, all referred to linked mastoids.

lowed by two or three sets of extinction trials in which the light alone was given without tone or response, leading to the gradual disappearance of the CNV. When possible, another set of twenty-five reconditioning or restoration trials was given to see whether the CNV returned to full value. At the end of the session, the child was encouraged to talk about his experience and he was assured that all went well in his testing.

The CNV developed in the flash, tone, and button sequence, and it reached its maximal amplitude at the vertex (C_z). Table 10-I presents the mean CNV amplitudes for the normal group.

The CNV reached the adult amplitude and pattern by age fifteen in the normal developmental group. A few CNV patterns in individual children of different ages are shown in Figure 10-2. It was present in all normal children tested by six years of age with a mean vertex amplitude in six year olds of 11 μv. The change in A-P distribution and amplitude with age is shown in Figure 10-3. Up to about the age of twelve, the CNV has a higher amplitude in the posterior half of the head, but after twelve, it tends to have a higher amplitude in the fronto-central region in most people. Some fully mature individuals however, have a higher CNV amplitude in the parietal region. The psychological significance of the distribution is not known; however, a significant asymmetry of the CNV in the two hemispheres is often found in cases with a unilateral brain lesion. Normally, the difference between the two hemispheres is not significant and the amplitudes lie within a 5 to 10 percent limit, primarily due to a function of the error of measurement.

Figure 10-4 shows comparisons of typical results of some LD children and age matched normal children. The CNV was reduced or absent in about 60 percent of the children with learning disabilities, being present to the normal degree in only sixteen of the forty-one children. Age is a significant factor in such cases; the average age of the children with no CNV was eight and one half years and those with normal or reduced CNVs averaged ten years of age. Few of the youngest children had a CNV, but it was absent in some of the older children as well.

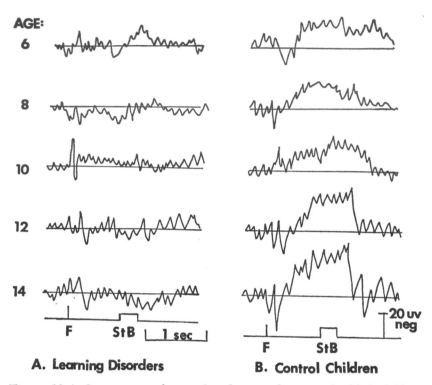

Figure 10-4. Comparison of normal and severe learning disabled children. Traces are averages of eight trials. Left column are five LD children of different ages and the right column has normal control children of the same age. Cases were selected to show absence of CNV in many cases of learning disabilities.

The traditional EEG clinical evaluation yielded only one possible abnormal record in the normal control group (all waking). This abnormal record had long runs of excessive fast activity synchronous over many channels. Eleven out of the forty-one LD children had abnormal records (most had sleep records), and most of those had CNV impairments. Only two of these Ss with normal CNVs had abnormal EEGs. One had generalized slow waves and one had excessive 7 and 14/sec positive spikes. One child had excessive slow activity with a poor CNV *but most* (8/11) of the EEG abnormalities were seen among the children who had no CNV. These included four cases of generalized slow waves, two cases with scattered spikes and sharp waves, one with paroxysmal occipital lobe delta activity and one with spike and wave transients. They also seemed to be most severely impaired in the psychoeducational area. Eight of the sixteen LDs with no CNVs had normal EEGs.

DISCUSSION OF RESULTS AND DIAGNOSTIC VALUE

Our experience indicates that the absence or poor development of a CNV is diagnostic of a functional learning disability (or lack of attention) while asymmetry of the CNV and ERs tends to relate to an organic disorder. Low (1973) on the other hand did not find a CNV decrement in his sample of MCD children. This is probably due to different populations and different scoring procedures.

Cohen ruled out specific syndromes of organic lesions in his group of subjects, while Low probably included a fair number of children with such syndromes in his MCD group. Low's group accepted the dc baseline as a computer determined value at the beginning of each epoch, while Cohen made a correction in the value of the baseline by eye if the computer determination seemed inappropriate based on the appearance of the data for the whole epoch. While this procedure may be more open to bias, it seemed to yield greater validity in the measured values. Otherwise, an apparently normal looking CNV occurring after an eye blink at the beginning of an epoch may be measured at an apparently incorrect value. The two studies are in agreement that the LD group have a higher probability of generalized EEG abnormalities in the theta and delta slow wave bands than in the normal groups.

The absence of the CNV in many cases of children with LD leads to the speculation that it may help to distinguish types of dysfunctions. The interpretation of an evoked potential and CNV record must be made in the light of the clinical EEG and all else that may be determined about the child through psychological and educational testing and a complete medical examination. Our general findings suggest that an asymmetry of more than 20 percent in the amplitude of ERs between the hemispheres is suggestive of a possible cortical, or subcortical lesion beneath the area of decrease in amplitude. Of course, this assumes that the techniques of recording and measurement are excellent and that the electrodes are carefully placed for monopolar recording to a common reference (linked mastoids in our experiments). A hemispherical asymmetry in the CNV is also thought to relate to an organic lesion, but more likely of a cerebral cortical localization if the ERs are symmetrical. This is often seen in patients with a lesion even when the background EEG is normal.

The presence of a CNV is found to be a favorable *prognostic indicator* in cases of LD.* The wave shape and amplitude of the CNV may suggest impaired function in a learning situation or possibly immaturity. The skull and scalp act as a spatial averager, and activity must be synchronized over large areas of cortical tissue to be seen at the surface. When the CNV is not seen, it does not mean that it does not accompany learning, but that it is below the signal to noise ratio necessary for detection. The psychological characteristics necessary for efficient learning are thought to include good intelligence, motivation, attention and lack of competing activity. If the CNV relates to any of those functions which may be impaired in LD children, then it is not surprising that it is reduced or absent in a wide spectrum of such children.

REFERENCES

Begleiter, H. and Platz, A.: Cortical evoked potentials to semantic stimuli. *Psychophysiology,* 6:91-100, 1969.

Birch, H. G. (ed.): *Brain Damage in Children: The Biological and Social Aspects.* Baltimore, Williams and Wilkins, 1964.

Black, S. and Walter, W. G.: Effects on anterior brain responses of variation in the probability of association between stimuli. *J Psychosom Res, 9:* 33-43, 1965.

Buchsbaum, M. and Fedio, P.: Visual information and evoked responses from the left and right hemispheres. *EEG Clin Neurophysiol, 26:*266-272, 1969.

Cant, B. R. and Bickford, R. G.: The effect of motivation on the contingent negative variation (CNV). *EEG Clin Neurophysiol,* 23:594, 1967. (Abst.)

---

* Recent evidence in our laboratory from head trauma and stroke patients indicates that CNV presence is also a favorable prognostic indicator for recovery.

Caspers, H.: Changes of cortical D. C. potentials in sleepwakefulness cycle. E. G. W. Wolstenholme and M. O'Connor (Ed.): *The Nature of Sleep,* Boston, Little, Brown, 1961.

Chalke, F. C. and Ertl, J.: Evoked potentials and intelligence. *Life Sci,* 4:1319-1322, 1965.

Clare, M. H. and Bishop, G. H.: Properties of dendrites; apical dendrites of the cat cortex. *EEG Clin Neurophysiol,* 7:85-98, 1955.

Clements, S. D.: Minimal Brain Dysfunction in Children. NINDB Monograph 3, PHS Bulletin 1415. Washington, D.C., U.S. Dept. of Health, Education and Welfare, 1966.

Cohen, J.: The contingent negative variation (CNV) and visual recognition. In W. C. McCallum and J. R. Knott (Ed.): *Event Related Slow Potentials and Behavior.* Second Int'l Conference on the CNV, *EEG Clin Neurophysiol Suppl 33,* 1973(a).

————: The CNV in children with special reference to learning disabilities. W. C. McCallum and J. R. Knott (Ed.): *Event Related Slow Potentials and Behavior.* Second Internat. Conf. on the CNV. *Electroenceph Clin Neurophysiol* Suppl. 33, 1972(b).

Cohen, J., Offner, F. and Blatt, S.: Psychological factors in the production and distribution of the contingent negative variation (CNV). Proceedings of the Sixth *Internat Congr of Electroenceph and Clin Neurophysiol,* Vienna, Sept. 5-10, 1965.

Cohen, J., Offner, F. and Palmer, C. W.: Development of the contingent negative variation in children. *EEG Clin Neurophysiol,* 23:77-78, 1967.

Cohen, J. and Walter, W. G.: The interaction of responses in the brain to semantic stimuli. *Psychophysiology,* 2:187-196, 1966.

Connors, C. K.: Cortical visual evoked responses in children with learning disabilities. *Psychophysiology,* 7:418-428, 1971.

Creutzfeldt, O. D. and Kuhnt, U.: The visual evoked potential: physiological, developmental and clinical aspects. W. Cobb and C. Morocutti (Ed.): *The Evoked Potentials.* Amsterdam, Elsevier, 1967.

Donchin, E. and Cohen, L.: Average evoked potentials and intramodality selective attention. *EEG Clin Neurophysiol,* 22:537-546, 1967.

Donchin, E. and Lindsley, D. B. (Eds.): *Average Evoked Potentials: Methods, Results and Evaluations.* Washington: U.S. Govt. Print. Off. NASA SP-191, 1969.

Dustman, R. E. and Beck, E. C.: Visually evoked potentials: amplitude changes with age. *Science,* 151:1013-1015, 1966.

Eason, R. G. and White, C. T.: Average occipital responses to stimulation of sites in the nasal and temporal halves of the retina. *Psychon Sci,* 7: 309-310, 1967.

Ertl, J. P. and Schafer, E. W. P.: Brain response correlates of psychometric intelligence. *Nature,* London, 223:421-422, 1969.

Fenelon, B.: Expectancy waves and other complex cerebral events in dyslexic and normal subjects. *Psychon Sci, 13*:253-254, 1968.

Freeman, R. D.: Special education and the electroencephalogram: marriage of convenience. *J Spec Educ, 2*:61-73, 1967.

Geschwind, N.: Neurological foundations of language. H. R. Myklebust (Ed.). *Progress in Learning Disabilities.* Vol. I, New York, Grune and Stratton, 1968.

Goff, W. R.: Evoked potential correlates of perceptual organization in man. Proceedings of Teddington Conf. on Attention in Neurophysiology, Teddington, Middlesex, England, Oct. 3-5, 1967.

Guibal, M. and Lairy, G. C.: Preliminary findings concerning the expectancy wave and the visually deficient child. *Electroenceph Clin Neurophysiol, 23*:579, 1967.

Gullickson, G. R.: CNV and behavioral attention of a glide-tone warning of interesting non-moving or kaleidoscopic visual or auditory patterns in two- and three-year-old children. Abstract, Second Internat. Conf. on the CNV, *Electroenceph Clin Neurophysiol* Supplement, 1972 (in press).

Haider, M., Spong, P., Lindsley, D. B.: Attention, vigilance and cortical evoked potentials in humans. *Science, 145*:180-182, 1964.

Hillyard, S. A.: The CNV and vertex evoked potential during signal detection: a preliminary report. E. Donchin and D. B. Lindsley (Eds.): *Average Evoked Potentials: Methods, Results, and Evaluations,* NASA SP-191, 1969, pp. 349-354.

Hillyard, S. A. and Galambos, R.: Effects of stimulus and response contingencies on the surface negative slow potential shift in man. *Electrophysiol Clin Neurophysiol, 22*:297-304, 1967.

Irwin, D. A., Knott, J. R., McAdam, D. W. and Rebert, C. S.: Motivational determinants of the contingent negative variation. *EEG Clin Neurophysiol, 21*:538-543, 1966.

Knott, J. R. and Irwin, D. A.: Anxiety, stress and the contingent negative variation (CNV). *EEG Clin Neurophysiol, 24*:286-287, 1968.

Knott, J. R. and Peters, J. F.: Sex, stress and interstimulus interval. In W. C. McCallum, and J. R. Knott (Eds.): *Event Related Slow Potentials and Behavior.* Second Internat. Conf. on the CNV. *EEG Clin Neurophysiol* Suppl. 33, 1973.

Liberson, W. T.: Study of evoked potentials in aphasics. *Amer J Phys Med, 45*:135-142, 1966.

Lindsley, D. B.: Average evoked potentials—achievements, failures and prospects. In E. Donchin and D. B. Lindsley (Eds.): *Average Evoked Potentials: Methods, Results and Evaluations.* Washington, U.S. Govt. Print. Off. NASA SP-191, 1969.

Low, M. D., Borda, R. P., Frost, J. D. and Kellaway, P.: Surface negative slow potential shift associated with conditioning in man. *Neurology, 16:* 771-782, 1966.

Low, M. D. and Stoilen, L.: CNV and EEG in children: maturational characteristics and findings in the MCD syndrome. In W. C. McCallum and J. R. Knott (Eds.): *Event Related Slow Potentials and Behavior.* Second Internat. Conf. on the CNV. *EEG Clin Neurophysiol* Suppl. 33, 1973.

Luria, A. R.: *Higher Cortical Functions in Man.* New York, Basic Books, 1964.

McCarthy, J. J. and McCarthy, J.: *Learning Disabilities.* Boston, Allyn and Bacon, 1969.

McCallum, W. C. and Walter, W. G.: The effects of attention and distraction on the contingent negative variation in normal and neurotic subjects. *EEG Clin Neurophysiol, 25:*319-329, 1968.

McGrady, H. J.: Learning disabilities: implications for medicine and education. *J School Health, 41:*227-234, 1971.

Paine, R. S.: Organic neurological factors related to learning disorders. J. Hellmuth (Ed.): *Learning Disorders,* Vol. 1, Seattle, Special Child Publ. 1965.

Penfield, W. and Roberts, L.: *Speech and Brain Mechanisms,* Princeton, Princeton Univ. Press, 1959.

Rhodes, L. E., Dustman, R. E. and Beck, E. C.: The visual evoked response: a comparison of bright and dull children. *EEG Clin Neurophysiol, 27:*364-372, 1969.

Rose, G. H. and Lindsley, D. B.: Development of visually evoked potentials in kittens: specific and non-specific responses. *J Neurophysiol, 31:*607-623, 1968.

Shields, D. T.: A study of evoked cerebral responses to visual stimuli in normal children and children with learning disabilities. Dissertation, Northwestern University, Evanston, Illinois, 1072.

Sperry, R. W.: Cerebral organization and behavior. *Science, 133:*1749-1757, 1961.

Spong, P., Haider, M. and Lindsley, D. B.: Selective attentiveness and cortical evoked responses to visual and auditory stimuli. *Science, 148:*395-397, 1965.

Sutton, S.: The specification of psychological variables in an average evoked potential experiment. In E. Donchin and D. B. Lindsley (Eds.): *Average Evoked Potentials: Methods, Results and Evaluations.* NASA SP-191, Wash., D.C., U.S. Govt. Print. Off., 1969.

Sutton, S., Braren, M., Zubin, J. and John, E. R.: Evoked potential correlates of stimulus uncertainty. *Science, 150:*1187-1188, 1965.

Tecce, J. J. and Scheff, N. M.: Attention reduction and suppressed direct-current potentials in the human brain. *Science, 164:*331-333, 1969.

Timsit, M., Koninckx, N., Dargent, J., Fontaine, O. and Dongier, M.: Study of the contingent negative variation in psychotic and pre-psychotic patients. *Annl Medico Psychol, 126*:424-435, 1968.

Walter, W. G.: Electrophysiologic contributions to psychiatric therapy. *Curr Psychiat Ther, 6*:13-35, 1966.

Walter, W. G., Cooper, R., Aldridge, V. J., McCallum, W. C. and Winter, A. L.: Contingent negative variation: an electric sign of sensorimotor association and expectancy in the human brain. *Nature*, London, *203*:380-384, 1964.

CHAPTER 11

STEADY POTENTIALS ACCOMPANYING PERCEPTION AND RESPONSE IN MENTALLY RETARDED AND NORMAL CHILDREN

Rathe Karrer and Judy Ivins*

* Ted Holden, Betty Karrer, and David Hoats collaborated in the RT study. Don Thor, Betty Karrer, and David Hoats collaborated in the DIT study. Thanks are due to Drs. Herman Spitz and John Winters for the use of the facilities at the Edward R. Johnstone Training and Research Center, Bordentown, New Jersey and facilitating the data collection. Anne Campbell, of the University of Illinois Medical School, Research Resources Laboratory, developed the programs used in the data reduction and analysis on the IBM/370. Without her diligent help the studies would never have been completed.

Various portions of this work have been presented at the sixth Gatlinburg Conference on Research and Theory in Mental Retardation, 1973; the Third International Congress on Event-Related Slow Potentials of the Brain, England, 1973; the Third International Congress of the International Association for the Scientific Study of Mental Deficiency, The Hague, 1973; and the Eastern Psychiatric Research Association Conference on Psychiatric Problems of Childhood, New York, 1974. The work was partially supported by NICHD Research Grant HD-03762-01. Figures 1, 4, 12 and 13 are reproduced, by permission, from W. C. McCallum and J. R. Knott (Eds.): *The Responsive Brain*. Bristol, Eng., John Wright, 1975.

MENTAL RETARDATION COMPRISES an extremely heterogeneous group of individuals whose main commonality is their reduced cognitive and social performance. This reduced performance has been variously attributed to motivation (Zigler, 1967), arousal (Clausen, 1966, 1972); orienting (Luria, 1963); attention (Zeaman and House, 1963); information processing (Spitz, 1968, 1973); and memory processes (Ellis, 1963, 1970; Fisher and Zeaman, 1973). It is probable that some (or all) of these processes are deficit in some retardates. It is improbable that a specific impairment characterizes all retardates. Therefore, a functional analysis of the brain-behavior relations accompanying efficient and inefficient performance as well as the conditions that give rise to these relations is a necessity.

There is a great need for novel approaches in research on mental retardation to resolve some of the present fragmentation of facts and theory. The investigation of steady potentials is one such approach that may contribute to theories of the retardates behavior and brain function.

Steady potentials, or DC potentials, (SP) have been under intensive investigation for decades (cf. Kohler and O'Connell, 1957; O'Leary and Goldring, 1964). Since Kohler's (1920, 1938) theorizing upon the importance of such potentials in perception and the development of an adequate technical methodology this research has slowly blossomed (Brazier, 1963; Kohler, Held and O'Connell, 1952; Rowland, 1968). Recently, Pribram (1971) has presented cogent and closely documented arguments that the critical neural phenomena for the integrative processes of psychological importance are the graded neural events of postsynaptic potentials and steady potentials. The occurrence of steady potential changes during specific tasks has been confirmed in a number of laboratories. Steady potentials have come to be an important cortical concomitant of specific behavioral states (Tecce, 1972; Rowland, 1968). They are reliable and promising physiological variables for understanding functional brain-behavior relations.

The contingent negative variation (CNV), an SP change which occurs during the foreperiod of a reaction time task, has especially come under intensive scrutiny because of its promise as a neurophysiological correlate of expectancy (see Chap. 10). The CNV has been considered to reflect increased cortical excitability and perceptual sensitivity (Walter, 1967; McAdam and Rubin, 1971). A main factor in the production of the CNV is the significance of the second of the stimuli pair to the subject. The second stimulus may acquire significance by requiring the subject to perform some action (either mental, verbal, or motor) or by being of specific interest or meaning to the subject. It is apparent that manipulation of the stimulus and response contingencies affects CNV amplitude (Karrer, Kohn, and Ivins, 1973). Also, an overt motor response does not seem to be a necessary condition (Donchin, et al., 1972). The present consensus is that the CNV is an electrophysiological concomitant of an attentional-motivational state in which the organism is set to receive and process information from the environment (Tecce, 1972).

Other negative SP changes are known to accompany increased arousal and orienting, while positive SP changes accompany decreased arousal, relaxation-relief, and reinforcing actions (Caspers, 1963; Rowland, 1968). It is evident that these electrocortical events are important to the organism's interaction with his environment. Recent studies have demonstrated SP events preceding enunciation of language sounds (McAdam and Witaker, 1971) and retrieval from memory (Rubin and McAdam, 1972). The involvement of SP phenomena in behavior such as attending, expectancy, memory and responding (in short the complex components of information processing) indicates the significance of the study of SP phenomena.

If it is true that changes in SP level toward greater negativity tend to increase cortical excitability and perceptual sensitivity, then the study of this phenomenon in an organism with perceptual, cognitive and performance difficulties might provide an insight into the processes and neurophysiological substrates responsible for the impaired behavior. Until the relations to cortical sensitivity are firmly established, however, it seems sufficient to stress that attending seems to be a necessary condition for the occurrence of the CNV. The importance of this phenomenon for studying the mentally retarded is clear. While orienting and attending have been seriously implicated in mental deficiency, little is known about these processes or even the physiological responsiveness of the mentally retarded (Berkson, 1963; Karrer, 1966). Previous work has concentrated upon autonomic functions as indicators of arousal and the OR (see Chaps. 2-7). Nothing has been reported on the CNV or other SP phenomena accompanying behavior in these subjects.

I will report two experiments designed to obtain basic information on SP characteristics in the retardate. The studies were also designed to contribute information to understanding the relation of SP changes to behavior. The experiments used a simple developmental paradigm to compare retardates to equal MA and equal CA normals. Two tasks, reaction time (RT) and dark interval threshold (DIT), allowed recording of the SP changes accompanying the traditional expectancy paradigm of the CNV (RT task) and in a more complex perceptual task (DIT). Both tasks require different aspects of temporal processing and preparation to respond. The DIT requires preparation to perceive the flashes, basic sensory temporal resolution, and a decision process on number of perceived flashes. The RT task requires preparation to respond as well as to perceive, a decision process to respond, and a basic motor temporal sequence. Since the preparatory time was constant, a process of temporal estimation is also appropriate to the preparatory sets in both tasks.

These tasks were chosen for their power to discriminate retardates from normals (retardates slower than normal) and their demonstration of developmental trends (young children slower than adults). The underlying strategy was to determine the functional relation between the specific behavior (RT and DIT) and the physiological component (SP) by varying parameters known to affect behavior. There are three main questions involved in this strategy: (1) What is the relation between changes in RT (or DIT) behavior and electrocortical events (SP)? Close scrutiny of deficits in behavior (e.g. the retardate) may provide a better understanding of this relation and its underlying processes. (2) Is the relation between change in RT (or DIT) and electrocortical SP the same over age and IQ? (3) Do these electrocortical-behavior relations indicate specific process differences of use in conceptualizing the retarded individual? The studies reported below are an initial step in answering these basic questions.

REACTION TIME PERFORMANCE

The speed with which an organism responds appropriately to an event is a measure of the organism's ability to process information. Speed is considered a major factor in most definitions of intelligence. Consequently, speed of response is often considered in the assessment of cognitive function (e.g. Sternberg,

1969). The efficiency of the information flow is one important limiting feature in the skills necessary in everyday action. The speed with which the individual comes to combine the various segments of behavior necessary for appropriate responding probably affects his motor performance. Our movements in everyday activity are fluid and smooth, appearing to flow one into the other at high rate. Nevertheless, each action can be performed only at some limit of speed. A pianist can play no more than about ten notes per second and simple drumming of fingers on the table is of the same order. It takes about 80-100 msec to perform the simplest action, a figure approximating the fastest laboratory reaction time. The simplest, and perhaps most basic speed task is reaction time (RT). This traditional task has been used extensively and productively as an index of input, central and motor processes (cf. Hohle, 1967; Sternberg, 1969; Teichner, 1954).

One pervasive characteristic of mental retardates is their slowness of response (Baumeister and Kellas, 1968). The RT task has reliably demonstrated the retardates' slowness on study after study. The RT task we selected utilized multimodality stimulation which is known to decrease RT of retardates (presumably via arousal increase, Holden, 1965). Bimodality input is also known to improve discrimination (Brebner, 1971) as well as signal detection in normals (Loveless, Brebner, and Hamilton, 1970).

The warning signal (WS) of the RT paradigm has an attention-getting (alerting or arousal) function. Consequently, it was hypothesized that if alerting or arousal processes underlying attention-getting are a factor in the performance of the retardate, a multi-modality WS (vs. a single modality WS) should carry more warning information and should increase arousal more for the retardate than for the normal. The latter's attention is probably sufficiently aroused by the warning information in a single modality WS to produce fast RT performance. Consequently, the retardate RT should be reduced more than the normals' RT by the multiple modality WS. The SP data should also indicate this by showing lower CNV amplitudes for retardates than for normals (reflecting the RT difference). If the CNV is a function of arousal the multimodality WS should increase CNV amplitude. The retardate CNV should also be increased more than for the normals by the multimodality WS. The rise time (slope) and latency of the CNV should also be slower in the retardates and young normals reflecting their less mature development.

Subjects and Procedure

Fifteen retardates were drawn from the population of Edward R. Johnstone Training and Research Center. Their ages were thirteen to eighteen ($\overline{X}$ = 16.1) with IQ 48 to 73 ($\overline{X}$ IQ = 63; $\overline{X}$ MA = 10.2). None had frank neurological impairment and all could perform the tasks adequately. Twenty-six normal children were drawn from public schools in the surrounding community of Bordentown, New Jersey. One group (CA) of thirteen was matched for chronological age (13 to 18, $\overline{X}$ = 15.1) to the retardates. Another group (MA) of thirteen normals was matched on presumed mental age (CA 9 to 12, $\overline{X}$ = 11.1) to the retardates. IQ data were not available on the normals.

The subject was seated at a table within a carrel with three sides and top. This backless chamber was painted flat black and illuminated by a lamp over the subject's head. The WS consisted of either auditory (600 Hz, 80 db tones) or tactile (vibration to the non-dominant wrist) stimulation, or the two combined. The reaction stimulus (RS) was a one inch diameter white light (0.8 foot-lambert) embedded in the wall of the cubicle facing the subject at eye level eighteen inches away. The preparatory interval (PI) between the WS and RS was a constant one second.

Twenty trials of each WS condition were presented in random order (60 trials per session). The subject was instructed to respond as fast as possible and was given practice trials until he understood, felt comfortable, and was not responding to the WS rather than the RS. Trials in which the subject's response anticipated the RS or had obvious movement artifacts in the EEG were repeated.

All subjects were brought into the situation and adapted to the setting and equipment. Much effort was put into establishing rapport with the subject. After explaining the task, the retardates were told they would receive fifty cents. All subjects reacted favorably and cooperated well. The RT task always followed the determination of the dark interval threshold (see below, Study 2).

Steady potentials were determined from EEG recordings of midline frontal (Fz) and vertex (Cz) sites referred to left mastoid. Vertical eye movement was monitored with electrodes in the center of the superior and inferior orbital ridges of the left eye. These data were recorded DC on a Grass (Model 5) polygraph with outputs to an Ampex (Model FR 1300) FM tape recorder for later analysis.

Because of anticipated trials, equipment malfunctions, and EEG artifacts from eye or body movement, some trials were discarded from the data. The remaining data comprised 70 percent, 52 percent, and 47 percent of the total trials respectively for the young normals, older normals and retardates. Two subjects in the retardate group had to be discarded because of both poor EEG records and unreliable RT performance.

Analog to digital conversion at 250 samples per second was performed on the EEG. The data comprised 5.2 sec epochs beginning 1.2 sec prior to the WS and averaged over trials in each WS condition. For each subject a *forward* average timelocked to the WS included three secs after the RS. *Backward* averages timelocked to the RS and continuing to the beginning of the trial were also computed. This system resulted in data with an accuracy of 2.5 μv. The following measures were determined for the forward averages and are demonstrated in Figure 11-1. The interval between the WS and 200 msec after the RS (1,200 msec) was divided into two 600 msec segments. The mean of the most positive 200 msec during the first segment after the WS was taken as the measure of peak *Post-WS positivity*. The mean of the 200 msec comprising the greatest negativity in the second segment was taken as the measure of peak *Pre-Response negativity* (CNV). In addition, *latency* was computed as the median of the last five points (20 msec) within 2.5 μv of the baseline prior to the CNV. *Peak time* was computed as the median point of the Post-WS and CNV peak scores. *Slope* was computed by subtract-

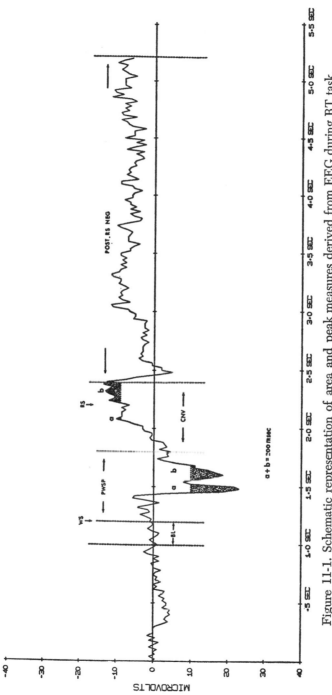

Figure 11-1. Schematic representation of area and peak measures derived from EEG during RT task.

ing latency from peak time. To determine SP changes following the RT response, the total negative area *(Post-R negativity)* and the total positive area *(Post-R positivity)* in the remaining three seconds (from 200 msec after RS to the end of the average) was computed. Baseline for all measures was determined from the last 200 msec prior to the WS. Comparable measures were computed from backward averages timelocked to the RT and extending for 2.2 sec prior to the response. Since these latter measures with few exceptions (slope and topography of frontal and vertex), correlated highly with the forward average measures they will only be considered where they add to the conceptualization.

Results

Behavior: Reaction Time

Means and standard deviations for each group and WS condition are presented in Table 11-I. A two-way Anova (Group × WS condition) of mean RT found that groups differed significantly (F 2/3 = 7.87, $p = < .002$) as did the WS conditions (F 2/72 = 18.18, $p < .001$). The predicted interaction was not significant. Retardates were slower than young normals who were slower than older normals. Both young normals and retardates also had significantly shorter RT for the compound WS (S + V) than for sound (S) or vibration (V) alone (F 2/24 = 8.97, $p < .002$; F 2/24 = 5/53, $p < .01$, respectively for the groups). For the older normals, RT to the compound WS was only signifi-

TABLE 11-I

MEANS AND SD's OF RT FOR
EACH GROUP AND WS CONDITION
(in msec)

		MA	CA	R
Sound	X	358.53	293.61	458.23
	SD	69.61	45.58	176.34
Vib.	X	342.84	280.84	446.76
	SD	55.62	42.24	172.48
S + V	X	311.0	264.07	404.84
	SD	36.03	25.62	159.79

cantly shorter than RT in the S condition (F 2/24 = 5.87, $p < .009$). This suggests that either the vibration stimulus had a preemptive role in reducing their RT or that the sound stimulus was particularly ineffective in reducing RT.

SP Measures: Description

Group averages for each WS condition are presented in Figure 11-2 for frontal and Figure 11-3 for vertex.

These figures show some interesting features. The baseline (zero) was calculated on the basis of activity 200 msec prior to the WS and all points were computed as the difference from this base. It is clear that there was no consistent trend or baseline drift as far as one second prior to the trials. There were consistent oscillations after the WS with four positive peaks discriminable. These peaks are larger in vertex than frontal, and larger for the V and S + V condition, than for the S condition. There appear to be group differences in the timing and amplitude of these peaks. At about 400-500 msec (after the fourth positive peak) in the V condition or about 300-400 msec (after the third peak) in the S and S + V condition, a large and consistent negative shift (CNV) becomes the dominant feature. While not apparent in the vertex lead, the beginning of the CNV in frontal starts immediately after the WS since the positive peaks are generally above baseline. The rising front of the CNV seems more abrupt in frontal than vertex. There seem to be no consistent group differences in CNV level. The CNV is resolved after the RT by a large positive peak which appears to interrupt a more slowly going positive trend toward baseline (especially in frontal and in the older normals and retardates). The return to baseline, however, is most often approximate and transitory. Considerable negativity remains as long as two to three secs after the RS. There appear to be group differences in this Post-RS negativity with the young normals showing larger areas in the V condition and retardates larger areas in the S and S + V conditions. Quantitative analysis of these data found the following.

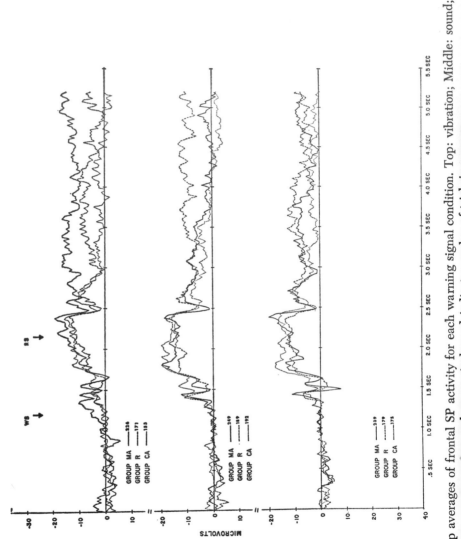

Figure 11-2. Group averages of frontal SP activity for each warning signal condition. Top: vibration; Middle: sound; Bottom:

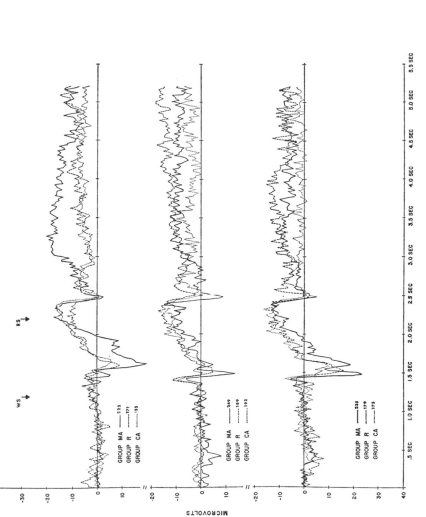

Figure 11-3. Group averages of vertex SP activity for each warning signal condition. Top: vibration; Middle: sound; Bottom: sound and vibration. Numbers after each group in legend indicate number of trials in average.

Post-WS Positivity

The most compelling feature of Figures 11-2 and 11-3 is the large Post-WS positivity, especially in the V and S + V conditions. Of some importance was the fact that for all groups together the vibration and compound WS produced larger positive shifts at about 300-400 msec than sound (F 2/27 = 7.57, 11.44, $p < .001$ for frontal and vertex respectively). To determine the uniformity of this effect between subjects a Kendall coefficient of concordance (Siegel, 1956) was performed on each group. There was significant concordance in vertex for both young (W = .25, $p < .05$) and old (W = .30, $p < .05$) normals while the retardates did not quite have significant concordance (W = .23, $p < .07$). The concordance indicated greatest positivity for the S + V condition and smallest positivity for the S condition. This trend was also present in the non-significant frontal lead.

While not analyzed here, it should be noted that the normal groups tend to have two positive peaks (especially for the S and S + V condition) generally falling between 300-400 msec. These peaks seem to be resolved into one wider peak for the retardates.

Young normals exhibited larger Post-WS positivity than the older normals and retardates (F 2/36 = 4.32, $p < .02$ vertex). Retardates had the longest frontal positivity peak times while the older normals had the shortest (F 2/36 = 3.34, $p < .047$). While both leads did not reach significance, the young normals were always slower than the older normals.

TOPOGRAPHY. The vertex minus frontal difference for combined WS conditions indicated smaller differences in amplitude and in peak time for the retardates (F 2/36 = 3.53, $p < .04$; F 2/36 = 6.65, $p < .003$ respectively). The younger normals had the greatest vertex-frontal difference for amplitude but the older normals had the greatest difference in peak time.

RELATION TO RT. The positivity paralleled the WS manipulation of RT (Fig. 11-4). The larger the peak positivity after the WS in frontal and vertex the faster the RT. However, only the young normal group had a significant correlation between positivity in the frontal lead and RT ($r = .564$, $p < .05$) for the

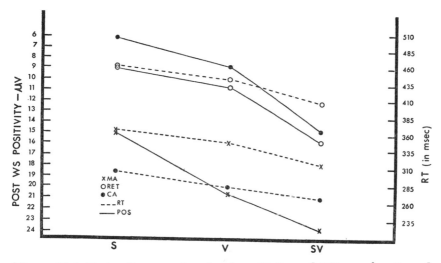

Figure 11-4. Vertex Post-warning signal positivity and RT as a function of warning signal condition.

S + V condition. In vertex, the sign of eight out of nine small correlations were in the proper direction in all WS conditions for the three groups.

To further tease this relation apart, the four fastest and four slowest RT subjects were compared. Only the young normals showed a consistent relation between RT extremes and positivity; fast RT subjects being more consistent than slow RT subjects (Fig. 11-5). The fast RT older normal and retardates also showed this relation of fast RT to large positivity in the frontal lead for the V and S + V condition but had a consistently reversed relation for vertex (larger positivity in slow RT individuals). This seems to reflect a developmental trend for the post-WS positivity that is also in the group averages.

Correlations of RT (intra-individual) with the positivity following the WS demonstrated no significant relation. However, for the young normals, five of six correlations ($\bar{X}$ r = .34), though small, indicated larger positivities in both frontal and vertex sites tended to precede faster RT. This was also reflected in a high *vs* low RT comparison. The older normals, while hav-

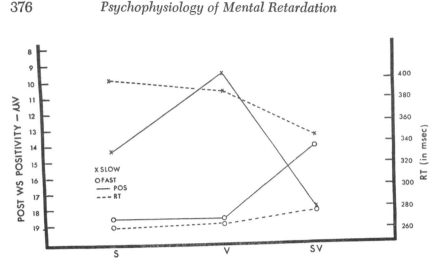

Figure 11-5. Vertex Post-warning signal positivity for fast and slow RT young normals.

ing consistent small correlations, showed no difference in positivity between high and low RT subjects. The retardates were inconsistent with the frontal lead showing this pattern but the vertex lead showing *smaller* positivity accompanying faster RT. This may again indicate a topographical difference in the processes underlying vertex positivity in the retardates. A developmental trend in the function of the positivity seems to be present.

INTERCORRELATIONS. The correlations between Post-WS positivity and CNV were quite low except for the frontal V condition (frontal: $r = 0.36$, 0.60, 0.36 and vertex: $r = 0.39$, 0.30, 0.30 for S, V, and S + V conditions respectively). With the exception of the last two all of these correlations were significant ($p < .05$). Nevertheless, the size of these correlations indicates that these two measures of peak activity early (positivity) and late (CNV) in the preparatory interval reflect relatively independent processes.

The frontal positivity showed some correlation to IQ in the retardates. Verbal and full scale IQ correlated 0.63 and 0.62 ($p < .05$) with positivity in the SV condition. MA level and performance IQ had the same trend ($r = 0.43$ and 0.52 respectively). Greater Post-WS positivity under some conditions, is moderately related to mental ability as measured by IQ. It is regrettable that IQ for the normals was not available for this analysis.

Pre-RS Negativity (CNV)

Combining groups there were larger CNVs in the S condition than in the V or S + V condition (F 2/72 = 7.24, $p < .002$; F 2/72 = 5.54, $p < .006$ for frontal and vertex respectively). This trend was the same in all three groups. Frontal latency was faster to leave the baseline in the S condition than in the S + V or V condition (F 2/72 = 8.01, $p < .001$), a consequence of the late positive peaks for the S condition not crossing the baseline (Fig. 11-2).

The groups did not differ in CNV amplitude for any WS condition. There was an interaction of groups and WS conditions for vertex measures of CNV latency, peak time, and slope (F 4/72 = 7.44, $p < .001$; F 4/72 = 3.83, $p < .007$; F 4/72 = 2.71, p < 0.37 respectively). The older normals had the longest, and younger normals shortest latencies and peak times for the V and S + V condition, with the reverse for sound alone. The retardates fell between the older and younger normals for latency and peak time. For the V and S + V conditions the vertex CNV slope of retardates was longer (slower rise time as predicted) than either normal group (shortest for older normals). In the S condition, by contrast, the older normals had the longest slopes, the young the fastest, with the retardates between.

TOPOGRAPHY. Interestingly, for all three WS conditions the slope of the frontal CNV was longer than vertex slope in both normal groups while the retardates had little difference, and in fact, slightly longer vertex slopes (mean difference vertex-frontal = −95, −105, +4 msec, for MA, CA, RET respectively; F 2/36 = 4.51, p < .018). Activity seems to build up in frontal areas at the same time as in vertex areas for the retarded.

It should be noted, while not significant, that the topographical relations for CNV peak time and amplitude were the same as for CNV slope and the post-WS positivity, i.e. smaller differences between vertex-frontal in the retarded.

RELATION TO RT. There were no significant correlations of mean RT to CNV within any group although they were always in the direction reported in previous studies (Hillyard, 1969a), i.e. the larger the CNV the shorter the RT. There was also no consistent relation between CNV and RT across the WS conditions for the three groups. The young normals gave larger CNV for WS conditions producing shorter RTs, while the older normals and the retardates showed a U-shaped relation of high CNV accompanying long as well as short RT (Fig. 11-6). Whether this reflects some developmental difference must be confirmed.

It is obvious that part of the variability resides in differential effects of the WS on fast and slow responders. An inspection of the four fastest and four slowest responders in each group indicated that fast retardate responders tended to have a larger vertex (and frontal) CNV than slow retardate responders (Fig. 11-7). There was no consistency and little difference between fast and slow normals. Therefore CNV seems only capable of discriminating individuals with extremes of RT that characterize fast and slow retardates.

It was reasoned that if the RT was related to CNV, then high RT variability among a subject's trials indicating fluctuations in attending may lead to lesser amplitude mean CNV. An analysis

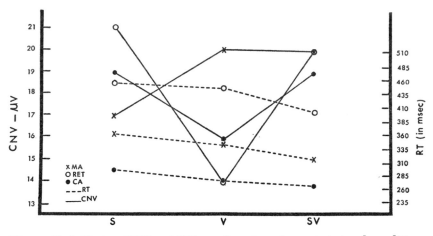

Figure 11-6. Vertex CNV and RT as a function of warning signal condition.

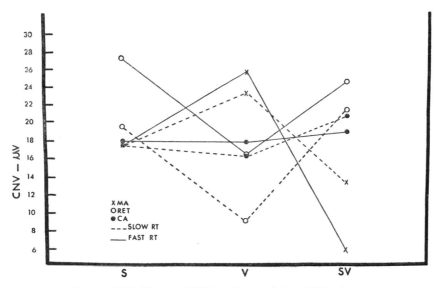

Figure 11-7. Vertex CNV for fast and slow RT subjects.

of subjects with greatest and lowest RT σ revealed different relations among the groups. For the young normals, high RT σ
accompanied smaller CNVs as expected. The older groups had
no relations between RT variability and CNV. Again, a possible
developmental difference in the relation of CNV to RT needs
confirmation.

INTERCORRELATIONS. There was a tendency for CNV amplitude
in frontal and vertex to be more highly correlated in old normals than in young normals (Table 11-II). The retardates seem
to be intermediate. This seems to indicate that the two brain

TABLE 11-II

CORRELATIONS BETWEEN FRONTAL
AND VERTEX CNV

	S	V	SV
MA	.37	.68†	.34
R	.73†	.51	.66*
CA	.68†	.57*	.61*

* 5 per cent significance level.
† 1 per cent significance level.

areas become more coordinated with age. There was no correlation between CNV and IQ or MA in the retardates.

Trends During the Session

To determine if there was a different growth of SP activity over trials, separate averages of four trials in the first and last half of the session were obtained (often the first four and last four trials). It can be seen in the group averages of the frontal EEG for the vibration WS (Fig. 11-8) that there was very little change in Post-WS positivity or CNV after the initial few trials (block 1) in the normals. For both measures the MA decline slightly while the CA increase slightly. On the other hand, there is considerable growth up to the final trials (block 2) in the retardates, especially for the CNV. This was accompanied by a decrease in RT by 70 msec. It should be noted that the group averages do not have an equivalent number of trials because of artifacts. It is an indication of the reliability of the data that the CA normals and retardates in the last block which had the fewest trials (14 and 24 respectively, all other blocks 52 trials), were no more variable than in the first block. Figure 11-9 shows a similar but less striking trend in the vertex EEG for the S + V condition. The MA normals again decline for the Post-WS positivity but increase slightly for the CNV, while the CA normals remain very stable for block 1 to 2. The retardates again show an increase in CNV above baseline both in amplitude and duration. This may be due to a somewhat reduced Post-WS positivity. The S condition in both frontal and vertex had a slight growth in the MA group but no change in either retardates or normals.

In general, there was a tendency for retardates to increase CNV over trials while the normal groups established a stable level and latency early in the session. Further study of these trends may prove fruitful.

Post-RS Negativity and Positivity

Although there seem to be large differences in area of negativity after the RS (Figs. 11-2 and 11-3) there were no significant differences between groups or WS conditions for this activity due to high variability.

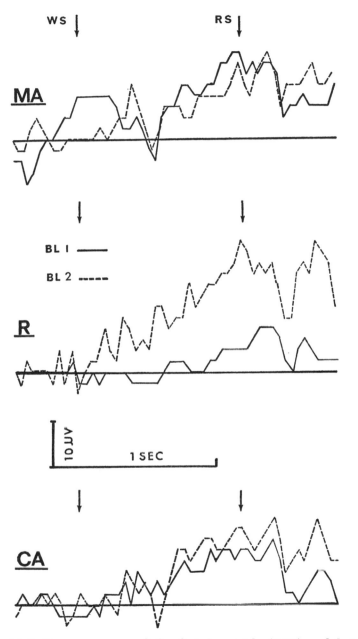

Figure 11-8. Group averages of the first four trials (BL1) and last four trials (BL2) of frontal SP activity during vibration WS condition.

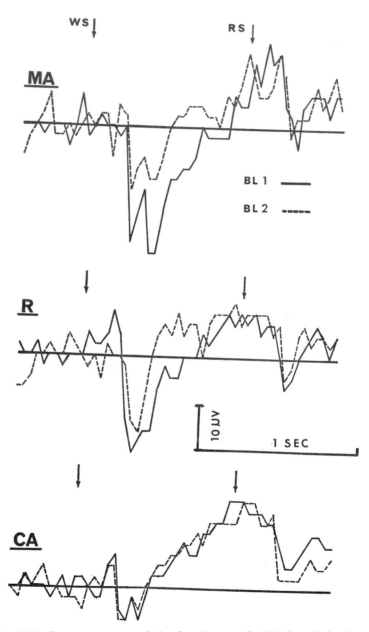

Figure 11-9. Group averages of the first four trials (BL1) and the last four trials (BL2) of vertex SP activity during S + V condition.

SP Activity Time-locked to RT (Backward Average)

An attempt to determine the motor readiness potentials (Vaughan, Costa and Ritter, 1968) or Bereitschafts-potential (Deecke, Scheid and Kornhuber, 1969) by averaging the activity time-locked to the response, found the correlation with CNV (activity time-locked to WS) to be quite high ($r = 0.81$ to 0.99). This implies that, in the RT paradigm, both the CNV and motor readiness potentials are inextricably confounded (cf. Tecce, 1972). The variability controlled by the type of time-locking is insufficient to wipe out the large amplitude and duration responses of the CNV and motor potentials. It is of interest, however, that the retardates had the lowest correlations. This might reflect that they do not "lock" into the requirements of the PI at WS onset.

Where there are differences between groups or WS conditions that are significant for one type of average (forward or backward) and not the other, a clue to the time-locked processes differentiating the groups or conditions is available. For example, the vertex CNV slope interaction of groups and WS conditions cited above was significant for forward but not backward averages. The same was true for the group difference in vertex-frontal CNV slopes. This means that the slope measure and its topography on the head which discriminates the retardates from normals is time-locked only to the WS and not to the RT. Similarly, the group differences for Post-WS positivity cited above were significant for forward but not backward averages. The forward average, obviously, reduces the variability to allow these effects to reach significance. Consequently, the differences between groups lies in activity time-locked to the WS only. Processes started by the WS early in the preparatory interval and prior to preparation to respond must be implicated. This strengthens the concept that the retardates do not "lock" into the task as quickly as do normals.

Discussion

Confirming much other work (Baumeister and Kellas, 1968), RT was slower in retardates than even younger normals. The greater alerting from the multimodality WS decreased RT. The predicted interaction that the retardates would be more affected by the multimodality WS, however, did not occur. There was some indication that the WS affected slow subjects more than fast subjects indicating the need for further study of extreme subjects (Karrer, in press). Also contrary to expectation, overall CNV amplitude did not differentiate retardates from normals nor young from old. Timing measures of the CNV (latency and slope) were fruitful. Retardates were slower in latency than the CA matched normals and tended to be slower in vertex CNV rise time than the younger normals. Retardates were also slower in reaching peak Post-WS positivity in frontal. Their slower SP activity is associated with the very beginning of the trial. They may not lock into the appropriate state or set early in the trial as do the normals. This would result in poorer preparation, and hence poorer processing, leading to impaired reaction time. The CNV also grows more over trials for retardates indicating that they not only take longer to lock into a trial but longer to develop over trials. Given these results, a more extensive analysis of behavioral and SP timing in retardates may be fruitful.

In general, there was a lack of differentiation (less difference in vertex and frontal) of the retarded for both Post-WS positivity and CNV. The normals tended to have large topographical differences in amplitude and peak times. The less differentiation of the timing of areas active in a task was more pervasive than topographical differences in amplitude in the retarded. This implies that the retardates may activate greater brain area than normals in performing a simple RT task (i.e. the frontal area is active at the same time as the vertex area in the retarded). When some retarded respond as fast as the normals their frontal activity remains simultaneous with vertex activity.

There were a number of developmental differences. Latencies were often shorter in younger normals. Only in the young normals was RT variability related to CNV amplitude, and RT related to Post-WS positivity. The Post-WS positivity was largest in young normals and smallest in CA normals. In these developmental trends the retardates always fell between MA and CA groups.

The complex WS condition is the one that produces the best performance in all three groups and, presumably, higher arousal and alerting. The Post-WS positivity followed this manipulation of arousal being larger in the SV condition that produced the faster RT and the only correlations of SP activity to IQ. The data make a strong point that the modality of the WS can effect the RT as well as the SP changes (PWSP) following the WS. The alerting property of the WS does not seem to be effective in modifying the CNV since the largest CNV was obtained for the sound WS. Neither did we find a consistent relation of CNV amplitude to RT or to fast or slow subjects, supporting Connor and Lang (1969).

The difference in latency among the groups and WS conditions for Post-WS positivity needs further specification. The present analysis did not look at evoked potential individual components which seem to make up much of the measure used here. It is possible, therefore, that the differences lie primarily in certain peaks of the four peaks discriminable (Fig. 11-2 and 11-3).

One possibility for the post-WS positivity is that it may be due to some specific evoked potential to vibration. The active electrode (Cz) is close to primary receiving areas for cutaneous stimuli to the wrist. This would explain the markedly reduced positivity in the S condition but not the almost additive effect of the S and V stimuli in the compound S + V condition. The developmental trend may reflect the same processes that produce larger visual evoked potentials in young children (Dustman and Beck, 1969; Gastaut and Regis, 1965; see Chap. 8). There is no direct evidence in the literature on vibratory evoked potentials to resolve this issue.

This Post-WS positivity may be similar to the P300 component seen in evoked potentials to visual and auditory stimuli. The P300 has been interpreted as reflecting selective attention (Donchin and Cohen, 1967). Similarly, Bull and Lang (1972) have found a linear relation between amplitude of positivity at about

300 msec and physical intensity of the stimulus which they interpreted as reflecting "response certainty." Paul and Sutton (1972) suggest that "P300 amplitude is increased whenever the 'salience' of a stimulus is enhanced." In the present paradigm, increased selective attention, response certainty, and/or stimulus salience would be produced by the WS and fed forward, facilitating a set to respond faster to the RS. Since the Post-WS positivity is affected by WS conditions and developmental factors, the selective attention, response certainty, and/or stimulus salience should follow a similar course. These arguments seem logically to fit the WS effects but the developmental trends would place greater selective attention, response certainty, and/or stimulus salience in the young normals and least in the older normals (the retardates falling between). The retardates would, by this reasoning, have greater amounts of these cognitive factors than the CA normals. This explanation does not seem tenable.

In the present study, the larger positivity in young children may be interpreted within the P300 conceptualization as reflecting greater conscious (cognitive) effort to perform the task. While this greater cognitive effort does not seem tenable if considered as greater attention or stimulus salience, it does seem tenable if considered as effort to control irrelevant activity and greater uncertainty in responding. This would be more consistent with the interpretations that the P300 component reflects a shift of attention associated with the orienting response (Ritter, et al., 1968) and that the P300 occurs at the resolution of uncertainty (Sutton, et al., 1967).

The Post-WS positivity, then, may reflect inhibitory processes that facilitate a motor response set. In this case, the young normals would require greater inhibition of activity irrelevant to the motor key press because of still relatively immature differentiation of motor skill performance. These inhibitory processes could take the form of voluntarily increasing conscious effort to respond, as well as more neurologically based inhibitory processes.

While a specific evoked potential to vibration may contribute to the positivity, the evidence favors the interpretation that the positivity reflects the voluntary or reflex inhibition of irrelevant motor activity which is largest in young normals and also necessary in the older retardates. This interpretation implies that once differentiation takes place, active inhibition is no longer necessary. The older normals would have differentiation of motor skill well established by age sixteen. The retardates, while the same age as the older normals, apparently lack complete motor skill differentiation for such a task and require greater inhibition of irrelevant motor activity than CA normals. This may be a further manifestation of the lag in differentiation indicated by the topographical analysis of the retardates SP activity.

IQ was only related to the Post-WS positivity in the S + V condition, the most arousing condition. The fact that there was this moderate relationship between the Post-WS positivity and IQ (also MA) in the retarded may indicate the loose relationship of IQ and MA to motor performance found by others (Clausen, 1966; Baumeister and Kellas, 1968). It is possible that increased inhibition of irrelevant motor activity goes with greater mental ability. That this should hold for the small sample of retardates indicates that further study of this relation may be fruitful.

DARK INTERVAL THRESHOLD PERFORMANCE

The DIT task is a measure of temporal processing of simple sensory information. Lower DIT thresholds reflect increased efficiency of information processing. Information processing time, of necessity, affects the amount of information in attention: attention span or capacity. The DIT task can also be considered a test of Spitz' (1963) Postulate II (see Chap. 9) that retardates should have slower recovery from a change induced in the nervous system. Slower information processing in retardates has been demonstrated in DIT and masking tasks using simple visual stimuli by a number of previous investigators (Galbraith and Gliddon, 1972; Spitz and Thor, 1968; Thor, 1970; Thor and Thor, 1970). However conceptualized, it seems certain that cognitive and central factors (intelligence, criterion and decision) are of primary importance to the high retardate thresholds for these simple stimuli (Thor and Thor, 1970: also Weisstein and Growney, 1969) even though flash stimuli are processed early in the visual system (Schiller, 1965).

It was expected that retardates should exhibit higher thresholds and longer decision times, the latter reflecting their decreased cognitive ability. Greater SP negativity preceding the two-flash occurrence should accompany more efficient perception, i.e. lower thresholds, greater certainty, and faster decisions of what was perceived. Therefore, less amplitude, greater variability and longer latency in SP negativity should be characteristics of the retardates and young normals. As detailed below, the DIT task allowed determination of SP shifts (1) accompanying orienting to each trial, (2) preceding motor activity (motor potential) associated with trial initiation, (3) accompanying the set to perceive, (4) accompanying decision making, and (5) associated with a verbal response (verbal motor potential). It was thought that all of these SP processes would be reduced in the retardate and that the decision and motor SP at verbalization may be of a different form than in normals. Regrettably, because of eye blink artifacts after the flashes, the analysis of the SP associated with verbalization was impossible.

Subjects and Procedure

Subjects were the same as in the RT study.

The flash stimuli were presented by a tachistoscope (Scientific Prototype, Model GB). A dim red fixation disc (15′ 32″, approx. 0.1 ft L) was presented by one channel superimposed on the area of the two equal intensity (6 ft L) test flashes (F1 and F2), each of 20 msec duration. A hand held push button allowed the subject to initiate the stimulus sequence at his own optimal readiness. Each trial consisted of a verbal "ready" (orienting) signal given by the experimenter followed by the subject's fixation of the red disc and voluntary button press which activated the T-scope one second later. After seeing the flashes the subject stated verbally (decision) whether he perceived one flash or two flashes. Inter-flash intervals of 20-200 msec in 20 msec steps were presented in random order for 40 test trials. Four lie trials of either 300 msec or 0 msec were interspersed in the session. Subjects were trained on 300 msec and 0 msec trials until it was clear that they understood the task and were responding consistently "one" to 0 msec and "two" to 300 msec. When the subject could not make a decision, the trial was repeated.

Steady potentials were recorded from frontal (FZ) and vertex (CZ) as described previously. For purposes of averaging the data over each subject's trials, indicator signals were collected on the data tape at the experimenter's "ready" signal, at the subject's button press, at the two flashes, and at the subject's verbal response. This allowed a number of analyses of the averaged EEG epochs beginning 0.2 sec prior to, and ending 7.2 sec after the ready signal. These analyses were performed on the EEG time-locked and averaged in two different ways as follows (1) The SP associated with orienting to the ready signal was determined from the averaged EEG *time-locked to the ready signal.* The area under the curve in the 0.6 sec after the ready signal, and prior to the subject's button press, was designated the *Orienting-Ready SP (ORSP).* (2) The SP activity associated with the subject's button press *(Pre-motor SP),* set to perceive *(CNV),* and decision processes *(DSP)* were determined from averages of EEG *time-locked to the subject's button press.* The SP area 0.5 sec prior to button press was designated the *Pre-Motor SP (MSP),* the motor readiness potential. The *Latency* of this MSP measure was taken as the median of the last 20 msec within 2.5 μV of baseline. The SP area during the foreperiod (1.2 secs) between button press and 200 msec after the first flash (the longest interflash interval) was designated the *CNV.* The SP area in the 400 msecs following the second flash defined the *Decision SP (DSP)* measure. These measures are demonstrated in Figures 11-10 and 11-11.

In order to determine the timing of these measures, peaks, as well as areas, were determined. In general, the peaks reflected the same effects as area measures. Peaks within each area were defined as the mean of the highest points yielding a 200 msec sample for that area. Peak time was taken as the latency of the median point for each 200 msec sample. For the long (1.2 sec)

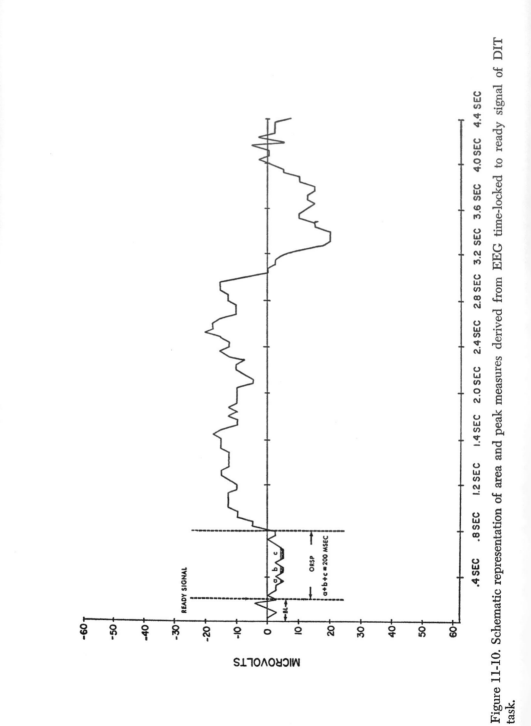

Figure 11-10. Schematic representation of area and peak measures derived from EEG time-locked to ready signal of DIT task.

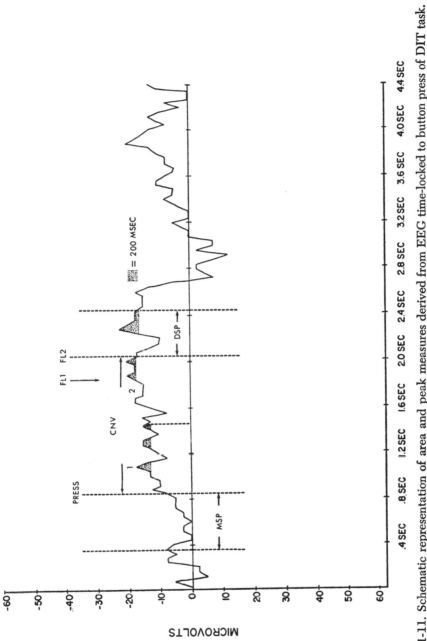

Figure 11-11. Schematic representation of area and peak measures derived from EEG time-locked to button press of DIT task.

CNV area two peaks and peak times were computed: an initial CNV peak in the first half and a final CNV peak in the last half of the foreperiod. These were equivalent CNV measures to those in the RT task. All measures were calculated as deviations from a baseline determined from the last 200 msec prior to the ready signal at the start of a trial.

The prevalence of artifacts prohibited the determination of SP measures during or after the vocal response or from averages time-locked to the vocal response. Artifacts, primarily movement and eye blinks, resulted in discarding many trials. The mean percent of artifact-free trials for each group was 56 percent, 45 percent, and 37 percent for the young normals, retardates, and older normals respectively.

Results

Behavior

Values for the three behavioral measures, threshold, press time and decision time can be seen in Table 11-3. The retardates had higher thresholds than either normal group who did not differ (F 2/35 = 3.52, $p < .04$). The data indicate that the retardates are about 26 percent slower than the CA normals. This confirms the previous studies finding slower processing for retardates.

There was no difference between groups in the time to voluntarily press the button to initiate a trial although the young normals tended to do so faster than older normals and retardates

TABLE 11-III

THRESHOLD (T), PRESS TIME (PT) AND DECISION
TIME (DT) MEANS AND STANDARD DEVIATIONS
(in msec)

	T	PT	DT
MA X̄	70	539	981
SD	18.3	100	111
R X̄	86	697	1145
SD	16.9	170	337
CA X̄	68	709	966
SD	18.7	347	226

(mean press times were 539, 709, and 697 msec respectively). This was due to the extreme variability within the groups for this measure. Decision time (DT), however, was significantly different with retardates slower than the two normal groups (mean DT = 1145, 982, and 966 for retardates, young and older normals respectively; $t = 2.06$, df 36, $p < .05$ for retardates, vs combined normals). These data indicate about a 19 percent slowing of retardate DT. Combining all three groups there was a tendency for fast decision times to accompany low thresholds ($r = .365$, $p < .05$). Those subjects with thresholds below their group median had faster decision times, but not significantly so ($F\ 1/32 = 2.91$, $p < .10$). Decision time was unrelated to age or MA but was correlated with IQ in the retardates ($r = -.644$, $-.601$, $p < .05$, for verbal and performance IQ respectively). Retardates with higher IQ had faster decision times.

The correlation of each subject's DIT threshold with his mean RT (for each WS condition of the RT task) suggested a developmental trend although all correlations were not significant. The MA group's correlations between threshold and RT were higher for all three RT conditions ($r = 0.55, 0.48, 0.52$, for V, S, and S + V respectively) than the retardates ($r = 0.26, 0.34$, 0.23, respectively) who were higher than CA normals ($r = 0.04$, 0.02, 0.21, respectively).

In summary, the behavioral measures, perceptual temporal resolution (thresholds) and time required to make a decision (decision time) discriminated the groups setting the ground for analysis of SP correlates of these differences.

SP Measures: Description

The basic averages that gave rise to the SP measures are shown in Figures 11-12 and 11-13. Figure 11-12 shows the total group averages of EEG activity time-locked to the ready signal initiating each trial. It is obvious from the similarity of the wave shapes between the groups that reliable processes are being recorded in this task. The first major feature in these curves is a late positive peak (ORSP) at 250-350 msec following the ready signal. This is greater in vertex than frontal. The young normals

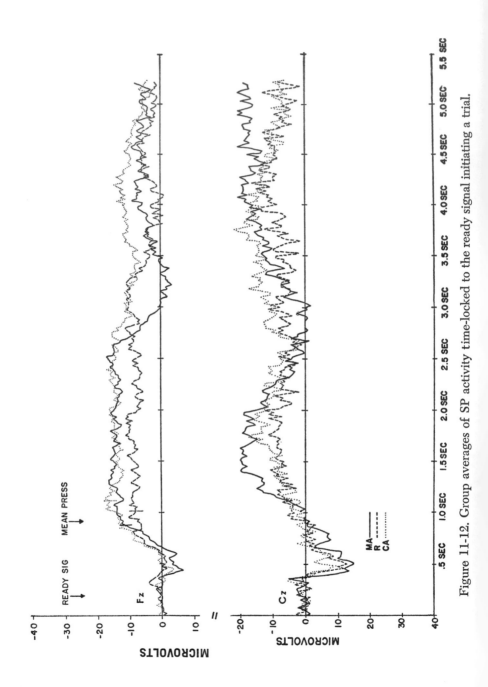

Figure 11-12. Group averages of SP activity time-locked to the ready signal initiating a trial.

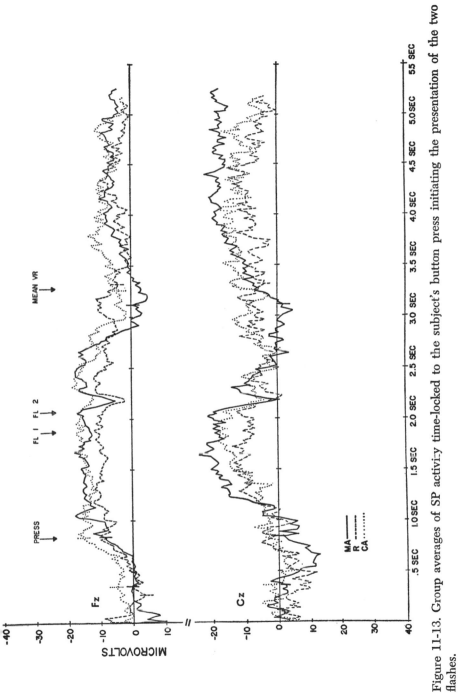

Figure 11-13. Group averages of SP activity time-locked to the subject's button press initiating the presentation of the two flashes.

have larger amplitudes than the other groups. This ORSP resolves into a long negative shift that reaches its peak in association with the mean press time in frontal, but continues rising after press time in vertex. This negativity after press is maintained until after the time that the two flashes occur. Retardates seem to have less of this negativity, especially in frontal, than the other groups.

Of some importance, methodologically and conceptually, is the fact that this average of activity time-locked to the ready signal is so regular and consistent even after the subject's button press. In fact, the button press seems to occur at the peak of the rising negativity (vertical line). Because measures of this activity were so correlated to those from the time-locked-to-button press average, we have chosen to use only that segment prior to button press from the ready signal time-locked data. This decision was based upon the reasoning that the button press would initiate SP activity independent of SP processes initiated by the ready signal. The unexpected regularity in the ready signal average well after (2-3 secs) the trial onset makes the assumption of independence obviously weak. It is apparent that the ready signal initiates activity that continues for some seconds even though the button press intervenes.

Figure 11-13 shows the total group averages of activity time-locked to the press. Since button press time varies between individuals, the curves at each end do not contain the whole group. The curves begin at that point prior to press in which 50 percent of the group is represented (the other 50% having longer press times). The whole group is represented at about 600 msec prior to press, reflecting the fastest press times.

There is a rather variable positive shift in vertex (not seen in frontal) at about 0.5 sec prior to press. This may be due to the activity time-locked to the ready signal (ORSP, see Fig. 11-12) and poorly time-locked to press. The first major feature of these curves is the sharp negative shift (MSP) beginning about 180-200 msec prior to press and is briefly interrupted by a positive peak after press. This MSP, in frontal, maintains its level after the press as the CNV. The CNV continues to grow in vertex until flash occurrence. The retardates, again, appear to have less CNV, especially in frontal. Following the first flash by about 300 msec is a large positive peak (P300?) which often resolves the CNV. This positive peak interrupts the negativity as it returns slowly to baseline after the flash (650-700 msec in vertex, longer in frontal). This "after" negativity (DSP) may be related to decision processes as its return to base tends to precede the verbal report.

Correlations (groups collapsed) between the measures of ORSP, MSP, CNV, and DSP found them quite independent. The ORSP was related to MSP: the greater the ORSP positivity the less the MSP negativity and the longer the MSP latency (frontal r's = .68 and .47, $p < .05$, respectively). This was due to the method of scoring the MSP (area in a certain time epoch rather than from peak ORSP to peak MSP). Neither the ORSP nor the MSP were significantly related to the CNV or DSP (r's = < .3). However, the CNV and DSP were significantly related to one another ($r = 0.78$ for frontal). For statistical analysis of all these measures, groups were split on median thresholds, median press times, as well as median decision times. Two-way anovas (Grps. × Thresholds, Grps. × Press Times, Grps. × Decision Times) were computed for each. These quantitative analyses gave the following results.

Ready Signal Average: ORSP

The area of vertex ORSP positivity was smaller ($\overline{X} = 36.2$ μV sec) for low threshold than for high threshold subjects ($\overline{X} = 150.3$ μV sec; F $1/32 = 3.99$, $p = .05$). But there was an interaction of groups by threshold for vertex peak ORSP amplitude (F $2/38 = 5.02$, $p < .01$). Low threshold normal subjects had less peak ORSP than high threshold normals while low threshold retardates had greater peak ORSP positivity than high threshold retardates. The interaction was also reflected in a significant difference between low threshold retardates ($\overline{X} = 31.2$ μv) and low threshold normals ($\overline{X}s = 9.0$ μv and 18.8 μV for CA and MA respectively; F $2/15 = 5.74$, $p < .015$).

The ORSP peak time was related to decision time in a complex interaction ($F\ 2/32 = 3.34$, $p < .04$). Slow DTs were preceded by shorter times of frontal ORSP peak in normals but not in retardates, while fast DTs showed no difference in ORSP peak time between groups.

Thus, better performance (threshold) was preceded by the occurrence of less ORSP positivity in vertex leads for the normals. On the contrary, the better performing retardates had larger ORSP positivity than either better performing normals or poorly performing retardates.

Press Time Average: Pre-Motor SP (MSP)

The MSP was usually a negative-going shift but quite often part or all of the MSP was on the positive side of the baseline.

There was no correlation of button press time and MSP nor were there MSP differences between fast button pressors and slow button pressors. The vertex MSP started closer to button press (230 msec) in young normals than in retardates or CA normals ($F\ 2/32 = 3.38$, $p < .04$) whose MSPs started at 515 msec and 507 msec prior to button press.

Low threshold subjects had larger vertex MSP negative area than high threshold subjects ($F\ 1/32 = 4.42$, $p < .04$). There was an interaction such that high threshold normals had vertex positive MSPs while low threshold normals had vertex negative MSPs ($F\ 2/32 = 3.48$, $p < .04$). The retardates had vertex positive MSPs with greater positivity for low threshold subjects; a reversal from the normals. There was also an interaction of fast/slow decision time and groups such that the slow decision time subjects had less frontal MSP negativity if they were retardates or young normals while the fast decision time subjects were equivalent among the groups ($F\ 2/32 = 4.28$, $p < .02$). The frontal MSP started sooner in slow decision time MA and CA normal subjects than comparable retardates. However, for fast DT subjects, the frontal MSP started sooner in retardates than in MA or CA normals ($F\ 2/32 = 5.10$, $p < .01$).

Thus, vertex MSPs began closer in time to the button press for young normals. Better performing (low threshold) normals tend to negative vertex MSPs, while inefficiently performing (high threshold) normals have positive (though negative-going) vertex MSPs. Retardates, on the other hand, tend to these positive vertex MSPs but with a reversed relation of greater positivity in more efficient (low threshold) performing retardates. Less frontal MSP negativity was associated with slow DT in both retardates and young normals. Fast decisions were associated with a late starting frontal MSP in normals but early starting MSP in retardates and slow DT normals.

TOPOGRAPHY. The topography of vertex and frontal MSP activity also differentiated the slow decision time groups. The slow CA normals had a greater vertex-frontal difference due to greater frontal MSP negativity than for fast decision time CA subjects ($t = 2.27$, df 11, $p < .04$). Retardate and MA normal slow decision time subjects had less of a vertex-frontal difference (because of their lesser frontal negativity) than slow CA normals (F $2/16 = 5.07$, $p < .02$). Among slow DT subjects the MSP started sooner in frontal than vertex but the groups did not differ in these V-F values (F $2/16 = 3.13$, $p < .07$). Among fast DT subjects, however, the MSP started at about the same time in frontal and vertex for normals but the frontal MSP started sooner than vertex for the retardates (F $2/16 = 7.33$, $p < .006$). This relation was also reflected by significant correlations between the size of the V-F latency difference and DT for CA normals ($r = -.56$, $p < .05$) and for retardates ($r - .58$, $p < .05$) but not for MA normals ($r = -.32$). The fast decision CA normals had less of a vertex-frontal MSP latency difference than did the slow CA normals ($t = 3.86$, df 11; $p < .003$). Apparently, shorter latency frontal than vertex MSPs tends to go with slow decision times, while little difference in vertex-frontal MSP latencies goes with fast decision times. The retardates had shorter latency frontal than vertex MSPs.

Preparatory Interval SP (CNV)

Correlations between the frontal and vertex CNV were moderate with young normals ($r = 0.56$, $p < .05$) and the retardates

($r = 0.51$, $p < 0.05$) having comparable values, while the CA normals had the highest correlation ($r = 0.77$, $p < .01$) as in the RT task above.

Contrary to expectation, there was no difference between the groups or between high vs. low threshold subjects on CNV amplitude. On the other hand, fast decision time subjects had larger CNVs than slow decision time subjects in both frontal and vertex (F $1/32 = 6.19$ and 6.09, $p < .02$ respectively). Also, slow decision time retardates had smaller frontal CNVs than age-matched normals ($t = 2.23$, df 11, $p < .025$).

The time to initial peak CNV clearly differentiated the groups in vertex. Older normals had longer time to peak than young normals (F $2/32 = 3.26$, $p < .05$ vertex; F $2/32 = 2.78$, $p < .07$ frontal) with retardates between. There was also an interaction with threshold. Initial and final frontal CNV peak times were faster for high threshold young normals than for high threshold retardates and older normals (F's $2/32 = 3.42$, 5.92, $p < .05$ for initial and final CNV). Fast decision time subjects reached initial vertex CNV peak faster than slow decision time subjects (F $1/32 = 9.61$, $p < .005$) with a similar trend in frontal (F $1/32 = 3.14$, $p < .07$). This was also true of time to final or maximum CNV prior to the flashes (F $1/32 = 5.41$, $p < .03$ for vertex).

TOPOGRAPHY. In the CA normals there were larger differences between vertex-frontal for CNV area of slow decision subjects than for fast subjects ($t = 2.79$, df 11, $p < .02$). This difference was due to larger frontal negativity in slow subjects. Retardates and MA normals did not reflect this topographical difference.

INTERCORRELATIONS. The CNVs from the DIT and RT studies were significantly correlated in only the MA group which had three of six correlations significant (frontal: sound WS, $r = .64$; vertex: vibration WS, $r = .65$, combined WS, $r = .72$, $p < .05$ for all). The retardates had only one significant correlation (frontal, vibration WS, $r = .74$, $p < .01$) while the CA group had none. These correlations between tasks follow the trend of the behavior correlations; greatest relationship in the young normals and least in older normals. The correlations also indicated that the retardates were similar to the young normals in their large size of frontal CNV correlations but like older normals in the small size of vertex CNV correlations (r's < 0.12). This implies a developmental trend in the differentiation of brain areas from task to task in the MA and retardate groups. The latter have appropriate differentiation for their age in vertex processes but lag behind in frontal process differentiation.

Decision SP (DSP)

The only difference in this activity was that, across groups, subjects with fast decision times had larger frontal and vertex negative areas (F $1/32 = 4.16$, 8.20 respectively, $p < .05$). There was no difference between groups or between low and high threshold subjects.

TOPOGRAPHY. As with the CNV there was a greater topographical difference in DSP negativity for slow decision CA normal subjects than fast CA subjects. Significantly smaller vertex negativity in the slow subjects again produced the effect ($t = 2.64$, df $11, p < .02$).

Variability of SP Measures

To assess the variability of the SP measures the standard deviation (SD) of each measure was computed for each subject over trials. There were no differences between groups for the SD of any measure. An interaction between groups and thresholds was found. High threshold retardates had significantly greater variability in frontal measures of ORSP, MSP, CNV, and DSP than low threshold retardates (t's $= 2.63, 2.29, 2.05, 1.87$, df $11, p < .05$) respectively. Normals did not differ significantly in frontal on any of these measures. On the other hand, in vertex, low threshold young normals had greater variability in the MSP and CNV than did high threshold subjects ($t = 2.39, 2.63$, $p < .05$, df 11, respectively). In this case retardates and older normals had no difference in vertex variability. There was also an interaction with decision time such that the slow decision time retardates had greater frontal variability for the pre-motor, and DSP measures than fast retardates. Again there was no difference between fast and slow decision time subjects in the normal groups.

In sum, inefficiently performing (high DIT, slow DT) retardates tend to greater variability in frontal SP measures, while efficiently performing (low DIT) young normals tend to greater variability in vertex SP measures.

Certainty vs Uncertainty SP Analysis

To better tease apart the relation of DIT threshold to SP activity each subject's data were averaged into two components. Those trials on which the probability of judging either one flash or two flashes was 100 percent were averaged together and designated *certainty* trials. Those trials on which the probability was less than 100 percent for a judgment of either one or two flashes were averaged together as *uncertainty* trials. These *uncertainty* trials were the trials in the threshold region. Since all subjects did not have *uncertainty* trials the data were from eight young normals, ten retardates, and seven older normals.

All but one normal subject had shorter decision times for *certainty* trials than for *uncertainty* trials ($t = 4.77$, df 7, $p < .003$ for MA; $t = 2.76$, df 6, $p < .03$ for CA). This reflects greater time to make a decision on the difficult discriminations around the threshold. While seven of ten retardates showed this relation the difference in decision time was not significant, indicating their tendency to take more time to make *certain* as well as *uncertainty* decisions.

Group averages of the SP data are seen in Figure 11-14 (frontal) and Figure 11-15 (vertex) for trials time-locked to the press (note: by definition, the beginning of such averages does not coincide with the beginning of the trial). It is immediately apparent that large and consistent negative shifts precede judgments that are consistent *(certainty)*. This negativity begins prior to button press and is maintained throughout the interval. Retardates (who have higher thresholds and, therefore, do more poorly on the task) seem to start their negative shift later and it is smaller than for either normal group. The *uncertainty* trials

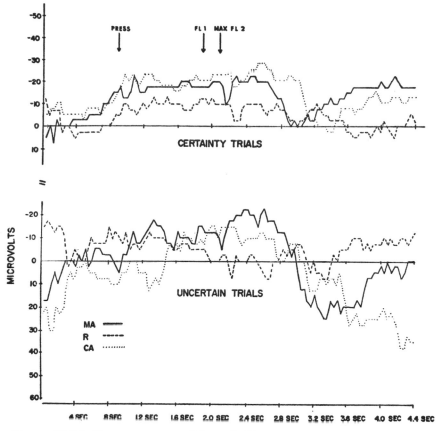

Figure 11-14. Group averages of frontal SP activity occurring on *certainty* and on *uncertainty* trials. Average was time-locked to the subject's button press.

show a dramatically different picture. The inconsistent judgments on *uncertainty* trials are preceded by smaller and less consistent negative SP amplitudes. There are large deviations from baseline prior to button press which may reflect a shifting baseline. Although there are negative shifts in the preparatory interval they tend to start later (normals) or decline during the interval (retardates).

Although the graphs are strikingly different between retardates and normals, there were no significant differences between

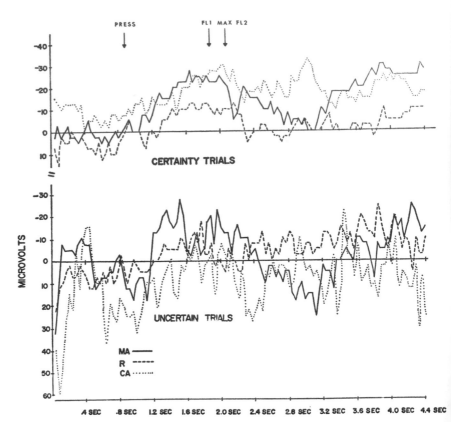

Figure 11-15. Group averages of vertex SP activity occurring on *certainty* and on *uncertainty* trials. Average was time-locked to the subject's press.

groups. This is undoubtedly due to the small number of subjects that could be used. There was an interaction between groups and *certainty-uncertainty* for the vertex MSP (F 2/24 = 3.69, *p* < .04). Groups did not differ in vertex MSP area for *certainty* trials, but young normals had greater negative MSP area than retardates or older normals for *uncertainty* trials.

The initial CNV peak after button press was significantly larger on *certainty* trials than on *uncertainty* trials across all three groups (F 1/24 = 5.45 and 6.86, *p* < .03 for frontal and vertex respectively). This reflects the later growth of the CNV on *uncertainty* trials (see Fig. 11-14).

TABLE 11-IV

GROUP MEANS FOR MSP AND CNV AREA AS A FUNCTION OF CERTAINTY-UNCERTAINTY TRIALS AND LOW VS. HIGH THRESHOLD SUBJECTS (in μv secs)

| | Frontal | | | | | | Vertex | | | | | |
| | MA | | R | | CA | | MA | | R | | CA | |
	H	L	H	L	H	L	H	L	H	L	H	L
MSP												
C	− 140	− 339	+ 43	− 95	+ 48	− 512	+ 222	− 133	+133	+ 283	+ 377	− 443
U	− 435	+ 492	− 430	+118	+ 249	+ 144	+ 150	− 824	+251	− 516	+ 742	+ 615
CNV												
C	−1473	−1389	− 568	−923	−1125	−1776	−1148	−1432	−136	− 661	−1556	−1393
U	−2869	−1154	−1368	+215	−1104	+ 43	− 882	−2509	−434	−1413	+ 927	− 25

The CA normals showed the *certainty-uncertainty* effects clearly for ORSP, MSP, and CNV in both frontal and vertex. The ORSP was less positive on *certainty* trials ($t = 2.86$, df 6, $p < .029$ for frontal; $t = 2.54$, df 6, $p < .04$ for vertex) and its peak on *certainty* trials was faster in frontal ($t = 3.21$, df 6, $p < .02$, not significant in vertex). Both the MSP and initial CNV had greater negativity on *certainty* trials (MSP; t's = 3.46, 5.30, df 6, $p < .01$ frontal and vertex respectively). The late CNV peak did not differ, reflecting the later CNV growth on *uncertainty* trials. DSP had the same trend of greater negativity on *certainty* trials ($t = 1.93$, df 6, $p < .05$, 1-tailed for frontal).

It is possible that the SP processes associated with *certainty-uncertainty* may differ for high and low threshold subjects. The *certainty-uncertainty* data were further divided into above vs. below median threshold in each group. The group means for these data are included in Table 11-IV. Inspection of this data indicated that in frontal, low threshold subjects in each group had considerably larger negative MSP and CNV on *certainty* trials than *uncertainty* trials. In fact, on *uncertainty* trials the means showed positive areas. On the contrary, high threshold retarded and MA subjects had greater negative MSP and CNV areas during *uncertainty* trials. There seems no such consistency for vertex, except that retardates may be seen to have a smaller CNV on *certainty* trials and this is most pronounced in high threshold subjects.

It should be noted that larger frontal CNV values are given by high threshold young normals and retardates on *uncertainty* trials, while low threshold older normals give the largest frontal CNV on *certainty* trials. In vertex, retardates and young normals of low threshold have the largest CNV on *uncertainty* trials, as compared to the largest CNV for high threshold older normals on *certainty* trials. These differences in which the young normals and retardates are similar may reflect cognitive strategies associated with thresholds that change with intellectual growth.

Discussion

The data confirm Thor and Thor (1971) that retardates have slower processing of perceptual information. Our prediction that they would have slower decision times was also confirmed. The fact that DT, and not threshold, was correlated to IQ confirmed our assumption that DT reflects primarily cognitive processes.

The developmental trend in the correlation between the two tasks (RT and DIT) implicates differentiation of processes underlying the two tasks. The older normals have rather completely differentiated these processes giving essentially zero correlations, while the retardates have done so incompletely.

Low thresholds were preceded by less positivity after the ready signal in the normal groups, while retarded low threshold subjects have more positivity. In fact, for the normals, high DIT thresholds were not only associated with larger positivities after the trial onset but slow decisions were associated with this positivity reaching peak quickly. This similarity between low threshold retardates and high threshold normals may indicate a promising lead for further analysis. It may imply different processes being utilized as the subject prepared to perceive the two flashes. If the SP positivity is related to an inhibitory function this must be detrimental to perceptual resolution in the normal but facilitate perceptual resolution in the retardate.

Greater differences in vertex and frontal activity went with better performance in the RT study. It is not clear, then, why the high threshold normals have the greatest difference in ORSP positivity with vertex predominant. It is reasonable to assume that differentiation of area and the predominance of vertex or frontal is dependent on the type of SP and the processes underlying the task. In the DIT task, less difference in frontal and vertex ORSP activity seems to accompany better performance. It is striking that the retardates with their significantly slower DIT thresholds had a large vertex-frontal difference and vertex predominance, even in low threshold subjects, for this positivity after the ready signal. The fact that the retardates do not always reflect the same effects (e.g. low threshold subjects have larger ORSPs and greater V-F difference) may also imply that the retardate uses different underlying processes in performing the task. These data need confirmation and extension.

The MSP was also related to threshold. Faster perceptual

processing was preceded by larger negative MSPs confirming Mc-Adam and Rubin (1971). Slow perceptual processing was accompanied by positive MSPs in all three groups but the low threshold retardates also have positive MSPs. This exception to the relation may also indicate different processes preceding adequate performance by the retardate.

MSP vertex latency followed a developmental trend that was counter to expectation, i.e. the young normals had shorter MSPs that began closer to their button press than the CA normals or retardates. Interactions again complicated the picture. Slow DT normals (CA and MA) also had such shorter frontal MSPs. Contrary to the RT Study, greater differences between frontal and vertex seemed to precede poorer performance, i.e. slower decision time. The CA normals most consistently showed this. Slow DT subjects had greater predominance in frontal amplitude and shorter frontal MSPs than fast DT subjects. This was different in the slow DT retardates and MA normals who had less of a vertex-frontal difference due to reduced amplitude frontal MSPs. These results again point to topography differences with development and with the adequacy of performance. It seems that slower decision times by older normals are preceded by short latency frontal predominance of activity that occurs before a motor response that initiates the preparation to process the information for the decisions. But in young normals and retardates slower decision times are preceded by reduced frontal negativity.

Contrary to expectations (and McAdam and Rubin, 1971), the CNV discriminated neither the groups nor high/low threshold subjects. On the other hand, fast DT subjects had larger CNVs than slow DT subjects. The CNV, therefore, seems more related to cognitive processes than to perceptual processes, an interpretation that would make our data compatible with the data from McAdam and Rubin's (1971) more complex perceptual task. Their task required cognitive processes more akin to our decision time than to our threshold for two flashes.

The slow DT CA normals had the largest vertex-frontal difference for the CNV and the slow DT young normals and retardates also reflected this trend. In fact, even the fast retardates had a large V-F difference. The slow DT retardates substantiated this trend by having the smallest frontal and vertex CNVs. Apparently, large CNVs in both frontal and vertex, with little V-F difference, are necessary for fast decisions.

The only developmental trend for the CNV resided in the correlations between tasks. This trend was the same as, but less dramatic than, the correlations of the RT and DIT: the CA normals had the greatest differentiation. In line with the other data, the retardates showed a lag in differentiation of the frontal CNV activity but not the vertex CNV.

These trends were further strengthened by the DSP. Thresholds or groups did not produce differences in DSP while DT did. Fast DTs were associated with larger negative DSPs than were slow DTs. The CA normal's topographical difference was again evident with slow DT subjects having the greatest difference due to very small vertex DSPs (also in MA and retardates).

The findings clearly indicate faster decision processes are accompanied by large negativity in both frontal and vertex. Since the DSP area also included the positive peak after the flashes (P300), it may be questioned if the relation to decision time is due to the P300 peak. However, if P300 were responsible, one would expect an inverse relation between size of the negative area and performance (i.e. faster decision times have smaller negative area, or larger P300). This was not the case.

The topography of SP activity early in the trial (ORSP, MSP) that accompanies efficient performance is similar to the topography of SP activity later in the trial (CNV, DSP) that accompanies efficient performance: frontal predominance and/or a small vertex-frontal difference.

It was also clear that high thresholds and slow DTs were associated with greater variability in frontal, but not vertex, SP measures in the retardate. The young normals greater variability in vertex, but not frontal, for low threshold subjects may reflect another developmental topographical difference. Perhaps, this is an expression of the growing differentiation of the processes in the two brain areas, leading to higher vertex variability in young subjects as cognitive and motor performance become independent and they begin to perform well.

The *certainty-uncertainty* comparisons found the CA normals to show the clearest differences. Less positivity in the ORSP and greater negativity in the MSP and initial CNV peak were associated with *certainty* trials. This was less evident in the DSP. The *certainty* trials in all three groups had larger initial CNVs than *uncertainty* trials reflecting an early growth of CNV during the PI interval on *certainty* trials. *Certainty* trials also had faster DT for normals but this was less so in the retardates. Even though their means show smaller negative MSPs and CNVs the retarded were not significantly different than normals.

This data seems to add support to the interpretation that the CNV accompanies increased efficiency in perceptual processing. Hillyard (1969b) and Hillyard, et al. (1971) found larger CNVs prior to correct detection in a threshold task. Our task did not have correct and incorrect trials. *Certainty* vs *uncertainty* trials are better considered a measure of consistency in perceptual processing and judgment while threshold (DIT) is a better measure of perceptual sensitivity.

In all groups low threshold subjects had larger negative frontal MSP and CNV areas on *certainty* trials, while *uncertainty* trials tended to positivity in frontal. Therefore, larger frontal negativity early in the trial leads to consistent judgments, while frontal positivity tends to lead to *uncertain* trials. This relation was the opposite for high threshold retarded and MA normal subjects, i.e. larger frontal negativity on *uncertainty* trials. Different criteria or strategies used by high vs low threshold subjects in the retarded and MA normals may explain this difference. It may be that high threshold retarded and MA subjects set higher criteria for judging the perception and thereby generate larger negativity. This trend was in the data (see Table 11-IV) but it is difficult to explain why this should produce differential effects on *certainty* and *uncertainty* trials. It is obvious, however, that the CNV is also related to cognitive processes (decision time, consistency of judgment, etc.) as well as perceptual processing.

Our data imply that the basic processes underlying the task are the same in retardates, MA, and CA normals. Only the timing and topography of these processes seem to differ between groups.

CONCLUSIONS

The slowest DIT processing of the retardates was on the order of 50-75 msec (26%) slower than CA normals while the slowest RT was on the order of hundreds of msecs (about 56% slower). If one accepts that of the discriminative behavior measures, the DIT is primarily perceptual, the RT both perceptual and motor, while the DT is perceptual, cognitive, and motor, then the retardate's slowness resides in input, central, and output processes. It can be further reasoned that there is a larger slowing in processes needed on demand from the environment than in processes under voluntary initiation i.e. the larger difference between groups in RT than in DT (only about 19% slower) even though the DT must include perceptual, cognitive, and motor processes. This implicates the process of responding (response organization or initiation) as a major factor in the retardates slowness. An analysis of the temporal sequences in performing an act could be of utmost importance to understanding this deficit and its remediation.

One source of SP shifts is thought to be widespread depolarization of apical dendrites in the upper layers of the frontal and premotor cortex. The CNV may act as a "primer" for the discharge of elements in motor cortex, ensuring synchrony and quickness of sensorimotor responses (Walter, et al., 1964). From this basis it was expected that retardates with slower cognitive and motor processes should also show slower CNV processes. It was not expected that they would have amplitudes equal to normal. However, in both tasks the retardates did have a different topography which often seemed to implicate the timing of frontal activity. This pervasive topographical difference between retardates and normals implies a lack of differentiation of processes underlying task performance and that timing of impulses arriving at the different brain areas is improper. The synchrony, phase, and timing of brain activity is crucial to adequate performance on any task. The present studies using only frontal and vertex midline sites point to a potentially lucrative payoff from studies using a full montage during simple and complex motor and cognitive tasks.

John (1972) has emphasized the importance of widespread topographical patterns of brain activity as the basis for cognitive processes. While his arguments were based upon the fast AC components of electrocortical activity, patterns of DC activity have also been uniquely demonstrated to accompany cognitive activity by DeMott (1970). These two aspects of electrocortical activity may conceivably follow the same or different patterns during a psychological process.

The larger Post-WS positivities in the RT task were interpreted as reflecting greater uncertainty and/or inhibition processes in the young normal (and retardate). However, the lack of larger positivity (ORSP) in the young normals during the DIT task (where one would expect just as great a degree of uncertainty and its resolution, especially on the *uncertainty* trials) argues for motor inhibition as the primary correlate of the Post-WS positivity. If the P300 wave comprises at least part of the Post-WS positivity a developmental analysis of the P300 and the Post-WS positivity found here using complex stimuli may yield important information on the development of the relation between cognition and cortical electrical activity. It may be that the increased amplitude in late components at about six to fourteen years mirrors the development of cognitive processes that foster uncertainty and its resolution in the information processing of the young child.

Since decision time was more productive of differences in CNV amplitude than the DIT or RT, the CNV must be more related to cognitive processes than to perceptual or motor processes. The fact that SP activity 1 to 1.5 secs prior to the critical stimuli is related to threshold certainty and decision time seems to implicate some general cognitive state that the organism adopts and focuses at the beginning of the trial. This must be an alerting and orienting or a set to attend in a particular way during the trial. In fact, the data would indicate that this cognitive state must develop sometime prior to .5 sec before the critical stimuli and, perhaps, reach a certain level as well. Some retardates and young normals do not do this and consequently have poor performance.

The present studies have only begun to scratch the surface of SP activity of the retardate and during development. The studies have demonstrated that evidence of retarded and developing brain function may be obtained and that the relation of SP activity to cognitive functions is a productive area. In general, the same processes are present in the retardate but in different patterns and with different timing quite often reflecting a developmental lag. The most compelling lack of the predominance of frontal activity, also often present in the younger normals, may reflect different underlying neurological processes and/or cognitive strategies.

Further work should follow up these leads by manipulating cognitive strategies in a task (e.g. appropriate strategies and inappropriate strategies). Such studies would tend to isolate the processes used by the young child and retardate leading to efficient or inefficient performance. They would also answer the question "do different cognitive strategies give different SP patterns?"

REFERENCES

Baumeister, A. A., and Kellas, G.: Distribution of reaction times of retardates and normals. *Am J Ment Defic,* 72:715-718, 1968.

Berkson, G.: Psychophysiological studies in mental deficiency. In N. R. Ellis (Ed.). *Handbook of Mental Deficiency,* New York, McGraw-Hill, 1963.

Brazier, M. A. B. (Ed.): *Brain Function.* Vol. 1. *Cortical Excitability and Steady Potentials; Relations of Basic Research to Space Biology.* Los Angeles, Univ. of California Press, 1963.

Brebner, J.: The refractoriness of regular responses. *Aust J Psych, 23(1):* 3-7, 1971.

Bull, K., and Lang, P. G.: Intensity judgments and physiological response amplitude. *Psychophysiology,* 9:428-436, 1972.

Caspers, H.: Relations of steady potential shifts in the cortex to the wakefulness-sleep spectrum. In M. A. B. Brazier (Ed.): *Brain Function.* Vol. 1. *Cortical Excitability and Steady Potentials; Relations of Basic Research to Space Biology.* Berkeley, Univ. California, 1963.

Clausen, J., *Ability Structure and Subgroups in Mental Retardation.* Washington, D.C., Spartan Press, 1966.

———: Arousal theory in mental deficiency. In M. Hammer; K. Salzinger, S. Sutton (Eds.): *Psychopathology*. New York, John Wiley, 1972.

Connor, W. H., and Lang, P. J.: Cortical slow-wave and cardiac rate responses in stimulus orientation and reaction time conditions. *J Exp Psy*, 82:310-320, 1969.

Deecke, L.; Scheid, P., and Kornhuber, H. H.: Distribution of readiness potentials, pre-motion positivity, and motor potential of human cerebral cortex preceding voluntary finger movements. *Exp Brain Res*, 7:158-168, 1969.

DeMott, D. W.: *Toposcopic Studies of Learning*. Springfield, Thomas, 1970.

Donchin, E., and Cohen, L.: Averaged evoked potentials and intramodality selective attention. *EEG Clin Neurophysiol*, 22:537-546, 1967.

Donchin, E.; Gerbandt, L. A.; Leifer, L., and Tucker, L.: Is contingent negative variation contingent on a motor response? *Psychophysiology*, 9: 178-188, 1972.

Dustman, R. E. and Beck, E. C.: The effects of maturation and aging on the wave form of visually evoked potentials. *EEG Clin Neurophysiol*, 26:2-11, 1969.

Ellis, N. R.: The stimulus trace and behavioral inadequacy. In N. R. Ellis (Ed.): *Handbook of Mental Deficiency*. New York, McGraw-Hill, 1963.

Ellis, N. R.: Memory processes in retardates and normals. In N. R. Ellis (Ed.): *International Review of Research in Mental Retardation*. Vol. 4, New York, Academic, 1970.

Fisher, M. A., and Zeaman, D.: An attention-retention theory of retardate discrimination learning. In Ellis, N. R. (Ed.): *International Review of Research in Mental Retardation*. Vol. 6, New York, Academic, 1973.

Galbraith, G. C., and Gliddon, J. B.: Backward visual masking with homogeneous and patterned stimuli: Comparison of retarded and nonretarded subjects. *Percept Mot Skills*, 34:903-908, 1972.

Gastaut, H., and Regis, H.: The visually evoked potentials recorded transcranially in man. In L. D. Proctor, and W. R. Adey (Eds.): *NASA Symposium on the Analysis of Central Nervous System and Cardiovascular Data Using Computer Methods*. NASA, Sp.-72, Washington, D.C., 1965.

Hillyard, S. A.: Relationships between the contingent negative variation (CNV) and reaction time. *Physiol Behav*, 4:351-357, 1969a.

Hillyard, S. A.: The CNV and the vertex evoked potential during signal detection: a preliminary report. In E. Donchin, and D. B. Lindsley (Eds.): *Averaged Evoked Potentials; Methods, Results, and Evaluations*. Washington, D.C., U.S. Government Printing Office, 1969b.

Hillyard, S. A.; Squires, K. C.; Bauer, J. W., and Lindsay, P. H.: Evoked potential correlates of auditory signal detection. *Science*, 172:1357-1360, 1971.

Hohle, R. H.: Component process latencies in reaction times. In L. P. Lipsitt, and C. C. Spiker (Eds.): *Advances in Child Development and Behavior:* Vol. 3. New York, Academic, 1967.

Holden, E. A.: Reaction time during unimodal and trimodal stimulation in educable retardates. *J Ment Defic Res*, 9:183-190, 1965.

John, E. R.: Switchboard versus statistical theories of learning and memory. *Science*, 177:850-864, 1972.

Karrer, R.: Autonomic nervous system functions and behavior: A review of experimental studies with mental defectives. In N. R. Ellis (Ed.): *International Review of Research in Mental Retardation*. Vol. 2, New York, Academic, 1966.

————: The attentional set of the mentally retarded and cortical steady potentials. In D. V. Siva Sankar (Ed.): *Studies on Childhood Psychiatric and Psychological Problems*. Westbury, N.Y., PJD, (In press).

Karrer, R.; Kohn, H., and Ivins, J.: Effects of varying the stimulus and response contingencies on the CNV. In W. C. McCallum, and J. R. Knott (Eds.): *Event Related Slow Potentials and Behavior. EEG Clin Neurophysiol*, Suppl. 33, 1973.

Kohler, W.: *Die Physischen Gestatten in Ruhe und in Stationären Zustand.* Braunschsveig, Friedr. Vieneg and Sohn, 1920.

Kohler, W.: *The Place of Value in a World of Facts*. London, Liveright, 1938.

Kohler, W.; Held, R., and O'Connell, D. N.: An investigation of cortical currents. *Proceedings of the American Philosophical Society*, 96:290-330, 1952.

Kohler, W., and O'Connell, D. N.: Currents of the visual cortex in the cat. *J Cellular Comp Physiol*, 49: suppl. 2, 1957.

Loveless, N. E.; Brebner, J., and Hamilton, P.: Bisensory presentation of information. *Psych Bull*, 73:161-100, 1970.

Luria, A. R.: Psychological studies of mental deficiency in the Soviet Union: In N. R. Ellis (Ed.): *Handbook of Mental Deficiency*. New York, McGraw-Hill, 1963.

McAdam, D. W., and Witaker, H. A.: Language production: Electroencephalographic localization in the normal human brain. *Science*, 172:499-502, 1971.

McAdam, D. W., and Rubin, E. H.: Readiness potential, vertex positive wave, contingent negative variation and accuracy of perception. *EEG Clin Neurophysiol*, 30:511-517, 1971.

O'Leary, J. L., and Goldring, S.: D-C potentials of the brain. *Physiol Rev*, 44:91-125, 1964.

Paul, D. D., and Sutton, S.: Evoked potential correlates of response criterion in auditory signal detection. *Science*, 177:362-363, 1972.

Pribram, K. H.: *Languages of the Brain*. Englewood Cliffs, Prentice-Hall, 1971.

Ritter, W.; Vaughan, H. G., and Costa, L. D.: Orienting and habituation to auditory stimuli: A study of short term changes in average evoked responses. *EEG Clin Neurophysiol, 25*:550-556, 1968.

Rowland, V.: Cortical steady potential (direct current potential) in reinforcement and learning. In E. Stellar, and J. M. Sprague (Eds.): *Progress in Physiological Psychology.* Vol. 2, New York, Academic, 1968.

Rubin, E. H., and McAdam, D. W.: Slow potential concomitants of the retrieval process. *EEG Clin Neurophysiol, 32*:84-86, 1972.

Schiller, P. H.: Monoptic and dichoptic visual masking by patterns and flashes. *J Exp Psychol, 69*:193-199, 1965.

Siegel, S.: *Nonparametric Statistics for the Behavioral Sciences.* New York, McGraw-Hill, 1956.

Spitz, H. H.: Field theory in mental deficiency. In N. R. Ellis (Ed.): *Handbook of Mental Deficiency.* New York, McGraw-Hill, 1963.

Spitz, H. H.: The role of input organization in the learning and memory of mental retardates. In N. R. Ellis (Ed.): International review of research in mental retardation. Vol. 3, New York, Academic, 1968.

Spitz, H. H.: Consolidating facts into the schematized learning and memory system of educable retardates. In Ellis, N. R. (Ed.): *International Review of Research in Mental Retardation.* Vol. 6, New York, Academic, 1973.

Spitz, H. H., and Thor, D. H.: Visual backward masking in retardates and normals. *Perception and Psychophysics, 4*:245-246, 1968.

Sternberg, S.: Memory-scanning: mental processes revealed by reaction-time experiments. *Am Scientist, 57*:421-457, 1969.

Sutton, S.; Tueting, P., and Zubin, J.: Information delivery and the sensory evoked potential. *Science, 155*:1436-1439, 1967.

Tecce, J. J.: Contingent negative variation (CNV) and psychological processes in man. *Psychol Bull, 77*:73-108, 1972.

Thor, D. H.: Discrimination of succession in visual masking by retarded and normal children. *J Exp Psychol, 83*:380-384, 1970.

Thor, D. H., and Thor, C. J.: The dark interval threshold and intelligence. *J Exp Psychol, 85*:270-274, 1970.

Teichner, W. H.: Recent studies in simple reaction time. *Psychol Bull, 51*: 128-149, 1954.

Vaughan, H. G.; Costa, L. D., and Ritter, W.: Topography of the human motor potential. *EEG Clin Neurophysiol, 25*:1-10, 1968.

Walter, W. G.; Cooper, R.; Aldridge, V. J.; McCallum, W. C., and Winter, A. L.: Contingent negative variation: An electric sign of sensorimotor association and expectancy in the human brain. *Nature, 203*:380-384, 1964.

Walter, W. G.: Slow potential changes in the human brain associated with expectancy, decision, and intention. In W. Cobb, and C. Morocutti (Eds.): *The Evoked Potentials.* Amsterdam, Elsevier, 1967.

Weisstein, N., and Growney, R.: Apparent movement and metacontrast: A note on Kahneman's formulation. *Percept and Psychophys*, 5:321-328, 1969.

Zeaman, D., and House, B. J.: The role of attention in retardate discrimination learning. In N. R. Ellis (Ed.): *Handbook of Mental Deficiency*, New York, McGraw-Hill, 1963.

Ziegler, E.: Familial mental retardation: a continuing dilemma. *Science*, 155:292-298, 1967.

CHAPTER **12**

ELECTROMYOGRAPHIC STUDIES OF SUBVOCAL REHEARSAL IN LEARNING

JOHN L. LOCKE AND FRED S. FEHR*

WHAT DO WE DO WHEN WE ATTEMPT to Learn? One approach to this question has been to ask ourselves and others what we think we are doing. Another is to infer processes and strate-

* This research was supported by Public Health Research Grant MH-07346 from the National Institute of Mental Health. The authors are indebted to Mr. Michael Fortner of the Champaign County Rehabilitation Center for encouraging retarded persons to participate, and to Miss Jean Lewis for secretarial and editorial assistance.

gies of learning from a loose admixture of what we know about the structure of the material to be learned, the preparedness of the learner, his level of remembering and pattern of forgetting. Variations on these schemes proliferate in our attempt to understand and influence the social development and learning of children, including those who appear, in some sense, to be "exceptional." This chapter reviews the methodology and findings of a series of developmental studies which suggest that certain covert learning behavior, previously vague and inferentially based, may be more objectively defined through the judicious use of electromyographic (EMG) recordings. Data are presented which support the presumed existence of covert phonetic behavior in memory processing and suggest that such peripherally reflected coding can be identified electromyographically. Findings are reviewed which show clear differences in the prerecall learning behavior of persons varying in chronological and mental age, differences potentially important not only to a fundamental grasp of learning but to the educational treatment of exceptional children. These findings, and the laboratory methods which fostered them, will be elaborated after some review of the theoretical notions and empirical yield on the learning processes of normal and exceptional children.

THEORY AND FINDINGS ON MEMORY PROCESSES OF NORMAL AND RETARDED CHILDREN

In 1970, Norman Ellis presented a selective review of the literature and the results of his own recent work on the memory processes of normal and mentally retarded persons. One of Ellis' conclusions was that "the retardate's deficiency is due to a failure of the rehearsal mechanism(s)." Although "rehearsal" was not defined, Ellis implied that it had something to do with language. His "rehearsal strategy deficiency hypothesis" was based largely on inspection of serial recall data.

Ellis' notion of a rehearsal deficiency in the mentally retarded is consonant with some work on developmental memory in normal children. It has been observed repeatedly that many preschool-age children do not show verbal mediation effects in recalling from short-term memory. They recall in a way which does not reflect their knowledge of oral language. One hypothesis suggests that young children use their verbal repertoire in memorizing but it lacks mediating value (Reese, 1962). This concept of a mediation deficiency was refined later to include another contingency, a production deficiency, attributing children's unmediated recall to their failure to produce potentially mediating terms (Flavell, Beach and Chinsky, 1966).

It is clear that rehearsal has been given a central role in the memory process, both in mentally retarded and normal children, and that it is not well understood. The literature is replete with reports of various methods used to infer the existence and function of rehearsal. Nearly all assume that rehearsal exists, and that it usually comprises minimal speech-like movements which affect recall. For example, the suppression technique assumes that subvocal rehearsal can be blocked, attenuated or disrupted by mechanical or temporal constraints, or by competing articulatory activity. An enhancement technique assumes that subvocal rehearsal must exist and must be a memory aid if, through experimenter induced subvocalization or vocalization, recall improves. Other methods of attempting to infer the existence of rehearsal have been the study of serial recall, response clustering, differential recall of high-low pronounceability or homophonous-non-homophonous lists, and confusion errors. Apparently, it has not been readily appreciated that subvocal rehearsal might be inferred more directly from electromyographic recordings. We have found only two published reports in which more direct observation was attempted without instrumental amplification or recording; and a series of laboratory investigations in which subvocalization during silent reading was addressed.

The production deficiency hypothesis referred to earlier rests on the naked-eye observation that relatively young children reveal less overt lip movement during a recall task than older children (Flavell, Beach and Chinsky, 1966). These authors presented twenty kindergarten, second and fifth grade children with a task requiring them to observe as seven familiar objects were pointed out to them in a specific sequence. Their task, either immediately or following a prerecall delay period, was to point to the objects in an identical sequence. The number of children who, through lip observation, appeared to rehearse increased rather dramatically from kindergarten to fifth grade. Since verbal mediation is thought to increase with age in childhood, this suggested that direct observation may yield relevant data. This was supported by a second experiment (Keeney, Cannizzo, and Flavell, 1967) in which children were separated into rehearsal and nonrehearsal groups on the basis of observed lip movement. In a task similar to the one just described above, the rehearsing children showed significantly better recall than nonrehearsing children, a difference which dramatically receded when the latter group was encouraged to rehearse. When left to their own methods these rehearsal-instructed children generally abandoned the practice, with subsequent fall in their recall levels. The work of Flavell and his associates is thought provoking but seemingly limited in its capacity to permit definitive statements regarding the nature and possible significance of so-called subvocal rehearsal.

As mentioned earlier, there have been several laboratory attempts to study vocal tract activity during silent reading (see reviews in Locke, 1970; McGuigan, 1970). EMG recordings have shown greater activity in chin-lip (McGuigan, Keller and Stanton, 1964; McGuigan, 1967; McGuigan and Rodier, 1968; McGuigan and Bailey, 1969) and laryngeal (Edfeldt, 1960; Hardyck, Petrinovich and Ellsworth, 1966; Hardyck and Petrinovich, 1969, 1970) sites than nonvocal control areas. In some cases, these recordings also have been observed to increase in test sites from quiet rest to the onset of silent reading. Unfortunately, though compelling at first glance, such studies do not provide evidence that the vocal tract activity observed has a linguistic identity. Is it a covert form of speech, as we know it in communicative contexts, or is it a vegetative nonspeech activity such as swallowing or lip-licking?

In this chapter a new method for studying rehearsal activity will be described which combines psychophysiological and descriptive linguistic techniques. The method is addressed specifically to eliciting, recording, and classifying the attenuated oral behavior which occurs during various cognitive tasks and is believed to reflect "verbal" rehearsal. We will review an investigation with normal adults, two experiments with normal children, and the results of a similar developmental study of retarded children. Since the methods used are comparable for this series of studies, they will be described at the beginning of the next section.

METHOD FOR ELECTROMYOGRAPHIC STUDY OF COVERT PHONETIC BEHAVIOR

Learning Task

Subjects are seated individually before a slide screen in a semidarkened, sound-attenuated and electrically shielded room. Voice communication is possible between the subject and the experimenter who monitors EMG, slide projection, and audio-recording equipment from an adjoining laboratory.

Subjects are instructed that they will see a list of familiar pictures or printed words on the slide screen and that their job is to try to remember them. Upon signal (a red light, usually 10-15 sec following the last item) the subject's task is to orally* recall the list in free or serial order. Usually the first two lists are sacrificed for pretraining purposes. In the case of very young children, or retarded young adults, an experimenter cues, coaches, and controls the subjects while sitting with them in the test booth. The prerecall delay period is included to elicit rehearsal activity, but only if subjects are naturally disposed to use it in that way.

EMG Procedures

Two Grass silver-chlorided surface electrodes (9 mm in diameter) are secured to the chin-lip area with Grass electrode cream and a small amount of surgical tape. One lead is placed immediately below the inferior surface of the lower lip, some 10 to 20 mm displaced laterally from midline. Midline recordings are not undesirable but are difficult because many adults have profound chin clefts which make secure contact difficult. A sec-

---

* We have also compared oral with graphic recall, visual with aural presentation (Locke and Fehr, 1972).

ond electrode for bipolar recording and integrated tracings is placed approximately 25 mm laterally and 10 mm inferiorally relative to the first lead. The placement of this latter electrode is not particularly critical except that the site should be a relatively inactive one on the lower chin and/or lower cheek. Presumably, the first (active) electrode is in the general area of the Quadratus labii inferioris, the second in the region of the trangularis (see Kaplan, 1960, p. 274), both of which may function in the production of certain bilabial phonemes (see Van Riper and Irwin, 1958, p. 396). However, the selection of recording sites is based more on exploratory observation than either physiological data or theory. We are not as interested in assessing the activity of certain muscles, which may be impossible due to their highly idiosyncratic locus, as we are in obtaining recordings which would reflect phoneme-bound activity of the lower lip. EMG recordings are obtained with a Grass Model 7 polygraph and 7P3A A.C. preamplifier and integrator.

Nonrecording dummy electrodes are placed in irrelevant areas to decrease the likelihood that subjects would focus their attention on the chin-lip site and possibly surmise the intentions of the investigation. This is why we also have not invaded the oral cavity. Electrode placement on the velum would provide for more interphonemic discriminations, increasing the rigor of the method, but possibly causing subjects to behave in unfortunate ways. Laryngeal recordings, which should not have this effect, may be an appropriate addition in that they may permit distinctions between voiced-voiceless cognates such as/p-b/(see Cooper, 1965). In studies with children, where there is some independent evidence of audible rehearsal (McGuigan, et al., 1964), a small but sensitive microphone is placed near the mouth for recording and subsequent playback over a high fidelity speaker.

Analysis of EMG data consists of visually identifying the greatest upward pen deflection within a recording period (presentation, rehearsal) and determining its magnitude (in μv). More recently, the same procedure has been carried out for each stimulus and each time period of roughly comparable length in the delay period. The phonemic identity of EMG-tracing activity is defined operationally by a significantly greater mean for labial than for nonlabial stimuli. Once obtained, if the degree of covert phonetic rehearsal is to be compared for two conditions, labial/nonlabial ratios or labial-nonlabial difference scores are used.

Stimuli

Stimuli have been selected to fit the following criteria: (1) half of them must contain labial phonemes in their pronunciation (e.g./p-b-m-w-f-v/) and half of them must not; (2) as determined by pre- or posttesting, all stimuli must elicit the same desired label or pronunciation (or, in some cases, an alternative response which does not violate the class to which the item belongs, e.g. oven and stove both contain /v/); (3) the stimuli in labial and nonlabial lists must be of roughly equal recallability (including familiarity and concreteness, sometimes informally determined); (4) the syllable length of stimuli must be matched across labial-nonlabial lists as closely as possible within the other constraints. Ideally, during postexperiment labeling, each subject's EMG values for overt speech would provide a reference for the analysis of covertly precipitated tracings.

Stimuli are presented either in pictorial or orthographic form by 35 mm slide projector, programmed by a tape reader or voice relay cued by audio pulses. EMG tracings record all stimulus-presentation and response-cueing events on the same time base as muscle potentials.

Experimental Rationale

The rationale underlying the chin-lip electrode placement and the use of labial-nonlabial materials is that covert speech activity, if it occurs, will yield greater labial than nonlabial tracings. Vegetative, nonspeech activity will occur no more frequently during one list than another, and should have no effect other than driving the recording pen to high voltage readings with no significant labial-nonlabial differences. Since speech and oral vegetative activity, in essence, share the same musculature, covert rehearsal must reduce or replace or block such nonlinguistic behavior. The labial-nonlabial distinction is not a totally discrete one. Nonlabial is being used loosely to describe English consonantal phonemes which do not require lower lip movement in their articulation. But many phonemes naturally have labial artifact; English phonology also possesses several lip-rounded vowels, such as /u/. So the observance of some activity during the presentation or rehearsal of nonlabial stimuli does not necessarily weaken the procedure since for linguistic and biological reasons a certain amount of this is natural and necessary.

EMG RECORDINGS AS AN INDEX OF SUBVOCAL-VERBAL ACTIVITY

In the initial experiment (Locke and Fehr, 1970a) procedures were developed to demonstrate that these EMG measurements were, in fact, related to subvocal verbal processes. As already indicated, we reasoned that greater EMG-related activity to labial than nonlabial (response-produced) stimuli would reflect these verbal processes and distinguish them from random or irrelevant muscle activity.

Normal adults were presented thirty disyllables, half of them containing two labial phonemes (e.g. BAFFLE) and half of them containing no labial phonemes (e.g. TICKET), the six five-word lists appearing in random order. Stimulus exposure time was 1 sec with 0.5-sec interitem intervals. The rehearsal and recall periods, both of 10 sec duration, were followed by a 28.5-sec control period.

As Table 12-I shows, tracings taken during the presentation

TABLE 12-I

PEAK EMG AMPLITUDES (μv) DURING LEARNING OF LABIAL AND NONLABIAL WORDS

	N	Presentation X	SD	t	N	Rehearsal X	SD	t
Labial	11	90.24	21.28	3.205*	11	93.92	22.16	3.838*
Nonlabial	11	69.32	16.56		11	67.96	29.46	

* p < .005.

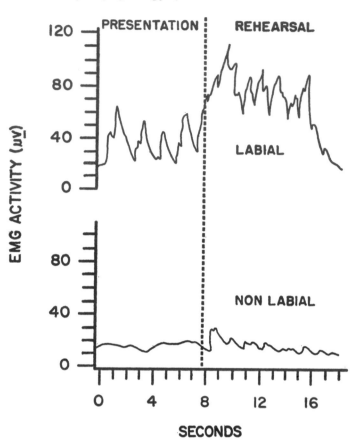

Figure 12-1. Selected electromyographic tracings from one subject (from Locke & Fehr, 1970a, by permission).

and rehearsal of words represented by labial pronunciations were significantly greater than nonlabial items.* Both labial and nonlabial values significantly exceeded control levels, although the labial-nonlabial distinction seems sufficient and more meaningful support for the existence of speech rehearsal. Table 12-I and also the representative EMG tracings in Figure 12-1 show

---

* Occasionally this apparent circumlocution "words represented by . . . " instead of the more direct "labial words" is our struggle not to lose sight of the fact that nothing "labial" is inherent in the stimulus, *the subject puts it there.* There are no labial graphemes and no labial pictures. Any labial "stimuli" are (motor-phonetic) response-produced.

slightly greater labial-nonlabial separations during rehearsal than during stimulus presentation, a trend which subsequent analysis showed to approach significance. At this point, it seemed that some of the covert oral activity during word-list learning was ascribable to phonetic coding or rehearsal and that a method existed with a potential for permitting additional observations. Recall data were not analyzed for this small study because the experiment was not designed to test a hypothesis regarding the function of phonetic rehearsal in learning, only whether it occurred. We concluded from these findings that even with intelligent adults (many were college students), covert phonetic behavior figures into the prerecall behavior arising both from presentation and delay periods. The existence of subvocalization in adults may reflect their implicit supposition that response-produced kinesthetic cues are a storable-retrievable aid to memory. Alternatively, such behavior may be a stimulus recycling which makes retrieval, as considered conventionally, unnecessary. The following child study was our first attempt to observe whether the production deficiency hypothesis discussed earlier would be borne out electromyographically.

COVERT PHONETIC BEHAVIOR OF FOUR AND FIVE-YEAR-OLD CHILDREN FOR PICTURES

This experiment (Locke and Fehr, 1970b) was designed to extend the EMG method to the study of young children. Four- and five-year-old children were presented thirty pictures arranged in five ensembles of three pictures representing labial phonemes (e.g. BEAR) and five ensembles of three pictures representing nonlabial phonemes (e.g. CHAIR). The ten ensembles were presented alternately, following two pretraining series. Stimulus exposure times were 4 sec, interstimulus intervals were 1.5 sec, with rehearsal and recall periods 12 sec each. After discarding from consideration the tracings associated with irrelevant utterances (19 percent) and inappropriate labeling (10 percent), the remaining records were analyzed in the manner described previously.

Tracing peaks arising during the presentation of labial pictures significantly exceeded values for nonlabial pictures with nonsignificant labial-nonlabial difference during rehearsal. The amount of relevant vocalization also decreased from presentation to rehearsal. Since later analysis showed that labial/nonlabial ratios during the presentation period significantly exceeded rehearsal ratios, it appeared that EMG activity noted during presentation might be a labeling or perception-bound behavior or a form of phonetic coding or rehearsal which does not continue into the delay period. The former notion is attractive in view of the production deficiency hypothesis of Flavell, et al. (1966) and our observation that the five-year-olds had higher labial-nonlabial ratios during rehearsal (1.33) than the four-year-olds (0.97). Since our frequency of whispering was less than that reported by McGuigan, et al. (1964), where six-year-olds read, we wondered whether this was due to our use of younger children or the processing of printed words rather than pictures. The latter possibility seemed reasonable since reading ordinarily is taught by a phonic method in which learners are encouraged to work through their phonetic repertoire in decoding words into semantic representations. So, possibly the whispering observed by McGuigan, et al. (1964) was the result of children "sounding out" the word stimuli. The next experiment was addressed to this and related matters.

COVERT PHONETIC BEHAVIOR OF SEVEN- AND EIGHT-YEAR-OLD CHILDREN FOR PICTURES AND PRINTED WORDS

In this study (Goldstein, Locke and Fehr, 1972) our prediction was that printed words would elicit more subvocalization than pictorial stimuli, during the presentation period where "sounding out" should occur, with relatively less or no difference during the rehearsal period. Subjects were twenty-six children who had successfully completed second or third grade one month prior to the experiment. Stimuli were a list of forty-eight labial and nonlabial pictures and a corresponding list of the pictures' labels. Each child was presented twelve four-item ensembles with an equal number drawn from labial pictures (LP), labial words (LW), nonlabial pictures (NP) and nonlabial words (NW). No child saw a single stimulus in both pictorial and orthographic forms. Stimulus exposure time was 2.25 sec with a 0.75 interstimulus interval. Following each series of four slides the subject waited 16 sec for a red light which signaled a 14-sec oral recall period. Thirteen percent of the tracings were discarded due to inappropriately applied labels or extraneous vocalization. Word recognition ability was near-perfect. Labial tracings significantly exceeded nonlabial values both for pictures and words in presentation and rehearsal. Labial-nonlabial ratios for pictures and words did not differ significantly in either period. Word ratios increased significantly from presentation to rehearsal, picture ratios also increased but not significantly so. Relevant audible whispering was detected on over 60 percent of the trials and was essentially similar in frequency for pictures and printed words. There were no differences in recall of pictures or words among children who showed marked and minimal subvocalization.

From these findings we cannot say that children do not work through their articulatory system in word decoding: it may be that when required to store stimuli for subsequent recall, picture-labeling articulatory activity is simply as apparent.

COVERT PHONETIC BEHAVIOR OF THE RETARDED IN PICTURE RECALL

Ellis (1970) based his notions regarding rehearsal deficiency on work with subjects whose CA ranged from thirteen to thirty-three years with an IQ range from forty-six to eighty-two. Our pilot study, similarly, was with seven subjects whose CA ranged from eighteen to forty-two with an IQ range of thirty-four to seventy-six. They were presented seven four-picture ensembles where the stimuli were represented by labels containing labial phonemes and seven ensembles whose labels contained no labial phonemes. With the exception of our use here of two additional ensembles, and exclusive use of pictures, the procedure was an exact replication of our third experiment and is comparable in major respects to our second one. Subjects were pretrained on two ensembles and monitored by an experimenter sitting beside them. Labial and nonlabial ensembles were presented alternately. Following the task, subjects were asked simply to label each picture as it was shown again. There was a 95 percent incidence of appropriate labeling. Analysis of recall data revealed a mean recall of 1.8/4.0 items per ensemble. EMG data were analyzed by identifying and assessing the amplitude (μv) of the single greatest tracing peak occurring within the 2.5 sec exposure of each stimulus and at four-sec intervals during the 16-sec delay period. Averaging across lists yielded labial means which slightly but nonsignificantly exceeded nonlabial means both for presentation and rehearsal periods. Two subjects were observed to silently articulate or whisper stimulus labels during the presentation period. When asked how one remembered the items, she replied, "I said them in my mind." The other denied his apparent use of subvocalization. Inspection of individual EMG records showed that only three of the seven subjects had greater labial than nonlabial values for the presentation period; these three cases included the two subjects described above.

From this pilot study it appeared to the authors that the EMG and learning procedures were appropriate for further analysis of retardate rehearsal processes. This is not to suggest that other laboratory approaches would not be appropriate or useful. We plan to continue our work with more mentally retarded of various chronological and mental ages.

CONCLUDING REMARKS

Phonetically mediated recall (Locke, 1971, a, b) and specifically covert motor-phonetic activity, may function significantly in the learning of normal and retarded children. While nonlaboratory investigations have yielded interesting findings regarding subvocal rehearsal, they have been limited by lack of sensitivity and precision in observing and recording such behavior. Laboratory studies as conducted previously have been unable to determine the linguistic identity, and therefore, the relevance of covert oral behavior. Nevertheless, these early studies, especially those of McGuigan and his colleagues, aided us in designing a

new approach which speaks to these shortcomings. EMG recordings from the labial area and the use of stimuli likely to be responded to either with labial or nonlabial motor gestures has
permitted fairly precise measurement and recording of activity
which is covert, relevant and identifiable as linguistically based.

A series of studies using this method have suggested that covert phonetic behavior occurs in normal adults during their exposure to, and even more so, during their rehearsal of printed
words. Young children reveal covert phonetic behavior during
their exposure to pictorial stimuli with markedly less activity
during their rehearsal. Older children behave essentially as
adults and show similar degrees of subvocalization for pictorial
and orthographic stimuli. Mentally retarded persons as a group
appear, as Ellis (1970) suggested, to show minimal subvocal rehearsal. Our work with retarded children, and very young children (3-4 years) is just beginning and we hope others will join
us in attempting to understand the nature and function of the
relationship between children's language and thought processes.

REFERENCES

Cooper, F. S.: Research techniques and instrumentation: EMG. *Proceed-
ings of the Conference: Communicative Problems in Cleft Palate. ASHA
Reports, 1:*153-168, 1965.
Edfeldt, A. W.: *Silent Speech and Silent Reading.* Chicago, University of
Chicago, 1960.
Ellis, N. R. (Ed.): *International Review of Research in Mental Retardation.* New York, Academic, 1970.
Flavell, J. H.; Beach, D. R., and Chinsky, J. M.: Spontaneous verbal rehearsal in a memory task as a function of age. *Child Dev, 37:*284-299,
1966.
Goldstein, J., Locke, J. L., and Fehr, F. S.: Children's pre-recall phonetic
processing of pictures and printed words. *Psychonomic Sci, 26:*314-316,
1972.
Hardyck, C. D.; Petrinovich, L. R., and Ellsworth, D. W.: Feedback of
speech muscle activity during silent reading; rapid extinction. *Science,
154:*1467-1468, 1966.
Hardyck, C. D., and Petrinovich, L. F.: Treatment of subvocal speech during reading. *J Read, 12:*361-369, 419-422, 1969.
Hardyck, C. D., and Petrinovich, L. F.: Subvocal speech and comprehen-

sion level as a function of the difficulty level of reading material. *J Verb Learn Verb Behav,* 9:647-652, 1970.

Kaplan, H. M.: *Anatomy and Physiology of Speech.* New York, McGraw-Hill, 1960.

Keeney, T. J.; Cannizzo, S. R., and Flavell, J. H.: Spontaneous and induced verbal rehearsal in a recall task. *Child Dev,* 38:953-966, 1967.

Locke, J. L.: Subvocal speech and speech. *ASHA,* 12:7-14, 1970.

Locke, J. L.: Phonetic mediation in four-year-old children. *Psychonomic Sci,* 23:409, 1970a.

Locke, J. L.: Acoustic imagery in children's phonetically mediated recall. *Psycholog Rep,* 32:1000-1002, 1971b.

Locke, J. L., and Fehr, F. S.: Subvocal rehearsal as a form of speech. *J Verb Learn Verb Behav,* 9:495-498, 1970a.

———: Young children's use of the speech code in a recall task. *J Exp Child Psychol,* 10:367-373, 1970b.

———: Subvocalization of heard or seen words prior to spoken or written recall. *Am J Psychol,* 85:63-68, 1972.

McGuigan, F. J.: Letters. *Science,* 157:579-580, 1967.

———: Covert oral behavior during the silent performance of language tasks. *Psychol Bull,* 74:309-326, 1970.

McGuigan, F. J., and Bailey, S.: Longitudinal study of covery oral behavior during silent reading. *Percept Mot Skills,* 28:170, 1969.

McGuigan, F. J., and Rodier, W. I.: Effects of auditory stimulation on covert oral behavior during silent reading. *J Exp Psychol,* 76:649-655, 1968.

McGuigan, F. J.; Keller, B., and Stanton, E.: Covert language responses during silent reading. *J Edu Psychol,* 5:339-343, 1964.

Reese, H. W.: Verbal mediation as a function of age level. *Psycholog Bull,* 59:502-509, 1962.

Van Riper, C., and Irwin, J. V.: *Voice and Articulation.* Englewood Cliffs, Prentice-Hall, 1958.

CHAPTER 13

SOME PUPILLARY CORRELATES OF MENTAL RETARDATION AND INFORMATION PROCESSING

ARNOLD LIDSKY[*]

A NECDOTAL AND HISTORICAL REFERENCES (Loewenfeld, 1958; Hakerem, 1967; Hess, 1972) to the significance of changes in the size of the pupil of the eye have been traced as far back as Archimedes (ca 200 B.C.) and Galen (ca A.D. 200). In more recent history, references contained in the *Encyclopedia of Medicine* compiled by Rhazes (ca A.D. 900), and a publication in

* The author is indebted to Dr. Johs Clausen for valuable comments on a preliminary version of this manuscript; to Dr. Mary Schmitt and Mr. Steven Richman for assistance in testing subjects and processing data; Diamantis Skinitis and Eugene Sersen for computer programming; Douglas Andersen for instrumentation help; and both Mike Donadio and Dennis Anderson for assistance in testing subjects. Portions of this chapter were presented at a joint meeting of the American Association on Mental Deficiency and the American Academy on Mental Retardation, Toronto, 1974.

1765 by Fontana (Loewenfeld, 1958) are notable. Jade dealers allegedly wear sunglasses to market, not only on sunny days, but to prevent communication of extreme interest in acquiring a gem through involuntary pupil dilation. One summary of available literature early in this century specifically suggests that pupil size and mental activity are closely related (Bumke, 1911). That the normal pupil responds to bright light by contracting and that darkness produces pupillary dilation have been known for centuries, and the significance for visual acuity and retinal protection has been documented. In fact, according to Lowenstein and Loewenfeld (1958, 1962), who together have perhaps done more for the body of knowledge concerning pupillometry in this century than any other researchers, the pupil's response to all natural stimuli is dilation, with contraction occurring to light stimulation only. Razran's review of the Russian literature (1961) also concluded that nonvisual stimulation consistently produces pupillary dilation as an initial response.

The firmness of the light-contraction reflex of the pupil has been established by studies in physiology, physics, anatomy, and psychophysiology. It is known to result from innervation of the parasympathetic nerve fibers from the Edinger-Westphal nucleus of the third nerve which, via the ciliary ganglion, causes the sphincter muscles of the iris to decrease the apparent size of the pupil.

The importance of changes in pupillary size as a diagnostic indicator in clinical medicine is known to every physician today, and Lowenstein and Loewenfeld (1958) have been instrumental in identifying specific loci of neurological lesions on the basis of precise pupillary measurements.

RATIONALE

At an embryological level the retina is a direct outgrowth of the brain and, to the extent that retinal stimulation determines pupillary responsiveness, which it apparently does (e.g. Lowenstein, Kawabata and Loewenfeld, 1964), measuring the pupil is equivalent to measuring a brain process. Furthermore, this measurement can be performed without the discomfort of electrode contact or abrading the skin of the subject, typical requirements in EEG, skin conductance, or heart rate recordings. In addition, the pupillary response per se is relatively automatic and involuntary and is free of confounding by certain vegetative functions inherent in cardiovascular correlates of behavior. The interplay of sympathetic and parasympathetic components of the autonomic nervous system, as well as adrenergic and cholinergic mechanisms, cannot be oversimplified for the pupillary system (e.g. Schaeppi and Koella, 1964). It is well accepted, however, that innervation of the iris' sphincter muscles is essentially a parasympathetic function, whereas the sympathetic cervical chain acts in relative opposition by exciting the radial muscles of the iris (e.g. Lowenstein and Loewenfeld, 1950). Additional dilatatory influences on the radial muscles derive less directly from cortical, posterior hypothalamic, reticular, and other subcortical areas (Loewenfeld, 1958). In other words, the pupillary system represents a reasonable model for studying integrated autonomic functions.

A substantial body of psychophysiological research relevant to mental retardation is being developed and is attested to by the present volume. Some of the work on autonomic correlates in mental retardation, and the concept of arousal is discussed in detail in the chapter by Clausen, Lidsky and Sersen (Chap. 2). Pervasive questions in this area concern operational definitions of arousal that have at least face validity, and whether retarded persons in general, or specific etiological groups in particular, can be identified as characteristically manifesting an arousal dysfunction. Largely on the basis of skin conductance and RT data, for example, Clausen, Lidsky and Sersen (see Fig. 9, Chap. 2) have very tentatively proposed that on one dimension of arousal Familial retardates are least aroused of all subjects, the normals as a group are optimally aroused (or they control arousal optimally), with Encephalopathic retardates, PKU's and possibly Down's subjects showing elevated sympathetic levels. Behavioral and psychophysiological consequences for responsivity to "arousing" stimulation are both demonstrated and predictable from this model, which almost certainly will require modification in the light of new data.

One problem with building an arousal model of mental retardation solely on a skin resistance measure is that, despite the fact that sweat glands of the palm are innervated via a cholinergic mechanism, the sweat glands have no parasympathetic neural innervation. That is, as far as we know, the sweat glands are innervated strictly by the sympathetic nervous system, where a typical stimulus-related response is unidirectional, i.e. decreasing *resistance* or increasing conductance, but not both an increase and decrease in either measure.

Thus, the pupil, on theoretical and practical grounds, has advantages for investigating arousal processes. Its reciprocal innervation mechanisms, and the light reflex with its predominantly parasympathetic mechanisms offer interesting alternatives. In the range of critical temporal response values, it is both *faster* than most autonomic variables (e.g. skin conductance, heart rate, blood pressure changes) yet is slower than CNS measures such as the EEG and evoked potentials. Unfortunately, careful pupillary measurements with mentally retarded subjects has barely begun, notwithstanding the substantial literature with other psychopathologies (e.g. Lowenstein and Westphal, 1933; May, 1948; Rubin, 1962; Lidsky, Hakerem and Sutton, 1971).

METHODOLOGY

As with any good physiological measure of behavior there can be technological and experimental design complications in teasing out the particular factor of primary interest. I wish to emphasize a few specific examples. One issue concerns the number of readings per second—which ranges in different studies from 1 or 2 per second to 30 to 60 per second, in effect discrete versus continuous measurement. Probably this issue is resolved by economic considerations, experimental stringency, and, most importantly the answers one is seeking. Psychologists measuring pupillary changes in relation to processes of affect, attention, discrimination, and thinking, have tended to use motion picture cameras with no more than two film exposures per second. Higher frequency electronic measurements suggest that the film-type recording is missing some early and rapid components, such as latency or peak response, which for light can occur anywhere from 150 to 1,500 msec after light onset. Nevertheless, the experimental paradigms used by Hess (1972), Kahneman and Beatty (1966, 1967), and others (e.g. Libby, Lacey and Lacey, 1973) using motion picture recording methods tend to concentrate on later components of the pupillary response (1.5 to 10 sec after stimulus onset) and have produced results of considerable interest for research in mental processing and mental retardation.

The evolution of techniques and instrumentation in pupil measurement has come to the point where electronic closed-circuit TV Systems, using infra-red illumination of the eye, are used to measure the pupil 60 times per second with a 1,000 line scanner unit—i.e. continuous measurement. Analogous to work with evoked brain potentials, computer averaging of time-locked 3-10 sec trials is used in conjunction with FM tape recordings of the voltage output of the pupillometer. The present studies used a Polymetric Company pupillometer, a Sanborn 7-channel tape system, and a Grass polygraph to display and store measurements.

Another serious problem, especially in working with institutionalized low-IQ subjects, or patients with ocular and neurological disorders, is that to measure pupillary size changes the eye must be open for a fixed period of time. While normal subjects can easily fixate on a dim red light for periods of five to seven seconds on command without blinking, we have tried to test certain mongoloid patients who after thirty minutes of practice do not exert such voluntary control for as little as one full second per trial. Fortunately, this is not such a serious problem until one drops to below 50 or 40 IQ. Nevertheless, our experience indicates that, in order to test people in that IQ range and below, it is necessary to devote considerable time to train subjects to fixate without blinking. The use of an upper eyelid retractor is, unfortunately, rather uncomfortable for most subjects.

It is also important, in studies using affective or cognitive visual stimulation (e.g. Hess, 1972), that experimental controls are adequate to distinguish between pupillary response characteristics attributable to psychological factors as distinct from physical light-dark contrast or color effects of the stimulus material.

STUDY 1: LIGHT REFLEX OF THE PUPIL

As a first pupillographic experiment using retarded subjects, we sought estimates of resting-level pupil diameters in retarded and normal subjects. In terms of the foregoing rationale, our understanding of the autonomic and arousal characteristics of retarded subjects would be extended by pupillary findings. It seemed desirable to obtain data on pupillary responsivity in retardates using a simple light-reflex paradigm, wherein certain approximate stimulus-response functions were predictable, and documented for normals, such as that between response amplitude and stimulus intensity.

We compared the pupillary light reflex in twenty Cultural-Familial residents of the Willowbrook Developmental Center with twenty Normal volunteers (Lidsky and Richman, 1973). The subjects ranged in age from twelve to forty-two years, with the patient and normal means being twenty-two and twenty years respectively. The mean retardate IQ was 61.4, with a range from 43 to 82. Subjects were individually tested in a soundproof and temperature controlled room under dark-adapted conditions. Obtaining such measurements under dark-adapted conditions reduces the within-subject variability of pupil diameter, since the effects of ambient light on the retina (and consequently on pupil size) are thus minimized.

Each stimulus was a 30 msec pulse of light delivered at 30 sec intervals to a half ping pong ball *(Ganzfeld)* located over the subject's left eye. Each of four stimulus intensity conditions were presented ten times in random sequence. Intensities (no light, 4 ftL, 9 ftL, and 18 ftL) were calibrated at the ping pong ball by a Pritchard photometer. Trials during which eyeblinks or other artifacts occurred were not analyzed. In the 18 ftL condition, the data from only nineteen normals and fifteen retardates could be analyzed.

Three-second response curves were averaged, by stimulus intensity, at the rate of 66 data points per second, and the resulting graph for each intensity for each subject was plotted separately, using a Hewlett-Packard computer system (2115) and a Versatec line printer. The averaged value during the first 135 msec following stimulation is referred to as the initial diameter (ID). The latency, the extent of contraction, and the time to reach the peak of the contraction (TTP), are all identified conventionally. The digital values for these and other variables, obtained from the individual's averaged curves, were then averaged across subjects for retardates and for normals.

Figure 13-1 shows two sets of average pupillary response curves to light stimulation obtained from one normal and one retardate subject. The two sets of curves are well representative of the data, as indicated in the group results of Table 13-I. The average initial diameter of the individual (Fig. 13-1) and the group (Table 13-I) remain constant across stimulus intensities as it should, since the intensities are randomly presented, and the ID is based on a period which precedes the actual response to light. Also with regard to the ID it is clear that the patient in Figure 13-1 and the Familial group in Table 13-I, consistently showed smaller pupils than the normal subject or group, without regard to stimulus intensity. The analyses of variance comparing the two groups yielded significant differences at each intensity (p's < .01).

Concerning the extent of contraction (XC) to different light intensities, again Figure 13-1 and Table 13-I show larger contractions in response to higher intensities of the 30 msec light pulses. For all subjects combined the difference in extent of contraction as a function of stimulus intensity (4 and 9 ftL) was highly significant ($F\ 1/36 = 149.33$, $p < .01$). At the 4 ftL intensity there was a significant group difference in XC ($F\ 1/36 = 13.7$, $p < .01$). At 9 ftL the difference was also significant ($F\ 1/36 = 4.69$, $p < .05$), but at 18 ftL the groups did not differ statistically. Furthermore, analyses of covariance, using the ID's as predictor variables for each intensity, confirmed the group differences in XC at the lowest stimulus intensity (4 ftL, $F\ 1/35 = 14.41$,

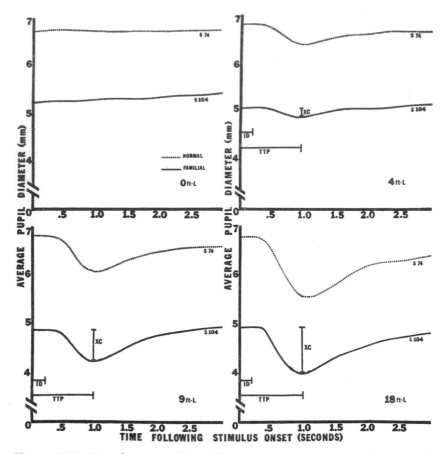

Figure 13-1. Sample averaged pupillary response curves as a function of light stimulus intensity. Each curve is the average of 10 or more trials. ID = initial diameter; TTP = time to peak contraction; XC = extent of contraction; ftL = footlamberts.

$p < .01$). An extension of this paradigm with six normals and nine patients, using a 300 msec duration pulse at 9 ftL, resulted in mean XC's for the two groups at this energy level that were virtually the same; 1.42 mm for Familials and 1.43 for controls.

Table 13-I also includes sample values of times to peak (TTP) responses, and rates of contraction. While statistical significance between groups was not as consistent with these measures, the group means indicate monotonic changes with increasing stimulus intensity (rate of contraction × intensity, $F = 108$, $p < .01$) as well as patient-normal differences at lower intensities.

Whereas each response variable was often significantly correlated across stimulus conditions, product-moment correlations between different variables were seldom and inconsistently significant for conditions or groups. For example, the r for initial diameter between the 4 ftL and 9 ftL conditions was .94 and .93 ($p < .01$) for normals and Familials respectively. The corresponding r for extent of contraction was .85 and .75 ($p < .01$) while TTP yielded an r of .63 ($p < .01$) for normals only. On the other hand, when ID and XC were correlated at 4 ftL, using all 40 subjects, the r was .21. Neither this, nor the separate correlations for Familials and normals, were significant, suggesting that the variables are relatively independent.

Concerning developmental changes and pupil size, the ID's of normals and Familials were significantly related to age. For normals, $r = -.54$ $p < .02$; for Familials, $r = -.47$, $p < .05$. That is, younger subjects within each group had larger pupils. For all 40 subjects combined, correlations with age were not significant, which was probably due to the group differences on initial di-

TABLE 13-I

MEAN PUPILLARY RESPONSES TO 30 msec LIGHT PULSES*

Intensity (ftL)	Group (N)	Initial Diameter (mm)	Extent of Contraction (mm)	Time to Peak (msec)	Rate of Contraction (mm/sec)
0	Normals 20	6.24	—	—	—
	Familials 20	5.57†	—	—	—
4	Normals 20	6.23	.38	922	.69
	Familials 20	5.53†	.18†	947	.45†
9	Normals 20	6.28	.68	959	1.04
	Familials 20	5.60†	.50†	940	.78
18	Normals 19	6.24	.97	1012	1.36
	Familials 15	5.79†	.93	1009	1.28

* SD's were not substantially different between groups or conditions. For example, the range of SD's for Normal and Familial ID's were .62 to .73 and .64 to .77, respectively; for extent of contraction, the Normal and Familial SD ranges were wider; .17 to .22, and .14 to .40.
† $p < .05$ or less.

ameter. Correlations with IQ in the retardate group were not significant in a consistent manner.

There are several possible lines of interpretation of these results, some of which might emphasize factors such as peripheral ocular disorders (e.g. Manley and Schuldt, 1970), accommodative or drug effects. However, such effects were minimized to the extent possible, by selecting patients whose medical records indicated no visual impairments, and requiring abstinence from psychoactive medication for at least twenty-four hours preceding testing. The results may thus be more parsimoniously viewed in conventional physiological terms of autonomic innervation of the pupillary system. Accepting the pupil as an indicator of arousal, these data indicate that Cultural-Familial retardates have a low sympathetic resting level of arousal (i.e. small initial diameter) and a reduced parasympathetic reactivity to light of near-threshold intensity. In emphasizing the reduced arousal level and responsivity these data are consistent with the theoretical arousal curve of Clausen, Lidsky and Sersen (Chap. 2) which was based on skin resistance data. Two important distinctions must be borne in mind in looking at these pupil data and interpreting them in relation to skin conductance. First, at highest light intensities the response difference between Familials and normals disappear, which means that these retardates can respond like normals if the stimulus intensity is appropriate. Indeed, such a possibility was raised by Karrer (1966) in reviewing the effects of strong or complex stimuli on the autonomic response of retardates (also see Chaps. 8, 9). On the other hand, whereas skin resistance suggested only sympathetic hypofunction in Cultural-Familials, the pupil data suggest *both* sympathetic hypofunction at rest *and parasympathetic* deficits in response to low intensity lights.

The above results raise a variety of interesting implications. If the Familial's deficient responsivity does indeed involve both sympathetic and parasympathetic systems then stimulation acting more directly on the pupil dilator system should also result in smaller than normal dilation responses. Using 5-sec duration pure

tones (800HZ) of several intensities, preliminary results with some
of the above subjects suggest that this is in fact what happens.

STUDY 2: PUPILLARY CORRELATES OF TASKS DEMANDS AND ARITHMETIC PROCESSING

Several reports of significant relationships between pupillary
dilation and cognitive processing in normal college students have
appeared within the last decade. Hess and Polt (1964), and
Bradshaw (1967), for example, concluded that the size of the
pupil increases with the level of difficulty in arithmetic problem-
solving. Similarly, during a pitch discrimination task, more difficult comparisons were correlated with greater pupillary dilation
(Kahneman and Beatty, 1967). Paivio and Simpson (1966) have
shown that when a subject imagines abstract words his pupils are
larger than with concrete words.

I have located only one published report in which retarded
and normal subjects were compared on pupillary dilation during
arithmetic problem solving (Boersma, Wilton, Barham, and
Muir, 1970). Their findings, derived from ten educable retardates (mean age = 10.5, IQ = 72) and ten normals (mean age =
11.0, IQ = 112), will be described in some detail. Six arithmetic
problems, consisting of three difficulty levels (either 2, 4, or 6
digits to be summed), were individually presented on stimulus
cards, while the subject's pupil was measured (30 readings per
second) for approximately 20 seconds. Key-press reaction times
and postsolution pupillary values were also obtained. Analysis of
the RT data, using the Newman-Keuls procedure in conjunction
with analyses of variance, demonstrated that normals had shorter RTs than retardates at all levels of difficulty, and both groups
had shortest RTs with the simplest problems.

The pupil dilation data, without regard to problem difficulty,
showed significantly larger responses in normals than in patients
during the response portion immediately preceding problem solutions. In fact, during the final period a trend was observed
wherein greater problem difficulty was associated with smaller
dilations than simpler problems for the retardates only. Without

regard to groups, on the other hand, significantly more dilation occurred with more difficult problems in those portions of the responses shortly after stimulus presentation. The authors interpret their results in terms of Berlyne's concept of attentiveness (Berlyne, 1970) and its probable interaction with arousal, with retardates and simple problems producing less attentiveness and arousal.

Unfortunately the authors did not report certain details of interest, such as correlations between key response variables and IQ, their method of handling eyeblinks during the rather lengthy problem exposures, and illumination conditions in the test room or on individual stimulus cards. Other useful information which could be derived from extending this experimental design, would be provided by using an MA-matched group, automated presentation of many more than six problems per subject, and reliability estimates of pupil diameter and RT data.

We have also been studying pupillary and skin conductance correlates of arithmetic processing. The theoretical framework and some of the procedural and analytical details, which differ from those of Boersma, et al. (1970), have been discussed earlier in this chapter. While only preliminary data on a limited number of subjects and variables have been obtained, the design and some data can be presented here.

The stimuli were fifty visually-presented slides, each containing three single digits in a vertical pattern, with the third digit representing a sum of two numbers. The addends ranged between numbers 1 and 5, with each addend appearing in ten slides. Twenty-five slides contained the correct sums, while the others were incorrect; ten slides (problems) had identical addends, five of which were correct and five incorrect. The slides were presented at the rate of two per minute. The subject, located in the dark test room, fixated a 4 × 4 inch screen, at a distance of 62 cm from the eye. Each slide was exposed for 5 sec, using automatic timing devices, a Carousel projector and a Lafayette tachistoscope shutter.

Pupillary activity (of the right eye) and skin conductance (of the fingers) were continuously recorded during the arithmetic processing of these highly practiced additions. Under certain conditions the subject was required to press one of two response keys which gave measures of motor reaction time and correctness of response. Three basic conditions of task demand were employed. These may be considered as manipulating levels of arousal (e.g. Zahn, 1964). *Passive* observation of the numerical displays involves minimal arousal (12 slides). In a *Detection* condition the subject pressed the same response key on every trial, as soon as the bottom digit on each slide had been identified, without regard to accuracy of the arithmetic (12 slides). The most demanding task, *Discrimination,* required that the subject distinguished between correct and incorrect sums, such as 2 2 4 or 2 2 3, and press one key for a correct sum and the other key for an incorrect sum (50 slides). Additional control conditions have also been used with the most recently tested subjects (blank slides, verbal discrimination response at the end of each trial, and detection with key press of "same" versus "different" numerical content on each slide). Each slide presentation, with the associated physiological and RT responses of the subject, constituted one trial. When a blink or other artifact occurred during the viewing of the slide or before the key press that trial was omitted from the analyses.

To date we have analyzed several parameters from seven normals and seven retarded subjects, ranging in age from ten to twenty-nine years. The mean CA for normals was 19.3 years; for retardates, CA was 22.5 with a mean MA of 10 years. Two of the retardates were diagnosed as high level Encephalopathies, and the others were Familials. None of these patients or normals were included in the data of Experiment 1.

Two illustrative curves, from the pupillary data of one retarded subject, are shown in Figure 13-2. The upper panel contains an average curve for the Detection condition, which clearly shows a much larger contraction (mean XC = 1.76 mm) and a much faster mean RT (773 msec) than in the Discrimination

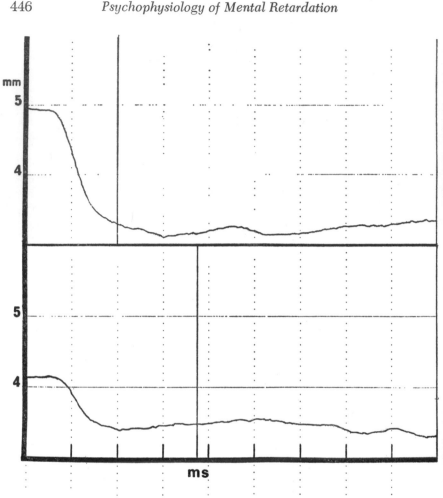

Figure 13-2. Sample averaged pupillary response curves in one subject to arithmetic problems. The dark vertical lines represent the mean motor reaction time for each condition. Upper panel = Detection condition; Lower panel = Discrimination condition. The horizontal axis represents time following stimulus onset (500 msec units); the vertical axis refers to average pupil diameter, in millimeters.

condition of the lower panel (mean XC = .78 mm and mean RT = 1642 msec).

Several statistically significant findings are also apparent from the data of Table 13-II and can be summarized as follows:

TABLE 13-II

AVERAGE PUPILLARY AND RT CORRELATES OF ARITHMETIC TASK
CONDITIONS

Condition	Initial Diameter M.R.	Norm.	Extent of Contraction M.R.	Norm.	Time to Peak M.R.	Norm.	Motor RT M.R.	Norm.
Passive	5.0*	5.8	.93	.92	1372*	836	—	—
Detection	5.2*	6.4	.84	1.04	1048	935	953	747
Discrimination ...	4.8*	6.1	.46*	.89	996	879	2598*	1213

* p < .05 or less; M.R. = Retarded Group; Norm. = Normal Group.

Reaction Time

RT's for normals were generally faster than for patients; during Discrimination, $t = 3.79$, with $p < .01$. For all subjects combined, Detection RT's were faster than Discrimination RT's ($t = 3.09$, $p < .01$), and the differences between conditions were significant both for the normals alone ($t = 2.75$, $p < .05$) and for the patients alone ($t = 4.28$, with $p < .01$). This is consistent with most relevant literature. On the other hand, the shorter Detection RT for normals was not significantly different from that of retardates.

Initial Diameter

The ID's *between* conditions for the same group never differed significantly, whereas *within* each condition the mean ID of normals was at least 0.7 mm greater than the mean ID of retardates. The significant difference between groups, during Discrimination and Detection, for example, involved t's of 2.61 and 2.35, with p's < .05. These differences are, of course, consistent with the ID findings in Study 1.

Pupillary Response

The smallest pupillary contractions and times to peak contractions in retardates tended to occur during the Discrimination task (XC: Passive vs. Discrim, $t = 2.58$, $p < .05$; Detect vs. Discrim, $t = 1.58$, $p < .10$). But for all subjects combined the statistical outcomes were not significant. Comparisons between patients and normals yielded significantly smaller patient contractions *only* during Discrimination ($t = 1.88, p < .05$). This is also an indication that the differential initial diameter of the groups, and the effects of the brightness of the projected slides in the Passive condition, where no voluntary response was required, did not differentially influence the extents of contraction in the two groups. During the Passive condition, the normal mean TTP (836 ± 256 msec) was significantly faster than the patient mean (1372 ± 426 msec), with $t = 2.64$, and $p < .05$.

The essential implication of these data are that difficulty levels (arousal) influence pupillary responses. Furthermore, there is some degree of relationship between pupillary activity and motor reaction time. During Discrimination the most consistent correlation with RT was obtained with the pupillary TTP. Combining the fourteen subjects, r equalled .65, ($p < .02$) while for the retardates and normals separately, r's equalled .75 and .61 respectively (two tailed p's $< .05$ and $> .10$). Neither ID nor extent of contraction attained this degree of association with RT. The correlation coefficient between XC and TTP in normals alone was significant ($r = .85, p < .01$), and for all subjects combined the initial diameter and extent of contraction were also positively related ($r = .57, p < .05$). With the exception of the TTP-RT correlation, and without regard to significance levels, the intercorrelations between the response variables discussed in this experiment were generally negative for the retardates and positive for the normals.

It will be noted that the pupillary variables referred to in this study were not discussed by Boersma, et al., since that experiment primarily analyzed late components of *dilation*. Because increased blink rates occur with longer periods of fixation, the present work emphasized early and pre-RT components of the pupillary responses. The recovery from contraction data ("redilation") and the skin conductance correlates of this study remain to be analyzed and compared. The present methodology and instrumentation has the capability of retrieving and analyzing individual responses and trials as a function of additional salient common characteristics. It is possible to further sort the individual content and physiological response correlates of the Discrimination condition stimuli as functions of both cognitive and motivational factors. The groups of problem slides containing identical addends (such as $1 + 1$ or $4 + 4$) and different addends (such as $3 + 2$ or $1 + 5$)—solutions which have generally been overlearned by most subjects—can be compared in terms of physiological correlates. The effects of the magnitude of the second addend (from 1 to 5), often considered a major factor in arithmetic processing (e.g. Parkman and Groen, 1971; Sekuler, Rubin and Armstrong, 1971), can be evaluated with the pupillary data. Similarly, the effects of correct versus incorrect sums (such as $3 + 3 = 6$ versus $3 + 3 = 5$) can be compared. Furthermore, the pupillary and skin conductance correlates, as well as RT's, can be analyzed with respect to correct or incorrect decisions (key presses) made by the subject. These analyses are in progress, but a further preliminary result is of interest.

Comparing the means between normal and retardate groups, as well as within groups, as a function of whether projected sums were either "Right" or "Wrong," contained "Same" or "Different" addends, both "Same and Right," "Same and Wrong," "Different Right," or "Different Wrong," certain patterns were evident. With one exception normals had faster RT, faster pupillary TTP, and slower skin conductance TTP (and, of course, larger initial diameters) during Discrimination. Under the single condition where slides contained *both* identical addends and correct sums ("Same Right"), the pupillary TTP for retardates was not only faster (856 ± 292 msec) than normals (992 ± 288 msec), but contained the shortest of all eight retardate TTP's and the longest of all eight normal TTPs. Across conditions this was where retardates also had their fastest mean RT (2353 ± 1104 msec). But the speed of the normal RT (1140 ± 402 msec) was no faster than for other conditions. The pupillary TTP values consistently preceded the motor RT values, often by one second or more. The possibility thus exists of identifying the subject's decision regarding the correctness or incorrectness of a particular sum *before* the appropriate reaction key has been pressed.

CONCLUDING REMARK

Other experimental paradigms which we are currently employing with retarded and normal subjects include two-tone discriminations of intensity in a method of standard comparisons (e.g. Kahneman and Beatty, 1967), pupillary resolution of brief double light pulses (e.g. Hakerem and Lidsky, 1969) separated by dark intervals of .2 to .9 sec, and pupillary dilation as it relates to evoked potential correlates of stimulus uncertainty and certainty (e.g. Sutton, Braren, Zubin and John, 1967). We are also attempting to extend the light reflex work to other etiological groups of the mentally retarded, especially with Down's Syndrome and Encephalopathic subjects (e.g. Lidsky and Richman, 1973). In conjunction with pupillary measurements, other psychophysiological variables should be compared. Present evidence suggests that, for certain tasks, the pupil is a more consistent discriminator than the galvanic skin response (Colman and Paivio, 1969), or heart rate (Kahneman, Tursky, Shapiro and Crider, 1969).

In terms of arousal theory, the present pupillary results may be interpreted as follows. If larger pupils are associated with higher arousal and attentiveness, and if the sympathetic system opposed by the parasympathetic is primarily responsible for enlarging pupils, then all of the present data show that Familial retardates have reduced arousal levels. If high light intensity stimulation produces large pupillary contractions, via the parasympathetic reflex, which are similar in these retardates and normals (as concluded in Study 1), then the Passive condition of the present study should yield no significant differences in extent of contraction between groups, which is indeed what happened for both Passive and simple Detection. However, when arousal demands were greatest, during Discrimination—especially for patients—sympathetic interference with the parasympathetic light reflex may have inhibited the extent of contraction, with the result that the smallest contractions occurred during Discrimination. Normals as a group tended to retain consistently large contractions across the three conditions.

It is premature to speculate further on the processes underlying these results. They are especially intriguing, but they require extension and verification. That is, larger numbers of subjects, both MA and CA matches, sex and etiological classifications, the contribution of motivational components, and additional control conditions—such as simpler choice RT based on "same" vs. "different" judgments *per se,* and stringent statistical evaluation, have all yet to be assessed. Nevertheless, the resources of pupillary data, and their potential contribution to understanding information processing in retarded and normal persons should not be underestimated. On the one hand, most aspects of the RT data are consistent with the evidence based on other choice RT studies, and the pupillary results are generally consistent with a psychophysiological arousal concept as it relates to what is known of the neural mechanisms of the pupillary system. It has been shown that parallels exist in performance and in pupillary activity in both normal and retarded persons.

REFERENCES

Berlyne, D.: Attention as a problem in behavior theory. In D. Mostofsky (Ed.): *Attention.* N.Y., Appleton-Century-Crofts, 1970.

Boersma, F.; Wilton, K.; Barham, R., and Muir, W.: Effects of arithmetic problem difficulty on pupillary dilation in normals and educable retardates. *J Exp Child Psychol,* 9:142-155, 1970.

Bradshaw, J.: Pupil size as a measure of arousal during information processing. *Nature, 216:*515-516, 1967.

Bumke, O.: *Die pupillenstörungen, bei geistes und nervenkrankheiten.* Jena, Fischer, 1911.

Clausen, J.; Lidsky, A., and Sersen, E.: Measurements of autonomic functions in mental deficiency. In: R. Karrer (Ed.): *Developmental Psychophysiology of Mental Retardation.* Springfield, Thomas, 1975.

Colman, F., and Paivio, A.: Pupillary response and galvanic skin response during an imagery task. *Psychonom Sci, 61:*296-297, 1969.

Hakerem, G.: Pupillography. In: Venables, P., and Martin, I. (Eds.): *Manual of Psychophysiological Methods.* Amsterdam, North-Holland, 1967.

Hakerem, G., and Lidsky, A.: Pupillary reactions to sequences of light and variable dark pulses. *Ann NY Acad Sci, 156:*951-958, 1969.

Hess, E. H.: Pupillometrics. In: Greenfield, N., and Sternbach, R. (Eds.): *Handbook of Psychophysiology.* N.Y., Holt, Rinehart and Winston, 1972.

Hess, E., and Polt, J.: Pupil size in relation to mental activity during simple problem solving. *Science, 140:*1190-1192, 1964.

Kahneman, D., and Beatty, J.: Pupil diameter and load on memory. *Science, 154:*1583-1585, 1966.

Kahneman, D., and Beatty, J.: Pupillary responses in a pitch discrimination task. *Percept Psychophysics, 2:*101-105, 1967.

Kahneman, D.; Tursky, B.; Shapiro, D., and Crider, A.: Pupillary, heart rate, and skin resistance changes during a mental task. *J Exp Psychol, 79:*164-167, 1969.

Karrer, R.: Autonomic nervous system functions and behavior. In Ellis, N. R. (Ed.): *International Review of Research in Mental Retardation.* Vol. 2. N.Y., Academic, 1967.

Libby, W.: Lacey, B., and Lacey, J.: Pupillary and cardiac activity during visual attention. *Psychophysiology, 10:*270-294, 1973.

Lidsky, A.; Hakerem, G., and Sutton, S.: Pupillary reactions to single light pulses in psychiatric patients and normals. *J Nerv Ment Dis, 153:*286-291, 1971.

Lidsky, A., and Richman, S.: Pupil size and responses to light in retardates and normals. Paper presented at *8th Colloqium on the Pupil,* Wayne State University, Detroit, 1973.

Loewenfeld, I.: Mechanisms of reflex dilation of the pupil. *Docum Ophthalmol, 12:* (suppl. 2), 185-448, 1958.

Lowenstein, O.; Kawabata, H., and Loewenfeld, I.: The pupil as indicator of retinal activity. *Am J Ophthalmol, 57:*569-596, 1964.

Lowenstein, O., and Loewenfeld, I.: Mutual role of sympathetic and parasympathetic in shaping of the pupillary reflex to light. *Arch Neurol Psychiat, 64:*341-377, 1950.

Lowenstein, O., and Loewenfeld, I.: Electronic pupillography. A new instrument and some clinical applications. *AMA Arch Ophthalmol, 59:* 352-363, 1958.

Lowenstein, O., and Loewenfeld, I.: The pupil. In Davson, H. (Ed.): *The Eye.* Vol. 3. *Muscular Mechanisms,* New York, Academic, 1962.

Lowenstein, O., and Westphal, A.: *Experimentelle und Klinische studien zur physiologie und pathologie der pupillenbewegung.* Berlin, Karger, 1933.

Manley, J., and Schuldt, W.: The refractive state of the eye and mental retardation. *Am J Optomet, 47:*236-241, 1970.

May, P. R.: Pupillary abnormalities in schizophrenia and during muscular effort. *J Ment Sci, 94:*89-98, 1948.

Paivio, A., and Simpson, H.: The effect of word abstractness and pleasantness on pupil size during an imagery task. *Psychon Sci, 5:*55-57, 1966.

Parkman, J., and Groen, G.: Temporal aspects of simple addition and comparison. *J Exp Psychol, 89:*335-342, 1971.

Razran, G.: The observable unconscious and the inferable conscious in current Soviet psychophysiology: Interoceptive conditioning, sematic conditioning, and the orienting reflex. *Psychol Rev, 68:*81-147, 1961.

Rubin, L.: Patterns of adrenergic-cholinergic imbalance in the functional psychoses. *Psychol Rev, 69:*501-519, 1962.

Schaeppi, V., and Koella, W.: Adrenergic innervation of cat iris sphincter. *Am J Physiol, 207:*273-278, 1964.

Sekuler, R.; Rubin, E., and Armstrong, R.: Processing numerical information: a choice time analysis. *J Exp Psychol, 90:*75-80, 1971.

Sutton, S.; Braren, M.; Zubin, J., and John, E. R.: Information delivery and the sensory evoked potential. *Science, 155:*1436-1439, 1967.

Zahn, T.: Autonomic reactivity and behavior in schizophrenia. *Psychiat Res Repts, 19:*156-173, 1964.

CHAPTER 14

DEVELOPMENTAL PSYCHOPHYSIOLOGY OF MR: SOME PROBLEMS AND TRENDS

RATHE KARRER

OVERVIEW

THERE IS PRESENTLY NO BODY of integrated knowledge that can be called developmental psychophysiology, much less a body of knowledge that deals with aberrant development. There has been little effort at accumulating this knowledge either during aberrant development or normal development.

In the development of ANS-behavior functioning, problems of response specificity, and of situational specificity have hardly been scratched. Even for such a basic problem as the relation of ANS response to base levels (the so-called "Law" of initial values (Wilder, 1950)) there is no developmental perspective. There has been slightly more research on the development of electrocortical activity (c.f. Ellingson, 1968; Dustman and Beck, 1969; also Chap. 8; Lindsley, 1939; Myslivecek, 1970; Scherrer, et al., 1970). Further, most of the existing research has not yet reached a level that inspires much theoretical deviation from the data base. There is a need for detailed psychophysiological analyses of specific processes (e.g. orienting, habituating, attending, information processing strategies, input organization, memory retrieval, RT, and response organization and the conditions for expression, inhibition, and modification of these processes in the developing individual). Only in this way can the deviant *individual's* behavior be included in any theoretical assertions.

There are many areas of investigation that should be included

454

in a developmental psychophysiology of MR that could not be included in this book. The aberrant infant's psychophysiology is one such area. While there is an increasing body of knowledge on the normal infant there is still a paucity of psychophysiological study of aberrant infants or the development of aberrance in the initial years (c.f. Hellmuth, 1967, 1971; Robinson, 1969; Sterman, McGinty and Adinolfi, 1971). The study of sleep of children and the MR individual constitutes another area of neglect. Of utmost importance is the psychophysiological study of social interaction during development of normal as well as aberrant behavior (for an interesting example see Minuchin, 1974, p. 7). All of these areas have inherent methodological and technical problems that need solution. The study of biofeedback effects cuts across all areas and has yet to be assessed as an effective tool in the study of development and MR. The success of Galbraith, et al. (Chap. 9) in modifying EEG patterns and thereby modifying performance will do much to answer this question for MR. The modification as well as the possibility of acquisition of voluntary control of physiological systems could be a powerful tool to unraveling some major questions in developmental psychophysiology, i.e. the development of response patterning, situational specificity, and the strength of the macrophysiological-behavior relation.

Another omission is the problem of electrocortical activity (e.g. latency of the EP) as a means of assessing intelligence (see review by Callaway, 1973; also Chaps. 8, 9). I believe this area is replete with commercialism, hasty assertions, and a paucity of hard data. Further, I do not believe it useful to replace the IQ with an even more complicated measure. Instead, the efforts should be to determine the physiological-behavioral bases for cognitive functioning (Chaps. 8, 9).

The zeitgeist of MR today is moving from nonfunctional administrative diagnoses (IQ, etc.) toward an emphasis on identifying functions that point to remedial action. Psychophysiological analysis can contribute to this trend in two ways. First, psychophysiological information can contribute to the extent that a macrophysiological event can become a specific and valid index of a behavioral function not easily assessed by other means. However, inferring a behavioral state from a physiological measure (e.g. attention to the stimulus from heart rate deceleration; arousal from heart rate or electrodermal activity) is currently a weak position. Given our present insufficient knowledge of behavioral physiology, if one feels compelled to infer behavior characteristics from the physiological data, then it is absolutely necessary to confirm the inference with a direct behavioral test. Second, if modifying macrophysiological activity (e.g. biofeedback) can effectively modify behavior (strong assumption) or assist in the modification of behavior (weak assumption) a powerful analytic and remedial tool is obtained. The potential of these approaches has yet to be fully fathomed.

The main contribution of psychophysiological research is to the understanding of the macrophysiological foundations of behavior so necessary to full understanding of complex action and its consequence. Psychophysiology is the interface of neurobiology to behavior, and as such, is necessary to a complete understanding of the organism. It can provide the translation function of the neurobiologist's information at the cellular and multicellular level to the human organism's complex behavior. This translation function should provide the clues for the identification of, for example, the neural processes or physiological system mediating specific behavior in all its affective-cognitive complexities.

Psychophysiological studies are of necessity multivariate studies for which a brief word on strategy is appropriate. One must treat a psychophysiological analysis in terms of an interaction of independent variables. Behavior (including experience) has physiological affects, and physiological process affects behavior (and experience). Both behavior and physiological process may work to modify the effective stimulus conditions. Therefore, the best one can do is maintain rigid stimulus control and analyze behavior and physiology as a function of states of the other (see discussion of this triangular paradigm by Sutton, 1969). By sorting the physiological variable along a behavioral dimension (e.g. slow to fast RT), and vice versa, sorting the behavioral variable along a physiological dimension (e.g. high to low amplitude), one can tease apart the coupling relationship under specific situational demands. It is essential that both sorts be done. These analyses require considering the variability along each dimension rather than disregarding it with central tendency measures. *Developmental* psychophysiological analysis requires consideration of a fourth interactive dimension of development along which behavior and physiology must be sorted. The determination of the behavior-physiology coupling at various levels of development is a first approximation for dealing with this dimension. Longitudinal studies and the manipulation of development also offer promise. However, serious problems of stimulus equivalence arise when one compares organisms with differing experiential and temporal backgrounds as well as differing physiological development.

It should be stressed that finding reliable and valid differences between individuals does not imply an "organic lesion" and such differences may have little to do with etiology. Such a finding reflects only a *different* psychophysiological relationship. The reason for any difference may be the learning during development of different social, cognitive, or emotional strategies for dealing with the situation and, thereby, different appropriate physiology. This is not to deny that a difference may also be a sign of a lesion of some physiological process. Psychophysiological investigation therefore implies only the truism of psychophysiological correspondence, or functional psychosomatic identity, and thereby, reflects the complex interaction of genetics, biological development and experience.

This is to say that all behavior is "organic." Quantitative and qualitative differences in performance are accompanied by quantitative and qualitative differences in physiological components. This is a simple truism unless one assumes psychological-behavioral events to be epiphenomena. Such a concept allows one to bypass the insidious concepts of "minimal brain dysfunction" or "organic" with all their causal implications and superfluous meanings bearing on prognosis. (I am not denying that physiological trauma can often be the cause of subsequent behavioral consequences, and vice versa.) It is reasonable to assume that during development retardates (and normal children) may learn inappropriate patterns of physiological activity as well as behavior. This point has been labored, but I believe it is essential to counteract much of the erroneous conceptualization of behavior-physiology in the developmental defects literature.

Are there emerging trends of a developmental psychophysiology? I believe there are many exciting results described in the foregoing chapters. All of the studies can be subsumed under a rubric of psychophysiological relations during information processing. They focus on arousal, the orienting reponse, attending behavior under a variety of situations, as well as preparatory behavior (the latter implies the organism is processing information and is getting set to act appropriately).

Many of the studies of retardates find phenomena similar to that in the normal literature. For example, the cardiac deceleration in preparation for a response (Chap. 3). The U-shaped function relating evoked potentials to the pleasantness-unpleasant stimulus dimension (Chap. 9) is similar to other findings using pupillography and heart rate (Lacey, et al., 1963; Libby, Lacey and Lacey, 1973; Hare, et al., 1971). It is reassuring to find analogous results reported in different systems or populations.

Serious problems arise in any attempts to derive a psychophysiology of MR. In the first place MR stands for an extreme heterogeneity of human characteristics. The theorist putting his facts together must deal with the incomparability of these individuals. Within any group of retardates the variability in performance on any task is usually greater than normal. Some retarded will approach or will overlap the normal distribution of performance. Given this situation one must analyze the process using the given variability as a tool for studying high and low performance (c.f. Baumeister, 1968; Berkson, 1973; Karrer, 1965; Karrer, in press).

This situation is no different when comparing different etiological classifications which may have physiological or behavioral consequences. Variables which affect heart rate, evoked potentials or RT in one way in Down's syndrome may affect the Familial

MR child differently. Clausen, et al. (Chap. 2) are wrestling with this problem by trying to define different patterns of ANS activity and arousal in some specifiable MR subgroups. The model of arousal-behavioral interaction adduced by these authors lends itself to empirical check. An increase in arousal for Familials should lead to more efficient performance while an increase in arousal for PKU, Down's, or Encephalopathics would lead to further degrading of performance. On the contrary, an arousal decrease should give more efficient performance in these latter categories. There are a few threads of converging evidence that may be supportive of this. Fehr (Chap. 7) finds a degradation of RT performance when Down's children were more aroused during his film distraction condition. Krupski (Chap. 3) finds lower basal heart rate (arousal) in high level retardates (presumably Familial). Lidsky (Chap. 13) finds that dark adapted pupillary diameter data also indicate lower arousal in Familial retardates. In Chapter 11, Karrer and Ivins report that increasing arousal with bimodality stimulation decreased the RT of their nonorganic retardates. Dustman, et al. (Chap. 8) report larger late evoked potential components in Down's syndrome that may imply greater reticular formation activation and, therefore, greater arousal (or less inhibitory process, see Bigum, et al., 1970). Galbraith, et al. (Chap. 9) have shown this effect is a function of stimulus intensity, i.e. low intensities gave no difference in visual evoked potential amplitude while high intensities gave larger evoked potentials in Down's syndrome. Further, Straumanis, et al. (1972) report that somatosensory evoked potential recovery functions are faster for Down's syndrome, as one might predict for a higher arousal state. Moskowitz and Lohman (1970) have found that a more intense stimulus was necessary to evoke an OR in Down's subjects. At first appraisal this appears counter to a higher arousal state. But, if the OR is considered a localized arousal increase, then it could be that a stronger eliciting stimulus is necessary because the organism is already adapted to a higher than normal arousal level.

It is reasonable to expect that an arousal deficit would affect processing of complex information and complex tasks more than processing of simple information (nonmeaningful sounds, flashes, figures, etc.) and simple tasks. Any processing is, however, also affected by the "arousal value" of the tasks and stimuli. This is difficult to assess. What is needed is a good criterion measure of the organism's arousal state. An arousal index is not simple since with response patterning and situational specificity one must be cautious in inferring a general arousal state. The dissociation between (and within) various ANS, electrocortical, and somato-motor measures, with the consequences for arousal theory has repeatedly been pointed out (Lacey, 1967; Lacey and Lacey, 1970). Naatanen (1973) has recently argued that the relation of arousal to performance is state dependent.

There is no agreement as to the way out of this dilemma so long as the concept of arousal still seems heuristic. For the present, it may be productive to do EEG frequency analyses to demonstrate putative levels of electrocortical arousal. So far there has been little attempt at using the recent sophistication with frequency analysis during task performance with retardates and during development. EEG base levels (DC) also offer promise as an index of arousal that may be more fruitful than frequency (c.f. Rowland, 1968; Caspers, 1963). In addition pupillary activity may offer a unique means of assessing arousal as demonstrated by Lidsky (Chap. 13). All of these approaches need considerably more study along with a situational analysis.

The arousal model places the retardates at the extremes of the skin resistance arousal dimension where it might be expected that homeostatic processes may be operating more strongly to reduce their higher arousal in the Down's, PKU, and Encephalopathics, but to increase the lower arousal of the Familials. This may result in greater homeostatic restraint processes (Karrer, 1966), a concept that may be able to avoid the unitary dilemma of the arousal concept when dealing with response and situational patterning of ANS responses. Each ANS variable (e.g. SR) has different physiologic (as well as cognitively based) homeostatic processes that must be considered individually and in complex interaction with behavior. Homeostatic restraint is also a concept that may be difficult to empirically assess. There are two measures that do seem to get at homeostatic processes. The correlation between pre and post-stimulation values (Lacey, 1956) is the simplest measure and it can be derived from any study of responsiveness. This measure has been used to demonstrate less homeostatic restraint in asthmatic children's heart rate OR (Hahn, 1966), and in adults with cardiovascular disease (Hord, Johnson and Lubin, 1964) as well as greater homeostatic restraint in nonorganic retardates (Karrer and Clausen, 1964; Karrer, 1966). The second measure requires manipulation of stimulus parameters (e.g. intensity) to determine the stimulus value that gives a crossover from heart rate acceleration to deceleration (Bridger and Reiser, 1959). This measure has been used to assess developmental changes.

Different etiologies of MR with specific physiological concomitants are obviously a source for studying various psychophysiological relations (see Chaps. 2 and 7). Fehr's studies (Chap. 7) demonstrate a promising approach to teasing apart the ANS-behavior linkage as well as to the evaluation of intervention procedures. Certain etiologies may be expected to have different electrophysiological processes. The consequences of hypothyroidism for MR is well known and probably has specific consequences for cortical activity (Bradley, Eayrs, and Schmalback, 1960). Hypothyroidism in rats, for example, leads to impaired learning and an overall decrease in dendritic density of the cortex (Eayrs, 1971). Hence SP shifts (CNV) should be less in such rats if SP shifts like the CNV arise from dendritic processes. Down's syndrome (trisomy 21) may also have an erratic and abnormal distribution of apical dendrite spines (Marin-Padilla, 1972). If there is a linkage between SP shifts and behavior, as strongly indicated in the literature (Chap. 11; Pribram, 1971; DeMott, 1970), then such etiologies may have different SP shifts and could be fruitful models for study of the SP-behavior linkage.

Repeatedly in the MR-ANS literature (Karrer, 1966) retardates are less responsive at low stimulus intensities but equal to or greater than normal at high intensities. Galbraith, et al. (Chap. 9) find Down's retardates to be similar to normals at low intensities but greater than normal at high intensities (as did Dustman, et al. (Chap. 8). Lidsky (Chap. 13) also finds this stimulus intensity dimension for the pupillary response. At low light intensities the pupillary response of normals is larger than for the retarded, while at high light intensity there is no difference. It would be of interest to determine the light intensity-pupillary response function for Down's cases since this may bear on the evoked potential data (Chaps. 8 and 9). All of these results may be explained by a different psychophysical scaling of intensity (or other stimulus attributes) by retardates. Their growth of subjective magnitude may be such that lower intensities are perceived as less bright than normals. Hence, less pupil contraction, slower rate of contraction, less response in other ANS systems and similar amplitude of primary EP. At higher intensities they may perceive greater brightness and hence larger EP and greater (or similar) ANS responding. This evidence is only suggestive but it warrants studies of basic psychophysical magnitude functions in retardates.

There seems a thread of evidence running through many of the studies that the retardate has less differentiation of activity (ANS, electrocortical, and somatomotor) than at least his normal peer (see Chaps. 2, 4, 7, 8, 9 and 11). This should be brought into focus, confirmed, and understood in terms of development.

Input organization is known to be impaired in retardates (Ellis, 1970; Spitz, 1966; 1973). One strategy for facilitating organization is covert repetition of the material in order to temporally compress or divide it into chunks as well as to emphasize the trace. Locke and Fehr (Chap. 12) demonstrate that muscle activity may be a promising index of rehearsal in the retardate and young child. Their preliminary findings also imply less differentiation of muscle activity during speech in these groups, reminiscent of Russian work (c.f. Luria, 1963).

Attending processes are also considered to be deficit in retardates (c.f. Luria, 1963; Karrer, in press; Zeaman and House, 1963). Consequently, heart rate deceleration in a task requiring attending should be attenuated along with the retardate's behavioral performance. Krupski (Chap. 2) has taken an important step in studying the RT-deceleration relation in retardates. She has indeed found attenuated deceleration during preparation to respond in retardates. By within-group analyses she adduces the concept that the retardate is unable to time his response appropriately. This concept of improper timing strategies is amenable to direct test by task manipulation and by training. It has some support in the fact that retardates are poor time interval estimators (McNutt and Melvin, 1968). Another convergent thread is the improper timing of electrocortical activity (SP) to different brain areas (Chap. 11).

Conditioning is a problem of information processing mechanisms. Related to the concept of time interval estimation is the effect of interstimulus interval on classical conditioning (Chap. 6). This temporal variable is crucial to obtaining retardate normal differences in conditioning (also see, Ross and Ross, 1973). It is the longer interval situations which accentuate deficits in retardates. This is also in accord with Krupski's RT and heart rate data during a 13 sec PI. There has been very little work with conditioning (either operantly or classically) autonomic (or electrocortical) activity in developmental defective children. Lockhart's intensive analysis of the existing studies offers promising leads. The most important to this writer is an extensive developmental analysis of multiple electrodermal responding during conditioning in retarded and normal children. If Lockhart's Pre-US-R is somehow related to cognitive activity during the ISI or at least to language capacity there should be definite predictable trends during development and in subjects independently assessed to have reduced cognitive and/or language capacity.

One compelling result (Chaps. 8, 9, 10 and 11) is the topographical difference in brain electrical activity during development and in the retardate. It is interesting that the retardate differences were found among various brain areas, types of comparisons, and electrical events by three different teams of experimenters (EEG coherence between areas and posterior to anterior fall-off of visual EP amplitude, Chap. 9; differences in left-right EP amplitude, Chap. 8; differences in frontal-vertex timing and amplitude measures of SP, Chap. 11). This implies that differing topography of activity underlying information processing performance may be a pervasive feature of the retardate (see also Richlin, et al., 1973). Dustman, et al. (Chap. 8), found asymmetry of the EP to be greater in conditions increasing attention. Asymmetry was also greater in the more intelligent. This is a promising lead that is especially intriguing when coupled with their concept of asymmetry of reticular formation (RF) function. Asymmetrical interaction of the RF with cortical processes could produce patterning of responses during arousal and attending. The result could be specific types of arousal or optimal states of brain processes associated with specific task requirements. Further understanding of this process could go far to unraveling the patterning of ANS and the topography of electrocortical events during information processing. The implication for lack of asymmetry in the retardate and during low attention is that the RF-cortical reciprocal relation is less differentiated into regional or hemispheric interaction.

Cohen (Chap. 10) has shown a developmental trend in topography of CNV amplitude such that there were larger amplitudes in posterior areas in the young child (age 6), but in anterior areas by age eighteen. There was some evidence (Chap. 11) of reduced frontal negativity (in relation to vertex) in retardates compared to equal age normals. Also the size of the correlations between the CNV of the RT and DIT task placed the retardates similar to the younger normals in frontal activity but similar to equal age normals in vertex activity. Whether these data reflect a posterior to anterior shift during development must remain for further study.

There are at least three possibilities for the presence of a different topography of cortical events in the mentally retarded and during development.

1. The retardate and developing child has learned to use different processes (strategy, motivation, etc.) in performing a task. The processes require utilization of different brain areas and/or mechanisms.

2. The retardate and young child does not have available certain neural processes (or other physiological structures) which

requires him to utilize alternate processes (and areas) leading to a different topography. Such processes may be lacking because of developmental immaturity or various lesions. It is apparent that 1 and 2 may not be mutually exclusive.

3. Different topographies are not specific to task requirements and are, therefore, of little use for understanding behavior. There is ample evidence accumulating that is counter to this possibility even for EEG frequency measures (see for example Galin and Ornstein, 1972). Systematic study of the topography of EEG frequency measures, early and late components of the EP, steady potential activity and motor potentials in the young child and the mental retardate seem imperative. These studies should utilize sensory and complex tasks designed to intercalate with the known deficits in retardate performance.

That the retardate (or the young child) has a different topography or pattern of shared neural activity accompanying different behavior cannot be taken as implying a causal relation. If psychophysiological identity is to be adhered to, specific behavior must reflect specific physiological processes and vice versa. Either component in the identity is capable of being changed via experience (learning, shaping, etc.). That behavior is capable of this type of change is putative. There is now considerable evidence that brain electrical activity, ANS activity and somatomotor activity can also be modified (Chap. 9; Barber, et al., 1971; Sterman, 1973). Therefore, by working from both sides (behaviorally and physiologically) of the organism it may be possible to produce more effective and rapid change. In actuality, we have not yet identified the physiological components of any behavior with any specificity. Consequently, we are left to work with and consider a less than perfect psychophysiological identity. We must, in effect, deal with a range of slop in the linkage of one to the other.

The studies of the OR (Chaps. 4, 5) are, frankly, puzzling in light of the Russian theory and data. Johnson (Chap. 4) found differences in the OR of (nonorganic or organic) retardates depending upon the type of stimuli used; weaker OR to signal stimuli. Simple stimulus parameters seem to produce equal effects in retardates as in normals. On the other hand, Das (Chap. 5) found no consistent difference between retardates and normals even to signal stimuli. It is of interest that a recent study of the same problem found a stimulus complexity dimension in OR habituation (Siddle and Glenn, 1974). Retardates took longer to habituate GSR to complex shapes than did the normals. The differences between these studies lie in a variety of factors that need further study. For example, the OR index favored here is HRD and GSR while the head and finger blood volume measures are favored in studies abroad. There are differences in methodology and in the derivation of OR measures that could effect results. There are also differences in the populations labeled MR (but Johnson found no difference between categories, Chap. 4). It may be as Luria points out (Das, Chap. 5) that the integrity of frontal cortex is the critical factor. It is clear that Johnson and Das have raised meaningful questions that must be answered.

The patterning of the OR indices is another unknown that warrants a closer look and may be related to the problem of stimulus and response specificity. The ontogeny of ANS patterning is at best a sticky problem, but one that may have great payoff. The one study that has tried to analyze patterns of ANS activity in MR (Karrer and Clausen, 1964) found an interesting homogeneity of response in the different ANS systems. This was interpreted in terms of greater homeostatic restraint which has yet to be followed up.

The OR could well stand further study along different lines. A phenomenological analysis of orienting to a stimulus finds multiple psychological processes involved that mean different things to the consequent behavior. For example: a completely novel stimulus would give rise initially to a "what is it?" response as the organism strives to extract relevant features of the stimulus. With repeated presentations habituation takes place as information from the stimulus is integrated with his past experience. In addition, however, after the first two or three presentations the subject also adopts a "when is it coming?" orientation that is an accurate expectancy depending on whether the interstimulus interval is fixed or variable, long or short. Therefore, after the first few stimuli the OR reflects a behavioral state changed in at least two different ways. Temporal discrimination and temporal expectancies are probably of special importance to the auditory system which is highly tuned to temporal analysis of information. Further compounding results if the stimuli do not occur in the same place each time and thereby generate uncertainty as to "where?" This localization process is of specific importance to the orientation of the visual system which has become highly specialized for spatial analysis. This type of phenomenological analysis could be carried much further in describing the usual task requirements we use. It would be fruitful to launch a systematic study of the OR in tasks requiring only "what," "when," "where" orientations followed by tasks involving combinations. It seems highly likely that the OR and its patterning changes with such state changes as well as with development and cognitive proficiency.

The magnitude, frequency, habituation and patterning of the OR are the important aspects. One unsolved problem is the relation of OR magnitude to speed of habituation. If the OR and its habituation are important to information processing via the establishing of some model of the stimulus (Sokolov, 1963; Lewis, et al., 1968; Jeffrey, 1968; Johnson, Chap. 4; Das, Chap. 5; Siddle and Glenn, 1974) then certain hypotheses can be generated for the weak or strong OR and fast or slow habituators. Johnson has stated some relevant hypotheses and it may be useful to follow them further. Assuming a solution to the OR magnitude-habituation problem, there are four combinations of OR and habituation outcomes to be found. (1) A weak OR and fast habituation, (2) A weak OR and slow habituation, (3) A strong OR and fast habituation, and (4) A strong OR and weak habituation. The first, weak OR and fast habituation, may imply (A) the "novel" stimulus was not novel to the subject (or discrepant from his previous experience); or (B) that the information in the stimulus was processed rapidly leading to a weak generalized OR and fast habituation; or (C) low arousal of the subject giving a weak OR and fewer aspects of the stimulus processed. And consequently (via feedback), lesser arousal and even fewer stimulus aspects processed on subsequent trials. For retardates, rapid processing (B) seems improbable so that (A) and (C) seem most probable. How could a novel stimulus (A) not be discrepant from his model? This could occur if the retardate is processing fewer aspects (especially distinctive dimensions) of the stimulus than the normal so that there would be fewer presentations needed to build his simpler model. He would, therefore, be expected to have a different psychophysical scaling of stimulus dimensions (intensity, quality, complexity, meaning, etc.) and, perhaps, different information seeking strategies (eye movement patterns, haptic search, exploratory behavior, play, etc.). He might prefer lower intensities and lesser complexity than the equal age normal but may be similar to the developmentally younger child. The alternative is (C)—that there is an arousal problem coupled with information processing that is adequate.

The second combination, weak OR and slow habituation would imply (A) that the stimulus was not very discrepant coupled with a state of low arousal, (B) not very discrepant and inefficient information processing, or (C) just low arousal. Slower information processing could be due to a different growth of subjective scaling, slower physicochemical neural processes or low arousal. Thus, this OR-habituation combination may be a function of inefficient information processing or low arousal.

The third combination, strong OR and fast habituation, implies good arousal plus (A) a novel stimulus and efficient information processing or (B) the novel stimulus is perceived more simply (i.e. different psychophysical scaling of stimulus dimensions) with fewer distinctive aspects and, consequently, less information to add to the model each trial. The retardate would be expected to be the latter (B).

The fourth, strong OR and slow habituation, would imply a novel stimulus and good arousal and (A) inefficient (slow) information processing (as above) or (B) a different subjective scaling of stimulus dimensions such that there are *more* distinctive features or information perceived in the stimulus. The retardate would be expected to be (A).

Obviously, then, all of these possible outcomes could be given by a retardate (or a younger normal) assumed to have low arousal, inefficient information processing or both. It is also obvious that it is difficult to isolate the process underlying the combination that may be found in any study without a series of subsequent studies to determine the role of arousal, novelty-familiarity, inefficient processing, and psychophysical scaling. And this assumes we know the relation between OR magnitude to speed of habituation. If this information processing model is to be productive we must have parametric developmental studies of these factors using a variety of stimulus dimensions relevant and irrelevant to the organism.

Some phenomena well known to psychophysiologists in normal adults should be studied in the developing normal child and retardate. For example, many studies in the psychophysiology literature demonstrate a relation between cardiac acceleration with stimulus "rejection" and/or internal cognitive processing and cardiac deceleration with stimulus "acceptance" or attending (Lacey, et al., 1963; Graham and Clifton, 1966). Investigation of this relation in retardates may further delineate the behavior-HR linkage as well as add to the knowledge of specific MR deficits (Chap. 3). It would be fruitful to compare retardates on the two types of tasks supposed to give cardiac acceleration and deceleration. Retardates are traditionally considered to be poor at cognitive processing. If acceleration is truly coupled with cognitive processing and blocking of the reception of external stimuli, then retardates should demonstrate less acceleration in a cognitive task than deceleration in a simple passive stimulus reception task. In the latter task they may exhibit similar or more deceleration than normal (c.f. Karrer, 1965).

The foregoing are only a few of the many threads weaving among the chapters. I hope that the reader will weave many of his own as he challenges, confirms, rejects, or modifies the facts and ideas presented. Neuroscience has been fluorishing of late and promises to provide exciting understanding of neurophysiological development processes. Psychophysiological analysis should also be providing exciting understanding of the actively engaged human from a vantage point that is unavailable elsewhere.

REFERENCES

Barber, T.; Di Cara, L. V.; Kamiya, J.; Miller, N.; Shapiro, D. and Stoyva, J. (Eds.): *Biofeedback and Self-Control.* Chicago, Aldine, 1971.

Baumeister, A. A.: Behavioral inadequacy and variability of performance. *Am J Ment Defic, 73:*477-483, 1968.

Berkson, G.: Behavior. In J. Wortis (Ed.): *Mental Retardation,* Vol. 5. New York, Grune and Stratton, 1973.

Bigum, H. B.; Dustman, R. E. and Beck, E. C.: Visual and somatosensory evoked responses from mongoloid and normal children. *EEG Clin Neurophysiol, 21:*202, 1970.

Bradley, P. B.; Eayrs, J. T. and Schmalbach, K.: The electroencephalogram of normal and hypothyroid rats. *EEG Clin Neurophysiol, 12:*467-477, 1960.

Bridger, W. H. and Reiser, M.: Psychophysiologic studies of the neonate: An approach toward the methodological and technical problems involved. *Psychosom Med, 21:*265-276, 1959.

Callaway, E.: Correlations between averaged evoked potentials and measures of intelligence. *Arch Gen Psychiat, 29:*553-558, 1973.

Caspers, H.: Relations of steady potential shifts in the cortex to the wakefulness-sleep spectrum. In M. A. B. Brazier (Ed.): *Brain Function Vol. 1. Cortical Excitability and Steady Potentials; Relations of Basic Research to Space Biology.* Berkeley, Univ California, 1963.

DeMott, J.: *Toposcopic Studies of Learning.* Springfield, Thomas, 1970.

Dustman, R. E. and Beck, E. C.: The effects of maturation and aging on the wave form of visually evoked potentials. *Electroenceph Clin Neurophysiol, 26:*2, 1969.

Eayrs, J. T.: Thyroid and developing brain: anatomical and behavioral effects. In M. Hamburgh and E. J. W. Barrington (Eds.): *Hormones in Development.* New York, Appleton-Century-Crofts, 1971.

Ellingson, R. J.: The study of brain electrical activity in infants. In L. P. Lipsitt and H. W. Reese (Eds.): *Advances in Child Development and Behavior.* Vol. 3, New York, Academic, 1968.

Ellis, N. R.: Memory processes in retardates and normals. In N. R. Ellis (Ed.): *International Review of Research in Mental Retardation.* Vol. IV. New York, Academic Press, 1970.

Galin, D. and Orstein, R.: Lateral specialization of cognitive mode: An EEG study. *Psychophysiology, 9:*412-418, 1972.

Graham, F. K. and Clifton, R. K.: Heart rate changes as a component of the orienting response. *Psychol Bull, 65*:305-320, 1966.

Hahn, W. W.: Autonomic responses of asthmatic children. *Psychosom Med, 28*:323-332, 1966.

Hare, R. D.; Wood, K.; Britain, S., and Frazelle, J.: Autonomic responses to affective visual stimulation: Sex differences. *J Exp Res Person, 5*:14-22, 1971.

Hellmuth, J. (Ed.): *Exceptional Infant. The Normal Infant.* Vol. 1. Seattle, Special Child Publ., 1967.

——— (Ed.): *Exceptional Infant. Studies in Abnormalities.* Vol. 2. New York, Brunner/Mazel, 1971.

Hord, D. J.; Johnson, L. C. and Lubin, A.: Differential effect of the law of initial value (LIV) on autonomic variables. *Psychophysiology, 1*: 79-87, 1964.

Jeffrey, W. E.: The orienting reflex and attention in cognitive development. *Psychol Rev, 75*:232-334, 1968.

Karrer, R.: Comparison of autonomic activity of mental defectives and normals: A sequential analysis of the heart rate response. *J Ment Defic Res, 9*:102-108, 1965.

———: Autonomic nervous system functions and behavior: A review of experimental studies with mental defectives. In N. R. Ellis (Ed.): *International Review of Research in Mental Retardation.* Vol. 2., New York, Academic, 1966.

———: The attentional set of the mentally retarded and cortical steady potentials. In D. V. Siva Sankar (Ed.); *Studies on Childhood Psychiatric and Psychological Problems.* Vol. 2. Westbury, New York, PJD Press (in press).

Karrer, R. and Clausen, J.: A comparison of mentally deficient and normal individuals upon four dimensions of autonomic activity. *J Ment Defic Res, 8*:149-163, 1964.

Lacey, J. I.: The evaluation of an autonomic response: Toward a general solution. *Ann NY Acad Sci, 67*:123-164, 1956.

Lacey, J. I.: Somatic response patterning and stress: Some revisions of activation theory. In M. H. Appley and R. Trumbull (Eds.): *Psychological Stress.* New York, Appleton-Century-Crofts, 1967.

Lacey, J. I. and Lacey, B. C.: Some autonomic central nervous system interrelationships. In P. Black (Ed.): *Physiological Correlates of Emotion.* New York, Academic Press, 1970.

Lacey, J. I.; Kagan, J.; Lacey, B. C. and Moss, H. A.: The visceral level: Situational determinants and behavioral correlates of autonomic response patterns. In P. H. Knapp (Ed.): *Expression of Emotions in Man.* New York, International Univ Press, 1963.

Lewis, M.; Goldberg, S. and Campbell, R.: A developmental study of information processing within the first three years of life: Response decrement to a redundant signal. *Child Dev Monogr, 33:* No. 133, 1968.

Libby, W. L.; Lacey, B. C. and Lacey, J. l.: Pupillary and cardiac activity during visual attention. *Psychophysiology, 10:*270-294, 1973.

Lindsley, D. B.: Electrical potentials of the brain in children and adults. *J Genet Psychol, 55:*197-213, 1939.

Luria, A. R.: *The Mentally Retarded Child.* New York, Macmillan, 1963.

Marin-Padilla, M.: Structural abnormalities of the cerebral cortex in human chromosomal aberrations: A Golgi study. *Brain Res, 44:*625-629, 1972.

McNutt, T. H. and Melvin, K. B.: Time estimation in normal and retarded subjects. *Am J Ment Defic, 72:*584-589, 1968.

Minuchin, S.: *Families and Family Therapy.* Cambridge, Harvard Univ. Press, 1974.

Moskowitz, H. and Lohmann, W.: Auditory threshold for evoking an orienting reflex in mongoloid patients. *Percept Mot Sk, 31:*879-882, 1970.

Myslivecek, J.: Electrophysiology of the developing brain—Central and Eastern European contributions. In W. A. Himwich (Ed.): *Developmental Neurobiology.* Springfield, Thomas, 1970.

Naatanen, R.: The inverted-U relationship between activation and performance: A critical review. In S. Kornblum (Ed.): *Attention and Performance, IV.* New York, Academic, 1973.

Pribram, K. H.: *Languages of the Brain.* Englewood Cliffs, Prentice-Hall, 1971.

Richlin, M.; Weinstein, S. and Giannini, M.: Development of neurophysiological indices of mental retardation: I. interhemispheric asymmetry of the auditory evoked cortical response. *Pediatrics, 52:*534-541, 1973.

Robinson, R. J. (Ed.): *Brain and Early Behavior.* New York, Academic, 1969.

Ross, L. E. and Ross, S. M.: Classical conditioning and intellectual deficit. In D. K. Routh (Ed.): *The Experimental Psychology of Mental Retardation.* Chicago, Aldine, 1973.

Rowland, V.: Cortical steady potential (direct current potential) in reinforcement and learning. In E. Stellar and J. M. Sprague (Eds.): *Progress in Physiological Psychology,* Vol. 2. New York, Academic, 1968.

Scherrer, J.; Verley, R. and Garma, L.: A review of French studies in the ontogenetical field. In W. A. Himwich (Ed.): *Developmental Neurobiology.* Springfield, Thomas, 1970.

Siddle, D. A. T. and Glenn, S. M.: Habituation of the orienting response to simple and complex stimuli. *Am J Ment Defic, 78:*688-693, 1974.

Sokolov, E. N.: Higher nervous systems; the orienting reflex. *Ann Rev Physiol, 25:*545-580, 1963.

Spitz, H. H.: The role of input organization in the learning and memory of mental retardates. In N. R. Ellis (Ed.): *International Review of Research in Mental Retardation,* Vol. II. New York, Academic, 1966.

Spitz, H. H.: The channel capacity of educable mental retardates. In D. K. Routh (Ed.): *The Experimental Psychology of Mental Retardation.* Chicago, Aldine, 1973.

Sterman, M. B.: Neurophysiologic and clinical studies of sensorimotor EEG biofeedback training; some effects on epilepsy. *Semin Psychiat,* 5:507-524, 1973.

Sterman, M. B.; McGinty, D. J. and Adinolfi, A. M. (Eds.): *Brain Development and Behavior.* New York, Academic, 1971.

Straumanis, J. J.; Shagass, C. and Overton, D. A.: Somatosensory evoked responses in Down's syndrome. *Arch Gen Psychiat,* 29:544-549, 1973.

Sutton, S.: The specification of psychological variables in an average evoked potential experiment. In E. Donchin and D. B. Lindsley (Eds.): *Average Evoked Potentials: Methods, Results, and Evaluations.* Washington, D.C., NASA, 1969.

Wilder, J.: The law of initial values. *Psychosomat Med, 12*:392, 1950.

Zeaman, D. and House, B. J.: The role of attention in retardate discrimination learning. In N. R. Ellis (Ed.): *Handbook of Mental Deficiency.* New York, McGraw-Hill, 1963.

AUTHOR INDEX

SUBJECT INDEX

A

Ability
  to learn, 6
  to process, 6
Abnormalities, 45
  see also specific
Achievement quotient, 8
Achievement tests, 8
Acoustic chamber, 47, 48
Acquisition/reversal, 152, 154, 156, 159, 164
Activation, 10, 29, 344
AEP, *see* Evoked potential, average
AER, *see* Average evoked response
AER, *see* Auditory evoked response
Aging and evoked responses, 274
Alcohol and evoked responses, 293, 294, 295, 301
Alerting, 366, 412
  processes, 366
Alertness, 228
Alpha
  activity, 328, 330, 339
  block, 22, 230, 231
  pattern, 17
  rhythm, 17, 19, 22, 29, 229, 230, 301
  see also Electroencephalogram
Anesthesia, 251
ANS, *see* Autonomic nervous system
Anticipation/feedback, 170, 171, 174
Anticipatory response, 149, 169, 170, 174
Anxiety, 224, 225, 227
  chronic, 346
  CNV in, 346
  level, 345
  scale, 227
AQ, *see* Achievement quotient
AR, *see* Anticipatory response
Area of psychophysiology, 455

Arithmetic processing, 443, 444, 445, 449
Arousal, 4, 10, 22, 29, 67, 84, 88, 177. 241, 303, 364, 366, 367, 435, 442, 450, 451, 456, 458, 459, 464, 466, 467
  assessing, 460
  autonomic, 67, 163
  behavioral aspects of, 45, 221, 343, 344, 459
  characteristics, 438
  decreased, 364, 459
  deficit, 84, 459
  definitions of, 435
  demands, 450
  differences in, 223
  dysfunction, 435
  faulty, 24
  from electrodermal activity, 456
  from heart rate, 456
  impaired, 19, 41
  increased, 364, 366, 459
  index, 11, 460
  indicator of, 442
  level of, 10, 84, 85, 221, 223, 230, 241, 442, 450
  low, 468
  malfunction, 20
  peak of, 345
  processes, 19, 366, 436
  reduced, 230, 460
  role of, 469
  state, 460
  theory, 450, 460
  value, 460
Artifact, 326, 392
  and GSR, 150
  and HR change, 168
  and movement, 43, 50, 65, 82, 134, 367, 392